# Heritage in Quilts

## Tennessee Society
## Daughters of the American Revolution

Turner Publishing Company
Paducah, Kentucky

# IN MEMORIAM

Mrs. Edith Burns Little was a fifty year member of the Daughters of the American Revolution at the time of her death May 5, 1999. As a dedicated chapter member, she helped forty five current members with their application papers. Mrs. Little served as the Chapter Registrar and also served in numerous chairmanships at the state level.

A 1930 graduate of Maryville College, she worked for seven years as the supervisor of the college's maid shop which designed quilt patterns and kits to raise funds. According to Mrs. Little, Maryville College was the first college to design quilt patterns. Her "Wild Rose" quilt, submitted for this book prior to her death, was assumed to have been made from one of these kits.

Following the death of this dedicated and experienced quilter, the Mary Blount Chapter TSDAR made a contribution to the TSDAR American Heritage Quilt Project as a memorial to Mrs. Little.

**TURNER PUBLISHING COMPANY**
412 Broadway • P.O. Box 3101
Paducah, Kentucky  42002-3101
(270) 443-0121

Copyright © 2000 Tennessee Society Daughters of the American Revolution
Mrs. James O. Shearer, State Regent
Mrs. Marilyn Johnson Baugus, Chairman

Vice-chairmen:
Mrs. Ann Haas, Chickasaw District     Mrs. Anne Hightower, Sequoia District
Mrs. Nancy Coleman, Cumberland District     Mrs. Hermena Litton, Cherokee District
Mrs. Betty Stevens, Appalachian District

Marilyn Baugus and Bridget Ciaramitaro, Editors
Chickasaw Bluff Chapter

Publishing Rights:  Turner Publishing Company
Turner Publishing Company Staff:
Randy Baumgardner, Editor
Shelley R. Davidson, Designer

Library of Congress Catalog Card Number 00-130146
ISBN:  1-56311-573-5

Printed in the United States of America.  Additional copies may be purchased directly from the publisher.  Limited Edition.

# INTRODUCTION

One of the goals of the Daughters of the American Revolution is to help preserve our rich American Heritage. The National Society of the Daughters of the American Revolution Museum has fulfilled this goal in many ways including an outstanding display of quilts which toured Japan in 1999 as the NSDAR's first international quilt exhibit. Many of the DAR Museum's quilts have also been featured in books and other exhibits. To further the appreciation of American Heritage in future generations, the Museum sponsors a Children's Quilt Camp each summer.

I chose as my theme for the 1999-2001 Tennessee State Regent's administration "Together We Serve Through Preservation, Education, and Affiliation." Inspired by the efforts of the NSDAR Museum, we decided to embark on a project that would preserve our Tennessee history by documenting quilts owned by the members of the Tennessee Society Daughters of the American Revolution.

Tennessee residents have been associated with quilts since the earliest settlers. Prior to the construction of interstate highways, anyone traveling through East Tennessee could see quilts displayed for miles in the yards of artistic quilt makers. Recent years have brought a phenomenal revival of interest in quilts. We are fortunate that many of our members have retained family heirloom quilts which are generations old. Quilts provide warmth, are decorative, and in many instances tell stories of family weddings, births, bicentennial celebrations, wars, special people, and events. These stories make our quilts special.

My earliest memory of owning a quilt goes back to my childhood. My mother's best friend, for whom I was named, gave me a handmade embroidered quilt for my doll bed. Years later I was fortunate to receive a full size quilt of the same pattern as a wedding gift. Today, I cherish these quilts and continue to be awed at the time and talent that go into the making of a quilt.

The TSDAR has some quilt stories of its own. In 1983, eight DAR Regents of the Knox County Regents Council presented a handmade quilt to Mrs. James O. Harrison, State Regent. The quilt depicted vari-

ous aspects of national and state government.. Of particular interest is the block featuring the Tennessee Flag. Mrs. Harrison authored the Pledge to the Tennessee Flag which was adopted by the Tennessee Legislature as the official Pledge. Unfortunately we are not aware of what happened to this quilt following Mrs. Harrison's death.

Another significant quilt was made during the administration of Mrs. James R. Quarles, Sate Regent 1995-1998. Chapters were chosen to make quilt blocks depicting various aspects of Tennessee History in celebration of the State's Bicentennial. This quilt is now housed at the Tennessee State Museum in Nashville.

I am indebted to the members of the Tennessee DAR who have shared their pictures and stories to enable us to prepare this book. Many quilts were handmade and reflect loving work by members or their ancestors. Others have been acquired as gifts or through purchase. Regardless of their origin, our goal has been to permanently preserve a record of these beautiful works of art for the present and future.

I am very grateful to Marilyn Baugus, Tennessee State American Heritage Chairman, for her many hours spent verifying quilt patterns, compiling information and editing this book. I express the appreciation of TSDAR members to Mrs. Baugus and her volunteer helpers for this accomplishment.  May our *TSDAR Heritage In Quilts* book provide many hours of enjoyment for you and your family.

Mrs. James O. Shearer
Tennessee State Regent 1998-2001

All of my life I have been interested in history, genealogy, and quilts. I was honored when Mrs. James O. Shearer, State Regent of the TSDAR, asked me to chair the TSDAR American Heritage Quilt Project. Our goal would be to collect pictures and stories about the quilts and coverlets owned by the members of the TSDAR. My committee and I were pleased that from the very beginning of this project, members responded with enthusiasm and support.

In the early stages, we decided to produce a video that could be taken to each and every chapter to promote the project so that every member would have the opportunity to participate. The video, produced by Bridget Ciaramitaro and Gary Witt, was shown at the 1999 TSDAR State Conference in Chattanooga, Tennessee at the American Heritage Brunch.

Inspired by the video and the opportunity to preserve our State's heritage, over 1900 pictures and stories were submitted by the July 1, 1999 deadline. With such an overwhelming response, we wanted to be certain that all pictures and stories would be included in the final outcome of this project, the *TSDAR Heritage in Quilts* book. We had just thirteen short months from the announcement of the project to the submission of the final manuscript to the publisher.

We researched the name of quilt patterns if the owner did not submit this information. We were able to identify all but a few of the quilt patterns. However, most of the coverlets were made before 1900 and many of their pattern names remain unidentified.

Unfortunately, some of the pictures and stories we received could not be included because they did not fit the criteria set forth in our

guidelines. In order to be included, a quilt or coverlet must be finished and must currently belong to a member of the TSDAR. For example, quilts owned by Mrs. Hillman P. Rogers, a former State Regent who is now deceased, were not included. They are housed in a museum along with other of Mrs. Davies' personal items.

This entire project has been a "labor of love." It could not have been done without the support and participation of many. My committee helped promote the project and gather pictures from the five state districts. I will be forever grateful for their enthusiasm, hard work,  and leadership. I am also grateful to friends and family who helped with the typing, proofing and other tasks involved in putting this book together. Bridget Ciaramitaro assisted with the editing. Nelda Grimes and Jane Ramsay, Chickasaw Bluff Chapter, worked faithfully to help identify patterns and proof the copy for this book. I would also like to thank each and every Daughter who sent in quilt and coverlet pictures and stories. This has been one gigantic, volunteer effort, proving again that Tennessee is truly the Volunteer State.

Marilyn Johnson Baugus, Editor

**Adams, Embry Hadley**
Rachel Stockley Donelson Chapter
Ancestor: Lt. Col. John Donelson, VA — #352074
This "Pinwheel" quilt was made in 1938-40 at Nashville, TN by the owner's mother, Sadie Aileen Burgess Hadley (born 11/27/1898 at Nashville, TN, married Howard Embry Hadley, died 2/25/1988 at Nashville).

**Aiken, Betty Jane Foster** (Charles)
Sarah Hawkins Chapter
Ancestor: Hugh Caldwell, Jr., PA —#674120
This "Tulip Variation" quilt was pieced in the 1920's by the owner's grandmother and finished in 1996 by the owner.

**Allen, Catherine McCullough** (Thomas Hunter)
Robert Lewis Chapter
Ancestor: James Coffey —#623587
This "Feathered Star" quilt was made in Marshall County, TN by the owner's grandmother's aunt, Hannah Irvin (born circa 1820 at Marshall County, TN). The owner's grandmother was named after the aunt who made this quilt.

**Allen, Nancy Quarles** (Wyatt, Jr.)
Caney Fork Chapter
Ancestor: William P. Quarles, VA — #610119
This original "Flags of the World" quilt was designed in the 1920's at Dixon Springs, TN by the owner's husband's uncle, William H. Cox (born 1919, died 1943). When William was a young boy he was fascinated by the flags of the different countries and drew the designs on paper. His mother, Lois R. Cox, commissioned young Bill's flag designs to be made into a quilt. Dixon Springs, TN neighbor, Kitty Corum, translated the boy's drawings into fabric and another neighbor, Vallie Bowman, hand quilted the quilt. Flags appear as they would have in the 1920's, thus the American Flag has only 48 stars. This flag quilt remains a special keepsake since William H. Cox was killed in action November 1943 during World War II.

**Amos, "Gerry" Large**
General William Lenoir Chapter
Ancestor: David Campbell, NC — #710060
This "Wandering Foot" quilt was made in the 1960's at Lenoir City, TN by the owner's mother, Viola Forrester Large. The quilt was passed to the owner at her mother's death in 1980.

**Amos, "Gerry" Large**
General William Lenoir Chapter
Ancestor: David Campbell, NC —#710060
This "Sunflower" quilt was embroidered in 1975 at Cincinnati, OH by the owner and quilted by her mother, Viola Forrester Large. "During the time of family problems, embroidering this quilt was therapy for my mother. This was the last quilt she made."

**Anderson, Katherine Baugh** (Sam O.)
Ft. Blount Chapter
Ancestor: John Richmond, SC —#669441
This "Broken Star" quilt was made circa the late 1900's by the owner's husband's grandmother, Lillie Ferguson Anderson (born 7/18/1875 at Hickman County, TN, married Sam Tucker Anderson, died 4/11/1964 at Hickman County).

**Anderson, Katherine Baugh** (Sam O.)
Ft. Blount Chapter
Ancestor: John Richmond, SC — #669441
This "New York Beauty/Sunrise Over the Rockies" quilt was made in the early 1930's at Gainesboro, TN by the owner's grandmother, Hallie Cooper Baugh.

**Anderson, Katherine Baugh** (Sam O.)
Ft. Blount Chapter
Ancestor: John Richmond, SC — #669441
The center of this "Grandmother's Flower Garden" quilt was purchased by the owner at an antique shop. She belongs to the Silver Threads Quilters Club. The members gathered their old flour sacks saved from the 1940's. With these materials, she reworked the blocks, added borders and hand quilted it. She carried the quilt to the Tennessee Valley Quilters Assembly Day in Cookeville, TN, where Georgia Bonesteel was guest speaker. She asked the guest speaker and officers of the association to quilt a few stitches making this quilt even more memorable.

**Anderson, Katherine Baugh** (Sam O.)
Ft. Blount Chapter
Ancestor: John Richmond, SC —#669441
This "Pineapple" quilt was made in the early 1930's at Gainesboro, TN by the owner's grandmother, Hallie Cooper Baugh (born 12/27/1878 in TN, died 11/3/1965 at Gainesboro).

**Anderson, Katherine Baugh** (Sam O.)
Ft. Blount Chapter
Ancestor: John Richmond, SC — #669441
This "Whole Cloth" quilt was made in 1996 by the owner (born 7/12/1924 at Gainesboro, TN). This quilt won a blue ribbon and People's Choice Award at the local quilt show in May 1996.

**Anderson, Katherine Baugh** (Sam O.)
Ft. Blount Chapter
Ancestor: John Richmond, SC — #669441
This "Whole Cloth" quilt was made in 1996 by the owner. This quilt won a blue ribbon and People's Choice Award at the local quilt show in May 1997.

**Anderson, Katherine Baugh**
(Sam O.)
Ft. Blount Chapter
Ancestor: John Richmond, SC —#669441
This "Christmas Log Cabin Wreath" quilt was made by the owner. This quilt also won a blue ribbon at the local quilt show.

**Anderson, Victoria Richards**
(George H.)
Charlotte Reeves Robertson Chapter
Ancestor: Thomas Dawson, VA — #580184
This "Nine Patch/Square in a Square" quilt was made during the winter of 1986 at Center Hill, TN by the Porters Chapel Homemakers Club. The owner bought two "chances" and was fortunate to win this quilt. The proceeds were used for Tennessee Homecoming 86 activities. Madeline Mason and Ernestine Lehto did most of the quilting because a big snow fell, roads were closed, and they were "shut in" with the quilt.

**Ansley, Merrill Everett**
(Sterling)
General James Winchester Chapter
Ancestor: James Roddye, NC —#717099
This "Wind Blown Square/ Balkan Puzzle" memory quilt was made by the owner's daughter-in-law, Katherine Zimmerman Ansley at Clarksville, TN in 1978.

**Armstrong, Mary Patton**
(Robert M.)
Margaret Gaston Chapter
Ancestor: Daniel Agee, VA —#702007
This "Lone Star" quilt was made prior to 1865 at Clay County, IL by the owner's great-great-great-grandmother, Margaret Herman (born circa 1800 at NC, married Francis Marion Herman, died after 1860 at Clay County, IL).

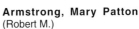

The owner inherited the quilt from her grandmother, Cora Patton. According to Cora, the quilt was in the trousseau of her mother, Mary Elizabeth Herman Patton, and was brought by her from Clay County, IL to Wilson County, TN in 1865 when she married Richard Patton. Cora always kept the quilt safely folded away in her chest because her grandmother had made it.

**Armstrong, Mary Patton**
(Robert M.)
Margaret Gaston Chapter
Ancestor: Daniel Agee, VA — #702007
This "Log Cabin" quilt was made between 1860-80 at Rutherford County, TN. It was purchased by the owner at the estate auction of Mrs. Birdie Holden of Watertown, TN.

**Arnette, Mary Jernigan** (James)
Robert Cooke Chapter
Ancestor: Sgt. John Garrett, NC — #775003
This "Rectangles" quilt was made in Tennessee about 100 years ago by the owner's grandmother, Amanda Jernigan (born 4/20/1857 at Rutherford County, TN, married Newton Jernigan, died 12/12/1941 at Nashville, TN).

**Arnette, Mary Jernigan** (James)
Robert Cooke Chapter
Ancestor: Sgt. John Garrett, NC — #775003
This "Strips in Squares" quilt was made in the 1920's in Tennessee by the owner's grandmother, Amanda Jernigan. The owner remembers, "I learned to sew at my grandmother's knee and some of the pieces in this quilt, I am sure I stitched."

**Ashton, Margaret Denton** (Harvell)
Jane Knox Chapter
Ancestor: Lt. John Black —#393301
This "Whig's Defeat" quilt was made circa 1855 at Maury County, TN by the owner's great grandmother, Caroline Matilda Faucett Galloway (born 8/20/1823 at Marshall County, TN, married Francis Marion Galloway, died 7/8/1895 at Maury County, TN). The quilt was made as a wedding gift for the maker's daughter, Margaret Jane Galloway Caskey, and handed down through the family.

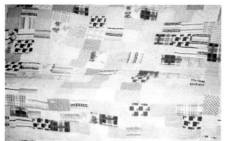

**Babin, Anne Dean** (Alan)
Commodore Perry Chapter
Ancestor: George Hammond, NC —#488252
This "Blocks" quilt was pieced circa 1930-35 at Collierville, TN by the owner's mother, Anna Gordon Davis Dean (born 7/9/1912 at Memphis, TN, married John Little Dean, died 7/14/1986 at Memphis). A local quilter finished the quilt.

**Babin, Anne Dean** (Alan)
Commodore Perry Chapter
Ancestor: George Hammond, NC —#488252
This pink and white quilt was made circa 1900-1910 at Trenton, TN by the owner's husband's maternal grandmother, Jessie S. Haste (born 8/27/1876 at Blue Earth County, MN married David Miles Haste, died 2/22/1959 at Memphis, TN). Jessie made this quilt as a young bride after she married in 1899.

**Babin, Anne Dean** (Alan)
Commodore Perry Chapter
Ancestor: George Hammond, NC —#488252
This "Log Cabin" quilt was made circa 1920-30 at Collierville, TN by the owner's paternal grandmother, Martha Little Dean (born 4/5/1885 at Marshall County, MS, married Charles Dean, died 9/21/1967 at Memphis, TN). The quilt is made from silk neckties. The borders and back are also made of silk.

**Babin, Anne Dean** (Alan)
Commodore Perry Chapter
Ancestor: George Hammond, NC —#488252
This "Nine Patch" quilt was made circa 1920 at Collierville, TN by the owner's paternal grandmother, Martha Little Dean.

**Babin, Anne Dean** (Alan)
Commodore Perry Chapter
Ancestor: George Hammond, NC —#488252
This "Brick" wool quilt was made circa 1920-30 at Collierville, TN by the owner's paternal grandmother, Martha Little Dean.

**Baker, Ailene Eddlemon** (Austin, Jr.)
Hatchie Chapter
Ancestor: Zachariah Melton, NC —#766876
This "Stairway to Heaven" variation of a "Log Cabin" quilt was made circa the 1930's in Hardeman County, TN. The owner purchased this quilt from Mrs. Francis Laney in the early 1960's for $15.00.

**Baker, Ailene Eddlemon**
(Austin, Jr.)
Hatchie Chapter
Ancestor: Zachariah Melton, NC — #766876
This "Dresden Plate" quilt was made circa 1930's in Hardeman County, TN by Mrs. Francis Laney. The owner bought this quilt from the maker in the early 1960's for $20.00.

**Baker, Ailene Eddlemon**
(Austin, Jr.)
Hatchie Chapter
Ancestor: Zachariah Melton, NC — #766876
This "Nine Patch" quilt was pieced in 1944-49 at Lake County, TN by the owner (born 10/20/1935 at Lake County, TN). She started this quilt in the summer of 1944 after she had undergone a tonsillectomy. Her mother thought piecing a quilt would "keep her still and quiet." The quilt was quilted circa 1967 by the Fayette County Home Demonstration Club.

**Baker, Ailene Eddlemon** (Austin, Jr.)
Hatchie Chapter
Ancestor: Zachariah Melton, NC —#766876
This "Double Wedding Ring" quilt was made circa 1932-1940 at Bolivar, TN by the owner's husband's grandmother, Willie Moorman Beck McAnulty (born 2/6/1872 at Salem, MS, married David Moorman McAnulty, died 8/3/1940 at Bolivar, TN). Willie's husband died in 1932. After his death, she made a number of quilts for her children and grandchildren.

**Baker, Ailene Eddlemon** (Austin, Jr.)
Hatchie Chapter
Ancestor: Zachariah Melton, NC — #766876
This "Texas Star" quilt was made circa 1935 at Lake County, TN by the owner's mother, Inez Marie Flowers Eddlemon (born 10/27/1915 at Benton County, TN, married Herbert Leon Eddlemon, died 9/20/1988 at Dyersburg, TN).

**Baker, Ailene Eddlemon** (Austin, Jr.)
Hatchie Chapter
Ancestor: Zachariah Melton, NC — #766876
This "Six Pointed Star" quilt was made circa 1932-40 at Bolivar, TN by the owner's husband's grandmother, Willie Moorman Beck McAnulty.

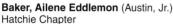

**Baker, Ailene Eddlemon** (Austin, Jr.)
Hatchie Chapter
Ancestor: Zachariah Melton, NC — #766876
This "Bow Tie/String" quilt was pieced in the early 1940's at Lake County, TN by the owner's grandmother, Gertrude May Lewis Eddlemon Jowers Hopkins (born 4/24/1885 at Weakley County, TN, married 1st Boyd Price Eddlemon, married 2nd A.L. Jowers, married 3rd Hopkins, died 8/1/1946 at Lake County, TN). The quilt was quilted in 1969 by the Fayette County Home Demonstration Club.

**Baker, Ailene Eddlemon** (Austin, Jr.)
Hatchie Chapter
Ancestor: Zachariah Melton, NC — #766876
This "Diamond Star/Eight Pointed Star" quilt was made in the early 1940's at Lake County, TN by the owner's grandmother, Gertrude May Lewis Eddlemon Jowers Hopkins.

**Baker, Ailene Eddlemon** (Austin, Jr.)
Hatchie Chapter
Ancestor: Zachariah Melton, NC — #766876
This "Sunbonnet Sue" quilt was made in the late 1930's at Lake County, TN by the owner's grandmother, Gertrude May Lewis Eddlemon Jowers Hopkins.

**Baker, Ailene Eddlemon** (Austin, Jr.)
Hatchie Chapter
Ancestor: Zachariah Melton, NC — #766876
This "Lily of the Valley/Tulip" quilt was made circa the 1920's at Lake County, TN by the owner's grandmother, Gertrude May Lewis Eddlemon Jowers Hopkins.

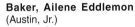

**Baker, Ailene Eddlemon** (Austin, Jr.)
Hatchie Chapter
Ancestor: Zachariah Melton, NC — #766876
This "Daisy" quilt was made circa 1935 at Lake County, TN by the owner's mother, Inez Marie Flowers Eddlemon.

**Baker, Ailene Eddlemon** (Austin, Jr.)
Hatchie Chapter
Ancestor: Zachariah Melton, NC — #766876
This "Duck Paddle/Goose Tracks" quilt was made circa 1935 at Lake County, TN by the owner's mother, Inez Marie Flowers Eddlemon.

**Baker, Ailene Eddlemon** (Austin, Jr.)
Hatchie Chapter
Ancestor: Zachariah Melton, NC — #766876
This "Arkansas Star" quilt was made circa 1935 at Lake County, TN by the owner's mother, Inez Marie Flowers Eddlemon.

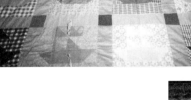

**Baker, Ailene Eddlemon** (Austin, Jr.)
Hatchie Chapter
Ancestor: Zachariah Melton, NC — #766876
This "The Mayflower" quilt was made circa 1935 at Lake County, TN by the owner's mother, Inez Marie Flowers Eddlemon.

**Baker, Ailene Eddlemon** (Austin, Jr.)
Hatchie Chapter
Ancestor: Zachariah Melton, NC — #766876
This "Grandmother's Flower Garden" quilt was made circa 1935 at Lake County, TN by the owner's mother, Inez Marie Flowers Eddlemon.

**Baker, Ailene Eddlemon** (Austin, Jr.)
Hatchie Chapter
Ancestor: Zachariah Melton, NC — #766876
This "Trip Around the World" quilt was made in the 1940's at Toone, TN by Miss Christine Kelly (born 1890, died 1978 at Toone).

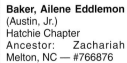

**Baker, Ailene Eddlemon** (Austin, Jr.)
Hatchie Chapter
Ancestor: Zachariah Melton, NC — #766876
This "Mrs. Hoover's Colonial" quilt was made in the 1940's at Toone, TN by Miss Christine Kelly.

**Baker, Ailene Eddlemon** (Austin, Jr.)
Hatchie Chapter
Ancestor: Zachariah Melton, NC — #766876
This "Bow Tie" quilt was made circa 1932-40 at Bolivar, TN by the owner's husband's grandmother, Willie Moorman Beck McAnulty.

**Baker, Ailene Eddlemon**
(Austin, Jr.)
Hatchie Chapter
Ancestor: Zachariah Melton,
NC — #766876
This "Grandmother's Flower
Garden" quilt was made circa 1932-40 at Bolivar, TN
by the owner's husband's
grandmother, Willie
Moorman Beck McAnulty.

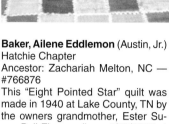

**Baker, Ailene Eddlemon** (Austin, Jr.)
Hatchie Chapter
Ancestor: Zachariah Melton, NC —
#766876
This "Drummer's Samples" quilt was
made in the early 1900's at
Hardeman County, TN by the
owner's husband's great grand-
mother, Ann Eliza Moorman Beck
(born 8/1/1845 at Tippah County,
MS, married Col. William Davis
Beck, died 5/22/1921 at Bolivar, TN).

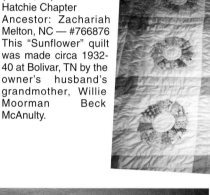

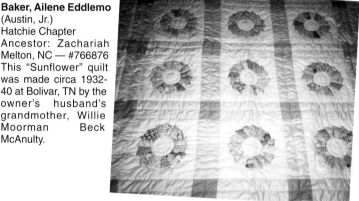

**Baker, Ailene Eddlemon**
(Austin, Jr.)
Hatchie Chapter
Ancestor: Zachariah Melton,
NC — #766876
This "Fruit Basket" quilt was
made circa 1932-1940 at
Bolivar, TN by the owner's
husband's grandmother,
Willie Moorman Beck
McAnulty.

**Baker, Ailene Eddlemon** (Austin, Jr.)
Hatchie Chapter
Ancestor: Zachariah Melton, NC —
#766876
This "Eight Pointed Star" quilt was
made in 1940 at Lake County, TN by
the owners grandmother, Ester Su-
san Bell Flowers (born 4/25/1885 at
Benton County, TN, married John
Albert Flowers, died 8/8/1943 at Lake
County, TN).

**Baker, Ailene Eddlemo**
(Austin, Jr.)
Hatchie Chapter
Ancestor: Zachariah
Melton, NC — #766876
This "Sunflower" quilt
was made circa 1932-
40 at Bolivar, TN by the
owner's husband's
grandmother, Willie
Moorman Beck
McAnulty.

**Baker, Barbara Simpson**
(Ross)
Samuel Doak Chapter
Ancestor: Stanley Moses,
VA — #775662
This "Double Wedding
Ring" quilt was made in
1953 in Hawkins County,
TN by the owner's grand-
mother, Nola Coward
Simpson (born 7/2/1889 at
Hawkins County, married
Henry Madison Simpson,
Sr., died 11/18/1954 in the
same county).

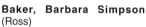

**Baker, Barbara Simpson**
(Ross)
Samuel Doak Chapter
Ancestor: Stanley Moses, VA —
#775662
This "Bald Eagle in Flight" quilt
was made in 1986 at Morristown,
TN by one of the best craftsmen
in Tennessee. The owner won
the quilt at the TFWC Conven-
tion at the Peabody Hotel in
Memphis, TN 4/21/1986. The
National emblem is quilted in the
center.

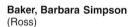

**Baker, Barbara Simpson**
(Ross)
Samuel Doak Chapter
Ancestor: Stanley Moses,
VA — #775662
This "Lone Star" quilt was
made in the 1940's in
Hawkins County, TN by the
owner's aunt's mother-in-
law, Bonnie Stapleton
Pearson.

**Baker, Barbara Simpson**
(Ross)
Samuel Doak Chapter
Ancestor: Stanley Moses,
VA — #775662
This "Dolly Madison Star"
quilt was made in Hawkins
County, TN by the owner's
aunt, Lois Simpson Arnott
(born 12/14/1922, married
Joseph Arnott).

**Baker, Barbara Simpson**
(Ross)
Samuel Doak Chapter
Ancestor: Stanley Moses,
VA — #775662
This "Eight Pointed Star"
quilt was made in
Hawkins County, TN by
the owner's aunt, Mary
Simpson Wood (born 10/
2/1927 at Hawkins
County, married Henry
Wood).

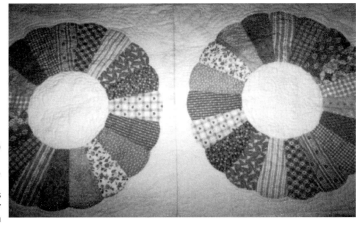

**Baker, Barbara Simpson** (Ross)
Samuel Doak Chapter
Ancestor: Stanley Moses, VA — #775662
This "Sampler" quilt was made in the 1980's at Hawkins County, TN by the owners aunt, Lois Simpson Arnott.

**Baker, Betty Mayes** (David F.)
Great Smokies Chapter
Ancestor: Absalom Hooper, Sr., GA —#746131
This "Dresden Plate" quilt was made in 1998 at Sevier County, TN by the owner (born 8/9/1945 at Sevier County). "I call this a prayer quilt because with every stitch, I said a prayer for "Aunt B" who would be the first to own the quilt."

**Bales, Laura McFalls** (Richard H.)
Moccasin Bend Chapter
Ancestor: Benjamin Seaton, VA —#604655
This "Double Wedding Ring" quilt was made in 1955 at Sevier County, TN by the owner's mother, Rowena Henderson McFalls (born 4/25/1929 at Sevier County, TN, married Ben C. McFalls).

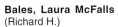

**Bales, Laura McFalls** (Richard H.)
Moccasin Bend Chapter
Ancestor: Benjamin Seaton, VA —#604655
This "Flowers of the States" quilt was made in 1962 at Sevierville, TN by the owner's mother, Rowena Henderson McFalls

**Ballard, Martha Powell** (Donald)
Commodore Perry Chapter
Ancestor: Lt. John Powell, SC—#778360
This "Flowers of Beauty" quilt was made in 1995 at Memphis, TN by the owner. "My daughter, Kathy, at the age of 36 had become paralyzed in May 1995. During the hours of 7:00AM to 7:00PM, I was allowed to sit in her ICU room at Methodist Hospital where I worked on this quilt. I finished this quilt while staying with her at HealthSouth during 1996, five days each week."

**Ballard, Martha Powell** (Donald)
Commodore Perry Chapter
Ancestor: Lt. John Powell, SC—#778360
This "Football" quilt of whole cloth printed with footballs was made in 1996 at Memphis, TN by the owner (born 12/7/1933 at Charleston, MS).

**Bales, Laura McFalls** (Richard H.)
Moccasin Bend Chapter
Ancestor: Benjamin Seaton, VA —#604655
This "Double Wedding Ring" quilt was made before 1937 at Sevier County, TN by the owner's maternal grandmother, Zelma Cannup Henderson (born 5/25/1906 at Sevier County, TN, married Steward Ray Henderson, died 3/6/1937 in the same county). The maker gave the quilt to the owner as a wedding present.

**Ballard, Martha Powell** (Donald)
Commodore Perry Chapter
Ancestor: Lt. John Powell, SC—#778360
This "Log house" quilt was made in 1998 at Collierville, TN by the owner.

**Ballard, Martha Powell**
(Donald)
Commodore Perry Chapter
Ancestor: Lt. John Powell,
SC—#778360
This "Floral Hearts" quilt
was made in 1996 at Memphis, TN by the owner using pre-printed fabric.

**Ballard, Martha Powell**
(Donald)
Commodore Perry Chapter
Ancestor: Lt. John Powell,
SC—#778360
This "Denim Stripes and
Stars" quilt was made in
1999 at Collierville, TN by
the owner using pre-printed
fabric.

**Ballard, Martha Powell**
(Donald)
Commodore Perry Chapter
Ancestor: Lt. John Powell,
SC—#778360
This "Floral Basket" quilt
was made in 1997 at
Collierville, TN by the owner
using pre-printed fabric.

**Ballard, Martha Powell** (Donald)
Commodore Perry Chapter
Ancestor: Lt. John Powell, SC—
#778360
This "Star" quilt was made in
1994 at Memphis, TN by the
owner using pre-printed fabric.

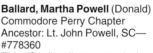

**Ballard, Martha Powell**
(Donald)
Commodore Perry Chapter
Ancestor: Lt. John Powell,
SC—#778360
This "Double Wedding
Ring" quilt was made in
1992 at Collierville, TN by
the owner using pre-printed
fabric.

**Ballard, Martha Powell**
(Donald)
Commodore Perry Chapter
Ancestor: Lt. John Powell,
SC—#778360
This "Patchwork" quilt was
made in 1998 at Collierville,
TN by the owner using pre-printed fabric.

**Ballard, Martha Powell**
(Donald)
Commodore Perry Chapter
Ancestor: Lt. John Powell,
SC—#778360
This "Triangle and Stars"
quilt was made in 1995 at
Collierville, TN by the owner
using pre-printed fabric.

**Ballard, Martha Powell**
(Donald)
Commodore Perry Chapter
Ancestor: Lt. John Powell,
SC—#778360
This "Floral Wreath" quilt
was made in 1993 at
Collierville, TN by the owner
using pre-printed fabric.

**Ballard, Martha Powell**
(Donald)
Commodore Perry Chapter
Ancestor: Lt. John Powell,
SC—#778360
This "Star" quilt was made
in 1999 at Collierville, TN by
the owner using pre-printed
fabric.

**Balsam, Jeanne Hanks** (John E.)
Moccasin Bend Chapter
Ancestor: Martin Shofner, NC —
#669947
This "Trip Around the World" quilt was
made circa 1920-24 in Murfreesboro,
TN by the owner's great grandmother, Cassie Green Gattas (born
11/1/1872 at Bedford County, TN,
married Isaac Newton Gattas, died
2/12/1945 at Murfreesboro, TN). The
quilt was made as a wedding gift for
the owner's grandmother, Ailene
Gattis Hill. When Ailene died in 1958,
the quilt was in the possession of the
owner's mother, Joan Hill Hanks.
When the owner married in 1980, her
mother presented the quilt as a wedding gift.

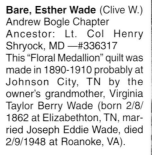

**Barber, Sarah Overton**
Charlotte Reeves Robertson Chapter
Ancestor: David Christopher, VA — #574162
This "Sampler" quilt was made in the 1970's at Bradford, TN by the owner's mother, Elsie Overton (born 11/25/1908 at Bradford, TN, married Paul Overton).

**Bare, Esther Wade** (Clive W.)
Andrew Bogle Chapter
Ancestor: Lt. Col Henry Shryock, MD —#336317
This "Floral Medallion" quilt was made in 1890-1910 probably at Johnson City, TN by the owner's grandmother, Virginia Taylor Berry Wade (born 2/8/1862 at Elizabethton, TN, married Joseph Eddie Wade, died 2/9/1948 at Roanoke, VA).

**Bare, Esther Wade**
(Clive W.)
Andrew Bogle Chapter
Ancestor: Lt. Col Henry Shryock, MD — #336317
This "Grapes and Leaves" quilt was made circa 1890-1910 probably at Johnson City, TN by the owner's grandmother, Virginia Taylor Berry Wade.

**Barnes, Hilda Hagar**
(Thomas F.)
Robert Cooke Chapter
Ancestor: George Hamilton, NC — #652477
This "Double Wedding Ring" quilt was made in 1950-1960 at Hermitage, TN by the owner's mother, Nova J. Hagar (born 10/20/1894 at Mt. Juliet, TN, married Emmett G. Hagar, died 3/20/1974 at Hermitage, TN).

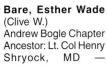

**Barnes, Hilda Hagar**
(Thomas F.)
Robert Cooke Chapter
Ancestor: George Hamilton, NC —#652477
This "Butterfly" quilt was made 1950-1960 at Hermitage, TN by the owner's mother, Nova J. Hagar.

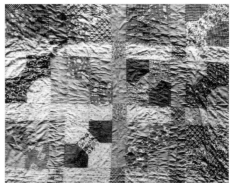
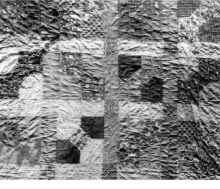

**Barnett, Peggy Johnson**
(Rex S.)
General William Lenoir Chapter
Ancestor: James Matthews, NC — #715119
This "Bow Tie" quilt was made in 1943 at Loudon County, TN by the owner's paternal grandmother, Mary Sherwood Johnson (born in 1882 at Anderson County, TN, married Joseph M. Johnson, died 1954 at Loudon County).

**Barnett, Peggy Johnson** (Rex S.)
General William Lenoir Chapter
Ancestor: James Matthews, NC — #715119
This "Trip Around the World" quilt was pieced in 1940 at Loudon County, TN by the owner's grandmother and mother.

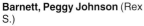
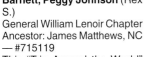

**Barnett, Peggy Johnson**
(Rex S.)
General William Lenoir Chapter
Ancestor: James Matthews, NC — #715119
This "Nine Diamond" quilt was made in 1940 at Loudon County, TN by the owner's maternal grandmother, Sammie Overton Tate. The quilt was passed from grandmother, to daughter, to owner.

**Barnett, Peggy Johnson** (Rex S.)
General William Lenoir Chapter
Ancestor: James Matthews, NC — #715119
This "Stair Step" quilt was made in 1950 in Loudon County, TN by the owner's mother, Elizabeth Tate Johnson, who gave it to the owner.

**Barnett, Peggy Johnson** (Rex S.)
General William Lenoir Chapter
Ancestor: James Matthews, NC — #715119
This "Dutch Doll/Sunbonnet Sue" quilt was pieced in the 1970's in Loudon County, TN by the owner's mother, Elizabeth Tate Johnson, and quilted by the owner's paternal aunt, Katherine Johnson Bright (born in 1915, married John Bright). Katherine is a member of TSDAR the General William Lenoir Chapter.

**Barnett, Peggy Johnson** (Rex S.)
General William Lenoir Chapter
Ancestor: James Matthews, NC —
#715119
This "Stair Step" quilt was made in
1940 by the owner's maternal grandmother, Sammie Overton Tate, who
passed it to the owner's mother. She
then passed it to the current owner.

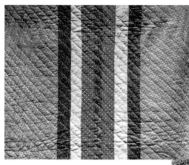

**Barnett, Peggy Johnson** (Rex S.)
General William Lenoir Chapter
Ancestor: James Matthews, NC —
#715119
This "Strip" quilt was made in 1900 at
Roane County, TN by the owner's
maternal great grandmother, Martha
Ridge Tate (born 1869 at Roane
County, TN, married Robert Byrd Tate,
died in 1946 at Roane County).

**Barnett, Peggy Johnson** (Rex S.)
General William Lenoir Chapter
Ancestor: James Matthews, NC —
#715119
This "Random Tack" quilt was
made in 1950 at Loudon County,
TN by the owner's mother, Eliza-
beth Tate Johnson.

**Barnett, Peggy Johnson** (Rex S.)
General William Lenoir Chapter
Ancestor: James Matthews, NC —
#715119
This "Patch" quilt was made in 1945
at Loudon County, TN by the
owner's mother, Elizabeth Tate
Johnson.

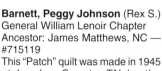

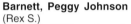

**Barnett, Peggy Johnson**
(Rex S.)
General William Lenoir
Chapter
Ancestor: James Matthews,
NC — #715119
This "Eight Pointed Star"
quilt was made in 1930 at
Roane County, TN by the
owner's maternal great
grandmother, Martha Ridge
Tate.

**Barnett, Peggy Johnson** (Rex S.)
General William Lenoir Chapter
Ancestor: James Matthews, NC —
#715119
This "Octagon/Snowball" quilt was
made in 1944 at Loudon County,
TN by the owner's mother, Elizabeth Tate Johnson, and her paternal grandmother, Mary Sherwood
Johnson. During WWII, the owner's
father, Glyn Johnson, was in Eu-
rope with the army. Her mother
lived at various times with her
mother or in-laws. While there, they
made several quilts. The owner inherited this quilt which was made
during this time.

**Barry, Helen Hines** (Elmo)
Old Glory Chapter
Ancestor: James Williams,
VA — #745177
This "Evening Star" quilt
was made in Kentucky in
1988. The owner acquired
it from the Amish in 1990.

**Barry, Helen Hines** (Elmo)
Old Glory Chapter
Ancestor: James Williams,
VA — #745177
This "State" quilt was made
in 1976 at Nashville, TN by
the 4th grade class at Glen-
dale School, the owner's
student's.

**Barton, Ruby Cole**
(Wade)
James Buckley Chapter
Ancestor: John Cole, VA —
#582508
This "Dresden Plate" quilt
was made 1929-30 at
Neshoba County, MS by
the owner.

**Bates, Shelby Fowler** (James C.)
Robert Lewis Chapter
Ancestor: Sgt Sherwood Fowler, VA
— #785381
This "Dutch Doll" quilt was made in
the early 1950's in Marshall County,
TN by Mrs. Aldridge who sold the
quilt to the current owner.

**Bassett, Nancy Woolf** (Don)
We-ah-tah-umba Chapter
Ancestor: George Darden, Sr., GA — #701548
This "Tulip" quilt was made in June 1891 at
Madisonville, Kentucky by the owner's great
grandmother, Mamie Ruby Pratt (born at
Madisonville, married Dr. Virgil Pratt, died in Atlanta, GA). The quilt was given to the owner's
grandmother on her wedding day, and eventually passed down to the owner's mother, and finally to the owner.

**Bates, Shelby Fowler** (James C.)
Robert Lewis Chapter
Ancestor: Sgt Sherwood Fowler, VA —
#785381
This "Log Cabin" quilt was made in the early
1980's in Summer County, TN by the owner's
mother-in-law, Annie Mai Bates (born 6/5/1917
at Macon County, TN, married Hilmer E.
Bates).

**Baugus, Heather Benet**
Chickasaw Bluff Chapter
Ancestor: Abner Alloway
Strange, VA — #780089
This "Cosmic Explosion" quilt
was pieced in 1998 in Memphis, TN by the owner (born 9/7/1973 at Memphis, TN) and
her grandmother, Marilyn
Johnson Baugus. In 1997,
when the owner knew she
would be leaving home for
graduate school, she asked
her grandmother to help her
make a quilt that would remind
her of home and keep her
warm in the cold Oregon winters. Heather selected the pattern, and pieced the quilt with

**Baugus, Marilyn Johnson**
(Clarence Earl, Jr.)
Chickasaw Bluff Chapter
Ancestor: Abner Alloway Strange, VA
— #621436
This "Dogwood" quilt was made
1975-78 at Memphis, TN by the
owner (born 8/27/1929 at Savannah,
TN). She bought this quilt kit at
Goldsmith's Department Store
around 1970. It is made completely
by hand including the quilting which
was done on her daughter's quilt
frame. The quilt is signed, "Finished
8/27/76, my 46th birthday."

instructions and encouragement from her grandmother who prepared the top for
quilting. It was quilted by Joyce Fratini.

**Baugus, Marilyn Johnson**
(Clarence Earl, Jr.)
Chickasaw Bluff Chapter
Ancestor: Abner Alloway
Strange, VA — #621436
This "Sunbonnet Sue Throughout the Year" quilt was appliqued 1998-99 by the owner at
Memphis, TN. It was quilted by
Joyce Fratini. A quilt shop in
Paducah, KY inspired th owner
to make the quilt. She was
drawn to the applique and the
creative possibilities of making
a one of a kind quilt using a traditional pattern as the base.
The owner said, "It was a joy to
know Sue, dress her, furnish her
with accessories and see her
happy in every season."

**Baugus, Marilyn Johnson** (Clarence Earl,
Jr.)
Chickasaw Bluff Chapter
Ancestor: Abner Alloway Strange, VA —
#621436
This "Elongated Octagon" quilt was made in
Hardin County, TN in the 1920's by the
owner's great grandmother, Missouri Ann
Melton Flannagan ( born 6/14/1855 at
Booneville, MS, married William Simpson
Flannagan, Sr., died 3/6/1936 at Savannah,
TN). Unlike many of the owner's quilts, this
one was not used as often as other quilts
and is, therefore, better preserved. The
owner remembers her great grandmother,
cutting the pieces, picking seeds from cotton bolls, carding the batts, and putting the
layers of the quilt together on the floor. Once
it was basted, the maker put it on a quilt
frame, made by her husband, and quilted it.
Through her great grandmother, the owner
developed a life long love of quilts.

**Baugus, Marilyn Johnson**
(Clarence Earl, Jr.)
Chickasaw Bluff Chapter
Ancestor: Abner Alloway
Strange, VA — #621436
This "String" quilt was made
sometime in the 1920's by the
owner's great grandmother,
Missouri Ann Melton
Flannagan. Even though this
quilt is "worn out," the owner
says, "this quilt is beautiful to
me because I have never
seen an ugly quilt."

**Baugus, Marilyn Johnson** (Clarence
Earl, Jr.)
Chickasaw Bluff Chapter
Ancestor: Abner Alloway Strange, VA —
#621436
This "Grandmother's Flower Garden" quilt was made circa 1946-47 by the owner's grandmother,
Daisy Ann Flannagan Fowler
(born 2/9/1885 at Hardin County,
TN, married Tone K. Fowler, died 5/17/1969 at Memphis, TN). "I remember my grandmother piecing this quilt.
It is small and light weight because she
could not sleep under heavy cover due to
her arthritis."

**Baugus, Marilyn Johnson**
(Clarence Earl, Jr.)
Chickasaw Bluff Chapter
Ancestor: Abner Alloway Strange, VA
— #621436
This original "Landscape Banner"
quilt was made in 1998 by Marilyn
Baugus, her granddaughter, Heather
Baugus, and her daughter, Bridget
Ciaramitaro. They designed and
made this quilt with other seniors in
the Memphis Community who are
active in Senior Leaders, Inc. The
quilt has been featured in four videos, on the cover of workbooks,
and in brochures about the Senior
Leaders organization.

**Bawcum, Julia Allen**
(Coy H.)
Glover's Trace Chapter
Ancestor: Sgt. John
Allen, VA —#769227
This "Lone Star" quilt was
made in 1946 at
Camden, TN by the
owner's mother, Ila Mai
Allen (born 1/30/1909 at
Benton County, TN, married Theo R. Allen, died
1/10/1985 at Gibson
County, TN).

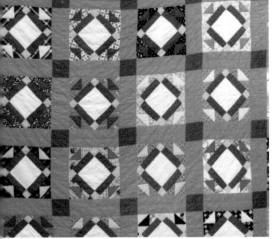

**Bawcum, Julia Allen** (Coy H.)
Glover's Trace Chapter
Ancestor: Sgt. John Allen, VA —#769227
This "Ducks on the Pond" quilt was made in 1935 at Benton County, TN by the owner's mother, Ila Mai Allen.

**Bawcum, Julia Allen** (Coy H.)
Glover's Trace Chapter
Ancestor: Sgt. John Allen, VA —#769227
This "Gemstone" quilt was made in 1975 at Benton County, TN by the owner (born 8/25/1929 at Camden, TN).

**Bawcum, Julia Allen** (Coy H.)
Glover's Trace Chapter
Ancestor: Sgt. John Allen, VA —#769227
This "Tulip" quilt was made in Camden, TN in 1940 by the owner's mother, Ila Mai Allen.

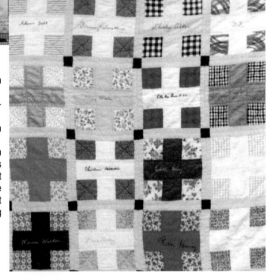

**Bawcum, Julia Allen** (Coy H.)
Glover's Trace Chapter
Ancestor: Sgt. John Allen, VA —#769227
This "Sunlight and Shadow" quilt was made in 1935 at Camden, TN by the owner's mother, Ila Mai Allen.

**Bawcum, Julia Allen** (Coy H.)
Glover's Trace Chapter
Ancestor: Sgt. John Allen, VA —#769227
This "Mystery Star/Wheel" quilt was made in 1937 at Camden, TN by the owner's mother, Ila Mai Allen.

**Bawcum, Julia Allen** (Coy H.)
Glover's Trace Chapter
Ancestor: Sgt. John Allen, VA —#769227
This "Nine Patch Friendship" quilt was made in 1952 at Bruceton, TN by the owner's co-workers at H.I.S. Manufacturing Company.

**Bawcum, Julia Allen** (Coy H.)
Glover's Trace Chapter
Ancestor: Sgt. John Allen, VA —#769227
This "Chicken Gizzard" quilt was made in 1972 at Benton County, TN by the owner.

**Bawcum, Julia Allen** (Coy H.)
Glover's Trace Chapter
Ancestor: Sgt. John Allen, VA —#769227
This "Diamond Field" quilt was made in 1975 at Camden, TN by the owner's mother, Ila Mai Allen.

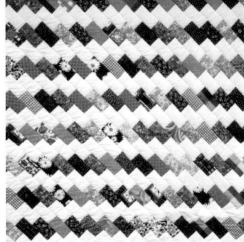

**Bawcum, Julia Allen**
(Coy H.)
Glover's Trace Chapter
Ancestor: Sgt. John
Allen, VA —#769227
This "Postage Stamp"
quilt was made in 1975
at Camden, TN by the
owner's mother, Ila Mai
Allen.

**Bawcum, Luwana**
Glover's Trace Chapter
Ancestor: Sgt. John
Allen, VA —#769706
This "Brick Walk" quilt
was made in 1969 at
Camden, TN by Ila Mai
Allen.

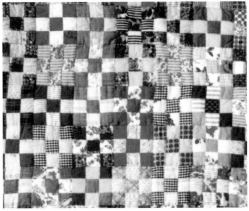

**Bawcum, Luwana**
Glover's Trace Chapter
Ancestor: Sgt. John
Allen, VA —#769706
This "Postage Stamp"
quilt was made in 1969
at Camden, TN by the
owner's grandmother,
Lela Myrtle Bawcum
(born 10/25/1895 at
Camden, married
James A. Bawcum, died
9/2/1981 at Camden).

**Beck, Norma Nuckolls**
(Eugene Jr.)
Charlotte Reeves
Robertson Chapter
Ancestor: Hudson Berry,
Sr., NC — #770265
This "Crazy" quilt was
made in 1888 by Mary
Hutchison Ogburn Draper
(born 11/24/1863 at
Springfield, TN, married
John Bryson Draper, died
2/17/1900 at Springfield).
"1888 AD" is embroidered
into the quilt. That is the
birth year of Mary Virgina
Draper, daughter of the
maker. The quilt was
passed from the maker, to
Mary Virgina Draper Par-
sons, to her daughter,
Louise Hutchison Par-
sons, to the current owner.

**Beck, Virginia Freeman**
(Eugene, Sr.)
Charlotte Reeves
Robertson Chapter
Ancestor: Thomas Farmer,
NC — #570725
This "Tulip" quilt was made
in 1937 at Nashville, TN by
the owner's cousins, Mrs.
Thomas H. (Nettie) Warren
and Mrs. Clarence Carter.

**Beck, Virginia Freeman**
(Eugene, Sr.)
Charlotte Reeves
Robertson Chapter
Ancestor: Thomas Farmer,
NC — #570725
This "Governor's Garden"
coverlet was inherited from
the owner's maternal an-
cestors. It was published in
Of Coverlets, the Lega-
cies—The Weavers by
Sadye Tune Wilson and
Doris Finch Kennedy. The
coverlet was also part of
the Tennessee Textile His-
tory Project.

**Beesinger, Lauran Elizabeth
(Beth) Jenkins** (David)
Fort Prudhomme Chapter
Ancestor: David Craig, NC —
#765994
This original design "Tennessee Bicentennial" crib quilt was made in
1996 at Campbell, MO by Amelda
Brauer Dees (born 1924 at
Wilhelminia, MO, married James
Dees). The quiltmaker is the owner's
friend's daughter-in-law's mother. In
1996 the owner's DAR chapter was
selling bicentennial posters. Mrs.
Dee's daughter took the poster to her
mother and suggested she make a
quilt using the design. This is one of
three quilts she made from the
poster. The owner's grandmother,
Delene Craig Smith, bought this quilt
as a gift for the owner's son, James
Winston Beesinger, who was just
two months old. The maker was 70 years old and was having trouble with cata-
racts when she made the quilt. Her other quilts have won awards.

**Beets, Marjorie Ewing**
(Robert)
Samuel Doak Chapter
Ancestor: Shadrac Inman,
NC —#385050
This "Double Wedding
Ring" quilt was purchased
by the owner at a shop in
Gatlinburg, TN in the late
1970's at an "end of the
season" sale.

**Beets, Marjorie Ewing** (Robert)
Samuel Doak Chapter
Ancestor: Shadrac Inman, NC — #385050
This "Drunkard's Path" quilt was made in 1935 at Grainger County, TN by the owner's mother-in-law, May Rich Beets (born 5/7/1893 at Grainger County, TN, married Henry Edgar Beets, died 2/18/1967 at Morristown, TN). The quiltmaker had five sons. She made a quilt for each one and embroidered his name on it. This one is labeled "Bobby Beets, March 1935". The quiltmaker kept a quilt frame hanging from the ceiling and quilted in her spare time. The maker gave this and other quilts to the owner.

**Bell, Laverne Melton** (Marvin)
Glover's Trace Chapter
Ancestor: Zachariah Melton, NC — #772544
This "Grandmother's Flower Garden" quilt was made in 1961 in Benton County, TN by the owner's mother, Florence W. Melton (born 6/5/1886 at Benton County, married Herbert B. Melton, died 9/14/1987 in the same county).

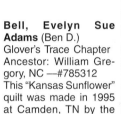

**Bell, Evelyn Sue Adams** (Ben D.)
Glover's Trace Chapter
Ancestor: William Gregory, NC —#785312
This "Devil's Puzzle" quilt was made in 1994 at Camden, TN by the owner (born 5/22/1928 at Lone Oak, KY).

**Bell, Evelyn Sue Adams** (Ben D.)
Glover's Trace Chapter
Ancestor: William Gregory, NC —#785312
This "Double Wedding Ring" quilt was made in 1997 at Camden, TN by the owner.

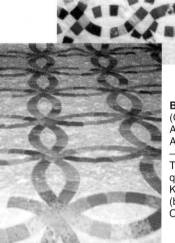

**Bell, Evelyn Sue Adams** (Ben D.)
Glover's Trace Chapter
Ancestor: William Gregory, NC —#785312
This "Kansas Sunflower" quilt was made in 1995 at Camden, TN by the owner.

**Bennett, Frances Williams** (Carl)
Andrew Bogle Chapter
Ancestor: Fredrick Emmert — #699800
This "Double Wedding Ring" quilt was made in 1994 in Knoxville, TN by the owner (born 8/12/1927 at Granger County, TN).

**Berger, Nellree Baker** (Ernest E.)
Moccasin Bend Chapter
Ancestor: John Cates, NC 605523
This "Dutch Doll" quilt was begun in 1933 by the owner when she was 12 years old as a summer project at Grandma Lena Keef Fry's home (married to Fred in 1895) in Elmo, TN. The owner's mother, Edna Fry Baker (born 10/19/1897, married John Joseph Baker 4/17/1917, died 3/18/1993 at Chattanooga, TN), finished piecing it in 1933 in Chattanooga, TN. It was quilted by the owner's paternal aunt, Harriet Baker Clark, at Lookout Mountain, GA. The owner remembers that when she visited her grandparents during the summer "we did not do much playing, but she taught us things, at least she tried. In the summer of 1933, she started the girls on making quilt blocks. Ten blocks were completed. Years later when Edna Baker finished piecing the quilt, it was turned over to master quiltmaker, Harriet Baker Clark. Harriet had finished many quilts for people in New York. She had even quilted one for First Lady, Jackie Kennedy, that was to be used at Mt. Vernon, VA.

**Berger, Nellree Baker** (Ernest E.)
Moccasin Bend Chapter
Ancestor: John Cates, NC 605523
This child's "Crazy" quilt was made in 1918 at Hamilton County, TN by the owner's great grandmother, Teleta Bridwell Fry (born 1/1/1837 at McMinn County, TN, married Houston Greenberry Fry, died 11/30/1918 at Hamilton County, TN). The quilt was made before the owner's older sister, Edythe Baker Crabtree, was born in 1918. It has been handed down to the owner. The owner says that this quilt has had a "hard life with four kids playing on it and also being used as a lap cover for winter sporting events. We didn't appreciate quilts then."

**Berger, Nellree Baker** (Ernest E.)
Moccasin Bend Chapter
Ancestor: John Cates, NC 605523
This "Cathedral Window" quilt was made in 1971-75 at Chattanooga, TN by the owner's mother, Mary Teleda (Eda) Fry Baker. The owner received it with the promise to pass it on to her niece, Estha Freeman. In 1981 the owner added 6 inches of blocks to the quilt.

**Berry, Ann Powers** (William J.)
Captain William Edmiston Chapter
Ancestor: John Tatom, NC — #495509
This "Robbing Peter To Pay Paul" quilt was made in 1916 at Bruceton, TN by the owner's paternal aunt, Eddie Powers Burch (born 2/2/1888 at Houston County, TN, married John Thomas Burch, died 12/26/1948 at Nashville, TN). This was one of two quilt's she made for her bachelor brother. She completed the quilt while her brother was in France in World War I. He served with the 81st Wildcat Division from 9/9/1917-6/29/1919. She presented the quilts to him when he arrived back home. Eventually he married and his wife took excellent care of the quilts. They are still beautiful today.

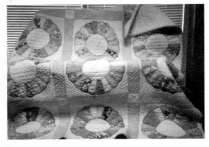

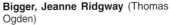

**Berry, Ann Powers** (William J.)
Captain William Edmiston Chapter
Ancestor: John Tatom, NC — #495509
This "Dresden Plate" quilt was made in 1917 at Bruceton, TN by the owner's paternal aunt, Eddie Powers Burch. This is the second of the two quilts she made for her brother while he served in WWI.

**Berry, Ann Powers** (William J.)
Captain William Edmiston Chapter
Ancestor: John Tatom, NC — #495509
This "Butterfly" quilt was made in 1910 at Vanleer, TN by the owner's husband's grandmother, Emma Hughes Pancher (born 4/26/1874 at Montgomery County, TN, married John Thomas Van Pancher, died 10/16/1960 at Vanleer, TN). The quiltmaker made the quilt for her daughter who loved butterflies. The quilt was given to the owner's husband by his mother, Ruby Prancher Berry on 5/31/1957.

**Bigger, Jeanne Ridgway** (Thomas Ogden)
Tullahoma Chapter
Ancestor: Jacob Flournoy, VA — #527400
This "Velvet Rose" coverlet was made circa 1865 at Perryville, KY by the owner's husband's grandmother and great grandmother. His grandmother, Molly Tewmey Bigger, was born 12/28/1849 at Perryville, KY, married John Thomas Bigger, and died 10/24/1924 at Harrodsburg, KY). The coverlet was passed from Ann Graves Penny Tewmey, to Molly Tewmey Bigger, to Lloyd B. Bigger, to Thomas Ogden Bigger, to Thomas Ridgeway Bigger, to the owner.

**Bigger, Jeanne Ridgway** (Thomas Ogden)
Tullahoma Chapter
Ancestor: Jacob Flournoy, VA — #527400
This "Crazy" quilt was made before the War Between the States at Perryville, KY by the owner's husband's grandmother and great grandmother, Ann Graves Penny (born 5/18/1834 at Perryville, KY, married Dr. Joseph R. Lewney, died 3/13/1897 at Harrodsburg, KY).

**Billips, Grace Edna Motley** (Woodrow W)
Campbell Chapter
Ancestor: David Motley, VA — #582261
This "Crazy" quilt was made circa 1928-32 at Pittsylvania County, VA by the owner (born 8/2/1918 at Pittsylvania County, VA). She started the quilt when she was 10 or 12 years old at the urging of her mother "who felt the need to teach me to sew and be occupied." The quilt is made of dresses and other fabrics from the home. Before finishing high school, the maker lost interest in the quilt, and it was stored carelessly in the attic trunk. The maker's fascination was renewed as a result of the "TSDAR American Heritage Quilt Project." At 80 years old, she completed the quilt in time for it to be included in this book.

**Billips, Grace Edna Motley** (Woodrow W)
Campbell Chapter
Ancestor: David Motley, VA — #582261
This "Lone Star" quilt was made circa 1939 at Pittsylvania County, VA by the owner's paternal grandmother, Nellie Catherine Bennett Motley (born 11/6/1870 at Pittsylvania County, married Josiah Coleman Motley, died 10/12/1961 at Danville, VA). It was presented to the owner 1939 as a wedding gift. The quilt remained stored on a shelf waiting for an "appropriate use." The TSDAR American Heritage Quilt Project has inspired the owner to remove the quilt from the closet, put it on display, and make sure it is passed to the next generation.

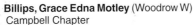

**Billips, Grace Edna Motley** (Woodrow W)
Campbell Chapter
Ancestor: David Motley, VA — #582261
This "Odd Fellows Patch" quilt was made circa 1938-39 at Bland County, VA by the owner's mother-in-law, Louvenia Jane Compton Billips (born 3/7/1877 at Tazwell County, VA, married William Floyd Billips, died 7/30/1964 at Bland County, VA). The quilt was given to the owner as a wedding gift in 1939. It was used for many years as a quilt for comfortable sleeping. In later years it was used on the back of a Duncan Phyfe sofa in memory of the maker.

**Bird, Mollie Burnett** (William Trump)
Captain William Edmiston Chapter.
Ancestor: Charles Champion, VA —#756826
This embroidered baby quilt was discovered in the owner's mother-in-law's attic after her death.

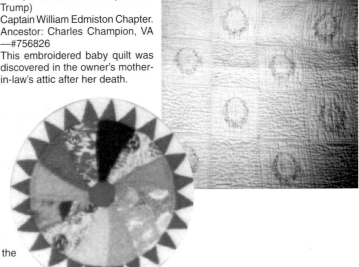

**Bird, Mollie Burnett** (William Trump)
Captain William Edmiston Chapter.
Ancestor: Charles Champion, VA —#756826
This "Rising Sun" quilt was also discovered in the owner's mother-in-law's attic after her death.

**Blair, Gwen Stallard** (Donald)
Samuel Doak Chapter
Ancestor: Walter Stallard, VA — #718005
This "Bow Tie" quilt was made in 1957-58 at Red Jacket, WV by the owner's mother, Esther Stallard (born 7/7/1937, married J.D. Stallard). It was given to the owner by her mother.

**Blair, Gwen Stallard**
(Donald)
Samuel Doak Chapter
Ancestor: Walter Stallard, VA — #718005
This "Lone Star" quilt was made in the 1970's at Red Jacket, WV by the owner's grandmother, Fannie Stallard (born 3/3/1911 at Omaha, VA, married the Rev. Ernest O. Stallard, died 1/8/1981 at Hernshaw, WV).

**Blair, Gwen Stallard**
(Donald)
Samuel Doak Chapter
Ancestor: Walter Stallard, VA — #718005
This "Fan" quilt was made in the 1960's at Red Jacket, WV by the owner's grandmother, Fannie Stallard. The quilt was passed from the maker, to her daughter-in-law, Esther Johnson Stallard (the owner's mother), to the owner.

**Bland, Joy Norwood** (Bobby)
John Babb Chapter
Ancestor: John Crockett, NC — #734145
This "Butterfly" quilt was pieced in 1932-33 at Henry County, TN by the owner's mother, Sunshine Miller Norwood (born 12/23/1915, married William Kirkman Norwood). The maker's aunts, Laura Hart and Lilly Miller, helped her quilt it. The butterflies are made from fabrics left over from family sewing projects.

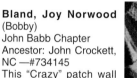

**Bland, Joy Norwood** (Bobby)
John Babb Chapter
Ancestor: John Crockett, NC —#734145
This "Friendship/Album" quilt was made in 1932 at Henry County, TN by the owner's mother, Sunshine Miller Norwood. The maker pieced some of the squares and friends and family pieced the others. Their names are embroidered on the centers.

**Bland, Joy Norwood**
(Bobby)
John Babb Chapter
Ancestor: John Crockett, NC —#734145
This "Crazy" patch wall hanging was made by the owner's great grandmother, Georgia Boyce Tharpe Atkins (born 8/29/1860 at Henry County, TN, married Thomas Kirk Atkins, died 7/4/1903 at Henry County). This wall hanging is all that remains of a beautiful quilt that was made of silk and velvet.

**Bland, Joy Norwood** (Bobby)
John Babb Chapter
Ancestor: John Crockett, NC — #734145
This "Tulip" quilt was made in the 1980's by the owner's aunt by marriage, Evelyn Allbritten Norwood (born 5/9/1919, married Priestly Alston Norwood, died 12/3/1994 at Paris, TN). Each year the maker and her husband spent many summer weeks camping at Land Between the Lakes. It was here that she pieced the quilt and then quilted it during the winter months. When she died, she left over 100 beautiful quilts all of different designs and patterns.

**Bledsoe, Anna Garrett**
(Duke)
Hatchie Chapter
Ancestor: Jonathon Jones, SC — #785238
This "Colonial Lady" quilt was made in the 1980's at Jackson, TN by the owner's mother, Bertha Ruth Garrett (born 10/28/1907, married John Shannon Garrett).

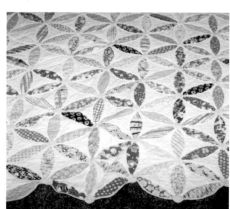

**Bledsoe, Anna Garrett**
(Duke)
Hatchie Chapter
Ancestor: Jonathon Jones, SC — #785238
This "Daisy Chain/Orange Peel" quilt was made in the 1920's in Humboldt, TN by the owner's husband's grandmother, Elizabeth Kimbrough Rose (born 12/5/1878 at Marshall County, TN, married James Alfred Rose, died 3/11/1964 at Humboldt, TN).

**Bledsoe, Anna Garrett**
(Duke)
Hatchie Chapter
Ancestor: Jonathon Jones, SC — #785238
This "Snowball" quilt was made in the 1930's at Humboldt, TN by the owner's husband's grandmother, Elizabeth Kimbrough Rose.

**Bledsoe, Anna Garrett** (Duke)
Hatchie Chapter
Ancestor: Jonathon Jones, SC — #785238
This mosaic "The House That Jack Built" quilt was made in the 1950's at Carroll County, TN by the owner's grandmother, Ada Laura Pugh (born 4/3/1880 at Carroll County, married Walker E. W. Pugh, died 9/19/1959 at Jackson, TN). The maker made a quilt for each of the children of her ten living children. This quilt was made of scraps of material from the owner's school dresses, so when she looks at the quilt she sees her first grade dresses. The quilt was given to the owner when she was ten years old.

**Bledsoe, Anna Garrett** (Duke)
Hatchie Chapter
Ancestor: Jonathon Jones, SC — #785238
This "Snow Flower" quilt was made in 1968 at Bolivar and Humboldt, TN by the owner (born 11/28/1944 at Jackson, TN and her mother-in-law, Nell Bledsoe (born 7/24/1907 at Humboldt, TN, died 7/29/1986 at Jackson, TN).

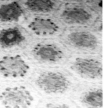

**Bledsoe, Anna Garrett** (Duke)
Hatchie Chapter
Ancestor: Jonathon Jones, SC — #785238
This "Grandmother's Flower Garden" quilt was made in the 1930's at Gibson County, TN by the owner's mother-in-law, Nell Bledsoe.

**Bledsoe, Anna Garrett** (Duke)
Hatchie Chapter
Ancestor: Jonathon Jones, SC — #785238
This "Tulip" cross stitch quilt was made in the 1970's at Humboldt, TN by the owner's mother-in-law, Nell Bledsoe.

**Bledsoe, Anna Garrett** (Duke)
Hatchie Chapter
Ancestor: Jonathon Jones, SC — #785238
This "Baby Block" quilt was made in the 1930's at Humboldt, TN by the owner's mother-in-law, Nell Bledsoe.

**Bledsoe, Anna Garrett** (Duke)
Hatchie Chapter
Ancestor: Jonathon Jones, SC — #785238
This "Rose" cross stitch quilt was made in the 1970's at Humboldt, TN by the owner's mother-in-law, Nell Bledsoe.

**Bledsoe, Anna Garrett** (Duke)
Hatchie Chapter
Ancestor: Jonathon Jones, SC — #785238
This "Floral" cross stitch quilt was made in the 1960's at Humboldt, TN by the owner's mother-in-law, Nell Bledsoe.

**Bledsoe, Anna Garrett** (Duke)
Hatchie Chapter
Ancestor: Jonathon Jones, SC — #785238
This "Wheel of Mystery/Winding Ways" quilt was made in the 1930's at Humboldt, TN by the owner's mother-in-law, Nell Bledsoe.

**Bledsoe, Anna Garrett** (Duke)
Hatchie Chapter
Ancestor: Jonathon Jones, SC — #785238
This "Colonial Lady" quilt was made in the late 1930's at Jackson, TN by the owner's grandmother, Ida Garrett (born 3/3/1861 at Carroll County, TN, married David Franklin Garrett, died 1/3/1942 at Madison County, TN).

**Bledsoe, Anna Garrett** (Duke)
Hatchie Chapter
Ancestor: Jonathon Jones, SC — #785238
This "Dogwood Blossoms" quilt was made in the late 1930's at Jackson, TN by the owner's grandmother, Ida Garrett.

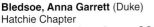

**Bledsoe, Anna Garrett** (Duke)
Hatchie Chapter
Ancestor: Jonathon Jones, SC — #785238
This "Cross and Crown" quilt was made in the 1950's in Carroll County, TN by the owner's grandmother, Ada Laura Boyd Pugh.

**Bledsoe, Anna Garrett** (Duke)
Hatchie Chapter
Ancestor: Jonathon Jones, SC — #785238
This "Kansas City Star/Blazing Star" quilt was made in the 1950's in Carroll County, TN by the owner's grandmother, Ada Laura Boyd Pugh.

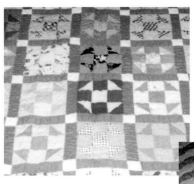

**Bledsoe, Anna Garrett** (Duke)
Hatchie Chapter
Ancestor: Jonathon Jones, SC —
#785238
This "Shoo-Fly" quilt was made in the
1950's by the owner's grandmother,
Ada Laura Boyd Pugh.

**Bledsoe, Anna Garrett** (Duke)
Hatchie Chapter
Ancestor: Jonathon Jones, SC —
#785238
This "Dutch Doll" quilt was made in
the 1970's at Jackson, TN by the
owner's mother, Bertha Garrett (born
10/28/1907, married John Shannon
Garrett).

**Bledsoe, Anna Garrett** (Duke)
Hatchie Chapter
Ancestor: Jonathon Jones, SC —
#785238
This "Love Ring" quilt was made in
1987 at Jackson, TN by the owner's
mother, Bertha Garrett.

**Bledsoe, Anna Garrett** (Duke)
Hatchie Chapter
Ancestor: Jonathon Jones, SC —
#785238
This "Improved Nine Patch" quilt was
made in Jackson, TN by the owner's
mother, Bertha Garrett.

**Bledsoe, Anna Garrett** (Duke)
Hatchie Chapter
Ancestor: Jonathon Jones, SC —
#785238
This "Dresden Plate" quilt was made
in the 1970's at Jackson, TN by the
owner's mother, Bertha Garrett.

**Bledsoe, Anna Garrett** (Duke)
Hatchie Chapter
Ancestor: Jonathon Jones, SC —
#785238
This "Double Wedding Ring" quilt was
made in the 1980's at Jackson, TN
by the owner's mother, Bertha Garrett.

**Bledsoe, Mary Massey**
(Charles)
King's Mountain Messenger
Chapter
Ancestor: Robert Stephen,
VA — #713291
This "Crazy" quilt was made
in 1890-95 at Lincoln County,
TN by the owner's great
grandmother's sister,
Phoebe Franklin (born 1830
at Lincoln County, married
Hiram Franklin, died 1916 in
Lincoln County near Kelso,
TN). This quilt was made
from pieces of fabric given by
friends and family. Phoebe
was listed in census records
as a weaver of tapestry. She
put the pieces of this quilt
together with beautiful

stitches and put the names on each piece. It is interesting that her name isn't on
any of the pieces. Evidently, she thought that "fools names like their faces are
always seen in public places," so she left her and her husband's names off.
Phoebe gave the quilt to her sister, Delphia Ann Franklin. Delphia Ann's daughter, Delia Canzadia Franklin married Robert Stiles and the owner's mother, Etta
Stiles Massey, was their daughter. Delia died when Etta was seven years old.
Her father had also died. Delphia Ann raised Delia and gave her the quilt when
she married circa 1895. Delphia Ann lost her mother, father and two sisters within
a short time due to a typhoid epidemic. Only she and her younger brother
survived."If this quilt could talk!"

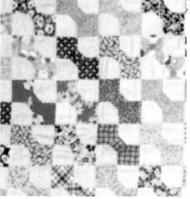

**Bolton, Marilyn Hunt** (Glenn)
Traveler's Rest Chapter
Ancestor: John Charles Lindsay, MD
—#781352
This "Bow Tie" quilt was made circa
1952 at Nashville, TN by the owner's
first husband's grandmother, Edith
Chilton Keller (born 11/08/1871 at
Bedford County, TN, married Charles
P. Keller, died 1/4/1967 at Nashville,
TN). The quilt was passed from
maker, to her daughter, Jennie Keller
Anderton, to the current owner.

**Bolton, Marilyn Hunt** (Glenn)
Traveler's Rest Chapter
Ancestor: John Charles Lindsay, MD
—#781352
This "Churn Dash" quilt was made
circa 1920 at Nashville, TN by the
owner's first husband's grandmother,
Edith Chilton Keller.

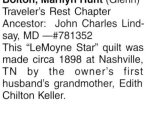

**Bolton, Marilyn Hunt** (Glenn)
Traveler's Rest Chapter
Ancestor: John Charles Lind-
say, MD —#781352
This "LeMoyne Star" quilt was
made circa 1898 at Nashville,
TN by the owner's first
husband's grandmother, Edith
Chilton Keller.

**Boscaccy, Carol** (Mike)
Chucalissa Chapter
Ancestor: Andrew Gibson, NC
—#772168
This "Improved Nine Patch"
quilt was made circa 1940 at
Walnut, MS by the owner's
great aunt, Myrtle Grantham
Cox (born 1904 at Hardeman
County, TN, married Buster
Cox, died 1995 at Bolivar, TN).
When the owner's house
burned in 1960, Aunt Myrtle
gave her this quilt. Since everything was lost in the fire, the
quilt was a very practical and
useful gift, and since Aunt
Myrtle made it, it meant even
more to the owner.

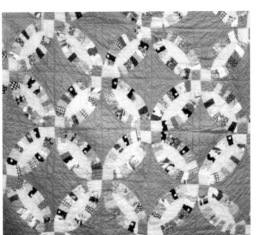

**Bourne, Ann Riley**
(Robert)
Glover's Trace Chapter
Ancestor: Alexander
Love, SC — #533017
This "Double Wedding
Ring" quilt was made
1930-40 at Memphis,
TN by the owner's
mother, Lena Harris
Riley.

**Bourne, Ann Riley**
(Robert)
Glover's Trace Chapter
Ancestor: Alexander
Love, SC — #533017
This "Double Wedding
Ring" quilt was made
1930-40 at Memphis,
TN by the owner's
mother, Lena Harris
Riley (born 10/31/1901
at DeSoto County, MS,
married John, died 12/
29/1977 at Benton
County, TN).

**Bowles, Bettye Milligan**
(M.P. "Pat")
French Lick Chapter
Ancestor: 2nd Lt. James
Lewis, VA — #693391
This "Cockscomb and
Currants" quilt was made
in 1910 at Winchester,
TN by the owner's grand-
mother, Sally Elizabeth
Hawkins (born 11/7/1874
at Winchester, TN, mar-
ried John Green
Hawkins, died 1/19/1966
at Dechard, TN at age
91).

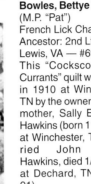

**Bourne, Ann Riley** (Robert)
Glover's Trace Chapter
Ancestor: Alexander Love, SC — #533017
This "Yo Yo" quilt was made 1924-29 at Marked Tree, AR by the owner's mother,
Lena Harris Riley.

**Bowman, Winnie J.**
Bonny Kate Chapter
Ancestor: Hugh Rogers,
NC —#750497
This original embroi-
dered doll size quilt was
made in the mid 1930's
at Walker County, GA by
the owner's mother,
Willa Mae Johnston
Bowman. The frayed
edge is the result of
playing with her dolls
too close to the fire
place.

**Bowman, Winnie J.**
Bonny Kate Chapter
Ancestor: Hugh Rogers, NC
—#750497
This "Dutch Doll/Sunbonnet
Sue" doll size quilt was
made circa 1930's, prob-
ably at Clay County, NC, by
the owner's mother, Willa
Mae Johnston Bowman
(born 12/25/1895 at Clay
County, NC, married
Charles Wilson Bowman,
died 9/8/1974 at Ft.
Ogelthorpe, GA). The
quilt was made for the
owner and her dolls.

**Bowman, Winnie J.**
Bonny Kate Chapter
Ancestor: Hugh Rogers, NC —#750497
This "State Flowers" quilt was made in the late 1920's at Chattanooga, TN
by the owner's mother, Willa Mae Johnston Bowman. Each block is embroidered with the flower of one of the 48 states. The quilt was entered in a fair
at Warner Park in Chattanooga, TN, but the owner does not think it won an
award.

**Bowman, Winnie J.**
Bonny Kate Chapter
Ancestor: Hugh Rogers, NC — #750497
This "Baby Roses" crib quilt was made circa 1930 at Clay County, NC by the owner's grandmother, Carrie Lee Anderson Johnston (born 9/23/1876 at Hayesville, NC, married Robert Lee Johnston, Sr., died 2/22/1961 at Asheville, NC). It was probably made for the owner's mother as a baby gift when the owner was born.

**Bowman, Winnie J.**
Bonny Kate Chapter
Ancestor: Hugh Rogers, NC — #750497
This coverlet was made in the 1920's at Clay County, NC by the owner's grandmother, Carrie Lee Anderson Johnston. The maker was talented in weaving, quilting and with other handwork. This coverlet was used in the owner's lifetime as a bed cover in houses without central heat. It was probably made as a wedding present for the owner's parents who married in 1922.

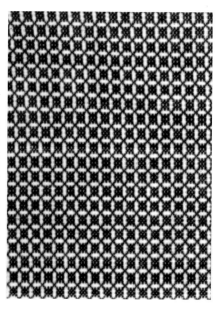

**Bowman, Winnie J.**
Bonny Kate Chapter
Ancestor: Hugh Rogers, NC — #750497
This coverlet was made circa 1930's at Clay County, NC by the owner's grandmother, Carrie Lee Anderson Johnston.

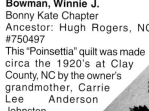

**Bowman, Winnie J.**
Bonny Kate Chapter
Ancestor: Hugh Rogers, NC — #750497
This coverlet was made circa 1930's at Clay County, NC by the owner's grandmother, Carrie Lee Anderson Johnston.

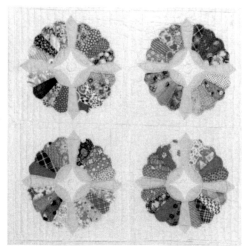

**Bowman, Winnie J.**
Bonny Kate Chapter
Ancestor: Hugh Rogers, NC —#750497
This "Dresden Plate" quilt was pieced circa the 1930's at Chattanooga, TN by the owner's mother, Willa Mae Johnston Bowman. In 1974, the quiltmaker requested that quilters at the Sevier County, TN Senior Citizen Center finish the quilt for the owner's birthday. After it was quilted, but before the binding was finished, the owner's mother died unexpectedly.

**Bowman, Winnie J.**
Bonny Kate Chapter
Ancestor: Hugh Rogers, NC — #750497
This "Poinsettia" quilt was made circa the 1920's at Clay County, NC by the owner's grandmother, Carrie Lee Anderson Johnston.

**Bowman, Winnie J.**
Bonny Kate Chapter
Ancestor: Hugh Rogers, NC —#750497
This "Duck Paddle/Frannies's Fan" quilt was made in the early 1930's in Georgia by the owner's mother, Willa Mae Johnston Bowman. The quilt was made for the maker's sister, Lenora Johnston Roberts, who gave it to the current owner not too long before she died in 1993. The owner's aunt pointed to a patch with large stitches. She told the owner, "These are the stitches you added as a little girl."

**Bowman, Winnie J.**
Bonny Kate Chapter
Ancestor: Hugh Rogers, NC —#750497
This "Ax Head/Double Ax Head" quilt was made circa 1930's in Georgia by the owner's mother, Willa Mae Johnston Bowman. The owner recognizes fabric from her mother's dresses throughout the quilt"

**Boyd, Margaret Davis** (Doyle A.)
Belle Meade Chapter
Ancestor: Thomas Boyd, PA —# 677689
This "Flower" quilt was made between 1877-1882 in Tennessee by the owner's grandmother, Martha Fitzgerald Davis (born 1852 at Hamilton County, TN, married William Davis, died 1882 in the same county). The maker was part Native American Indian. She died at age 30 from tuberculosis. The dye for the fabric is from things in nature. The owner's father's hand was quilted on the corner when he was five years old. "My mother passed the quilt down with the wish that we keep the family quilt."

**Boyter, Dale Dean** (Alfred)
Charlotte Reeves Robertson Chapter
Ancestor: John Millspaugh, NY —#639197
This "Log Cabin/Sunshine and Shadows" quilt was made in 1985 at Shelbyville, TN by Ann Throneberry.

**Boyter, Dale Dean** (Alfred)
Charlotte Reeves Robertson Chapter
Ancestor: John Millspaugh, NY —#639197
This "Square in a Square" quilt was made in 1974 at Springfield, TN by the owner's friend, Mrs. George P. Glover (Grace).

**Boyter, Dale Dean** (Alfred)
Charlotte Reeves Robertson Chapter
Ancestor: John Millspaugh, NY —#639197
This "Teddy's Alphabet" quilt was made in 1983 by the United Methodist Women of the New Chapel Methodist Church in Springfield, TN.

**Boyter, Dale Dean** (Alfred)
Charlotte Reeves Robertson Chapter
Ancestor: John Millspaugh, NY —#639197
This "Colonial Plymouth" quilt was made in 1974 at Springfield, TN by the owner (born 2/8/1955 at Nashville, TN). The quilt won a 2nd place ribbon at the Robertson County Fair in Springfield, TN.

**Boyd, Sarah**
Bonny Kate Chapter
Ancestor: John Moore, SC -- #777607
This "Lone Star" quilt was purchased by the owner.

**Boyd, Sarah**
Bonny Kate Chapter
Ancestor: John Moore, SC -- #777607
This "Milky Way/Star" quilt was made in Texas in 1996 by the owner.

**Boyd, Sarah**
Bonny Kate Chapter
Ancestor: John Moore, SC -- #777607
This "Dutch Doll/Sunbonnet Sue" quilt was inherited by the owner.

**Braddock, Virginia Eleazer** (Benjamin H.)
Hermitage Chapter
Ancestor: Col. George Waller, VA — #566351

This "Basket" quilt was made in Tiptonville, TN by the owner's grandmother, Tennessee Ann Tipton Jamison (born 12/9/1886 at Tiptonville, TN, married William Terry Jamison, died 2/8/1971 at Dyersburg, TN).

**Brawley, Dorothy Perry** (William G.)
William Cocke Chapter
Ancestor: John Snider, GA — #771742

This "Trip Around the World" quilt was made in the 1930's at Savannah, GA by the owner's grandmother, Emma May Snyder Perry (born 5/18/1879 at Effingham County, GA, married Orrin Bonaparte Perry, died 1/6/1946 at Savannah, GA). This quilt was passed from maker, to her daughter-in-law, Ruth N. Perry, to her daughter-in-law, Claire C. Perry, to the current owner.

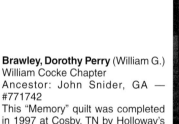

**Brawley, Dorothy Perry** (William G.)
William Cocke Chapter
Ancestor: John Snider, GA — #771742

This "Memory" quilt was completed in 1997 at Cosby, TN by Holloway's Country Home Quilts, a working craft studio located in Cosby, TN. For the owner's 70th birthday, her daughter Laura, contacted family and friends and asked each of them to make a square for a memory quilt for a birthday gift. Laura started about two years before the owner's 70th birthday. It was amazing how many friends and family sent squares. Then about 3-4 months before the big event, she took them to Holloway's Quilts to be pieced together and quilted. Maria Holloway was amazed with the number and diversity of the squares. Instead of one quilt, there were four. They are all hanging in the owner's home and every time she passes them she feels the warmth and love of wonderful friends and family. The owner says, "I treasure my 70th birthday quilts, but mostly the love and friendship they represent."

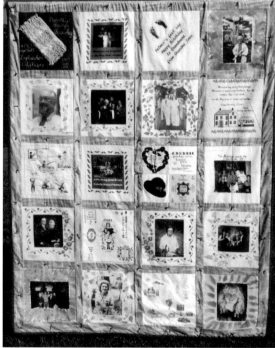

**Breazeale, Virginia Montgomery**
(William Mack)
General William Lenoir Chapter
Ancestor: Capt. Andrew Colville —
#754119
This "Irish Chain Variation" quilt was made in 1870 at Loudon County, TN by the owner's great grandmother, Lucy Ann Barton Griffitts (born 1/31/1829, married William Houston, died 2/16/1910). This quilt was given by the maker to her son, Bruner Griffitts, who moved to Oregon. He gave it to his son, Asa Griffitts who mailed it back to the owner's mother, Margaret Griffitts Montgomery, who gave it to the owner.

**Brewer, Elizabeth Petree** (James)
French Lick Chapter
Ancestor: Nicholas Gibbs, NC — #787358
This "Nose Gay/ Brides Bouquet" quilt was made in 1930 in Knoxville, TN by the owner's aunt, Ruth Petree (born 1897 at Greeneville, TN, married Colbert G. Petree). The maker gave the quilt to the owner.

**Brewer, Elizabeth Petree** (James)
French Lick Chapter
Ancestor: Nicholas Gibbs, NC — #787358
This "Grandmother's Flower Garden" was purchased at the Country Store.

**Brewer, Elizabeth Petree** (James)
French Lick Chapter
Ancestor: Nicholas Gibbs, NC —#787358
This "Bow Tie" quilt was made in 1940 in Mississippi by the owner's mother-in-law, Mary Davis Brewer (born 12/30/1901 at Waynesboro, MS, married Albert Brewer, died 4/27/1990 at Nashville, TN). The quilt was given to the owner's husband by his mother.

**Brewer, Rebecca Lee**
French Lick Chapter
Ancestor: Nicholas Gibbs, NC —#787358
This "Glorified Nine Patch" quilt was made in the early 1940's in Mississippi by the owner's grandmother, Mary Davis Brewer (born 12/30/1901 at Waynesboro, MS, married Albert Brewer, died 4/27/1990 at Nashville, TN).

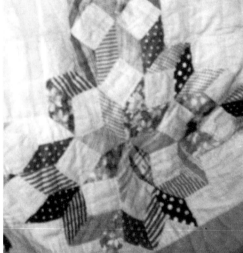

**Brewer, Rebecca Lee**
French Lick Chapter
Ancestor: Nicholas Gibbs, NC —#787358
This "Dutch Rose/Optical Star" quilt was made in the 1930's in Mississippi by the owner's grandmother, Mary Davis Brewer. It was a gift from the maker to the owner.

**Bridgeman, Bernice Smith** (Earl N., Jr.)
Watauga Chapter
Ancestor: Robert Dowdell, SC
This "Daisy Chain" quilt was made in the 1980's at Batesville, AR by the owner's sister, Ermile Smith McNeill (born 12/16/1915 at Boswell, AR, married Elmo McNeill, died 5/14/1990 at Memphis, TN). The maker gave the quilt to the owner.

**Bridgeman, Bernice Smith** (Earl N., Jr.)
Watauga Chapter
Ancestor: Robert Dowdell, SC
This "Flower Basket and Butterflies" quilt was made in the 1950's at Boswell, AR by the owner's sister, Ermile Smith McNeill. The maker gave the quilt to the owner.

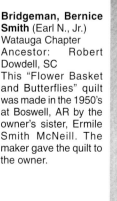

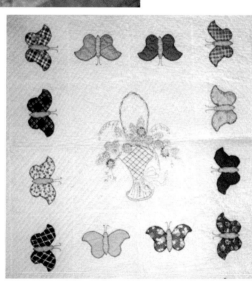

**Bridgeman, Bernice Smith** (Earl N., Jr.)
Watauga Chapter
Ancestor: Robert Dowdell, SC – #735016
This "Rose" quilt was made in the 1980's at Batesville, AR by the owner's sister, Ermile Smith McNeill. The maker gave the quilt to the owner.

**Bridgeman, Bernice Smith** (Earl N., Jr.)
Watauga Chapter
Ancestor: Robert Dowdell, SC – #735016
This "Star Within A Star" quilt was made in the 1950's at Boswell, AR by the owner's sister, Ermile Smith McNeill. The maker gave the quilt to the owner.

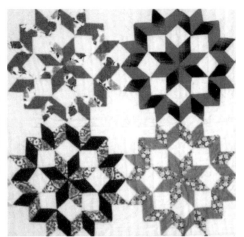

**Bridgeman, Bernice Smith** (Earl N., Jr.)
Watauga Chapter
Ancestor: Robert Dowdell, SC – #735016
This "Squares" quilt was made in the 1980's at Batesville, AR by the owner's sister, Ermile Smith McNeill. The maker gave the quilt to the owner.

**Bridgeman, Bernice Smith** (Earl N., Jr.)
Watauga Chapter
Ancestor: Robert Dowdell, SC – #735016
This "Dresden Plate" quilt was made in the 1930's at Boswell, AR by the owner's mother, Edna Combs Smith. This quilt was passed from maker, to owner's sister, to owner.

**Bridgeman, Bernice Smith** (Earl N., Jr.)
Watauga Chapter
Ancestor: Robert Dowdell, SC – #735016
This "Tulips in a Basket/ Goose Tracks" quilt was made in Boswell, AR by the owner's mother, Edna Combs Smith (born 10/19/ 1896 at Boswell, AR, married S.C. Smith, died 5/6/1982 at Batesville, AR). This quilt was passed from maker, to owner's sister, to owner.

**Bridgeman, Bernice Smith** (Earl N., Jr.)
Watauga Chapter
Ancestor: Robert Dowdell, SC – #735016
This "Dutch Doll" quilt was made in the 1930's at Boswell, AR by the owner's mother, Edna Combs Smith. This quilt was given to the owner as a gift.

**Bridgeman, Bernice Smith** (Earl N., Jr.)
Watauga Chapter
Ancestor: Robert Dowdell, SC – #735016
This "Nine Patch" quilt was made in 1936/37 at Boswell, AR by the owner's mother, Edna Combs Smith. The owner assisted her mother in making this quilt.

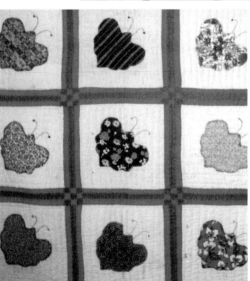

**Bridgeman, Bernice Smith** (Earl N., Jr.)
Watauga Chapter
Ancestor: Robert Dowdell, SC – #735016
This "Butterfly" quilt was made in the 1940's at Boswell, AR by the owner's mother, Edna Combs Smith. The maker gave the owner this quilt after she married.

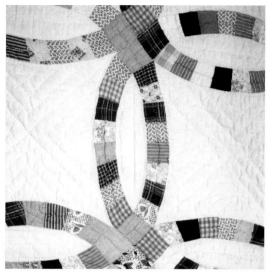

**Bridgeman, Bernice Smith** (Earl N., Jr.) Watauga Chapter Ancestor: Robert Dowdell, SC – #735016 This "Double Wedding Ring" quilt was made in the 1930's at Boswell, AR by the owner's mother, Edna Combs Smith. The quilt was passed from maker to Ermile McNeill, to current owner.

**Bridgeman, Bernice Smith** (Earl N., Jr.) Watauga Chapter Ancestor: Robert Dowdell, SC – #735016 This "Baby Double Wedding Ring" quilt was made in the 1930's at Boswell, AR by the owner's mother, Edna Combs Smith. The quilt was passed from maker, to Ermile McNeill, to current owner.

**Bridgeman, Bernice Smith** (Earl N., Jr.) Watauga Chapter Ancestor: Robert Dowdell, SC – #735016 This "Dresden Plate" quilt was made in the 1930's at Boswell, AR by the owner's paternal grandmother, Ida Ellen West Smith (born 3/26/1872 at Izard County, AR, married Henry Whitfield Smith, died 3/15/1941 at Boswell, AR). The quilt was passed from maker, to owner's mother, to owner.

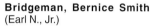

**Bridgeman, Bernice Smith** (Earl N., Jr.) Watauga Chapter Ancestor: Robert Dowdell, SC – #735016 This "Bow Tie" quilt was made circa 1936/37 at Boswell, AR by the owner's paternal grandmother, Ida Ellen West Smith. As a little girl the owner became interested in the art of making quilts. With Grandmother Smith's help, she cut and sewed many of the blocks in this quilt.

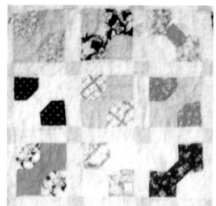

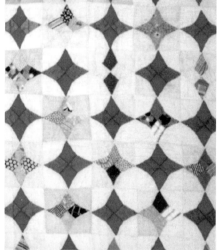

**Bridgeman, Bernice Smith** (Earl N., Jr.) Watauga Chapter Ancestor: Robert Dowdell, SC – #735016 This "Star/Snowball" quilt was made in the 1940's at Izard County, AR by the owner's maternal aunt, Miss Martha Ann Conrad (born 1872 at Izard County, died 1961 at Melbourne, AR). The quilt was passed from maker, to owner's mother, to owner's sister, to owner.

**Bridgeman, Bernice Smith** (Earl N., Jr.) Watauga Chapter Ancestor: Robert Dowdell, SC – #735016 This "Stars and Squares" quilt was made in the 1940's at Boswell, AR by the owner's maternal grandmother, Nancy Lee Conrod Combs (born 10/6/1867 at Warren County, TN, married Jackson Combs, died 4/7/1962 at Boswell, AR). The quilt was passed from maker, to owner's mother, to owner's sister, to owner.

**Bridgewater, Modena Wilburn** (Elmo) Caney Fork Chapter Ancestor: Bry Gregory, NC — #746215 This "Flower Pot" quilt was made in 1937 at Riddleton, TN by the owner (born 5/1/1922 at Dixon Springs). In 1937 the owner's grandmother, Clementney Glascow Richmond Jenkins, died. The family brought some of her personal things to Modena's home. In these things she found a quilt she liked, but it was well worn, so she cut a pattern from newspaper and made this quilt. She was 15 years old at the time. Neighborhood women helped quilt it.

**Bridgewater, Modena Wilburn** (Elmo) Caney Fork Chapter Ancestor: Bry Gregory, NC —#746215 This "Flower Basket" quilt top was found in the trunk of the owner's husband. He does not know who pieced it. The owner quilted it.

**Bright, Katherine Johnston** (John)
General William Lenoir Chapter
Ancestor: James Matthews, NC — #693557
This "Grandmother's Flower Garden" quilt was begun in 1939 at Rossville, GA by the owner (born 10/8/1915 at Roane County, TN). She was unable to finish this quilt at that time because of family responsibilities related to raising four children. So the quilt was delayed until after she retired. She made several other quilts and then, about 1992, she finished this quilt. Now it is one of her favorites.

**Bright, Katherine Johnston** (John)
General William Lenoir Chapter
Ancestor: James Matthews, NC — #693557
This "Victorian Crazy" quilt was made in 1890 at Roane County, TN by the owner's grandmother, Martha Katherine Johnston (born 7/24/1838 at Roane County, married Marquis D. L. Johnston, died 7/18/1921 in the same county). The maker lived in a remote area of Roane County where she and her family sewed their own clothing, saved the scraps, and pieced the quilts. They were self-sufficient and made their living from the earth. Religion was very important. They cared for the sick and were always willing to help in time of need. The Bible, mail order catalog, and school books were their only sources of reading material. "Things sure have changed since these times."

**Bright, Priscilla**
General William Lenoir Chapter
Ancestor: James Matthews, NC — #702161
This "Stars and Nine of Diamonds" quilt was pieced in 1945 by the owner's grandmother, Fannie Bright (born 4/7/1885 at Monroe County, TN, married William Carra Bright, died 3/20/1957 at Loudon, TN). The maker was a widow and didn't have money to buy materials for quilts. She often used fabric scraps given to her by neighbors. After the maker died, the quilt top was given to the owner's mother who quilted it and gave it to the owner. This makes the quilt even more special!

**Bright, Priscilla**
General William Lenoir Chapter
Ancestor: James Matthews, NC — #702161
This "Cathedral Window" quilt was made in 1960 at Lenoir City, TN by the owner's mother, Katherine Bright (born 10/8/1915 at Roane County, TN, married John Bright). The maker was working outside the home when she made this quilt. It took her six years or longer to finish it.

**Bright, Priscilla**
General William Lenoir Chapter
Ancestor: James Matthews, NC — #702161
This "Starburst' quilt was made in 1970 by the owner's mother, Katherine Bright.

**Britton, Eudine Morgan** (Floyd Earl)
Chief John Ross Chapter
Ancestor: Nathaniel Overall, TN — #600938
This "Snowball" quilt was made 1935-40 at St. Elmo, TN by the owner's husband's grandmother, Amanda Caroline Hufstedler Short (born 3/28/1859 in Georgia, married William Eli Short (1853-1913 TN), died 5/2/1942 at Chattanooga, TN).

**Britton, Eudine Morgan** (Floyd Earl)
Chief John Ross Chapter
Ancestor: Nathaniel Overall, TN — #600938
This "Feather/Pineapple" quilt was made circa 1880 at Walker County, GA by the owner's great aunt, Elizabeth Matilda Massey (born 6/21/1843 at Walker County, GA, married Reuben, died 5/14/1917 in Walker County). Her husband was killed at the Battle of Chickamauga during the War Between the States. The quilt was passed from owner's grandmother, Sarah Abercrombie Morgan (1854-1935, married to John Wesley), to owner.

**Britton, Eudine Morgan** (Floyd Earl)
Chief John Ross Chapter
Ancestor: Nathaniel Overall, TN — #600938
This "Dresden Plate" quilt was made circa 1935 at Chattanooga, TN by the owner's husband's mother, Myrtle Bell Short Britton (born 12/12/1899 at Shellmound, TN, married Lawrence Walter Britton (1896-1975), died 6/23/1976 at Chattanooga, TN).

**Britton, Eudine Morgan**
(Floyd Earl)
Chief John Ross Chapter
Ancestor: Nathaniel Overall, TN — #600938
This "Lone Star" quilt was made before 1925 in Tennessee by the owner's mother, Minnie Louvenia Overall Morgan (born 6/5/1882 at Rutherford County, TN, married Thomas Richard Clinton Morgan, died 4/10/1972 at Chattanooga, TN).

**Britton, Eudine Morgan**
(Floyd Earl)
Chief John Ross Chapter
Ancestor: Nathaniel Overall, TN — #600938
This "Feather/Pineapple" quilt was made at Walker County, GA by the owner's great aunt, Emma Bryan Morgan (born 11/17/1857 at Walker County, GA, married Benjamin Franklin Morgan, died 8/18/1936). She made it before her marriage in 1880. The quilt was given to the owner by the maker's daughter, Lillie Eurania Morgan Ransom, who died in 1986 at age 101).

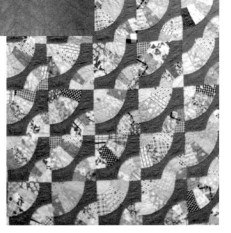

**Brooks, Dorothy Watts**
Glover's Trace Chapter
Ancestor: Jack Walton, VA — #582159
This "Double Fan/Whirling Fan" quilt was made circa 1940 at Trenton, KY by the owner's aunt, Mary Rilley Watts Fox (born 2/1/1893 at Todd County, KY, married Ben Franklin Fox, died 1/11/1976 at Hopkinsville, KY). The quilt was given to the owner by the maker.

**Brooks, Dorothy Watts**
Glover's Trace Chapter
Ancestor: Jack Walton, VA — #582159
This "Basket" quilt was made in 1958 at Trenton, KY by the owner's mother, Wilhelmina M. Watts (born 10/22/1898, married Frank P. Watts, died 8/9/1975 at Hopkinsville, KY). The quiltmaker gave the quilt to the owner for her 40th birthday April 23, 1958. She made it to be used for cover, not for "show."

**Brown, Guylene Carter**
(Ray)
Zacariah Davies Chapter
Ancestor: George Tubbs — #724442
This "Large Texas Star" quilt was made circa 1950's at Paducah, KY by the owner's husband's aunt, Mary E. Brown (born 5/25/1896, married Bernie Bryant Brown). The maker planted, picked, and carded the cotton by hand for this quilt. She gathered weeds from the field to dye the lining on the back of the quilt, then began the process of cutting, piecing together, and quilting. There are 5,508 diamond blocks in this quilt.

**Brown, Guylene Carter**
(Ray)
Zacariah Davies Chapter
Ancestor: George Tubbs — #724442
This "Fan" quilt was made by the owner's husband's maternal grandmother, Mamie Hensley Clowes (born 2/8/1886 at Covington, TN, married Bruce Oliver Tolley(1873-1914), married Chancey C. Clowes (1888-1947), died 10/16/1974 at Quito, TN). The owner received the quilt upon the death of her husband's mother.

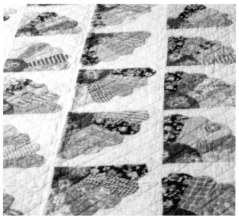

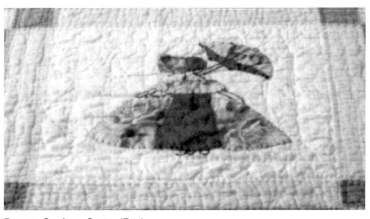

**Brown, Guylene Carter** (Ray)
Zacariah Davies Chapter
Ancestor: George Tubbs — #724442
This "Colonial Lady" quilt was made in 1959 as a gift for the owner's high school graduation at Covington, TN. The quilt was made by the owner's grandmother, Nannie Lee Meadows Owen (born 11/27/1876 at Benton County, MS, married Charles Christopher "Burk" Owen, died 3/8/1973 at Covington, TN).

**Brown, Guylene Carter**
(Ray)
Zacariah Davies Chapter
Ancestor: George Tubbs — #724442
This original design crib quilt was made July/August 1967 by the owner's sister, Carolyn Carter Ulery (born 1/27/1938 at Drew County, AR, married Bobby Lee Butler).

**Brown, Guylene Carter** (Ray)
Zacariah Davies Chapter
Ancestor: George Tubbs — #724442
This "Texas Star" quilt was made in 1960 for college twin beds by the owner's grandmother, Nannie Lee Meadows Owen. The owner also has the other quilt.

**Brown, Guylene Carter** (Ray)
Zacariah Davies Chapter
Ancestor: George Tubbs — #724442
This "Spider Webb" quilt was made circa 1850's by the owner's great great grandmother, Miriam Thomas Burton (born 5/12/1830 in NC, married William J. Burton, died 11/7/1906 at Lincoln County, AR). The owner bought the quilt from a long time acquaintance of her mother who turned out to be very distantly related and knew this was the owner's line.

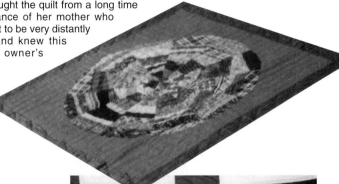

**Brown, Lillian Irene Walker** (Dan Jr.)
Cavett Station Chapter
Ancestor: John Chestnut, VA —#609162
This "United States History" quilt was made in 1985 at Clinton, TN by the owner (born 11/9/1913 at Manchester, KY). She made it for her grandson, Morris Calloway, Jr. The Pattern for some of the blocks was obtained from the Louisville Courier-Journal in 1927. Other blocks were designed by the maker.

**Brown, Lillian Irene Walker** (Dan Jr.)
Cavett Station Chapter
Ancestor: John Chestnut, VA —#609162
This "Bible History" quilt was made in 1980 at Clinton, TN by the owner and her grandmother, Lillian Irene Walker Brown. This design is from the Louisville Courier-Journal .

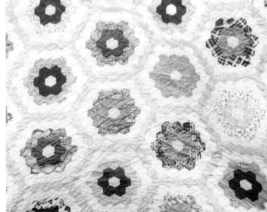

**Brown, Lillian Irene Walker** (Dan Jr.)
Cavett Station Chapter
Ancestor: John Chestnut, VA —#609162
This "Grandmother's Flower Garden" quilt was made in 1950 at London, KY by the owner.

**Brown, Lillian Irene Walker** (Dan Jr.)
Cavett Station Chapter
Ancestor: John Chestnut, VA —#609162
This "Flower Basket" quilt was made in the 1920's at Manchester, TN by a patient of the owner's father, Dr. David L. Walker. The quilt was payment for dental work.

**Brown, Lillian Irene Walker** (Dan Jr.)
Cavett Station Chapter
Ancestor: John Chestnut, VA —#609162
This "Colonial Lady" quilt was made in the 1980's at Clinton, TN by the owner.

**Bruce, Mary Frances Hagar** (William R)
Robert Cooke Chapter
Ancestor: George Hamilton, NC — #658446
This "Dutch Girl/Sunbonnet Sue" quilt was made in 1950-60 at Hermitage, TN by the owner's mother, Nora Jenkins Hagar (born 10/20/1894 at Mt. Juliet, TN, married Emmett G. Hagar, died 3/20/1974 at Hermitage, TN). The quilt was passed to the owner when her mother died.

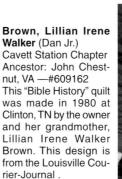

**Bruce, Mary Frances Hagar** (William R)
Robert Cooke Chapter
Ancestor: George Hamilton, NC — #658446
This "Cathedral Window" quilt was made circa 1965 at Hermitage, TN by the owner's mother, Nora Jenkins Hagar. The quilt was passed to the owner when her mother died.

**Bruch, Mary Frances Ballard** (Donald J., Sr.)
Zachariah Davies Chapter
Ancestor: Capt William Brockett, SC — # 750703
This "Variation of a Nine Patch" quilt was made circa 1930 at Nashville, TN by the owner's mother, Tennie Hackett Ballard (born 1902 at Pleasant Shade, TN, married Albert Fred Ballard, died 1973 at Carthage, TN. The quilt was passed from maker to current owner.

**Bruch, Mary Frances Ballard** (Donald J., Sr.)
Zachariah Davies Chapter
Ancestor: Capt William Brockett, SC —# 750703
This "String" quilt was made circa 1930 at Nashville, TN by the owner's mother, Tennie Hackett Ballard. The pieces were stitched together using a newspaper pattern. When the entire piece had been stitched, the paper was removed. The quilt was passed from maker to current owner.

**Bruch, Mary Frances Ballard** (Donald J., Sr.)
Zachariah Davies Chapter
Ancestor: Capt William Brockett, SC —# 750703
This "Variation of a Nine Patch" quilt was pieced at Gallatin, TN by the owner's maternal aunt, Mary Hackett Beasley (born 1900 at Pleasant Shade, TN, married Dewey Beasley, died 1990 at Gallatin, TN). The quilt was quilted by the ladies of the church. The quilt was made for the owner.

**Bruch, Mary Frances Ballard** (Donald J., Sr.)
Zachariah Davies Chapter
Ancestor: Capt William Brockett, SC —# 750703
This "Double Wedding Ring" quilt was made in the 1930's at Nashville, TN by the owner's mother, Tennie Hackett Ballard.

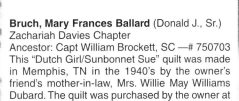

**Bruch, Mary Frances Ballard** (Donald J., Sr.)
Zachariah Davies Chapter
Ancestor: Capt William Brockett, SC —# 750703
This "Dutch Girl/Sunbonnet Sue" quilt was made in Memphis, TN in the 1940's by the owner's friend's mother-in-law, Mrs. Willie May Williams Dubard. The quilt was purchased by the owner at an estate sale.

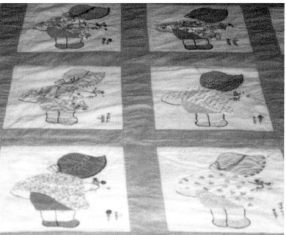

**Bruch, Mary Frances Ballard** (Donald J., Sr.)
Zachariah Davies Chapter
Ancestor: Capt William Brockett, SC —# 750703
This "Log Cabin" quilt was made circa 1880 at Pleasant Shade, TN by the owner's great grandmother, Nancy Ann Hesson Ballard (born 1854 at Smith County, TN, married Allen Ballard, died 1926 in the same county). The quilt was pieced from scraps of dresses and shirts worn by members of the family. The quilt was passed from the maker, to her grandson, Fred Ballard, to the current owner.

**Bruch, Mary Frances Ballard** (Donald J., Sr.)
Zachariah Davies Chapter
Ancestor: Capt William Brockett, SC —# 750703
This "Lone Star" quilt was made circa 1940 at Memphis, TN. The quilt was a gift to Dr. Horton Dubard, a Memphis surgeon, by one of his patients. It was purchased at the estate sale of Mrs. Horton Dubard.

**Bruch, Mary Frances Ballard** (Donald J., Sr.)
Zachariah Davies Chapter
Ancestor: Capt William Brockett, SC —# 750703
This coverlet was purchased at an estate sale in Memphis, TN. It is made of wool with a cotton lining.

**Buck, Laura Kathleen**
Fort Assumption Chapter
Ancestor: Thomas Montague, VA — #778514
This "Single Irish Chain" quilt was acquired by the owner after the death of her grandfather, Laird LaMarck Ward. According to the owner's grandmother, Patricia Ward Buck, the quilt was probably made by ladies in one of the Methodist Churches served by her grandfather, Dr. Richard Brooks Ward. In 1900, he was minister in Oakland MD, so the quilt may have been made there. The quilt belonged to Katherine O'Dell Metcalf Ward, Dr. Ward's wife. It is interesting to note that Mrs. Ward's mother came from Ireland and the quilt pattern is "Single Irish Chain."

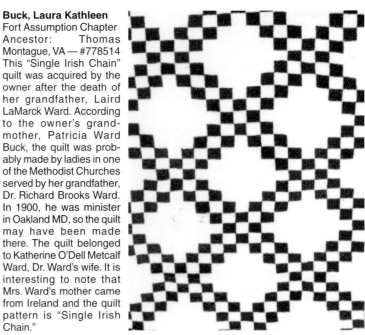

**Buck, Mary Margaret McClure** (James)
Ft. Assumption Chapter
Ancestor Henry Banta, PA —#526791
This woven coverlet was made in the 1800's in Kentucky. The owner received the coverlet in 1984 from her aunt, Nancye, who had received it circa 1929-30 from her uncle. The thread was spun and the coverlet woven in a log cabin in Kentucky. It was made by family members of the owner's great uncle by marriage. He gave it to Nancye Boardman McClure Park after the death of his wife, Ollie.

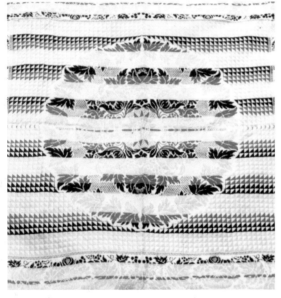

**Buck, Mary Margaret McClure** (James)
Ft. Assumption Chapter
Ancestor Henry Banta, PA —#526791
This "Hummingbird" quilt was made in the 1870's in Kentucky by the owner's great great grandmother, Mary Gillispie Wilson (born 9/11/1812 at Montgomery County, KY, married Uriah Wilson, died after 1882). The authenticity of this quilt was documented at the Memphis Pink Palace Museum by experts in 1985. The quilt was pieced by the maker for granddaughter and namesake, Mary Eliza Boardman, the owner's grandmother. In 1894, Mary Eliza married Dr. Phillip Leslie McClure. The quilt was in possession of their daughter, Nancye B. McClure Park, in 1984 when it was given to the current owner.

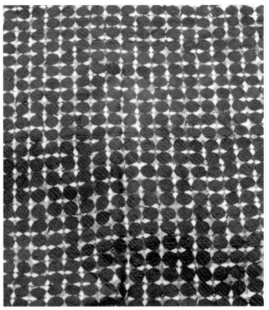

**Buck, Mary Margaret McClure** (James)
Ft. Assumption Chapter
Ancestor Henry Banta, PA —#526791
This "Tea Leaves" quilt was made in the 1890's at Bourbon County, KY by the owner's great grandmother, Minerva Wilson Boardman (born 9/16/1830 at Bourbon County, KY, married Harry Boardman, died 10/17/1921 in the same county). The quilt was made for the maker's daughter, Minnie Olive Boardman, born in 1872. It was probably made when Ollie married in 1893. She died in 1929 and the coverlet was given to her niece, Nancye Boardman McClure Park, by Hiram Ewing, Ollie's husband. It was then given to the current owner, Mrs. Park's niece.

**Buck, Mary Margaret McClure** (James)
Ft. Assumption Chapter
Ancestor Henry Banta, PA —#526791
This "Wheel Variation" quilt was made circa 1900 at Bourbon County, KY by the owner's great grandmother, Minerva Wilson Boardman. It was made for her granddaughter, Minerva Sue Boardman, second cousin of the owner (born 10/11/1900). Cousin Sue, who married Richard Hopkins, gave the quilt to her first cousin, Nancye Boardman McClure Park, who gave it to her niece, the current owner.

**Buell, Grace Harbison** (David A)
Caney Fork Chapter
Ancestor: Giles Harding, VA — #786275
This "Wine Goblet" quilt was made circa 1910 at Bellwood, TN by the owner's great great grandmother, Flora Blackwell Robertson Bell (born 10/1/1847 at Leeville, TN, married William Anzi Bell on 9/24/1868 at Wilson County, died 4/22/1917 at Bellwood, TN). Flora made it for her grandson, James Harding, who is the owner's grandfather. He gave the quilt to the owner.

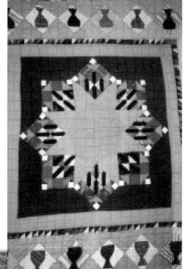

**Bullington, Joyce Enochs** (Ernest)
Old Reynoldsburg Chapter
Ancestor: Capt. Enoch Enoch, PA — #67-9316
This "Owl" quilt was made in 1970 at McEwen, TN by the owner's mother-in-law, Mattie Zeal Choate Bullington (born 12/6/1900 at McEwen, TN, married William Willis Bullington, died 10/23/1987 at McEwen). She enjoyed making hundreds of quilts. Her mother, Martha Choate, taught her to make the tiniest of neat stitches. Her quilting was her pride and joy. She made this quilt for her son, Ernest, the owner's husband.

**Bullington, Joyce Enochs** (Ernest)
Old Reynoldsburg Chapter
Ancestor: Capt. Enoch Enoch, PA — #67-9316
This tied "Block" quilt was made in 1965 at McEwen, TN by the owner's mother, Annie Davis Enochs (born 9/17/1905 at Dickson County, TN, married Wilbert Nathan Enochs, died 7/12/1978 at Dickson). This quilt is made of old coats. It was made for the owner to take to APSU to keep warm in bed. She made it on a cold snowy day and tied it. She also made a lot of these quilts during the depression because she did not have any other fabric.

**Bullington, Joyce Enochs** (Ernest)
Old Reynoldsburg Chapter
Ancestor: Capt. Enoch Enoch, PA — #67-9316
This "Photo" quilt was made at McEwen, TN by the owner's daughter, Patricia Bullington Davis (born 10/31/1955 at Waverly, TN, married Dorris Davis). The quilt was made for the owner's 45th wedding anniversary.

**Bumpus, Anne Shirley** (James Jones)
Tenassee Chapter
Ancestor: George Murphy, VA —#526085
This "Double Wedding Ring" quilt was made circa 1980 by the owner's mother-in-law, Addie Grace Scott Bumpus (born 5/14/1899 at Maury County, TN, married John Sidney Bumpus, Jr., died 1/29/1992 at Columbia, TN). The quilt was made for the owner and her husband.

**Bumpus, Anne Shirley** (James Jones)
Tenassee Chapter
Ancestor: George Murphy, VA —#526085
This "Nine Patch" quilt was made in 1986 by the owner's mother-in-law, Addie Grace Scott Bumpus, for her son. This is the last quilt pieced by Mrs. Bumpus.

**Bumpus, Anne Shirley** (James Jones)
Tenassee Chapter
Ancestor: George Murphy, VA —#526085
This "Double Wedding Ring" quilt was made 1976 by the owner's mother-in-law, Addie Grace Scott Bumpus. The maker made the quilt for her granddaughter, Jane Anne Bumpus, as a present for her high school graduation.

**Bumpus, Anne Shirley** (James Jones)
Tenassee Chapter
Ancestor: George Murphy, VA —#526085
This "Dutch Doll/Sunbonnet Sue" quilt was made in 1929 at Mt. Pleasant, TN by the owner's husband's grandmother, Annie M. Nichols Bumpus (born 12/3/1869 at Maury County, TN, married Dr. John Sidney Bumpus, died 10/5/1953 at Tullahoma, TN).

**Bumpus, Anne Shirley**
(James Jones)
Tenassee Chapter
Ancestor: George Murphy,
VA —#526085
This "Log Cabin" quilt
was made circa 1980 at
Mt. Pleasant, TN by the
owner's mother-in-law,
Addie Grace Scott
Bumpus. The quilt
was purchased by
the owner.

**Burkhalter, V. Jean**
Fort Nashborough Chapter
Ancestor: Michael Burkhalter,
SC — #716362
This "Tulip Garden" quilt was
made in the 1930's at Flat
Rock, AL by the owner's mother, Ila Moore Burkhalter (born 3/23/1890 at Henagar, AL, married John B. Burkhatler, died 12/22/1980 at Nashville, TN).

**Burks, Alice Moore** (Cleve E., Jr.)
Key Corner Chapter
Ancestor: Benjamin Hart, GA — #642680
This "Octagonal Star/Dutch Rose" quilt was made in the early 1900's at Obion
County, TN by the owner's grandmother, Emma Alice Swiggart Foute (born 10/
14/1866 at Obion County, TN, married Daniel Davis Foute, died 7/6/1946 at Washington, DC). The quilt was passed from maker, to Mary Foute Moore, to current
owner. The owner believes the quilt to be made before her birth in 1917 because
during those
years her grand-
mother was do-
ing quite a bit of
handwork in-
cluding quilting,
tatting, embroi-
dery and cro-
cheting. By the
time the owner
was born, her
grandmother
was diagnosed
with diabetes
and her vision
began to & fail.

**Burks, Alice Moore**
(Cleve E., Jr.)
Key Corner Chapter
Ancestor: Benjamin
Hart, GA — #642680
This "Crazy" quilt
was made in the
early 1900's at
Obion County, TN by
the owner's grand-
mother, Emma Alice
Swiggart Foute. The
quilt was passed
from maker, to Mary
Foute Moore, to cur-
rent owner.

**Burows, Suzanne Porter** (Richard W.)
Long Island Chapter
Ancestor: William Brizendine, VA—
#513659
This "Rose of Sharon" quilt was
made in Carroll County, VA
in 1969 by the owner's
mother, Virginia
McMillan Porter
(Mrs. Walter A.)

**Burows, Suzanne Porter** (Richard W.)
Long Island Chapter
Ancestor: William Brizendine, VA —#513659
This "Carolina Lily" quilt was made in Carroll County, VA by the owner's great
grandmother, Sarah Alice Jenkins Porter. The quilt was passed to the owner's
mother, Virginia McMillan Porter (Mrs. Walter A.). Mrs. Porter is a 50 year DAR
member and the organizing regent of the Applachian Trail Chapter of the VADAR
in Hillsville, VA.

**Burows, Suzanne Porter** (Richard W.)
Long Island Chapter
Ancestor: William Brizendine, VA — #513659
This "Irish Chain" quilt was pieced in Illinois by Elsie Amiden, aunt of Lavon Amiden Wilcox. It was quilted by the Exchange Place Quilters in Kingsport, TN. The quilt was passed to the owner by her husband's aunt, Lavon Wilcox.

**Burows, Suzanne Porter** (Richard W.)
Long Island Chapter
Ancestor: William Brizendine, VA —#513659
This "Churn Dash" quilt was pieced in Illinois by Elsie Amidon, aunt of Lavon Amiden Wilcox. It was quilted by the Exchange Place Quilters in Kingsport, TN. The quilt was passed to the owner by her husband's aunt, Lavon Wilcox.

**Burows, Suzanne Porter** (Richard W.)
Long Island Chapter
Ancestor: William Brizendine, VA — #513659
This "Double Wedding Ring" was made in Fox, VA in 1934. It is the last quilt made by Rosa Eudora Hash McMillan, the owner's grandmother. The quilt was passed to the maker's daughter, Virginia McMillan Porter (Mrs. Walter A.)

**Burows, Suzanne Porter** (Richard W.)
Long Island Chapter
Ancestor: William Brizendine, VA — #513659
This "Grandmother's Flower Garden" quilt was made by Elsie Amidon, aunt of Lavon Amiden Wilcox. The quilt was passed to the owner by her husband's aunt, Lavon Wilcox.

**Bush, Mary Pratt** (Dennis)
Old Glory Chapter
Ancestor: John S. Smithson — #725842
This "Bird of Paradise" cross stitch quilt was made in 1980 by the owner (born 5/26/1942 at Wilson County, TN).

**Bush, Mary Pratt** (Dennis)
Old Glory Chapter
Ancestor: John S. Smithson —#725842
This "LeMoyne Star" quilt was made in 1959 by the owner's grandmother, Mattie Givens Hoskins (born 9/16/1896, died 9/21/1966).

**Bush, Mary Pratt** (Dennis)
Old Glory Chapter
Ancestor: John S. Smithson —#725842
This "Bouquet of Roses" quilt was made in 1960 by the owner's mother, Esther Pratt (born 1/22/1921 at Williamson County, TN).

**Burroughs, Mary Raulston** (James)
Judge David Campbell Chapter
Ancestor: Robert Bean, NC —#717539
This "Tulip" quilt was made in 1853 in Tennessee by the owner's great grandmother, Laura Elizabeth Youngblood Raulston (born 10/28/1837 in Middle TN, married James Wallace Raulston, died in 1911 in Middle TN). The quilt was passed from the maker, to the owner's grandmother, to her mother, and finally to the owner.

**Bush, Mary Pratt** (Dennis)
Old Glory Chapter
Ancestor: John S. Smithson
—#725842
This "Grandmother's Fan"
quilt was made in 1966 by the
owner.

**Cabage, Grayce Hannah** (Harold N.)
Mary Blount Chapter
Ancestor: James Taylor, NC —
#596121
This "Double Nine Patch" quilt was
made in the early 1900's at Blount
County, TN and was given to the
owner's father as payment for a doc-
tor bill.

**Calvert, Julia "Judy" Catherine
Light** (James William)
Clinch Bend Chapter
Ancestor: James Dinsmore, NC —
#564284
This "Job's Troubles" quilt was made
in the late 1930's in Kentucky by the
owner's mother, Nattie Cameron Light
(born 1886 at Trigg County, KY, mar-
ried James L. Light, died 1962 at
Cadiz, KY).

**Cabage, Grayce Hannah** (Harold N.)
Mary Blount Chapter
Ancestor: James Taylor, NC —
#596121
This "Dogwood" quilt was made in the
1970's at Blount County, TN by the
owner's sister, Gladys H. White (born
and died in Blount County).

**Campbell, Joan Dring**
(Russell C.)
Campbell Chapter
Ancestor:        Joseph
Washburn, NY —#555067
This "Crazy" quilt was made
circa 1882 at Peekskill, NY
by the owner's maternal
grandmother, Eleanor Clark
Vredenburgh (born 11/1868
at Peekskill, married Richard Vredenburgh, died 11/
1963 at New York, NY). The
owner's great grandfather,
George F. Clark, had an im-
porting business in New
York. This provided many of
the beautiful "scraps" for
this quilt.

**Campbell, Sandra**
Spencer Clack Chapter
Ancestor: James Owenby, NC
—#762013
This "Rainbow Tile/Diamond
Field" quilt was pieced in 1975-
80 at Sevier County, TN by the
owner's great grandmother, Lillie
Jane Day (born 5/1887, died 10/
1975 at Sevierville, TN) and the
owner finished the quilt.

**Campen, Cynthia Brady** (Marvin)
Lt. James Sheppard Chapter
Ancestor: James Snodgrass, VA —
#747760
This "Postage Stamp" quilt was re-
ceived through the owner's
husband's aunt, Daisy Womack.

**Campen, Cynthia Brady**
(Marvin)
Lt. James Sheppard Chapter
Ancestor: James Snodgrass, VA
—#747760
This "Crazy" quilt was was re-
ceived through the owner's
husband's aunt, Daisy Womack.

**Canady, Carol Lawson**
(James Donald)
Old Glory Chapter
Ancestor: James Lawson, PA
—#638655
This "String" quilt was made in
Hickman County, TN by the
owner's husband's grand-
mother, Florence McCord
Canady (born in 1882 at
Hickman County and died in
1970 in the same county).

**Canady, Carol Lawson** (James
Donald)
Old Glory Chapter
Ancestor: James Lawson, PA —
#638655
This "Double Wedding Ring" quilt
was made in the late 1960's at
Centerville, TN by the owner's
mother-in-law, Dorothy Canady
(born 1913 at Richmond County,
married Curtis).

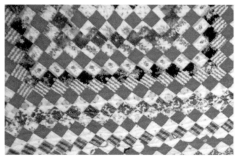

**Canady, Carol Lawson**
(James Donald)
Old Glory Chapter
Ancestor: James Lawson,
PA —#638655
This "Trip Around the World"
quilt was made at Hickman
County, TN by the owner's
husband's paternal great
uncle, Neut Cord (born and
died in Hickman County).

**Cantrell, Maymee Miller**
(Harvey)
Old Reynoldsburgh Chapter
Ancestor: John Rucker, Sr.,
VA —#563917
This "Dutch Doll/Sunbonnet
Sue" quilt was made in 1933
at Smyrna, TN by the owner's
mother, Mrs. J.R. Miller (born
9/30/1884 at Smyrna, died 10/
23/1964 in the same town).
The quilt was made as a gift
for the owner.

**Cantrell, Maymee Miller**
(Harvey)
Old Reynoldsburgh Chapter
Ancestor: John Rucker, Sr.,
VA —#563917
This "Sixteen Patch" quilt
was pieced in 1915 at
Smyrna, TN by the owner's
mother, Mrs. J. R. Miller. It
was quilted in 1992.

**Carley, Leila Shively** (Alfred)
The Crab Orchard Chapter
Ancestor: Thomas Williams,
MD —#703219
This "Star/Feathered Star" quilt
was pieced in 1934 in Ohio by
the owner's great grandmother,
Samantha Hart Wilson (born
1842, married Alexander
Robinson Wilson, died 1936 at
Barnesville, OH). The quilt was
given to the owner in 1958 by
her aunt, Margaret Thomas, at
Jerusalem, OH. She informed
the owner that her great grandmother had started the quilt
and it was finished by her
daughter, Leila Wilson Henershot. The owner was named after her great aunt.

**Carney, Louise Rosson**
Charlotte Reeves Robertson
Chapter
Ancestor: David Mims —
#747719
This "Crazy" quilt was made
circa 1895 at Guthrie, KY by
the owner's mother's child-
hood "live in" nurse, Tennie
Frey (died circa 1914 at
Nashville, TN). The quilt was
passed from the maker, to

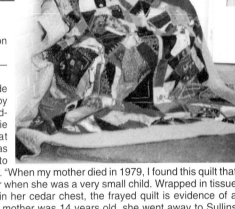

Sadie Mimms, to the owner. "When my mother died in 1979, I found this quilt that
her nurse had made for her when she was a very small child. Wrapped in tissue
paper and lovingly stored in her cedar chest, the frayed quilt is evidence of a
child's long use. When my mother was 14 years old, she went away to Sullins
Prepatory School in Bristol, VA. While she was there, her nurse died. She told
me, 'When Tennie died, it broke my heart.'"

**Carney, Louise Rosson**
Charlotte Reeves Robertson
Chapter
Ancestor: David Mims —
#747719
This coverlet was made prior
to 1844 in Ireland by the
owner's great grandmother.
The owner acquired the coverlet in 1979 at the death of
her mother, Sadie Mimms
Rosson. It was passed down
from the owner's father's
family, Matilda Moore and
George Adams, who emi-
grated to America from Ireland.

**Carpenter, Chris Thomas** (John)
Rhea-Craig Chapter
Ancestor: Robert Cooke, VA —
#500834
This "Dutch Girl/Sunbonnet Sue" quilt
was made in Madisonville, TN by the
owner's grandmother, Mrs. Cooke
Carson (born in1897 at Burnside, KY,
died in 1976 at Madisonville, TN).

**Carpenter, Chris Thomas**
(John)
Rhea-Craig Chapter
Ancestor: Robert Cooke, VA
—#500834
This "Dutch Girl/Sunbonnet
Sue" quilt was made in the
1930's at Easley, SC by the
owners husband's grand-
mother, Emmie Carpenter
(born at Andersen, SC, married James L. Carpenter,
died in 1949 at Easley, SC).

**Carpenter, Grace Marie**
Coytee Chapter
Ancestor: Capt. Samuel
Wear, VA —#782910
This "Dresden Plate" quilt
was made in 1940 at Madisonville,
TN by the owners great
grandmother, Grace Wear
Kirkpatrick (born 7/25/1912 in
TN, married William Elmo
Kirkpatrick).

**Carpenter, Janella Hooper** (J. Beecher)
William Cocke Chapter
Ancestor: Fredrick Jones, VA —#611614
This "Orange Peel/Variation of a Daisy
Chain" quilt was made circa 1935 by a fam-
ily member as a wedding gift to the owner.

**Carpenter, Janella Hooper**
(J. Beecher)
William Cocke Chapter
Ancestor: Fredrick Jones, VA
—#611614
This "Crazy" quilt was made in the 1970's at Knoxville, TN by the owner's aunt, Lela Carpenter Nichols (born 11/8/1897 at Jefferson County, TN, married Clyde Nichols, died 11/4/1977 at Knoxville TN). The owner recognizes fabrics in the quilt that were left from the many "aprons her aunt made to sell at church bazaars at the Fountain City United Methodist Church.

**Carpenter, Sheila Wolfe**
(James F.)
Coytee Chapter
Ancestor: Capt. Samuel Ware, VA —#697426
This "Ohio Star/Nine Patch" quilt was made in 1941 at Madisonville, TN by the owner's grandmother, Grace Wear Kirkpatrick (born 7/12/1912 at Vonore, TN, married William Elmo Kirkpatrick. The quilt was passed from the maker, to the owner's mother, to the owner.

**Carrell, Ruth Eggers** (Don)
Mary Blount Chapter
Ancestor: Willoughby Rogers, NC —#490648
This "String" quilt was made circa 1900 at Blount County, TN by the owner's grandmother, Florence Taylor Leatherwood (born 4/28/1871 at Blount County, TN, married John Leatherwood, died 1/9/1918 at Blount County).

**Carter, Edna Swann** (Willard)
Samuel Doak Chapter
Ancestor: Jacob Boyer, VA —#775349
This "Dresden Plate" quilt was pieced around 1930 at Greene County, TN by the owner's great aunt, Anne Burnett Stephens (married Charles Stephens). It was quilted by G. V. Osborne. It was given to the owner by the maker's daughter, Katherine Anne Stephens.

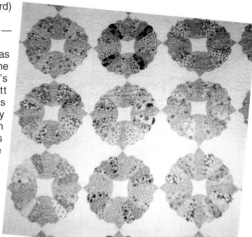

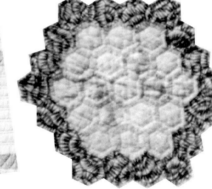

**Carter, Martha Atkins** (Carlos)
Bonnie Kate Chapter
Ancestor: Samuel Sharp — #685258
This "Dutch Girl/Sunbonnet Sue" quilt was made in the 1930's at Maynardville, TN by the owner's mother, Margaret L. Hamley Atkins (born 8/28/1913 at Knox County, TN, married Horace Edward Atkins, died 7/2/1995 at Knox County).

**Carter, Martha Atkins** (Carlos)
Bonnie Kate Chapter
Ancestor: Samuel Sharp — #685258
This "Grandmother's Flower Garden" quilt was made in the 1930's at Maynardville, TN by the owner's mother, Margaret L. Hamley Atkins.

**Carter, Martha Atkins**
(Carlos)
Bonnie Kate Chapter
Ancestor: Samuel Sharp —#685258
This "Rag" quilt was made in 1917 at Maynardville, TN by the owner's grandmother, Nila Louvenia Walton Atkins (born 8/15/1884 at Union County, TN, married George Wesley Atkins, died 12/2/1964 at Union County). The maker grew the cotton, carded it, and made the batting for her quilts.

**Carter, Martha Atkins** (Carlos)
Bonnie Kate Chapter
Ancestor: Samuel Sharp —#685258
This "Irish Puzzle/Kansas Trouble" quilt was made in 1918/1920 at Maynardville, TN by the owner's grandmother, Nila Louvenia Walton Atkins.

**Carter, Martha Atkins**
(Carlos)
Bonnie Kate Chapter
Ancestor: Samuel Sharp —
#685258
This embroidered "Cardinal"
quilt was made in the 1920's
at Maynardville, TN by the
owner's grandmother, Nila
Louvenia Walton Atkins.

**Carter, Phyllis Talbert**
(James H. Jr.)
Judge David Campbell
Chapter
Ancestor Adam Egle, PA —
#720421
This "Butterfly" quilt was
made in 1935-36 at
Salisbury, NC by the owner's
mother, Grace Hoffman
Talbert (born 9/28/1917 at
Salisbury, married Richard L.
Talbert). The maker embroi-
dered and appliqued the quilt
in her last year of high school
and quilted it the year follow-
ing her graduation. The
owner received the quilt from
the maker.

**Carter, Phyllis Talbert** (James
H. Jr.)
Judge David Campbell Chapter
Ancestor Adam Egle, PA —
#720421
This "Double Wedding Ring" quilt
was made circa the 1930's at
Salisbury, NC by the owner's
grandmother, Minnie Bailey
Talbert (born 6/2/1879 at
Randolph County, NC, married
James Lawrence Talbert, died 5/
13/1971 at Salisbury, NC.). This
quilt is very heavy. It is stuffed
with genuine sheep's wool from
sheep raised by the owner's
grandparents. The quilt was
passed to the owner at her
grandmother's death.

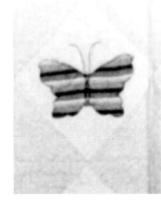

**Casey, Martha Belle Reid** (R. Fentress)
Henderson Station Chapter
Ancestor: Alsalon Haston, VA —#694730
This "Butterfly" quilt was made in 1934 at
Henderson, TN by the owners mother, Archie
Bell Williams Reid (born 10/30/1899 at
Chester County, TN, married Gordon Eli Reid,
died 11/30/1982 at Henderson County, TN).
The maker gave each of her daughters a doll
quilt and a "Butterfly" quilt.

**Chaffin, Betty Gay Littrell**
(Sherrill T.)
Buffalo River Chapter
Ancestor: Thomas Killen, NC
—#592584
This "Four Pointed Star" quilt
was made circa 1890-1900 at
Loretto, TN by the owner's
great grandmother, Alice
Riddle White (born 7/4/1867 at
Lawrence County, TN, married
Henry Andrew White, died 1/
24/1945 at Loretto, TN) and by
the owner's grandmother, Sa-
rah Eveline White Reeves.
This quilt and the "Turkey
Tracks" quilt they made were
stored in Sarah's trunk in 1919

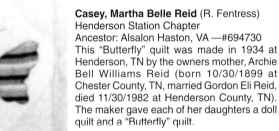

**Chaffin, Betty Gay Littrell**
(Sherrill T.)
Buffalo River Chapter
Ancestor: Thomas Killen, NC
—#592584
This "Turkey Tracks" quilt was
made made circa 1890-1900 at
Loretto, TN by the owner's great
grandmother, Alice Riddle White
and by the owner's grandmother,
Sarah Eveline White Reeves (born
4/3/1884 at Lauderdale County, AL,
married William Cleveland Reeves,
died 1/15/1919 at Loretto, TN).

at the time of her death from Spanish Flu that was brought back by solders who
fought in WWI. The quilts in the trunk were handed down to the owner's mother,
Neva Reeves Littrell, and then to the owner.

**Chaffin, Betty Gay Littrell**
(Sherrill T.)
Buffalo River Chapter
Ancestor: Thomas Killen, NC
—#592584
This "French Doll" quilt was
hand appliqued in 1958 at
Loretto, TN by the owner
(born 10/11/1942 at Mobile,
AL) when she was 16 years
old. She chose the colors
from a popular song of the
time "Lavendar Blue." It was
quilted by the owner's
mother, Neva Reeves Littrell,
in the early 1960's.

**Chaffin, Betty Gay Littrell**
(Sherrill T.)
Buffalo River Chapter
Ancestor: Thomas Killen, NC
—#592584
This cross stitch sampler quilt
was made circa 1974 at
Loretta, TN by the owner's
mother, Neva Reeves Littrell
(born 11/10/1909 at Loretta,
TN, married Clayton Lee
Littrell, died 12/26/1990 at
Huntsville, AL).

**Chaffin, Betty Gay Littrell**
(Sherrill T.)
Buffalo River Chapter
Ancestor: Thomas Killen, NC
—#592584
This "Grandmother's Flower Garden" quilt was made circa 1975 at Loretto, TN by the owner's mother, Neva Reeves Littrell.

**Chaffin, Betty Gay Littrell**
(Sherrill T.)
Buffalo River Chapter
Ancestor: Thomas Killen, NC
—#592584
This "Tulip Basket" quilt was made circa 1976 at Loretto, TN by the owner's mother, Neva Reeves Littrell.

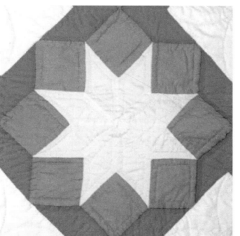

**Chaffin, Betty Gay Littrell**
(Sherrill T.)
Buffalo River Chapter
Ancestor: Thomas Killen, NC —#592584
This "Lone Star" quilt was made circa 1970 at Loretto, TN by the owner's mother, Neva Reeves Littrell. The owner says, "looking at these quilts brings back 'warm' memories. — Mother had a dress out of that print. — I remember wearing a play suit like that."

**Chaffin, Betty Gay Littrell**
(Sherrill T.)
Buffalo River Chapter
Ancestor: Thomas Killen, NC —#592584
This "Double Wedding Ring" quilt was made circa 1930 at Loretto, TN by the owner's mother, Neva Reeves Littrell.

**Chaffin, Judith Harlan**
(James A. )
Chief Piomingo Chapter
Ancestor: Aaron Harlon, NC —#728156
This "Eight Pointed Star" quilt was made in 1980 in Illinois by the owner's aunt, Glenna Harlan Schumacher (born 10/11/1920 at Craighead County, AR, married Lawrence J. Schumacher). The quilt was given to the owner by the maker.

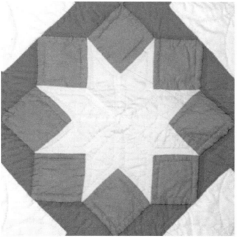

**Chaffin, Judith Harlan**
(James A. )
Chief Piomingo Chapter
Ancestor: Aaron Harlon, NC —#728156
This "Pinwheel/Sugar Bowl" quilt was made approximately 50 years ago and was purchased by the owner at a flea market in Memphis, TN in the early 1980's.

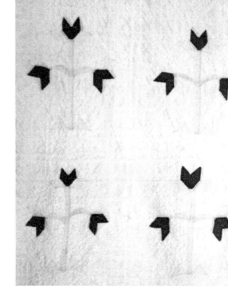

**Chaffin, Judith Harlan**
(James A. )
Chief Piomingo Chapter
Ancestor: Aaron Harlon, NC —#728156
This "Lilly" quilt was made approximately 75 years ago and was purchased by the owner at a flea market in Memphis, TN in the early 1980's.

**Chaffin, Judith Harlan** (James A. )
Chief Piomingo Chapter
Ancestor: Aaron Harlon, NC —#728156
These "Zig Zag" quilts were made in 1979 at Jonesboro, AR by the owner's mother-in-law, Geraldine Cole Chaffin (born 1/5/1921 at Jonesboro, AR, died 9/16/1992 at Jonesboro). They were given to the owner's son, Brett Harlan Chaffin, for Christmas. These quilts won a blue ribbon at the Craighead County, AR Fair.

**Cherry, Effie Lee Aman** (Frank)
Colonel Jethro Sumner Chapter
Ancestor: Phillip Aman, NC —
#770711
This "Log Cabin" quilt was made in 1903 at Onslow County, NC by the owner's grandmother, Effie Ann Simpson Higgins (born 5/11/1878 at Onslow County, married Manley Albert Higgins, died 11/3/1927 at Jacksonville, NC). The owner is named after her grandmother. The quilt was made in the first year of Effie's marriage. After the wedding, Effie's mother, Annie Elizabeth Horn Simpson, traveled to Maysville, NC to purchase material for the new bride so that she could make her first quilt. Family lore has it that the maker wanted this quilt to be inherited by the granddaughter named for her.

**Cherry, Linda Hudson** (Kenneth)
Charlotte Reeves Robertson Chapter
Ancestor: William Booker, VA —#746606
This "State Flowers" quilt was made in 1993-96 at Celina, TN by the owner's mother-in-law, Mary Elizabeth Kyle Cherry (born 6/22/1916 at Celina, TN, married Ray K. Cherry). It was given to the owner as a present.

**Ciaramitaro, S. Bridget Baugus** (The Rev. Vincent Ira)
Chickasaw Bluff Chapter
Ancestor: Abner Alloway Strange, VA —#780907
This original "Dinosaur" quilt was made in 1991 at Memphis, TN by the owner (born 5/1/1950 at Savannah, TN). It is machine pieced and quilted and it reflects the maker's son, Donovan's, love of dinosaurs.

**Ciaramitaro, S. Bridget Baugus** (The Rev. Vincent Ira)
Chickasaw Bluff Chapter
Ancestor: Abner Alloway Strange, VA —#780907
This "Friendship" quilt was presented to the owner's husband by the congregation of the Forked Deer United Methodist Church in Haywood County, TN in 1990. He pastored this church from 1989-1992. In 1998, Vincent had quadruple bypass heart surgery. He chose this quilt to sleep under during his surgery because it is light weight and holds such fond memories.

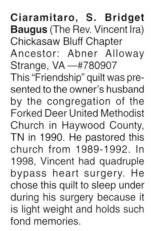

**Ciaramitaro, S. Bridget Baugus** (The Rev. Vincent Ira)
Chickasaw Bluff Chapter
Ancestor: Abner Alloway Strange, VA —#780907
This "Log Cabin" quilt was lovingly made in 1987 by members of Freeman's Chapel United Methodist Church at Martin, TN. It was given by the congregation to the owner's husband as a Christmas gift when he served the church as the minister.

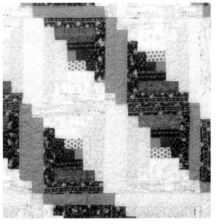

**Ciaramitaro, S. Bridget Baugus** (The Rev. Vincent Ira)
Chickasaw Bluff Chapter
Ancestor: Abner Alloway Strange, VA —#780907
This "Grandmother's Flower Garden" quilt was made in Memphis, TN from 1973-76 by the owner. "I chose this pattern because of its simplicity and it reminded me of my 'Grandma Fowler' and her quilts and flowers. I pieced this quilt while searching for my first job out of college and watching the Nixon Impeachment Proceedings."

**Ciaramitaro, S. Bridget Baugus** (The Rev. Vincent Ira)
Chickasaw Bluff Chapter
Ancestor: Abner Alloway Strange, VA —#780907
This "Gingham Dog and Calico Cat" baby quilt was made in 1986 by the owner's mother, Marilyn Johnson Baugus (born 8/27/29 at Savannah, TN, married Clarence Earl Baugus, Jr.). She made the quilt while waiting for her new grandchild, Donovan Westley Ciaramitaro.

**Ciaramitaro, S. Bridget Baugus** (The Rev. Vincent Ira)
Chickasaw Bluff Chapter
Ancestor: Abner Alloway Strange, VA —#780907
This "Friendship" quilt was made by the members of St. Paul United Methodist Church in Wingo, KY and given to the owner's husband as a Christmas gift in 1987. "The blocks reflect the lives of the members — from a young boy who my husband inspired to run track — to a baby born during his tenure as minister. There are flowers that repressent a member's love of gardening. I was so proud of Vincent to know both of his congregations loved him enough to make quilts for him in 1987."

**Ciaramitaro, S. Bridget Baugus** (The Rev. Vincent Ira)
Chickasaw Bluff Chapter
Ancestor: Abner Alloway Strange, VA —#780907
This "Symbol of Home" quilt was made in 1985 by the owner's mother, Marilyn Johnson Baugus. She made the quilt as a wall hanging for the owner and her husband. It is still hanging in their living room in 1999.

**Ciaramitaro, S. Bridget Baugus** (The Rev. Vincent Ira)
Chickasaw Bluff Chapter
Ancestor: Abner Alloway Strange, VA —#780907
This "Overall Bill" quilt was made in Memphis, TN in the 1976 by Ruby Duren, a close friend of the owner's mother, Marilyn Johnson Baugus. The quilt has a large "1976" embroidered in the middle since it was made in celebration of the Bicentenial. This quilt was purchased from the maker by the owner in 1977.

**Ciaramitaro, S. Bridget Baugus**
(The Rev. Vincent Ira)
Chickasaw Bluff Chapter
Ancestor: Abner Alloway Strange, VA —#780907
This "Dove/Peace" quilt was made in the 1970's at Memphis, TN by Ruby Duren, a close friend of the owner's mother, Marilyn Johnson Baugus. This quilt was purchased from the maker by the owner in 1977.

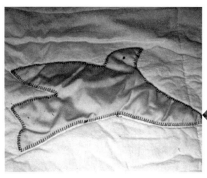

**Ciaramitaro, S. Bridget Baugus** (The Rev. Vincent Ira)
Chickasaw Bluff Chapter
Ancestor: Abner Alloway Strange, VA —#780907
This "Maple Leaf" quilt was made in the 1940's or 50's at Savannah, TN. The owner purchased this quilt at an antique shop in Savannah.

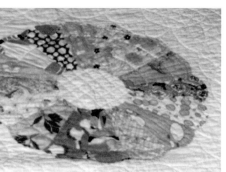

**Clapsadle, Christina Eye**
(Raymond)
Chucalissa Chapter
Ancestor: Jacob Harper, VA —#735754
This "Dresden Plate" quilt was made in the early 1900's at Randolph County, WV by the owner's great aunt, Ella Harman Dunkle (born 7/15/1898 at Pendleton Co., WV, married Roy O. Dunkle, died 12/26/1982 at Houston, TX). The owner inherited the quilt from her great aunt and uncle.

**Clapsadle, Christina Eye** (Raymond)
Chucalissa Chapter
Ancestor: Jacob Harper, VA — #735754
This "Nine Patch" quilt was made circa 1940 in Richmond, VA by the owner's godmother, Pat Kelles. It was given to her when she was a child.

**Clapsadle, Christina Eye** (Raymond)
Chucalissa Chapter
Ancestor: Jacob Harper, VA — #735754
This cross stitch embroidery quilt was made at Deer Run, WV in 1968 by the owner's grandmother, Etta Mae Dunkle Eye (born 7/30/1892 at Pendleton Co., WV, married Whitney W. Eye, died 4/20/1973 at Deer Run, WV). It was a wedding gift to the owner.

**Clevenger, Mary Nell Butler** (D. Wayne)
Mary Blount Chapter
Ancestor: Charles Butler, NC — #695156
This "Pinwheel" quilt was pieced in 1985 at Ventura, CA by the owner's sister, Nelda J. Butler Beem (born 2/1/1928, at Weatherford, TX, married Arthur G. Beem). The owner quilted the quilt at Maryville, TN .

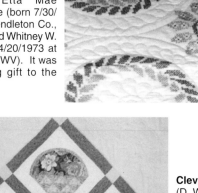

**Clevenger, Mary Nell Butler**
(D. Wayne)
Mary Blount Chapter
Ancestor: Charles Butler, NC — #695156
This "Basket" quilt is an original design made by the owner's sister, Nelda Jean Butler Beem. This quilt was made especially for the owner.

**Clevenger, Mary Nell Butler** (D. Wayne)
Mary Blount Chapter
Ancestor: Charles Butler, NC — #695156
This "Friendship" quilt was made in 1935 in Texas by friends, neighbors and family members of Mary Emma Neal Butler, the owner's grandmother (born 6/4/1895 at Walker County, GA, married Daniel Butler, died 8/8/1955 at Weatherford, TX). They surprised "Granny Butler" on her 62nd birthday. Each one had made a square for her. "Granny" and a friend quilted it. It was given to the owner by her aunt, Rosa Lena Butler Cobb.

**Clifton, Jamie Tomlinson** (James R.)
Colonel Jethro Sumner Chapter
Ancestor: Col. James Robertson, NC — #737592
This "Variation of a Trip Around The World" quilt was made in 1998 at Lebanon, TN by the owner's great aunt, Dorothy Ashley (married Earl). The quilt is signed and dated by the maker. In the summer of 1997, Dorothy and Earl Ashley saw a quilt like this one hanging on a wall in an antique shop in Bardstown, KY. No pattern being available, they counted the squares in each section, and she drew a quick sketch of it to take back home. With Earl's help, they figured the size of the squares and border widths, so she was able to duplicate the quilt. It is made of scraps. The only fabric purchased for it was the muslin for the borders.

**Clifton, Jamie Tomlinson**
(James R.)
Colonel Jethro Sumner Chapter
Ancestor: Col. James Robertson, NC — #737592
This "Flower Garden Sampler" was made in 1991 at Lebanon, TN by the owner's aunt, Dorothy Ashley. In 1992, it won 2nd place at the County Fair at Lebanon, TN. The quilt won "Best of Show" in 1994 at the October Fest in Lebanon.

**Coady, Marie Moore** (Joe)
Henderson Station Chapter
Ancestor: Anthony Hart, VA — #778693
This "Blooms 'n Butterfly" quilt is an original pattern made circa 1965 at Jackson, TN. The owner bought the top which is hand painted and every block is different. She quilted the quilt and plans to "will" it to her descendants.

**Coady, Marie Moore** (Joe)
Henderson Station Chapter
Ancestor: Anthony Hart, VA — #778693
This candlewick quilt was made in 1980 in Chester Co., TN by the owner.

**Cobb, Jane Kimbrough** (Carl)
Cavett Station Chapter
Ancestor: Robert Cook, VA — #663425
This "Tulip" quilt was made circa 1920 - 30's in Monroe Co., TN by the owner's grandmother, Minnie Williams Kimbrough (born 8/3/1858 Monroe Co., TN, married George Washington Kimbrough, died 3/1941 Madisonville, TN.) The quilt was passed from grandmother, to her son, James Claude, the owner's father, to the owner.

**Clifton, Jamie Tomlinson**
(James R.)
Colonel Jethro Sumner Chapter
Ancestor: Col. James Robertson, NC — #737592
This "Seven Sisters" quilt was made in 1998 at Lebanon, TN by the owner's aunt, Dorothy Ashley.

**Clifton, Jamie Tomlinson**
(James R.)
Colonel Jethro Sumner Chapter
Ancestor: Col. James Robertson, NC — #737592
This "Sampler" quilt was made in 1987 in Steger, IL by the owner's aunt, Dorothy Ashley. It one First place at a show in Momence, IL in 1987. The quilt won 2nd place in 1994 at Wilson Bank and Trust October Fest quilt show.

**Clifton, Jamie Tomlinson** (James R.)
Colonel Jethro Sumner Chapter
Ancestor: Col. James Robertson, NC — #737592
This "Mariners Compass Medallion" is an original pattern made in 1989 at Steger, IL by the owner's aunt, Dorothy Ashley. It has won several 1st place awards at various shows. In July 1989, it won a "Best of Show" at Will County Fair in Peotone, IL, 2nd place at the Wilson County, TN Fair in 1990, and 1st place in 1992 at the Southern Home Furniture Show.

**Coady, Marie Moore** (Joe)
Henderson Station Chapter
Ancestor: Anthony Hart, VA — #778693
This "Prairie Star" quilt was made circa 1975 at Chester Clounty, TN by the owner's husband's Aunt Morris (born 1918 at Chester County, married J.T. Morris).

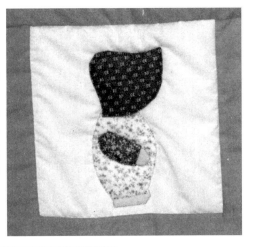

**Cobb, Jane Kimbrough**
(Carl)
Cavett Station Chapter
Ancestor: Robert Cook,
VA — #663425
This "Sunbonnet Kids"
quilt was made in 1988 in
Knoxville, TN by the owner
(born 6/23/1930 at San
Francisco, CA).

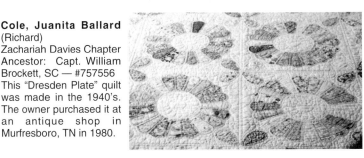

**Cobb, Jane Kimbrough**
(Carl)
Cavett Station Chapter
Ancestor: Robert Cook, VA
— #663425
This "Sun" quilt was made in
1930 in Monroe County, TN
by the owner's grandmother,
Minnie Williams Kimbrough.

**Cole, Estha**
Buffalo River Chapter
Ancestor: Robert Meanes,
NC —#687913
This "Flower Basket" quilt
was made by 1870 in
Hamilton Co., TN by the
owner's cousin, Elizabeth
Russell Burrell (born 6/23/
1836 at Hamilton Co., TN,
married Thomas Burrell,
died 1/12/1916 at Hamilton
Co., TN). The quilt was
handed down from the
owner's cousin to her
grandmother, to her aunt,
and then to the owner. The
quilt has been exhibited at
the Parthenon in Nashville
and in local quilt shows.

**Cole, Juanita Ballard**
(Richard)
Zachariah Davies Chapter
Ancestor: Capt. William
Brockett, SC — #757556
This "Dresden Plate" quilt
was made in the 1940's.
The owner purchased it at
an antique shop in
Murfresboro, TN in 1980.

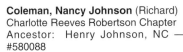

**Cole, Juanita Ballard** (Richard)
Zachariah Davies Chapter
Ancestor: Capt. William Brockett, SC
— #757556
This "Grandmother's Flower Garden"
quilt was made in the 1930's at Pleasant Shade, TN by the owner's great
aunt, Mary "Aunt Sis" Sloan (born
1859 at Pleasant Shade, TN). The
owner purchased the quilt from a family member.

**Cole, Suzanne**
Zachariah Davies
Chapter
Ancestor: Capt.
William Brockett,
SC — #760859
This "Lone Star"
quilt was made circa
1950 at Pleasant
Shade, TN by the
owner's grand-
mother and great

grandmother, Tennie Ballard and Alice Hackett Toney. Tennie was born in1902
at Pleasant Shade, TN, married Albert Fred Ballard, and died 1973 at Carthage,
TN. "The pieces in this quilt were remnants of uniforms made for an ice cream
store called "Sidebottom" in Nashville, TN during World War II. It was a time
when patriotism was high. Everything was red, white and blue. "The quilt was
made for my mother's hope chest, and now it is in my hope chest!!"

**Coleman, Nancy Johnson** (Richard)
Charlotte Reeves Robertson Chapter
Ancestor: Henry Johnson, NC —
#580088
This "Nine Patch" quilt was made in 1986
in Robertson County, TN by the owner's
mother, Irene S. Johnson (born 11/17/
1908, married Will Irvin Johnson) She
was 77 years old when she made the
quilt. She signed it "ISJ, 86".

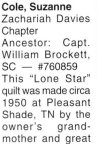

**Coleman, Nancy Johnson**
(Richard)
Charlotte Reeves Robertson
Chapter
Ancestor: Henry Johnson,
NC — #580088
This "Umbrella Girl" quilt was
already "old" in 1942 when we
moved to my grandmother's
house. It was found between
the mattress and springs on
an upstairs bed where it remained until 1973. It had
been put there to protect the
mattress.

**Coleman, Nancy Johnson** (Richard)
Charlotte Reeves Robertson Chapter
Ancestor: Henry Johnson, NC —
#580088
This "String" quilt was made circa
1918-19 in Robertson Co., TN by a
neighbor, Ada Fisher, (born 1891 at
Robertson Co, TN, died 1980 at
Robertson Co., TN, married Herschel
Fisher who was born in 1887 and died
in 1981). According to the owner, "Mr.
and Mrs. Fischer did not drive. When
Miss Ada got sick, I would take them
to the doctor in Springfield or to the
grocery. I would not accept pay and
one day when I went for them they
came to the car with this quilt. She
told me the batting was Mr. Herschel's
World War I army blanket that he
brought home after serving in France.
They had no children and I never saw
one without the other. On the first an-
niversary of her death in 1981, he committed suicide by hanging himself in their
home. He was 94 years old. They had been married 73 years."

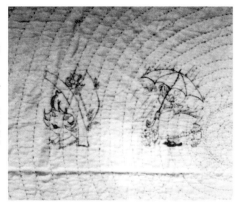

**Collins, Judy Rutherford**
(Sebert, Jr.)
James White Chapter
Ancestor: Michael Ault, PA —
#776555
This embroidered quilt with childhood scenes was made at Knoxville, TN in 1975 by the owner, (born 12/20/1947 at Knoxville, TN).

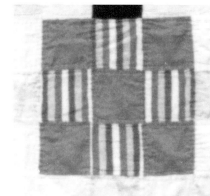

**Collins, Judy Rutherford**
(Sebert, Jr.)
James White Chapter
Ancestor: Michael Ault, PA —
#776555
This "Nine Patch" quilt was made by a neighbor, Kelly Sprangler, in 1978 at Knoxville, TN. When Virginia Alline and Cecil Rutherford's home burned January 11, 1978, she gave this quilt to them. The owner inherited the quilt from the Rutherfords.

**Collins, Judy Rutherford**
(Sebert, Jr.)
James White Chapter
Ancestor: Michael Ault, PA —
#776555
This "Allover Block" quilt was made in 1977 at Knoxville, TN by the owner's mother-in-law, Hester Price Collins, (born 12/8, married Sebert Collins, Sr., died 11/24/92 at Knoxville, TN). Hester gave the quilt to the owner.

**Collins, Judy Rutherford**
(Sebert, Jr.)
James White Chapter
Ancestor: Michael Ault, PA
— #776555
This embroidered "Pooh" quilt was made in 1997 at Luttrell, TN by the owner, (born 12/20/1948 at Knoxville, TN, married Sebert Collins, Jr.)

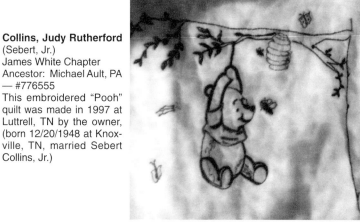

**Connell, Nan Duncan** (Michael M.)
Capt. William Edmiston Chapter
Ancestor: Jesse Nevill, NC —
#785082
This "Bow Tie" quilt belonged to the owner's husband's grandmother when he was still a little boy. Her name was Maude Connell (born 8/11/1885 in Albany GA, married 1/3/1909 to Fred Connell, died 1/4/1953. ) Her husband died in 1958 and left the quilt with their son and daughter-in-law, Marshall and Katherine Connell. After Katheryn died the quilt was left to their son and his wife, the current owners.

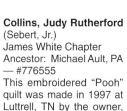

**Conners, Marcia Alexander**
(James)
Rhea-Craig Chapter
Ancestor: William Baker, VA
— #750656
This "Butterfly" quilt was made circa 1980 at Paris, TX. It was a gift to owner by Syble Alexander of Paris, TX and was made by her mother.

**Conners, Marcia Alexander**
(James)
Rhea-Craig Chapter
Ancestor: William Baker, VA —
#750656
This "Octagonal Star" was purchased in Maryland. The letter "S" is embroidered in one Corner. It was made by a professional quilter whose name was Shirley.

**Conners, Marcia Alexander**
(James)
Rhea-Craig Chapter
Ancestor: William Baker, VA —
#750656
This "LeMoyne Star" quilt was made by a neighbor, Reba, (born about 1910 and died 1985 at Russellville, AR). The owner received it as a gift.

**Conners, Marcia Alexander**
(James)
Rhea-Craig Chapter
Ancestor: William Baker, VA
— #750656
This "Crosses and Losses/Old Maid's Puzzle/Hour Glass" quilt was made before 1921 in Nebraska by the owner's grandmother, Eva Franzmann Thompson (born 1902 at Franklin, Iowa, married Andrew Thompson, died 1996 Fayetteville, AR). The owner's grandmother gave the quilt to her.

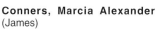

**Conners, Marcia Alexander**
(James)
Rhea-Craig Chapter
Ancestor: William Baker, VA —
#750656
This "Rose Dream" quilt is not documented by the owner.

**Conrey, Emily Granstaff**
(William "Bill")
French Lick Chapter
Ancestor: Capt. John
Medearis, NC—#782451
This "Dresden Plate" quilt was
made in 1991 in Ohio by the
owner's husband's aunt,
Roberta Conrey Morgan (born
7/22/1914, married Harold).
The quilt was a gift to the
owner.

**Conrey, Emily Granstaff**
(William "Bill")
French Lick Chapter
Ancestor: Capt. John
Medearis, NC—#782451
This "Double Wedding Ring"
quilt was made in 1940 at
Ohio by owner's husband's
grandmother, Hazel Conrey,
(born 1896 at Ohio, married
Curtis Conrey, died 1978 at
Ohio). The quilt was given
to Grace Conrey, who gave
it to the owner.

**Cooper, Dorothy Pisor**
(Warren A.)
Andrew Bogle Chapter
Ancestor: Michael
Gotshall, PA — #325554
This woven coverlet was
made circa 1845 in
Ohio. The weaver is un-
known. The coverlet be-
longed to the owner's
great great great aunt,
Phebe Loveridge. The
descent of the coverlet
is from Phebe to Eliza-
beth Loverage, to Anna
Mendenhall, to Mary
Gotshall, to Myrtle Pisor,
to owner.

**Cooksey, Bobby Lancaster**
(Howell)
Caney Fork Chapter
Ancestor: Capt. William
Jarrard — #673791
This "Drunkard's Path" quilt
was made before 1900 at
Lancaster, TN by the owner's
grandmother, Matilda Cowan
Lancaster, (born 3/4/1842,
married Robert Lancaster, died
1/30/1913 at Lancaster, TN).
The quilt descended from
grandmother, to mother, to the
current owner.

**Cooper, Elizabeth Painter**
(Neil S.)
Lydia Russell Bean Chapter
Ancestor: Joseph Hedges, MD
— #705714
This "Patchwork" quilt was
made in the 1930's at Knoxville,
TN by the owner's grand-
mother, Evy Wright Bynum
(born 11/1874 Edwin, Henry
Co., AL, married James J.
Bynum, died 9/1951 at Knoxville, TN). The quilt is made
from discontinued fabric
swatches. The quilt was given
by the owner's grandmother, to
her mother, and then to her.

**Cope, Anna Lisa Mims** (Scott)
William Cocke Chapter
Ancestor: John Huff, —#773570
This "Postage Stamp" quilt was
made in 1979 in Cocke County, TN
by a friend of the owner, Rosetta
McCarter (born 6/21/1939 at
Sevier Co., TN, married Doug
McCarter) The quilt was given to
the owner's mother who passed it
to the owner.

**Cossentine, Bette Goddeke** (Douglas)
Coytee Chapter
Ancestor: Stephen Webster, MA — #777003
This "Dresden Plate" quilt was made in Minnesota by the owner's great grandmother, Louisa Siebrasse Henderson
(born 8/10/1869 at Fisher, MN, died
7/19/1950 at Fisher, MN). The
quilt was passed down in the
family from great grand-
mother, to mother, to owner.

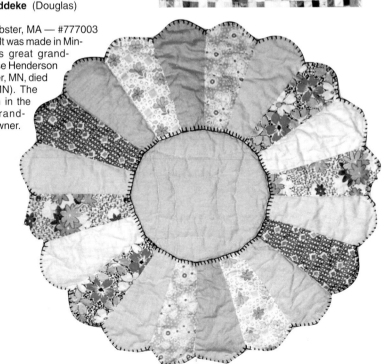

**Coppage, Pauline Martin**
(Quinton)
Robert Cooke Chapter
Ancestor: John McMurty,
PA — #539110
This "Sunbonnet Sue/
Dutch Girl" quilt was made
by the owner's aunt, Eva
Jennings (born 1910 at
Sumner Co., TN died at
Memphis, TN)

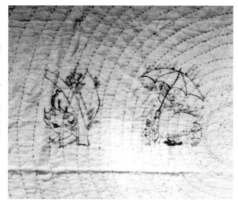

**Collins, Judy Rutherford**
(Sebert, Jr.)
James White Chapter
Ancestor: Michael Ault, PA —
#776555
This embroidered quilt with
childhood scenes was made
at Knoxville, TN in 1975 by
the owner, (born 12/20/1947
at Knoxville, TN).

**Collins, Judy Rutherford**
(Sebert, Jr.)
James White Chapter
Ancestor: Michael Ault, PA —
#776555
This "Nine Patch" quilt was made
by a neighbor, Kelly Sprangler, in
1978 at Knoxville, TN. When Virginia Alline and Cecil Rutherford's
home burned January 11, 1978,
she gave this quilt to them. The
owner inherited the quilt from the
Rutherfords.

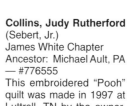

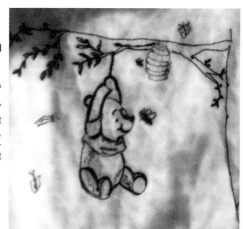

**Collins, Judy Rutherford**
(Sebert, Jr.)
James White Chapter
Ancestor: Michael Ault, PA —
#776555
This "Allover Block" quilt was
made in 1977 at Knoxville, TN
by the owner's mother-in-law,
Hester Price Collins, (born 12/
8, married Sebert Collins, Sr.,
died 11/24/92 at Knoxville,
TN). Hester gave the quilt to
the owner.

**Collins, Judy Rutherford**
(Sebert, Jr.)
James White Chapter
Ancestor: Michael Ault, PA
— #776555
This embroidered "Pooh"
quilt was made in 1997 at
Luttrell, TN by the owner,
(born 12/20/1948 at Knox-
ville, TN, married Sebert
Collins, Jr.)

**Connell, Nan Duncan** (Michael M.)
Capt. William Edmiston Chapter
Ancestor: Jesse Nevill, NC —
#785082
This "Bow Tie" quilt belonged to the
owner's husband's grandmother
when he was still a little boy. Her
name was Maude Connell (born 8/
11/1885 in Albany GA, married 1/3/
1909 to Fred Connell, died 1/4/
1953. ) Her husband died in 1958
and left the quilt with their son and
daughter-in-law, Marshall and
Katherine Connell. After Katheryn
died the quilt was left to their son
and his wife, the current owners.

**Conners, Marcia Alexander**
(James)
Rhea-Craig Chapter
Ancestor: William Baker, VA
— #750656
This "Butterfly" quilt was made
circa 1980 at Paris, TX. It was
a gift to owner by Syble
Alexander of Paris, TX and
was made by her mother.

**Conners, Marcia Alexander**
(James)
Rhea-Craig Chapter
Ancestor: William Baker, VA —
#750656
This "Octagonal Star" was purchased in Maryland. The letter "S"
is embroidered in one Corner. It
was made by a professional quilter
whose name was Shirley.

**Conners, Marcia Alexander**
(James)
Rhea-Craig Chapter
Ancestor: William Baker, VA —
#750656
This "LeMoyne Star" quilt was
made by a neighbor, Reba, (born
about 1910 and died 1985 at
Russellville, AR). The owner re-
ceived it as a gift.

**Conners, Marcia Alexander**
(James)
Rhea-Craig Chapter
Ancestor: William Baker, VA
— #750656
This "Crosses and Losses/Old
Maid's Puzzle/Hour Glass"
quilt was made before 1921
in Nebraska by the owner's
grandmother, Eva Franzmann
Thompson (born 1902 at
Franklin, Iowa, married An-
drew Thompson, died 1996
Fayetteville, AR). The owner's
grandmother gave the quilt to
her.

**Conners, Marcia Alexander**
(James)
Rhea-Craig Chapter
Ancestor: William Baker, VA —
#750656
This "Rose Dream" quilt is not
documented by the owner.

**Conrey, Emily Granstaff**
(William "Bill")
French Lick Chapter
Ancestor: Capt. John
Medearis, NC—#782451
This "Dresden Plate" quilt was made in 1991 in Ohio by the owner's husband's aunt, Roberta Conrey Morgan (born 7/22/1914, married Harold). The quilt was a gift to the owner.

**Conrey, Emily Granstaff**
(William "Bill")
French Lick Chapter
Ancestor: Capt. John
Medearis, NC—#782451
This "Double Wedding Ring" quilt was made in 1940 at Ohio by owner's husband's grandmother, Hazel Conrey, (born 1896 at Ohio, married Curtis Conrey, died 1978 at Ohio). The quilt was given to Grace Conrey, who gave it to the owner.

**Cooksey, Bobby Lancaster**
(Howell)
Caney Fork Chapter
Ancestor: Capt. William Jarrard — #673791
This "Drunkard's Path" quilt was made before 1900 at Lancaster, TN by the owner's grandmother, Matilda Cowan Lancaster, (born 3/4/1842, married Robert Lancaster, died 1/30/1913 at Lancaster, TN). The quilt descended from grandmother, to mother, to the current owner.

**Cooper, Dorothy Pisor**
(Warren A.)
Andrew Bogle Chapter
Ancestor: Michael Gotshall, PA — #325554
This woven coverlet was made circa 1845 in Ohio. The weaver is unknown. The coverlet belonged to the owner's great great great aunt, Phebe Loveridge. The descent of the coverlet is from Phebe to Elizabeth Loverage, to Anna Mendenhall, to Mary Gotshall, to Myrtle Pisor, to owner.

**Cooper, Elizabeth Painter**
(Neil S.)
Lydia Russell Bean Chapter
Ancestor: Joseph Hedges, MD — #705714
This "Patchwork" quilt was made in the 1930's at Knoxville, TN by the owner's grandmother, Evy Wright Bynum (born 11/1874 Edwin, Henry Co., AL, married James J. Bynum, died 9/1951 at Knoxville, TN). The quilt is made from discontinued fabric swatches. The quilt was given by the owner's grandmother, to her mother, and then to her.

**Cope, Anna Lisa Mims** (Scott)
William Cocke Chapter
Ancestor: John Huff, —#773570
This "Postage Stamp" quilt was made in 1979 in Cocke County, TN by a friend of the owner, Rosetta McCarter (born 6/21/1939 at Sevier Co., TN, married Doug McCarter) The quilt was given to the owner's mother who passed it to the owner.

**Cossentine, Bette Goddeke** (Douglas)
Coytee Chapter
Ancestor: Stephen Webster, MA — #777003
This "Dresden Plate" quilt was made in Minnesota by the owner's great grandmother, Louisa Siebrasse Henderson (born 8/10/1869 at Fisher, MN, died 7/19/1950 at Fisher, MN). The quilt was passed down in the family from great grandmother, to mother, to owner.

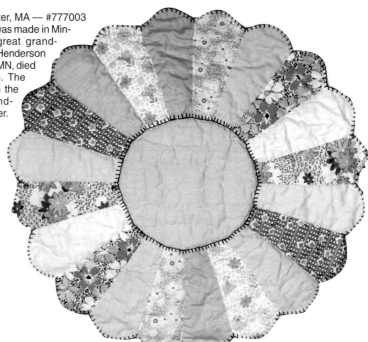

**Coppage, Pauline Martin**
(Quinton)
Robert Cooke Chapter
Ancestor: John McMurty, PA — #539110
This "Sunbonnet Sue/ Dutch Girl" quilt was made by the owner's aunt, Eva Jennings (born 1910 at Sumner Co., TN died at Memphis, TN)

**Cossentine, Bette Goddeke** (Douglas)
Coytee Chapter
Ancestor: Stephen Webster, MA — #777003
This "Crazy Quilt" was made circa 60 years ago in Minnesota by the owner's great grandmother. It was given to the owner's mother who passed it to the owner.

**Cowart, Kara Smith** (Craig A.)
Zachariah Davies Chapter
Ancestor: James Garrison, NC — #721106
This "Clay's Choice" quilt was made in 1977 by the owner's mother, Karen Fusselman Smith, (born 9/5/— at St. Louis , MO, married Dr. John W. Smith). The quilt was a gift from mother to owner.

**Cowart, Kara Smith** (Craig A.)
Zachariah Davies Chapter
Ancestor: James Garrison, NC — #721106
This original quilt is called "Camille's Bunnies" and was made in 1995 at Cordova, TN by the owner's mother. She made it as a baby shower gift for her first grandchild, Camille Olivia Cowart.

**Cowart, Kara Smith** (Craig A.)
Zachariah Davies Chapter
Ancestor: James Garrison, NC — #721106
This "Nursery Rhymes" quilt was made in 1996 at Moss Point, MS by a Mrs. Wilkerson. The owner's mother-in-law bought it for the owner's daughter, Camille. The quilt theme is "Humpty Dumpty and Hey Diddle Diddle."

**Cowart, Kara Smith** (Craig A.)
Zachariah Davies Chapter
Ancestor: James Garrison, NC — #721106
This "Nursery Rhymes" quilt was made in 1996 at Moss Point, MS by Mrs. Wilkerson, who gave it to owner and husband for their baby.

**Cowart, Kara Smith** (Craig A.)
Zachariah Davies Chapter
Ancestor: James Garrison, NC — #721106
This quilt, called by the owner "Kara's Animal Quilt," was made in 1969 by the owner's grandmother, Rose Anne Sansoucie Smith (born 10/28/1916 at Klondike, MO, married Eldon John Smith, died 2/6/1999 at De Soto, Mo.) She made the quilt for the owner before she was born.

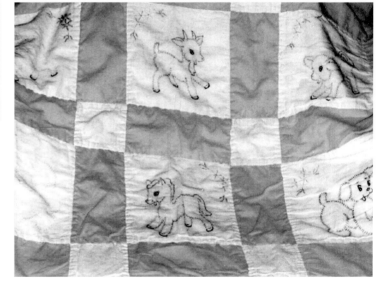

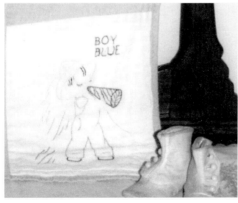

**Cowart, Kara Smith** (Craig A.)
Zachariah Davies Chapter
Ancestor: James Garrison, NC — #721106
This crib quilt, called "Kara's Doll Quilt," was made by the owner's grandmother in 1971 at De Soto, MO. The maker gave it to the owner.

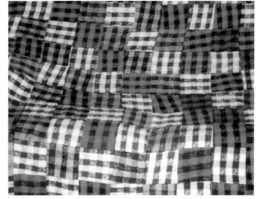

**Cowart, Kara Smith** (Craig A.)
Zachariah Davies Chapter
Ancestor: James Garrison, NC — #721106
This "Four Patch" quilt was made in 1991 at Moss Point, MS by Mrs. Wilkerson who gave the quilt to the owner.

**Cowart, Kara Smith** (Craig A.)
Zachariah Davies Chapter
Ancestor: James Garrison, NC — #721106
This "Four Patch" quilt was made in 1991 at Moss Point, MS by Mrs. Wilkerson as a gift for the owner and her husband.

**Cowart, Kara Smith** (Craig A.) Zachariah Davies Chapter Ancestor: James Garrison, NC — #721106 This "Nine Patch" quilt was made in 1970 at Rockford, IL by the owner's great great aunt, Edith Belle Dawdy Friend Roen, who gave the quilt to the owner".

**Cowart, Kara Smith** (Craig A.) Zachariah Davies Chapter Ancestor: James Garrison, NC — #721106 This "Nine Patch" quilt was made in 1971 at De Soto, MO by owner's grandmother, Rose Anne Sansoucie Smith. The owner received the quilt to the maker.

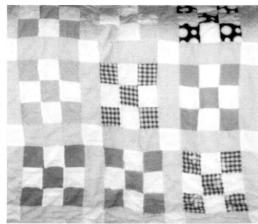

**Crabtree, Sue Merony** (Charles) Jane Knox Chapter Ancestor: Capt. Philip Delancy Maroney, MD — #737924 This "Dresden Plate" quilt was made in 1961 at Mt. Pleasant, TN by the owner's grandmother, Louisa Brymer Vernon (born 3/20/1888 at Maury Co., TN, married Ward Green Vernon, died 5/23/1973 at Maury Co., TN) Her grandmother gave the quilt to the owner.

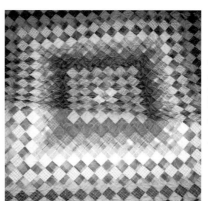

**Cranford, Alice Parrish** James Buckley Chapter Ancestor: Reuben Morgan, VA — #637183 This "Trip Around The World" quilt was made in 1960 at Chester County, TN by the owner.

**Cranford, Alice Parrish** James Buckley Chapter Ancestor: Reuben Morgan, VA — #637183 This "Iris" quilt was made circa 1970 at Chester County, TN by the owner.

**Cranford, Alice Parrish** James Buckley Chapter Ancestor: Reuben Morgan, VA — #637183 This "Improved Nine Patch" quilt was made in the 1960's at Chester County, TN by the owner.

**Cranford, Alice Parrish** James Buckley Chapter Ancestor: Reuben Morgan, VA — #637183 This "Log Cabin" quilt was made in 1960 at Chester County, TN by the owner. It is made of silk scraps.

**Cranford, Alice Parrish** James Buckley Chapter Ancestor: Reuben Morgan, VA — #637183 This "Spider Web" quilt was made in 1980 at Chester County, TN by the owner. The United Methodist Women helped the owner with the quilting.

**Craven-Smith, Sue Godshall** (John)
Andrew Bogle Chapter
Ancestor: Col. Jonathan Buck, MA —#773347
This coverlet was made in 1841 in Allentown, Pennsylvania by Benjamin Hausman. The owner's mother purchased it and gave it to her.

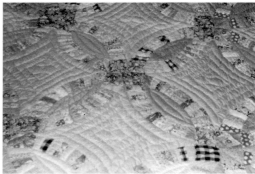

**Creasy, Helen Miller** (Lloyd)
Adam Dale Chapter
Ancestor: William Edmiston, VA — #567732
This "Double Wedding Ring" quilt was made in 1938 at Memphis, TN by the owner's husband's grandmother, Annie Jane Kennedy (born 1867 at Decatur Co., TN married William J. Kennedy, died 1963 at Memphis, TN). The quilt was a gift for the owner's husband from his grandmother.

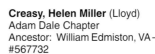

**Creasy, Helen Miller** (Lloyd)
Adam Dale Chapter
Ancestor: William Edmiston, VA — #567732
This "Bow Tie" quilt was made in the 1950's at Memphis, TN by the owner's mother, Kate Crenshaw Miller (born 10/9/1889, married John Bell Miller, died 5/5/1971 at Memphis, TN.) Kate gave the quilt to her daughter.

**Creasy, Helen Miller** (Lloyd)
Adam Dale Chapter
Ancestor: William Edmiston, VA — #567732
This "Double Wedding Ring" quilt was made in early the 1930's at Gibson County, TN by a Mrs. Taylor. The quilt was given to the owner's mother by her sister, Mary S. Crenshaw who gave the quilt to the owner.

**Creasy, Helen Miller** (Lloyd)
Adam Dale Chapter
Ancestor: William Edmiston, VA — #567732
This quilt is made of blue and red bandanas and is reversible. It was a gift from the maker to her husband.

**Creasy, Helen Miller** (Lloyd)
Adam Dale Chapter
Ancestor: William Edmiston, VA — #567732
This "Ocean Waves Variation" quilt was a wedding gift to the owner's mother, Kate Crenshaw Miller. The owner does not know who made the quilt or where it was made.

**Crosby, Juanita Irwin** (Samuel C.)
Clinch Bend Chapter
Ancestor: John "Raccon" Miller, NC — #769146
This "Lazy Daisy" quilt was made between 1930 and 35 at Clinton, TN, by the owner's mother, Sarah Elizabeth Heatherly Irwin (born 11/22/1893, at Campbell County, TN, married James Polk Irwin, died 11/9/1965 at Knoxville, TN.) The descent of the quilt is from maker to owner.

**Crosby, Juanita Irwin** (Samuel C.)
Clinch Bend Chapter
Ancestor: John "Raccon" Miller, NC — #769146
This "Churn Dash" quilt was made in 1985 at Andersonville, TN by a friend of the owner, Crea Elizabeth Longmire Lambdin (born 9/2/1913 at Andersonville, TN married James Lester Lambdin, died 3/11/1999 at Heiskell, TN).

**Crosby, Juanita Irwin** (Samuel C.)
Clinch Bend Chapter
Ancestor: John "Raccon" Miller, NC — #769146
This "Tea Leaf/Bay Leaf" quilt was made circa 1935 at Anderson Co., TN by the owner's mother, Elizabeth Heatherly Irwin.

**Culp, Martha Street**
(Delos P.)
John Sevier Chapter
Ancestor: John Miller, SC
— #488638
This original design "Rose Tree" quilt was made by the owner's friend, Ruth Tipton.. The owner bought the quilt when her friend's husband died.

**Culp, Martha Street**
(Delos P.)
John Sevier Chapter
Ancestor: John Miller, SC — #488638
This "Sunburst" quilt was made about 1860 in Upper East Tennessee. The owner bought the quilt at a sale.

**Culp, Martha Street**
(Delos P.)
John Sevier Chapter
Ancestor: John Miller, SC — #488638
This "Feathered Star" quilt was probably made circa 1860. It was purchased from a person who had quilts stored as "junk" in a smokehouse.

**Culp, Martha Street**
(Delos P.)
John Sevier Chapter
Ancestor: John Miller, SC — #488638
This "Southern Cross" quilt was made in 1975 by the owner (born 11/4/1915 at Gadsden, AL, married Delos P. Culp)

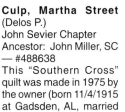

**Culp, Martha Street**
(Delos P.)
John Sevier Chapter
Ancestor: John Miller, SC — #488638
This coverlet was made circa 1848 in Pennsylvania and has the name "Susan Green Ewalt" and the date "1848" woven into the design.

**Culp, Martha Street**
(Delos P.)
John Sevier Chapter
Ancestor: John Miller, SC — #488638
This "Ocean Waves" quilt was made from 1992 to 1994 in Johnson City, TN by the owner. She made it in honor of her 60th wedding anniversary. The quilt has won two blue ribbons.

**Culp, Martha Street**
(Delos P.)
John Sevier Chapter
Ancestor: John Miller, SC — #488638
This "Feathered Star" quilt was made about 1985 at Unacoi, TN by a friend of the owner, Margaret Fletcher (born 1900, married Rev. Phillip Fletcher, died 1995). The owner bought the quilt at an auction or estate sale.

**Currin, Helen Merrell**
(Barron)
King's Mountain Messenger Chapter
Ancestor: William McLaurine, VA — #705254
This "Double Wedding Ring" quilt was made circa 1930 at Giles Co., TN by the owner's aunt, Dena Merrell (born 6/8/1906 at Giles Co., TN died 5/22/1985 at Giles Co., TN.) The quilt was given to the owner by her aunt.

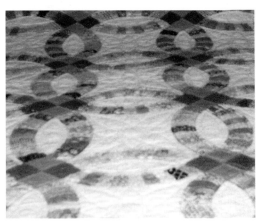

**Currin, Helen Merrell** (Barron)
King's Mountain Messenger Chapter
Ancestor: William McLaurine, VA — #705254
This "Log Cabin Light and Shade" quilt was made circa 1900 at Giles Co., TN by the owner's grandmother, Jeanette Harris Merrell (born 2/22/1870, married William P. Merrell, died 7/18/1935 at Giles Co., TN). It was given to the owner by her aunt, Dena Merrell.

**Currin, Helen Merrell**
(Barron)
King's Mountain Messenger Chapter
Ancestor: William McLaurine, VA — #705254
This "Barrister's Block" quilt was made in 1989 at Ardmore, TN by the owner. It has won prizes at different quilt shows and state fairs.

**Danford, Geraldine Smith**
Clinch Bend Chapter
Ancestor: Thomas Edwards, NC — #731907
This embroidery baby quilt was made in 1958 at Pleasant City, OH by the owner's mother-in-law, Agnes Danford (born 5/5/1902 at Pleasant City, OH, married Edgar Danford, died 8/1/1992 in the same town).

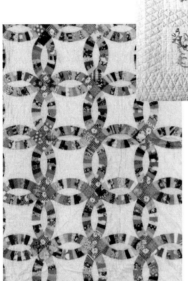

**d'Armand, Virginia "Penny" Carlisle**
Bonny Kate Chapter
Ancestor: Peter Keener, VA —#523959
This hand woven coverlet was made on a "weave-it" loom in the 1950's at Knoxville, TN by the owner (born 10/13/1934 at Knox County, TN).

**d'Armand, Virginia "Penny" Carlisle**
Bonny Kate Chapter
Ancestor: Peter Keener, VA —#523959
This "Double Wedding Ring" quilt was pieced 1920-1930 by the owner's paternal grandmother, Loudem Vasti McCalman d'Armand (born 10/26/1869 at Gaylesville, AL, married John Rosecrans DeArmond, died 5/13/1951 at Knoxville, TN). The maker made one for the owner and each of her siblings. This one was made for the owner's brother, Noel.

**Davidson, Carolyn Bigham** (Thomas A.)
Robert Lewis Chapter
Ancestor: Tyree Harris, Sr., NC —#749528
This "Slashed Diagonal" quilt was made in 1972 at Lewisburg, TN by the owner's mother, Katherine Malone Bigham (born 4/15/1914 at Giles County, TN, married David A. Bigham, Jr., died 9/8/1986). The owner inherited the quilt from her mother.

**Davidson, Carolyn Bigham** (Thomas A.)
Robert Lewis Chapter
Ancestor: Tyree Harris, Sr., NC —#749528
This "Crazy" quilt was made in 1970 at Lewisburg, TN by Katherine Malone Bigham.

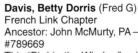

**Davidson, Carolyn Bigham** (Thomas A.)
Robert Lewis Chapter
Ancestor: Tyree Harris, Sr., NC —#749528
This "Lilly of the Valley" quilt was inherited from the owner's mother.

**Davidson, Carolyn Bigham** (Thomas A.)
Robert Lewis Chapter
Ancestor: Tyree Harris, Sr., NC —#749528
This "Grandmother's Flower Garden" quilt was made in 1980 at Lewisburg, TN by Katherine Malone Bigham, the owner's mother.

**Davis, Betty Dorris** (Fred G)
French Link Chapter
Ancestor: John McMurty, PA —#789669
This "Bird in the Window" quilt was made in the 1950's or 60's at Robertson County, TN by the owner's mother, Viola McMurtry Dorris (born 2/6/1893 at Sumner County, TN, married Albert Walter Dorris, died 6/11/1989 at Hendersonville, TN). "I rescued this quilt from my brother's 'store all' house a few years ago when I found it being used as an outside insulator around a box of his canned tomatoes — to keep them from freezing, no less! When I lectured him, he seemed truly amazed, then asked if I would like to have this quilt."

**Davis, Betty Dorris** (Fred G)
French Link Chapter
Ancestor: John McMurty, PA — #789669
This "Nine Patch" quilt was made in the 1950's at Robertson County, TN by the owner's mother, Viola McMurtry Dorris. This quilt was a gift to the owner when she married 3/19/1954.

**Davis, Betty Dorris** (Fred G)
French Link Chapter
Ancestor: John McMurty, PA — #789669
This "Boshie's Version of Dresden Plate" quilt was made in the 1960's at Robertson County, TN by the owner's mother, Viola McMurtry Dorris. The maker was not pleased with this quilt and when the owner was a little girl, she too thought it was "tacky." However, the owner now says, "Today, I consider it an honor to possess this quilt and to be able to see pieces of my mother's dresses, as well as some of my own."

**Davis, Betty Dorris** (Fred G)
French Link Chapter
Ancestor: John McMurty, PA — #789669
This "Yorktown" quilt was made between 1960 and 1982 at Madison and Davidson Counties in TN by the owner (born 9/2/1929). She received this Buscilla Quilt Kit No. 3286 from her husband as a Christmas gift in 1960. Due to caring for her very young sons, the owner stored the kit for three years. Once she began the quilt she "hauled it all over—camping, swimming, son's ball games," but mostly it was done when her younger son was having

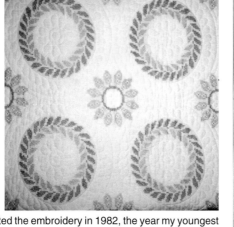

piano lessons. "I finally completed the embroidery in 1982, the year my youngest son graduated from college." The owner immediately engaged a master quilter to do the quilting.

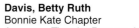

**Davis, Betty Ruth**
Bonnie Kate Chapter
Ancestor: Timothy Reagan, MD — #710915
This "Field of Pansies/Whole Cloth" quilt was made circa 1900-1920 by the owner's grandmother, Mary Theodocia Abbott Davis (born 10/20/1869 at Sevier County, TN, married George C. Davis, died 5/2/1938 at Knoxville, TN). This quilt was made to be used. Although it became very faded, the fabric was still good. The owner's mother, Ethel McDonald Davis, covered the quilt with pansy patterned fabric. Ethel was born 7/20/1903 at Knoxville, TN, married Robert Ernest Davis, and died 5/30/1984 in the same town.

**Davis, Betty Ruth**
Bonnie Kate Chapter
Ancestor: Timothy Reagan, MD —#710915
This "Pots of Flowers" quilt was made circa 1900-1920 at Knoxville, TN by the owner's grandmother, Mary Theodocia Abbott Davis. Over the years the owner's grandmother made many quilts for use in the home. Many wore out. The owner feels fortunate to have a few examples of the maker's handiwork remaining.

**Davis, Betty Ruth**
Bonnie Kate Chapter
Ancestor: Timothy Reagan, MD —#710915
This "Dutch Doll/Sunbonnet Sue" quilt was made circa 1930 at Knoxville, TN by the owner's mother, Ethel McDonald Davis and her grandmother, Mary Theodocia Abbott Davis. The owner's mother pieced two "Dutch Doll" quilts. This one, put together with blue, was for the owner. The other one was made for the owner's sister, Dorothy Kathryn Davis Muncy, and it is put together with pink.

**Davis, Betty Ruth**
Bonnie Kate Chapter
Ancestor: Timothy Reagan, MD —#710915
This embroidered cross stitch quilt was made 1970-75 in TN by the owner's mother, Ethel McDonald Davis. After her children were away in their own homes and her husband died, the maker wanted something to do. She made this quilt using a kit which came with printed pattern on the fabric and included the embroidery floss. She liked it because it came in strips and she could take it with her and work on it as she felt inclined. After she finished the top, the quilting group at the Fountain City United Methodist Church in Knoxville, TN quilted it.

**Davis, Louise**
Ancestor: George Hamilton —#756467
This "Buggy Rug" quilt was made as a wedding present for the owner's parents, Emmett and Nova Jenkins Hagar, who were married in November 1912. It was given to them by Emmett's sister, Myrtle Hagar Carter.

**Davis, Patricia Bullington** (Dorris)
Old Reynoldsburgh Chapter
Ancestor: Capt. Enoch Enoch, PA — #679317
This "Broken Star" quilt was made in 1960 at McEwen, TN by the owner's grandmother, Mattie Zeal Choate Bullington (born 12/6/1900 at McEwen, TN, married William Willis Bullington, died 10/23/1987 at McEwen). When the owner was ten years old in 1965, she attended the Bullington Family Reunion. "Grandma Mattie had put seven quilts in brown grocery bags. At that time there was only seven grandchildren. She called us together and told us to pick a bag. The tops were covered with another grocery bag so that we could not see what was inside. The sack I chose was this "Broken Star" quilt. It is just as lovely today as it was when I opened the bag." This quilt won first prize at the Humphreys County, TN Fair.

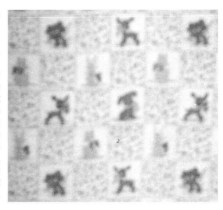

**Davis, Patricia Bullington**
(Dorris)
Old Reynoldsburgh Chapter
Ancestor: Capt. Enoch Enoch, PA — #679317
This baby quilt was made in 1986 at McEwen, TN by the owner (born 10/21/1955 at Waverly, TN). This quilt is made from one feed sack found among the owner's grandma, Anne Enoch's, sewing things. The material dates back to 1928, during the great depression years. The owner made this quilt in 1986 for her first son, Nathan.

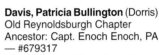

**Davis, Patricia Bullington** (Dorris)
Old Reynoldsburgh Chapter
Ancestor: Capt. Enoch Enoch, PA — #679317
This "Double Wedding Ring" quilt was pieced in 1984 at Dickson, TN by the owner's great aunt, Neugie Davis Shawl (born 11/28/1916 at Garrett Hollow, TN, married J. W. Shawl). The top was given to the owner as a Christmas gift. She later quilted the quilt.

**Davis, Patricia Bullington**
(Dorris)
Old Reynoldsburgh Chapter
Ancestor: Capt. Enoch Enoch, PA — #679317
This "Indian Double Wedding Ring" quilt was made in 1989 at McEwen, TN by the owner's second cousin, Maybel Matlock Holland (born 10/27/1910 at McEwen, married Manuel Holland). The owner paid the maker to piece and quilt the quilt. Maybel was in her 80's when she made the quilt.

**Davis, Patricia Bullington** (Dorris)
Old Reynoldsburgh Chapter
Ancestor: Capt. Enoch Enoch, PA — #679317
This "Bronze Photo" quilt was made in 1987 at McEwen, TN by the owner's second cousin, Maybel Matlock Holland. The quilt is made of family pictures that have been put on cotton.

**De Courley, Flora Tidwell**
(James Claude)
Chickasaw Bluff Chapter
Ancestor: Francis Cypert, Jr., NC—#706157
This "Pinwheel 50th Anniversary" quilt was made in 1991 in Missouri as a gift to the owner from her family. It was presented to her at the DeCourley Reunion.

**De Courley, Flora Tidwell** (James Claude)
Chickasaw Bluff Chapter
Ancestor: Francis Cypert, Jr., NC—#706157
This "Double Wedding Ring" quilt was made in the 1960's at Hardin County, TN by the owner's mother, Lillie Abell Tidwell (born 6/30/1895 at Hardin County, married Joe A. Tidwell, died 7/1/1975 in the same county). Lillie made the quilt for her daughter, the current owner.

**De Courley, Flora Tidwell** (James Claude)
Chickasaw Bluff Chapter
Ancestor: Francis Cypert, Jr., NC—#706157
This candlewick quilt was made in 1983 at Memphis, TN by the owner (born 7/21/1921 at Hardin County, TN). This was her first project when she retired from Sears Roebuck and Co. in 1983. Candlwick was the popular needlework of the time.

**De Courley, Flora Tidwell**
(James Claude)
Chickasaw Bluff Chapter
Ancestor: Francis Cypert, Jr.,
NC—#706157
This "Fan" quilt was made at
Hardin County by the owner's
mother, Lillie Abell Tidwell.
This quilt was on the bed of
the owner's father when he
died in 1983.

**De Courley, Flora Tidwell**
(James Claude)
Chickasaw Bluff Chapter
Ancestor: Francis Cypert, Jr.,
NC—#706157
This "Rolling Star" quilt was
made in the 1930's at Hardin
County, TN by the owner's
mother, Lillie Abell Tidwell.

**De Courley, Flora Tidwell**
(James Claude)
Chickasaw Bluff Chapter
Ancestor: Francis Cypert,
Jr., NC—#706157
This "Fan" quilt was made
in the 1940's at Hardin
County, TN by the owner's
mother, Lillie Abell Tidwell.

**De Courley, Flora Tidwell**
(James Claude)
Chickasaw Bluff Chapter
Ancestor: Francis Cypert,
Jr., NC—#706157
This "Log Cabin" quilt was
made before 1916 at
Calhoun County, MS by the
owner's mother-in-law,
Catherine Smith De Courley
(born 3/6/1876 in TN, mar-
ried James Claude De
Courley, Sr., died 2/1920 at
Pochahontas, AR). The quilt
is backed with flour sacks
with a company name
printed on them.

**De Courley, Flora Tidwell** (James
Claude)
Chickasaw Bluff Chapter
Ancestor: Francis Cypert, Jr., NC—
#706157
This coverlet was made in Hardin
County, TN by the owner's great great
grandmother, Catherine Polk Tidwell
(born 12/7/1836 in South Carolina,
married Thomas Tidwell, died 3/19/
1926 at Hardin County, TN). The coverlet is made from wool. The family
raised the sheep and sheared and
spun the wool. It was hand loomed
in two panels and then sewn together.
The owner inherited the coverlet from
her father.

**De Friese, Ruth Liggett** (Frank)
Lydia Russell Bean Chapter
Ancestor: George Ewing, Sr., VA
—#556712
This "Prairie Star and Tea Leaf"
quilt was made in the early 1820's
at Bedford County, TN by the
owner's great grandmother,
Teressa Fenville Ewing (born 3/
16/1817 at Bedford County, married Samuel Ewing, died 8/28/
1894 in the same county). This
quilt was featured in Quilt With the
Best, published by Oxmoor House
and it also appeared in Southern
Living.

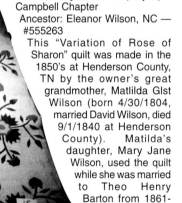

**Dennis, Mary T. Burton** (Roy J.)
Campbell Chapter
Ancestor: Eleanor Wilson, NC —
#555263
This "Variation of Rose of
Sharon" quilt was made in the
1850's at Henderson County,
TN by the owner's great
grandmother, Matlilda Glst
Wilson (born 4/30/1804,
married David Wilson, died
9/1/1840 at Henderson
County). Matilda's
daughter, Mary Jane
Wilson, used the quilt
while she was married
to Theo Henry
Barton from 1861-
1865. Mary Jane
was the mother of
the owner's father, J.W. Barton. Henry Barton married Virginia Douglass. Following her death in 1931, the quilt was sent to the owner's father.

**Dennis, Mary T. Burton** (Roy J.)
Campbell Chapter
Ancestor: Eleanor Wilson, NC —
#555263
This "Double Irish Chain" quilt was
made in the 1940's at Sharon, TN by
the owner's mother, Fannie
Bondurant Burton (born 7/22/1874 at
Sharon, TN, married James William
Burton, died 10/3/1973 at Nashville,
TN). The owner's mother made
"fancy" quilts and "service" quilts. She
and her sisters, Mary and Eddie
Bondurant, were considered the best
quilters in the area. They combed the
cotton to make the batts, so the quilt
would be soft and fluffy making it
easier to take ten stitches to the inch.
Fannie gave the quilt to her granddaughter, Elizabeth Waggoner, and
then she gave it to her daughter,
Martha.

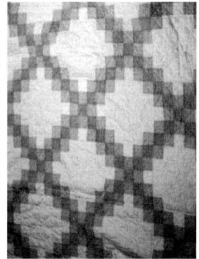

**Dennis, Mary T. Burton** (Roy J.)
Campbell Chapter
Ancestor: Eleanor Wilson, NC — #555263
This "Brown Goose" quilt was made circa 1875 at Weakley County, TN by the owner's
great great aunt, Patience Tansil Rogers (born 2/20/1802 at NC, married John Wesley
Rogers, died 6/3/1881 in Longview, TX). The quiltmaker was the oldest of nine children
of Edward Albert and Piety Thomas Tansil. At age 20, she went as a new bride to
Weakley County, TN. One son was born in route and ten others by 1842. She later
moved with her husband and children to East Texas. Her husband died in 1852. During
her widowhood, she returned every five years to Weakley County to spend several
months with her Tansil "kin." She insisted on making each child, born between visits, a
quilt and getting it quilted for the girls to have in their hope chests. She made her last
visit in 1880. The owner now has the quilt made for her aunt, Eddie Bondurant.

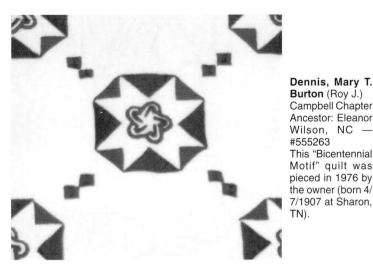

**Dennis, Mary T. Burton** (Roy J.)
Campbell Chapter
Ancestor: Eleanor Wilson, NC — #555263
This "Bicentennial Motif" quilt was pieced in 1976 by the owner (born 4/7/1907 at Sharon, TN).

**Dennis, Mary T. Burton** (Roy J.)
Campbell Chapter
Ancestor: Eleanor Wilson, NC — #555263
This "Strip" quilt was made in 1983 in TN by Mrs. Lee Danner. She used the owner's husband's ties to piece the quilt. It was quilted by the owner.

**Dennis, Mary T. Burton** (Roy J.)
Campbell Chapter
Ancestor: Eleanor Wilson, NC — #555263
This patchwork velvet quilt was made in the 1960's at Sharon, TN by the owner. This quilt is made from a dress and matching coat.

**Dennis, Mary T. Burton** (Roy J.)
Campbell Chapter
Ancestor: Eleanor Wilson, NC — #555263
This "Flower Basket" quilt was made in the 1850's at Henderson County, TN by the owner's paternal great grandmother, Matlilda Wilson.

**Dennis, Mary T. Burton** (Roy J.)
Campbell Chapter
Ancestor: Eleanor Wilson, NC — #555263
This "Dresden Plate" quilt was pieced in the 1930's at Senath, MO by the owner's friend, Mrs. Will Lanier (born at Obion County, TN, died in Senath, MO). The maker gave it to the owner as appreciation for a favor she had done for her. The owner's mother, Fannie Britmton, quilted it.

**Dennis, Mary T. Burton** (Roy J.)
Campbell Chapter
Ancestor: Eleanor Wilson, NC — #555263
This "Wreath of Roses" quilt was made in the 1930's at Sharon, TN by the owner's mother, Fannie Bondurant Burton.

**Dickenson, Anna Kathryn Tipton** (James E.)
Hermitage Chapter
Ancestor: Maj. George Waller, VA —#758509
This "Weather Vane" quilt was made in Castlewood, VA by the owner's husband's grandmother, Eliza Mason Dickinson (married Charles Sulins Dickenson, died at Abington, VA). The maker gave the quilt to the owner as a wedding present. She said she "put lots of red in it for happiness."

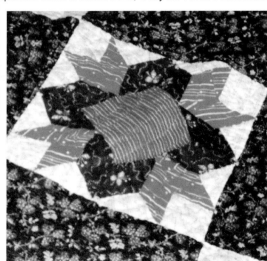

**Dickenson, Anna Kathryn Tipton** (James E.)
Hermitage Chapter
Ancestor: Maj. George Waller, VA —#758509
This "Fan" quilt was made circa 1915 by the owner's grandmother, Maude Beatrice Alford Johnson (born 4/8/1886, married Edward M. Johnson) and great grandmother, Margaret Melinda Craig Alford (born 6/17/1859, married Noah Jesse Thomas Alford). Ernestine (the owner's mother) remembers her mother and grandmother with several ladies quilting. Ernestine thought that since everyone was busy, she could go next door to "grandmom's" house and get some cookies. She got a chair, climbed up to the pie safe and "oops," she accidentally pulled it over. "Grandpa was big and fat and could hardly walk. He called, 'Ernestine is that you?' As he came through the door to see what was the matter, he fell!" All Ernestine could think of was, "if he gets up, I'm in trouble!" She grabbed the chair and put it on top of him, then ran home and crawled up under the quilt. She was so quiet that "grandmom" decided to go home and check things. The next thing she knew, "Here came grandma, stripping the leaves off a switch, her skirt tails just a flapping."

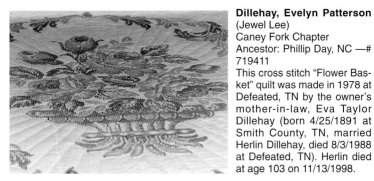

**Dillehay, Evelyn Patterson** (Jewel Lee)
Caney Fork Chapter
Ancestor: Phillip Day, NC —# 719411
This cross stitch "Flower Basket" quilt was made in 1978 at Defeated, TN by the owner's mother-in-law, Eva Taylor Dillehay (born 4/25/1891 at Smith County, TN, married Herlin Dillehay, died 8/3/1988 at Defeated, TN). Herlin died at age 103 on 11/13/1998.

**Dillehay, Evelyn Patterson** (Jewel Lee)
Caney Fork Chapter
Ancestor: Phillip Day, NC —# 719411
This "Grandmother's Flower Garden" quilt was pieced in 1989 at Carthage, TN by the owner (born 1/8/1929). At age 76, Hattie Kittrell quilted the quilt for the owner. The maker pieced four "Grandmother's Flower Garden" quilts for her grandchildren before deciding to make one for herself. She was unable to quilt them herself due to "arthritic hands."

**Dixon, Addie Canupp** (Walter)
Spencer Clack Chapter
Ancestor: Johann Martin Shultz, NC —#770210
This "Mariners Compass" quilt was made in 1996 at Sevier County, TN by the owner (born 12/15/1908 at Sevier County). The owner says about herself, "This 90 year old lady is still piecing and quilting to this day."

**Dooney, Bertha Carpenter** (Robert L.)
Adam Dale Chapter
Ancestor: Charles Cogbill, VA — #729908
This "Scrap" quilt was made in 1943-44 at Moscow, TN by the descendant of a slave in the owner's family's past, "Aunt Cint" Heaslett. The maker was not sure of her age but she was born in Fayette County, TN and died in the 1950's at Moscow, TN. The owner and her husband were married on 5/6/1944 and the quilt top was made as a wedding present. This was during WWII, and material was hard to get. Bundles of scraps were sold, but they were not made up of the most desirable fabrics or colors. Money was also scarce, but the maker somehow managed to buy enough to make this quilt top. "Aunt Cint" could neither read nor write, but she could quote many of the Bible's verses.

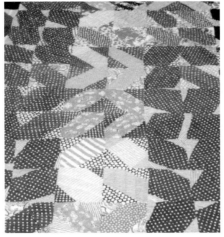

**Donnelly, Polly Watkins** (Russell A.)
Ocoee Chapter
Ancestor: John Anderson, VA —#605958
This "Crazy" quilt was made circa 1880 at Birchwood, TN by the owner's paternal great grandmother, Martha Jane Grigsby DeFriese (born 1/21/1837 at Bradley County, TN, married Dr. Thomas J. DeFriese, died 8/19/1919 at Hamilton County, TN). The maker gave the quilt to the owner's father who willed it to her in 1969. The quiltmaker was one of the first babies born in Bradley County, TN. Her father, James Grigsby, Jr. was among the first settlers and taxpayers in the county which was organized in 1836. Martha married (circa 1854) Dr. Thomas J. DeFriese, one of the earliest doctors in the county. They later moved to northern Hamilton County where he was a surgeon for the Confederacy.

**Dorman, Virginia Thomas** (Frank)
Volunteer Chapter
Ancestor: Jacob Thomas, PA — #671461
This "Fan" quilt was pieced by the owner's mother, Lola Pyle Thomas (born 9/24/1885 at Sullivan County, TN, married Joseph Kellor Thomas, Sr., died 5/1978 at Warren County, TN). It was quilted by the maker's friends at "quiltings" where women would gather and sew all day for fellowship. The quilt was "set up" on a stretcher frame in the "spare" room during the quilting process.

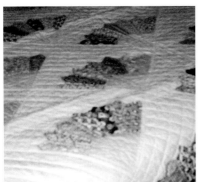

**Dorris, Dorothy Kelso** (C. Glen)
Colonel Jethro Sumner Chapter
Ancestor: Hugh Kelso, NC — #774876
This "Double Irish Chain" quilt was made in Bynum, TX by the owner's grandmother, Emma Barbara Himmel Johnson (born 2/10/1865 at Mason County, IL, married Daniiel R. Johnson, died 2/6/1932 at Brandon, TX). This quilt was the last one the maker pieced and quilted before she died. It was given to the owner's mother, who passed it on to her.

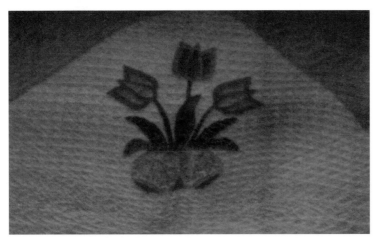

**Dorset, "Dee" Ingram** (Earle)
Ancestor: John Kennedy, Sr., VA — #657387
This "Tulip Vases" quilt was pieced in Brunswick, GA by the owner's friend, Willadean Colson Frost (born in Brunswick, GA, married Edwin Frost, died in Nashville, TN). It was quilted by a woman at the McKendree Methodist Church.

**Dotson, Glenda, L.** (Joe)
Coytee Chapter
Ancestor: Leroy Taylor, NC — #703538
This "Cathedral Window" quilt was made circa the 1960's by the owner's mother-in-law, Ivalee King Dotson (born 6/28/1909 at Sevier County, TN, married Luke Dotson, died 8/21/1993 at Blount County, TN).

**Dotson, Glenda L.** (Joe)
Coytee Chapter
Ancestor: Leroy Taylor, NC — #703538
This "Fan" quilt was made circa 1940's at Lenoir City, TN by the owner's aunt, Mary Long (born 8/11/1903 at Greenback, TN, died 5/9/1982 at Greenback). The quilt was given to the owner at the death of the maker.

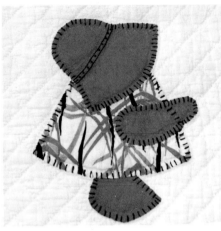

**Dotson, Glenda, L.** (Joe)
Coytee Chapter
Ancestor: Leroy Taylor, NC — #703538
This "Dutch Girl/Sunbonnet Sue" quilt was made circa 1930's by the owner's grandmother, Dora Poole Thompson (born 8/26/1875 at Jasper, AL, married Robert L. Thompson, died 1956 at Greenback, TN). The quilt was passed from maker, to the owner's mother, to the owner.

**Douglas, Inez Ingram** (Milton Larry)
Fort Prudhomme Chapter
Ancestor: William Ingram, VA —#638735
This "Sunbonnet Sue" quilt was made circa 1927 at Whiteville, TN by the owner's mother, Inez (Girlie) Ingram (born 10/14/1905 at Whiteville, married Lloyd Hicks Ingram, died 10/21/1998 at Ripley, TN). Inez made this quilt for her daughter's baby bed and she has had it ever since.

**Douglas, Inez Ingram** (Milton Larry)
Fort Prudhomme Chapter
Ancestor: William Ingram, VA — #638735
This cross stitched quilt was made in the 1970's by members of the owner's Home Demonstration Club. Each one made a block for the owner and then she put the blocks together. Joella Boyd of Stanton, TN quilted the quilt.

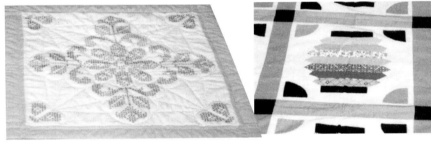

**Douglas, Inez Ingram** (Milton Larry)
Fort Prudhomme Chapter
Ancestor: William Ingram, VA —#638735
This "Japanese Lantern" quilt was made circa 1930 at Whiteville, TN by the owner's mother, Inez (Girlie) Hizer Ingram.

**Douglas, Inez Ingram** (Milton Larry)
Fort Prudhomme Chapter
Ancestor: William Ingram, VA — #638735
This "Double Wedding Ring" quilt was pieced before 1933 at Trenton, TN by the owner's grandmother, Nancy (Nannie) Lawrence Ingram (born 9/16/1864 at Gibson County, TN, married Charles Cephas Ingram, died 7/22/1933 at Trenton, TN). The maker made the top for the owner and in the late 1970's, she had it quilted by Joella Boyd of Stanton, TN.

**Douglas, Inez Ingram** (Milton Larry)
Fort Prudhomme Chapter
Ancestor: William Ingram, VA — #638735
This "Diamond Field" quilt was pieced in the 1940's at Ripley, TN by the owner's mother, Inez (Girlie) Ingram, and her grandmother, Lillie Jacobs Hizer (born in Hardeman County, TN, married William H. Hizer, died 3/14/1960 at Memphis, TN). It was quilted in the late 1970's by Joella Boyd of Stanton, TN.

**Douglas, Inez Ingram** (Milton Larry)
Fort Prudhomme Chapter
Ancestor: William Ingram, VA —#638735
This "Robbing Peter To Pay Paul" quilt was acquired by the owner's grandmother in 1909. She said it was very old then and had been in the family. She was told that the quilt was 100 years old and that the beige and tan pieces were dyed with bark. The owner has had the quilt since 3/14/1960, the date of her grandmother's death. Her name was Lillie Jacobs Hizer.

**Douglass, Shirley McGee** (John)
Lt. James Sheppard Chapter
Ancestor: John McGee — #703838
This "Star" quilt was made by an unknown middle TN quilter and acquired by the owner in the summer of 1998.

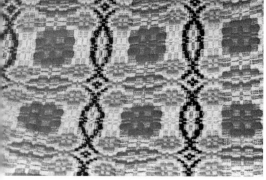

**Dowell, Cindy Rose** (Steve)
Caney Fork Chapter
Ancestor: William New, NC—
#777875
This coverlet was made circa 1895 at Smith County, TN by the owner's great great grandmother, Minerva J. Lamberson (born 10/20/1842 at Smith County, married John Gideon Reynolds, died 7/14/1929 at DeKalb County, TN). Electa Reynolds and Ira Bolivar Rose married on 1/3/1895. They received this coverlet as a wedding gift from Electa Reynold's mother, Minerva J. Lamberson. The family raised the sheep, and carded their own wool at that time. Walnut stain was used to get the brown color. Various other berries were used to dye the yarn red and aqua. The coverlet was woven on a loom. Today the coverlet is displayed in the home of Mr. and Mrs. Jerry Rose in Cookeville, TN.

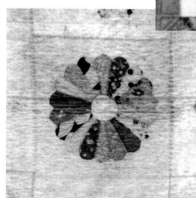

**Draper, Helen Maxwell** (Ward)
Fort Blount Chapter
Ancestor: Corporal Joseph Morgan — #679988
This "Dutch Mill" quilt was made in 1994 by the Silver Threads Quilt Guild at Gainesboro, TN. This guild was organized in 1986 with nine charter members becoming the 14th guild of the Tennessee Valley Quilters Association. This quilt was awarded a blue ribbon in 1995 at the quilt show associated with the "Poke Sallet Festival" at Gainesboro, TN.

**Dugger, Jane Granstaff** (Keith A.)
French Lick Chapter
Ancestor: Capt. David Phillips, PA —#720496
This "Variation of a Simplicity Pattern" quilt was made in TN before 1950. In the 1970's, it was a gift to the owner from her mother-in-law, Kathleen Johnson Dugger.

**Dugger, Jane Granstaff** (Keith A.)
French Lick Chapter
Ancestor: Capt. David Phillips, PA—#720496
This "Dresden Plate/Friendship Ring" quilt was probably made in TN, and to the owner, it seems very old. It was possibly made by the owner's husband's great grandmother, Sarah Elizabeth Oakley Grissom (born 9/15/1860 at Wilson County, TN, married James Grissom, died 10/17/1951 probably at Wilson County). James Grissom was born 11/30/1854 and died 8/16/1926. The quilt was passed from maker to Ruby Mae Grissom Johnson to Kathleen Johnson Dugger to current owner.

**Dugger, Jane Granstaff** (Keith A.)
French Lick Chapter
Ancestor: Capt. David Phillips, PA —#720496
This "Log Cabin" quilt was purchased in the 1970's by the owner.

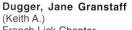

**Dugger, Jane Granstaff** (Keith A.)
French Lick Chapter
Ancestor: Capt. David Phillips, PA —#720496
This "Broken Star/Star with Diamonds/Carpenter's Wheel" quilt was purchased in the 1970's at a Nashville flea market. This quilt hangs in the foyer of the owner's home.

**Dugger, Jane Granstaff** (Keith A.)
French Lick Chapter
Ancestor: Capt. David Phillips, PA —#720496
This "Four Patch" quilt was made in the early 1980's at Maysville, NC by the owner's husband's grandmother, Ruby Mae Grissom Johnson (born 4/24/1902 at Wilson County, TN, married Grady George Johnson, died 6/2/1992 at Maysville, NC). The quilt was a gift from the owner's husband's aunt after the death of his grandmother with the request that the owner pass it on to her daughter, Laura Jane Dugger.

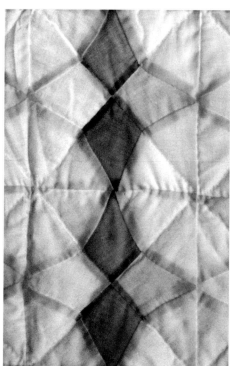

**Dugger, Jane Granstaff** (Keith A.)
French Lick Chapter
Ancestor: Capt. David Phillips, PA —#720496
This "Arkansas Snowflake" quilt was made 1979-80 at Maysville, NC by the owner's husband's grandmother, Ruby Mae Grissom Johnson. The maker made this quilt to celebrate the birth of her great grandson, Christopher John Dugger, born 6/7/1979. The owner plans to give the quilt to him when he has his own home.

**Dugger, Jane Granstaff** (Keith A.)
French Lick Chapter
Ancestor: Capt. David Phillips, PA —#720496
This "Sunbonnet Babies" quilt was purchased at a Nashville flea market in the 1970's by the owner.

**Durisch, Joanne Ferrell** (Lawrence)
King's Mountain Messenger Chapter
Ancestor: Hanchrist Carlock, VA — #547087
This "Grandmother's Flower Garden" quilt was made in 1930 at Chattanooga, TN by the owner's mother, Blanche Brown Bailey Ferrell (born 6/29/1909 at Mulberry, TN, married Floysce Joe Ferrell). The owner intends to copy a sample of the maker's signature and embroider it on the quilt. When Blanche made the quilt she was a young bride. She and her friend, Nancy Sue Alexander, bought quilt fabric together. They shared the fabric, so there is a quilt with similar fabric made by Nancy. Blanche gave this quilt to her grand daughter, Anne Bailey Durisch, when she was in high school. Anne Bailey is now a young bride, married June 20, 1998.

**Dyor, Mary Martha Hemby** (Neil A.)
Key Corner Chapter
Ancestor: Thomas Hamilton, NC — # 523963
This coverlet was made by the owner's great great grandmother, Mary Margaret Carothers Jordan (born 5/4/1828 at Williamson County, TN, married Stephen A. Jordan, died 3/29/1901 at Halls). This quilt was passed from great grandmother, to grandfather, to current owner.

**Dyor, Mary Martha Hemby** (Neil A.)
Key Corner Chapter
Ancestor: Thomas Hamilton, NC — # 523963
This "Crazy" quilt was made in 1875 at Lauderdale County, TN by the owner's great grandmother, Martha Jordan Mitchell (born 8/1/1847 at Williamson County, TN, married DeWitt C. Mitchell, died 4/28/1934 at Halls, TN).

**Dyor, Mary Martha Hemby** (Neil A.)
Key Corner Chapter
Ancestor: Thomas Hamilton, NC — 523963
This "Yo Yo" quilt was made in 1934-35 at Halls, TN by the owner's mother, Detra Hart Mitchell (born 8/1/1897 at Dyer County, TN, married James Archie Mitchell, died 12/22/1964 at Memphis, TN). The quilt was passed from the maker, to the owner.

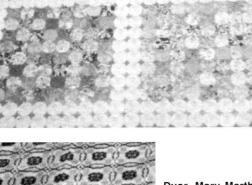

**Dyor, Mary Martha Hemby** (Neil A.)
Key Corner Chapter
Ancestor: Thomas Hamilton, NC — # 523963
This "Heart" quilt was made in the early 1800's at Williamson County, TN by the owner's great great great grandmother, Elsye Blair Corothers (born 4/19/1798 at Williamson County, TN, married Robert Corothers, died 9/11/1837 in the same county). The quilt was brought from Williamson County to Lauderdale County by the owner's great great grandmother. The quilt was passed from maker, to owner's great–great–grandmother, to her great–grandmother, to her grandfather, to her mother, and finally to the current owner.

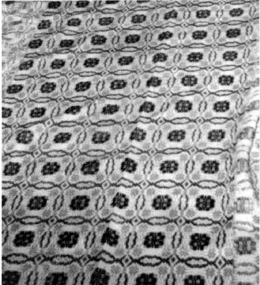

**Dyor, Mary Martha Hemby** (Neil A.)
Key Corner Chapter
Ancestor: Thomas Hamilton, NC — # 523963
This coverlet was made before 1850 at Williamson County, TN and passed from the owner's great great grandmother, to her great grandmother, to her grandfather, to her mother, and finally to the current owner.

**Dyor, Mary Martha Hemby** (Neil A.)
Key Corner Chapter
Ancestor: Thomas Hamilton, NC — # 523963
This coverlet was made before 1850 at Williamson County, TN and passed from the owner's great great grandmother, to her great grandmother, to her grandfather, to her mother, and finally to the current owner.

**Ead, Darlene Phillips** (Arthur)
Kings Mountain Messenger Chapter
Ancestor: Joseph Jewett, CT — #774632
This "Pinwheel" quilt was made by the owner and others from 1939-1976 in Ohio and New Hampshire. The pieces of the quilt were cut out by the owner's maternal grandmother, Dottie Dell Parrish Lauderbaugh, in 1939. The owner's mother, Vinnie Vyrtle Lauderbaugh pieced together the quilt while waiting for the owner to be born. The quilt top was put away for safe keeping not to be seen again until 1975 when it was given to the owner. While living in Lyndeborough, NH, the owner, her husband, and their children quilted what had come to be known as "The Quilt." The owner's aunt, Laura May Lauderbaugh Criss, bound the quilt. It is now displayed in the home of the owner in Taft, TN.

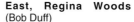

**East, Regina Woods** (Bob Duff)
Henderson Station Chapter
Ancestor: Edward Trice, NC #617126
This "Bicentennial Eight Pointed Star" quilt was pieced in 1976 at Henderson, TN by the owner's grandmother, Mary Williams Christopher and her mother, Rebecca C. Woods. Mary was born 5/29/1892 at Chester, TN, married Hal Carroll Christopher, died 1/13/1981 at Henderson, TN. The quilt was quilted by a professional quilter and then given to the owner by her mother.

**Edgman, Regina Jean Buck** (Victor W.)
Andrew Bogle Chapter
Ancestor: Sgt. William Buck, MA — #485150
This "Pink Dogwood" quilt was made in the 1970's/1995 at Chattanooga and Knoxville, TN by the owner's mother-in-law, Beulah Edgman Blevins (born 5/31/1903 at Chickamauga, GA, married George Blevins, died 5/5/1984 at Chattanooga, TN) and the owner. The quilt was started by Beulah in the 1970's. When she died, the quilt was passed to the owner. In 1993, the owner finished the appliqué and begin quilting it. The quilt was finished in 1995.

**Edgman, Regina Jean Buck** (Victor W.)
Andrew Bogle Chapter
Ancestor: Sgt. William Buck, MA — #485150
This "Basket" quilt was made in the 1930's at Rossville, GA by the owner's grandmother, Mary Slater Williams (born 5/7/1874 at Chattanooga, TN, married Clarence Williams, died 9/15/1969 at Knoxville, TN). Mary lived across the street from the owner when she was growing up. Mary made many quilts and Jean enjoyed watching her especially when she was using scraps from her dresses to piece the quilts. This "Basket" quilt was one of Jean's favorites. It was owned by her mother until her death. It was one of several quilts left to the owner by her mother.

**Edmands, Isabel Robinson** (Donald)
Campbell Chapter
Ancestor: Andrew Kennedy, NC — #352063
This "Crazy" quilt was made circa 1956 in NC by the owner's great grandmother, Lavinia Arsilla Hill (born 7/27/1838 at Horse Cove, NC, married Barak Pickeral Norton, died 4/20/1858 at Whitesides Cove, NC). Two round pieces, one blue and one red, were from the maker's husband's and father's hats worn on her wedding day, 12/15/1855.

**Edmands, Isabel Robinson** (Donald)
Campbell Chapter
Ancestor: Andrew Kennedy, NC — #352063
This "Bow Tie" quilt was made circa 1937 at Knox County, TN by the owner (born 7/26/1921 at Knox County).

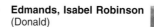

**Edmands, Isabel Robinson** (Donald)
Campbell Chapter
Ancestor: Andrew Kennedy, NC — #352063
This "Cathedral Window" quilt was made circa 1950 at Knox County, TN by the owner's mother, Edith Kennedy Robinson (born 11/19/1896 at Monroe County, married John Siler Robinson, died 11/7/1996 at Blount County, TN).

**Edmands, Isabel Robinson** (Donald)
Campbell Chapter
Ancestor: Andrew Kennedy, NC — #352063
This "Grandmother's Flower Garden" quilt was made in 1900 at Macon County, NC by the owner's grandmother, Ittie Norton Robinson (born 10/29/1857 at Horsecove, NC, married Jesse Robinson, died 3/27/1927 at Osyka, MS).

**Edmands, Isabel Robinson** (Donald)
Campbell Chapter
Ancestor: Andrew Kennedy, NC — #352063
This "Irish Chain" quilt was made in 1895 at Monroe County, TN by the owner's grandmother, Annie Ruth Hall Kennedy (born 6/12/1874 at Monroe County, married Dr. Walter B. Kennedy, died 3/8/1958 in the same county).

**Edwards, Sue Hairston** (Jimmy D.)
Traveller's Rest Chapter
Ancestor: George Hairston, VA — #682771
This "Dutch Girl" quilt was pieced in the 1970's at Salem, VA by the owner's husband's grandmother, Ethel May Counts Farris (born 9/10/1895 at Abingdon, VA, married Robert Anderson Farris, died 10/16/1989 at Salem, VA). The quilt was quilted by Mrs. Rose Beckett, a German Baptist lady who lived with Ethel Harris after her husband died.

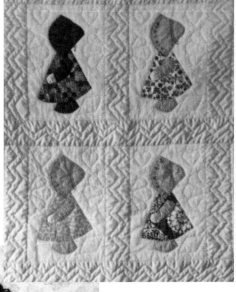

**Elder, Pattie-Anne Harris** (William)
River City Chapter
Ancestor: Capt. Robert Harris, VA —#743577
This "Sunbonnet Sue" quilt was made circa 1931 at Fresno, CA by the owner's aunt, Martha King Harris Hays (born 9/12/1869 at Gallatin, TN, married Amazon Scholl Hays, died 3/1948 at Fresno).

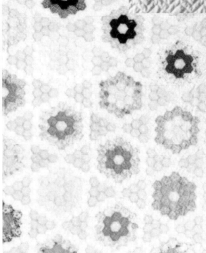

**Elder, Pattie-Anne Harris** (William)
River City Chapter
Ancestor: Capt. Robert Harris, VA —#743577
This "Grandmother's Flower Garden" quilt was made in the 1920's at Toledo, IL by the owner's husband's paternal grandmother, Dora Belle Ferris Elder (born 10/25/1874 at Toledo, married James William Elder, died 5/25/1945 at Toledo).

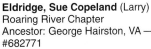

**Elder, Pattie-Anne Harris** (William)
River City Chapter
Ancestor: Capt. Robert Harris, VA —#743577
This "Pineapple" quilt was made in the 1920's at Toledo, IL by the owner's husband's maternal grandmother, Mary Elizabeth Seely Huffman (born 10/22/1860 at Toledo, IL, married William Asbury Huffman, died 12/22/1949 at Toledo).

**Eldridge, Sue Copeland** (Larry)
Roaring River Chapter
Ancestor: George Hairston, VA — #682771
This "Christmas Tree" quilt was pieced in the 1970's at Livingston, TN by the owner's husband's grandmother, Florence "Granny" Langford (born 10/24/1896 at Overton County, TN, married Andy Paul Langford, died 7/4/1985 at Livingston, TN). Florence's sister, Sallie Mae Pigg Thrasher quilted the quilt.

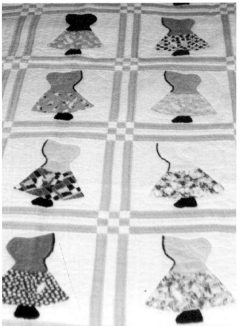

**Eldridge, Sue Copeland** (Larry)
Roaring River Chapter
Ancestor: George Hairston, VA — #682771
This "Dutch Doll" quilt was made in Overton County, TN by owner's husband's grandmother, Florence "Granny" Langford.

**Eldridge, Sue Copeland** (Larry)
Roaring River Chapter
Ancestor: George Hairston, VA — #682771
This "Lone Star" quilt was made in Overton County, TN by owner's husband's grandmother, Florence "Granny" Langford.

**Eldridge, Sue Copeland** (Larry)
Roaring River Chapter
Ancestor: George Hairston, VA — #682771
This "Lone Star" quilt was made in Overton County, TN by owner's husband's grandmother, Florence "Granny" Langford.

**Eldridge, Sue Copeland** (Larry)
Roaring River Chapter
Ancestor: George Hairston, VA — #682771
This "Grandmother's Fan" quilt was made in 1938-42 by the owner's grandmother, Nora Savage Gore (born 4/5/1880 at Overton County, TN, married Claborne Gore, died 11/26/1944 in the same county). The pieces were cut by maker's daughter, Alice Gore Copeland.

**Eldridge, Sue Copeland** (Larry)
Roaring River Chapter
Ancestor: George Hairston, VA — #682771
This "Bow Tie" quilt was made in 1938-42 at Overton County, TN by the owner's grandmother, Nora Savage Gore.

**Eleazer, Virginia Jamison** (Luther Edwin)
Hermitage Chapter
Ancestor: George Waller, VA —#564987
This "Improved Nine Patch" quilt was made at Tiptonville, TN by the owner's mother, Tennessee Ann Tipton Jamison (born 12/19/1886 at Tiptonville, married William Terry Jamison, died 2/8/1971 at Dyersburg, TN).

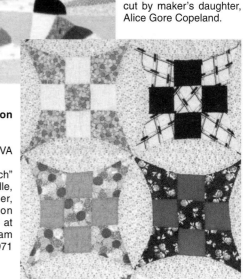

**Ellis, Isabel Wilkes** (Paul T.)
Robert Cartwright Chapter
Ancestor: William Abbott, NH — #538183
This "Maple Leaf" quilt was made circa 1960 at Athens, TN by the owner's husband's stepmother, Bess Terrill Ellis (born 3/18/1895 at Marble, NC, married George Blair Ellis, died 1/4/1989 at Athens, TN).

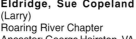

**Ellis, Isabel Wilkes** (Paul T.)
Robert Cartwright Chapter
Ancestor: William Abbott, NH — #538183
This "Scrap" quilt was made circa 1897 at Atlanta, GA by the owner's great grandmother, Jane Coulter Mackey (born 1843 in England, married John Samuel Mackey, died 1/3/1913 at Atlanta, GA). The maker made the quilt for her granddaughter's crib. The owner's mother left the quilt to her.

**Ellis, Isabel Wilkes** (Paul T.)
Robert Cartwright Chapter
Ancestor: William Abbott, NH — #538183
This coverlet was made by the owner's husband's grandmother, Nancy Jane Owen Wade (born 3/22/1859 at McMinn County, TN, married William Daniel Wade, died 8/18/1901). The maker gave the coverlet to the owner in 1946.

**Ellis, Isabel Wilkes** (Paul T.)
Robert Cartwright Chapter
Ancestor: William Abbott, NH — #538183
This "Crazy" quilt was made in Georgia by the owner's great grandmother, Jane Coulter Mackey. The quilt was passed from the maker, to her daughter, Isabel, to her grand–daughter, Isabel, and finally to her great great grand daughter, the current owner. The maker immigrated from Ireland during the Potato Famine, first to St. John's New Brunswick in 1859. Her husband came on a different ship and they moved together to Indian Reservation in North, GA, where he opened a store. Then they moved to Atlanta, GA.

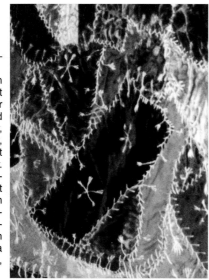

**Emery, Ella Reynolds** (Almon C.)
Chucalissa Chapter
Ancestor: Lt. William Hill, NC — #713989
This "Pinwheel" quilt was pieced in Conway, AR by the owner's cousin, Dana Carmichael (born circa 1895 at Faulkner County, AR, married Berman, died 1964 at Conway, AR). The owner's mother bought the top from Dora because everyone had made fun of the bright colors. The owner found a bright blue sheet for the lining and sent it to Darling, MS where some women were quilting to pay for their church. They quilted it for $25.00. It has polyester batting and the owner loves the modern colors.

**Emery, Ella Reynolds** (Almon C.)
Chucalissa Chapter
Ancestor: Lt. William Hill, NC — #713989
This "Double Wedding Ring" quilt was made in 1985 at Allgood, TN and was purchased by the owner from an ad in a Cookeville, TN newspaper.

**Emery, Ella Reynolds** (Almon C.)
Chucalissa Chapter
Ancestor: Lt. William Hill, NC — #713989
This "Dutch Doll" quilt was made by the owner's paternal grandmother, Mahallia Jane (Jennie) Fulmer Reynolds (born 6/16/1872 at Fulmer's Gap, Cadron Township, AR, married William Henry Reynolds, died 6/29/1949 at Conway, AR). The quilt was made for the owner.

**Emery, Ella Reynolds** (Almon C.)
Chucalissa Chapter
Ancestor: Lt. William Hill, NC — #713989
This "Nine Patch" quilt was made in AR. The top was in the owner's mother's trunk when she died. The quilt is made of polyester knit. It was hand quilted by the church women in Darling, MS.

**Erickson, Luanne Marie Vierkandt** (Daniel)
Zachariah Davies Chapter
Ancestor: James Baldwin, VA —#675958
This "Sampler" quilt was made in 1990 at Memphis, TN by Jo Harvey, who introduced the owner to her husband.

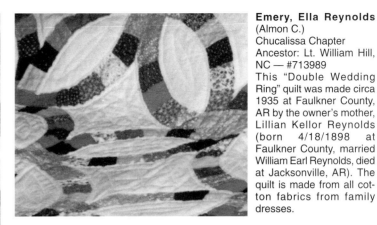

**Emery, Ella Reynolds** (Almon C.)
Chucalissa Chapter
Ancestor: Lt. William Hill, NC — #713989
This "Double Wedding Ring" quilt was made circa 1935 at Faulkner County, AR by the owner's mother, Lillian Kellor Reynolds (born 4/18/1898 at Faulkner County, married William Earl Reynolds, died at Jacksonville, AR). The quilt is made from all cotton fabrics from family dresses.

**England, Mary Crowder** (Thurman)
Rock House Chapter
Ancestor: William Norton, NC —#725907
This "Baskets of Flowers" quilt was made in White County, TN circa 1860 by the owner's great–grandmother, Jane Johnson when she was 16 years old. Jane was born 11/10/1844 at White County, TN and died 7/1916 in the same county. After the War Between the States, she married John Jacob Robinson, who had been injured in the war. Jane gave the quilt to the owner's mother who gave the quilt to the owner.

**Erickson, Evelyn Krueger** (Edward E.,Jr.)
Tullahoma Chapter
Ancestor: Isaac Baldwin, NH — #496038
This "Dogwood" quilt was made in 1941 at Chicago, IL by the owner's mother-in-law, Gladys Nelson Erickson (born 8/2/1900 at Chicago, married Edward E. Erickson, Sr., died 12/3/1947 at Chicago).

**Erickson, Luanne Marie Vierkandt** (Daniel)
Zachariah Davies Chapter
Ancestor: James Baldwin, VA —#675958
This "Double Wedding Ring" quilt was made in 1986 at Memphis, TN by Jo Harvey, who introduced the owner to her husband. It was given to the owner as a wedding present. "Luanne and Dan July 12, 1986" is stitched on the quilt.

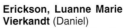

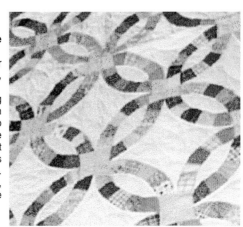

**Erickson, Luanne Marie Vierkandt** (Daniel)
Zachariah Davies Chapter
Ancestor: James Baldwin, VA —#675958
This "Sampler" quilt was made at Memphis, TN in 1990 by Jo Harvey, who introduced the owner to her husband. The quilt is signed "Made especially for Robert Andrew Erickson by Jo Harvey, Memphis, TN, December 17, 1990).

**Eubanks, Marie Harris** (Glen)
Captain William Lytle Chapter
Ancestor: Sgt. Hugh Baskin, SC —#773003
This "Bicentennial Star" quilt was made 1975-85 at Murfreesboro, TN by the owner (born 5/25/1941). Her mother helped her quilt the quilt,

**Fandrich, Julia Willis** (John Samuel, Sr.)
General James Winchester Chapter
Ancestor: Adam Caperton —#261378
This "Princess Feather" quilt was made in 1925 by the owner's husband's grandmother, Anna Graber Ruch (born 4/6/1845 in Mt Eaton, OH, married John H. Ruch, died 8/2/1930 at Belvidere, TN). The owner received the quilt as a wedding gift 9/11/1925. The owner lives in the same house in her 95th year and is still using this quilt today.

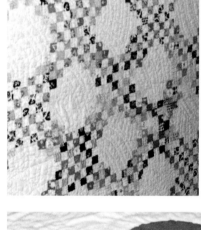

**Feldmann, Martha Johnson** (Larry)
Chucalissa Chapter
Ancestor: Michael Luther, MD —#775723
This "Triple Irish Chain" quilt was made in the early 1900's in Middle TN by the owner's great grandfather's sister, Emma Burk Todhunter (born circa 1870 probably at Wilson County, TN, died in 1940 at Nashville, TN). The quilt was given to the owner by her great aunt, Patty Burk Spencer, in 1968. "Aunt Emma was not known for her domestic skills so she made this quilt to prove that she had some."

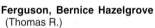

**Ferguson, Bernice Hazelgrove** (Thomas R.)
Hatchie Chapter
Ancestor: Zachariah Fortune, VA —#659147
This "Sunflower" quilt was made in 1934 at Whiteville, TN by the owner's mother-in-law, Irene Thompson Ferguson (born 8/12/1891 at Hardeman County, TN, married James Flynt Ferguson, died 1/29/1895 at Bolivar, TN). The quilt was made for the owner's husband when he graduated from the Whiteville High School in 1934. The petals of the flowers are embroidered with information about the pastor of each church in Whiteville in 1934, the names of the speakers at graduation, 1934 class officers, the name of each member of the boys' and girls' basketball teams, and the name of each member of the graduating class.

**Ferguson, Bernice Hazelgrove** (Thomas R.)
Hatchie Chapter
Ancestor: Zachariah Fortune, VA —#659147
This "Star of 76" quilt was made from a kit in 1976 at Bolivar, TN by the owner (born 5/24/1919 at Hardeman County, TN). This quilt officially recognized the commemoration of the American Revolution. It was authorized under public law, 93-179, license # 76-19-0551 according to the label on the quilt.

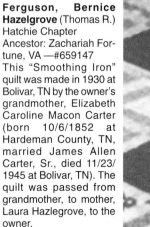

**Ferguson, Bernice Hazelgrove** (Thomas R.)
Hatchie Chapter
Ancestor: Zachariah Fortune, VA —#659147
This "Smoothing Iron" quilt was made in 1930 at Bolivar, TN by the owner's grandmother, Elizabeth Caroline Macon Carter (born 10/6/1852 at Hardeman County, TN, married James Allen Carter, Sr., died 11/23/1945 at Bolivar, TN). The quilt was passed from grandmother, to mother, Laura Hazlegrove, to the owner.

**Ferguson, Bernice Hazelgrove** (Thomas R.)
Hatchie Chapter
Ancestor: Zachariah Fortune, VA —#659147
This "Grandmother's Flower Garden" quilt was made in 1993 at Bolivar, TN by the owner. The label on this quilt reads "B. Ferguson 1990-1993."

**Ferguson, Bernice Hazelgrove** (Thomas R.)
Hatchie Chapter
Ancestor: Zachariah Fortune, VA—#659147
This "Cathedral Window" quilt was made in 1983 at Bolivar, TN by the owner.

**Ferguson, Bernice Hazelgrove** (Thomas R.)
Hatchie Chapter
Ancestor: Zachariah Fortune, VA—#659147
This coverlet was made in the mid 1800's in Hardeman County, TN by the owner's great–grandmother, Martha Ann Fortune Macon McKinnie (born 8/9/1832 at Salusbury, TN, married 1st Bailey Macon, married 2nd William McKinnie, died 12/20/1906 at Bolivar, TN). This coverlet was passed from maker, to grandmother, Betty Carter, to mother, Laura Hazlegrove, to owner. It was passed to the owner before her mother's death in 11/7/1957.

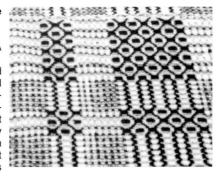

**Ferguson, Bernice Hazelgrove** (Thomas R.)
Hatchie Chapter
Ancestor: Zachariah Fortune, VA —#659147
This "Snowflower" cross stitch quilt was made in 1984 at Bolivar, TN by the owner. It is made from Paragoon Kit #01142.

**Ferguson, Bernice Hazelgrove** (Thomas R.)
Hatchie Chapter
Ancestor: Zachariah Fortune, VA —#659147
This "Clay's Choice" quilt was made in 1975 at Bolivar, TN by the owner.

**Ferguson, Bernice Hazelgrove** (Thomas R.)
Hatchie Chapter
Ancestor: Zachariah Fortune, VA—#659147
This "Double Wedding Ring" quilt was made in 1945 at Bolivar, TN by the owner's mother, Laura Carter Hazlegrove (born 8/25/1876 at Hardeman County, TN, married Walter W. Hazlegrove, died 11/9/1957 at Bolivar, TN). The quilt was passed from mother, to daughter.

**Ferguson, Bernice Hazelgrove** (Thomas R.)
Hatchie Chapter
Ancestor: Zachariah Fortune, VA —#659147
This "Poppy Basket" quilt was made from a kit in 1944 at Bolivar, TN by the owner.

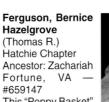

**Ferguson, Eloise Odam** (J.H.)
Hatchie Chapter
Ancestor: Redden McCoy, SC —#670652
This "Wagon Wheel" quilt was made in 1930-35 at Navarro County, TX by the owner's grandmother, Mary Ann Odam Birdwell (born 6/22/1857 at Parker County, TX, married 2nd Alvy Birdwell, died 10/8/1940 at Navarro, TX). The maker made each of her granddaughters a quilt. She gave this one to the owner.

**Ferguson, Bernice Hazelgrove** (Thomas R.)
Hatchie Chapter
Ancestor: Zachariah Fortune, VA—#659147
This "Crazy Ann" quilt was made in 1936 at Bolivar, TN by the owner.

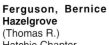

**Field, Suzanne Polk** (Robert Max)
We-Ah-Te-Umba Chapter
Ancestor: Charles Polk, NC —#460937
This "Irish Chain" quilt was made in the early 1900's at Oaktown, IN by the owner's great grandmother, Urania Sarter Polk (born 8/12/1849 at Brownsville, IN, married Charles Polk, died 1/30/1920 at Oaktown, IN).

**Field, Suzanne Polk** (Robert Max)
We-Ah-Te-Umba Chapter
Ancestor: Charles Polk, NC —#460937
This "Grandmother's Flower Garden" quilt was made in 1930 at Knox County, IN by the owner's grandmother, Faye Winemiller Latshaw (born 1/19/1890 at Knox County, IN, married John Melvin Latshaw, died 5/27/1976 at Oaktown, IN). John was born 2/6/1882 and died 3/26/1943. The maker and her husband resided on a farm of 487 acres just east of Oaktown which they purchased in 1834. They raised wheat, corn, oats and beans as well as a small herd of dairy cows. Each year Faye made a quilt from scraps of dress fabric and quilted it on a frame hung in the kitchen. She was often assisted by Fannie Latshaw. This "Grandmother's Flower Garden" quilt is especially appropriate since she had a beautiful garden which supplied the family and friends with food each year.

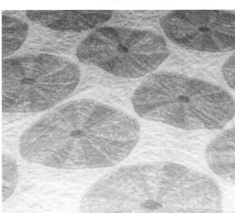
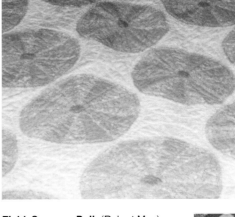

**Field, Suzanne Polk**
(Robert Max)
We-Ah-Te-Umba
Chapter
Ancestor: Charles
Polk, NC —#460937
This "Irish Chain" quilt
was made in the
1920's at Oaktown, IN
by the owner's grand-
mother, Edith Sheperd
Polk (born 4/24/1883 at
Oaktown, IN married
Claude Barton Polk,
died in 1980 at
Freelandville, IN).

**Field, Suzanne Polk**
(Robert Max)
We-Ah-Te-Umba Chapter
Ancestor: Charles Polk,
NC —#460937
This "Six Pointed Star"
quilt was made in the
1890's in Oaktown, IN by
the owner's great grand-
mother, Urania Sarter
Polk. This wool quilt was
made from the family wool
suits and coats, lined with
cotton flannel, and used
for warmth when riding in
a buggy or sled.

Claude was born 3/7/1885 and died 1/19/1919. He died when the owner's father
was two years old, leaving Edith a young widow.

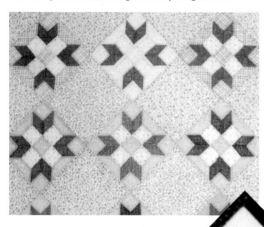

**Field, Suzanne Polk**
(Robert Max)
We-Ah-Te-Umba
Chapter
Ancestor: Charles Polk,
NC —#460937
This "Farmer's Daugh-
ter" quilt was made in
the 1940's at Oaktown,
IN by the owner's
grandmother, Edith
Sheperd Polk.

**Field, Suzanne Polk**
(Robert Max)
We-Ah-Te-Umba Chapter
Ancestor: Charles Polk,
NC —#460937
This "Nine Patch" quilt
was made in the 1920's
at Oaktown, IN by the
owner's grandmother,
Edith Sheperd Polk.

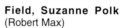

**Field, Suzanne Polk** (Robert Max)
We-Ah-Te-Umba Chapter
Ancestor: Charles Polk, NC —
#460937
This "Churn Dash" quilt
was pieced in the
1920's at Oaktown,
IN by the owner's
great grand-
mother,
Urania
Sarter
Polk.

**Field, Suzanne Polk**
(Robert Max)
We-Ah-Te-Umba Chap-
ter
Ancestor: Charles Polk,
NC —#460937
This "Six Pointed Star"
quilt was made in the
1920's at Oaktown, IN by
the owner's grand-
mother, Edith Sheperd
Polk.

**Field, Suzanne Polk**
(Robert Max)
We-Ah-Te-Umba
Chapter
Ancestor: Charles
Polk, NC —
#460937
This "Field of Dia-
monds" quilt was
made in Oaktown, IN
by the owner's grand-
mother, Edith Sheperd
Polk. The quilt was passed
from the maker, to the
owner's father, to the owner.

**Fink, Mary Vaughn**
(Charles S.)
Sarah Hawkins
Chapter
Ancestor: William
Vaughn, Jr., VA —
#559375
This "Tulip" quilt was
made by the
owner's great great
grandmother,
Phoebe Jane Ward
(born at Grayson
County, VA).

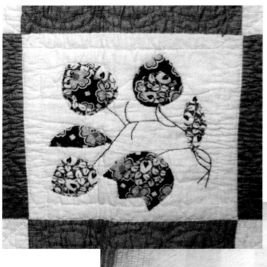

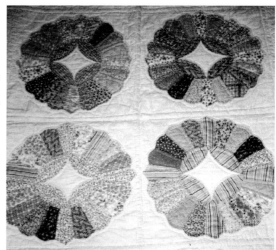

**Finks, Elizabeth**
(Tom)
Volunteer Chapter
Ancestor: John
Bruton, GA —
#752877
This "Tulip" quilt was
made in 1918 at
Jefferson County,
GA by Cornelia
Powell Ratchford.

**Finks, Elizabeth**
(Tom)
Volunteer Chapter
Ancestor: John
Bruton, GA —
#752877
This is a "Dresden
Plate Variation"
quilt.

**Finks, Elizabeth**
(Tom)
Volunteer Chapter
Ancestor: John
Bruton, GA —
#752877
This "One Patch"
quilt was made in
1910 at Sullivan
County, TN by Mary
Powell Thomas
(born in Sullivan
County).

**Finks, Elizabeth**
(Tom)
Volunteer Chapter
Ancestor: John
Bruton, GA —
#752877
This "Basket of
Flowers" quilt was
made in 1920 at
Jefferson County,
GA by Cornelia
Powell Ratchford.

**Fitts, Alice Mitchum**
(William Emmett)
Jane Knox Chapter
Ancestor: Thomas
Polk, NC —#698399
This "Nine Patch Varia-
tion "quilt was made
before 1850 at
Humboldt, TN by the
owner's great grand-
mother, Ann Hampton
Hamilton Adams (born
6/6/1821, married
Jeremiah Mitchell
Adams, died 5/19/
1919). Mrs. Adams
was born in Davy
Crockett's home in

**Fitts, Alice Mitchum**
(William Emmett)
Jane Knox Chapter
Ancestor: Thomas
Polk, NC —#698399
This "One Patch" quilt
was made in 1920-30
at Anadarka, OK by a
member of the owner's
husband's family, the
Dutchers. The owner's
husband received it
from his mother, Mar-
guerite Fitts

Lawrence County, TN. The quilt was probably made in McNairy County, TN. The
maker made 85 quilts. She had eight boys and two girls. She was the community
nurse for birth and death. Three of her sons fought in the battle of Shiloh.

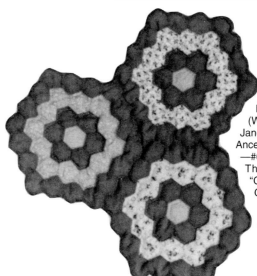

**Fitts, Alice Mitchum**
(William Emmett)
Jane Knox Chapter
Ancestor: Thomas
Polk, NC —#698399
This "Crazy" quilt was
found in a trunk in the
owner's father's home.
It may have been made
by the Campbells,
Pointers, or Polks.

**Fitts, Alice Mitchum**
(William Emmett)
Jane Knox Chapter
Ancestor: Thomas Polk, NC
—#698399
This variation of a
"Grandmother's Flower
Garden" quilt was
owned by Christine
Fiveash in Memphis,
TN.

**Fitts, Alice Mitchum**
(William Emmett)
Jane Knox Chapter
Ancestor: Thomas Polk,
NC —#698399
This "Eight Pointed Star"
quilt was found in a trunk
in the owner's father's
home. It may have been
made by the Campbells,
Pointers, or Polks.

**Fitzgerald, Nell Thompson**
(Curtis R.)
Jane Knox Chapter
Ancestor: Ambrose Hadley —
#607462
This "Crazy" quilt was made in
the 1930's at Columbia, TN by
the owner's aunt, Gertrude Thompson Freeman (born 9/20/
1896 at Maury County, TN, married George L. Freeman, died 10/
20/1976 at Columbia, TN). The
center is pieced from old neck
ties. The owner received the quilt
after the death of the maker.

**Fitzgerald, Nell Thompson**
(Curtis R.)
Jane Knox Chapter
Ancestor: Ambrose Hadley
—#607462
This "Postage Stamp" quilt
was made in the early 1930's
at Columbia, TN and left to
the owner after the death of
her aunt, Gertrude T. Freeman.

**Fitzgerald, Nell
Thompson** (Curtis
R.)
Jane Knox Chapter
Ancestor: Ambrose
Hadley —#607462
This "Sampler" quilt
was made in 1988
at Columbia, TN by
the owner (born 1/
24/1919 at Maury
County, TN). The
maker made the
quilt as she taught
a class in lap quilt-
ing at Columbia
State Community
College.

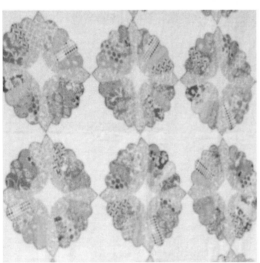

**Fitzgerald, Nell
Thompson** (Curtis
R.)
Jane Knox Chapter
Ancestor: Ambrose
Hadley —#607462
This "Fancy Dresden
Plate" quilt was made
in 1950 at Los Ange-
les, CA by the owner's
aunt, Nell Meroney
Gary (born 7/11/1894
at Maury County, TN,
married J. Marshall
Gary, died 6/13/1970
at Columbia, TN). The
owner received the
quilt at the death of
the maker.

**Fitzgerald, Nell Thompson**
(Curtis R.)
Jane Knox Chapter
Ancestor: Ambrose Hadley —
#607462
This "Princess Feather" quilt was
made in the 1930's at Columbia,
TN and left to the owner after the
death of her aunt, Gertrude T.
Freeman.

**Fitzgerald, Nell Thompson**
(Curtis R.)
Jane Knox Chapter
Ancestor: Ambrose Hadley
—#607462
This "Broken Star" quilt was
made in the 1930's at Co-
lumbia, TN and left to the
owner after the death of her
aunt, Gertrude T. Freeman.

**Fitzgerald, Nell Thompson**
(Curtis R.)
Jane Knox Chapter
Ancestor: Ambrose Hadley —
#607462
This "Sampler" quilt was
made in 1980 at Columbia,
TN by the owner. The maker
made the quilt as she taught
a class in lap quilting at Columbia State Community College.

**Fleenor, Mary Louise McChesney** (C. Warren)
Volunteer Chapter
Ancestor: Samuel McChesney, VA — #505011
This wool "Crazy" quilt was made in 1935-40 by the owner's grandmother, Mittie A. Byars McChesney (born 1/28/1859 at Glade Spring, VA,

married J.D. McChesney, died 12/22/1952 at Glade Spring). The owner noticed that one piece of fabric in the quilt was from the first dress she made in 4-H Club.

**Fleenor, Mary Louise McChesney** (C. Warren)
Volunteer Chapter
Ancestor: Samuel McChesney, VA — #505011
This "Pinwheel" quilt was made in 1939 at Glade Springs, VA by the owner's grandmother, Mittie A. Byars McChesney.

**Fleenor, Mary Louise McChesney** (C. Warren)
Volunteer Chapter
Ancestor: Samuel McChesney, VA — #505011
This "Star" quilt was made with strip piecing in 1939 by the owner's grandmother, Mittie A. Byars McChesney or by her aunt.

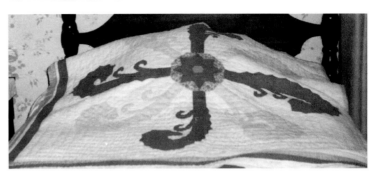

**Fleenor, Mary Louise McChesney** (C. Warren)
Volunteer Chapter
Ancestor: Samuel McChesney, VA —#505011
This "Princess Feather" quilt belonged to the owner's mother-in-law, Josephine Delarney St. John Fleenor, who gave it to the owner in 1942.

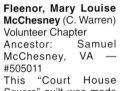
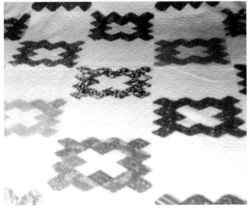

**Fleenor, Mary Louise McChesney** (C. Warren)
Volunteer Chapter
Ancestor: Samuel McChesney, VA — #505011
This "Court House Square" quilt was made in the early 1900's at Glade Spring, VA by the owner's grandmother, Mittie A. Byars McChesney. She made this quilt for her oldest daughter, Linnie A. McChesney Lester. "Over the years, it became my daddy's quilt, Dr. W.W. McChesney (died 1986), who was a veteran of WWI." The owner inherited the quilt when she put her parents house up for sale after her mother died in 1988.

**Fleenor, Mary Louise McChesney** (C. Warren)
Volunteer Chapter
Ancestor: Samuel McChesney, VA —#505011
This "Crazy" quilt was made in the early 1900's. The quilt is signed "I.M."

**Foley, Alice King** (James D.)
Chickasaw Bluff Chapter
Ancestor: Abraham Seay, VA —#747887
This "Square in a Square" quilt was begun in the 1930's at Arapaho, OK by the owner's sister, Margaret King (born 9/25/1923 at Custer, County, OK, married John W. Spencer). The top was finished by the owner in the 1980's and quilted by Clara Fullgrabe of Cordell, OK.

**Foley, Alice King** (James D.)
Chickasaw Bluff Chapter
Ancestor: Abraham Seay, VA —#747887
This "Double Wedding Ring" quilt was pieced in the 1930's at Arapaho, OK by the owner's mother, Lydia Lucile Dowler King (born 4/8/1898 at Crawford, MO, married William Jasper King, died 5/4/1993 at Custer County, OK). It was quilted by the owner in the 1980's at Memphis, TN. The pattern for the quilt was taken from the Kansas City Star. The Star circulated throughout the midwest as a weekly newspaper, mostly for farm families. Quilt patterns were in this publication from 1928 into 1961.

**Foley, Alice King** (James D.)
Chickasaw Bluff Chapter
Ancestor: Abraham Seay, VA
—#747887
This "Log Cabin" quilt was made in the 1970's at Meridian, MS by the owner (born 11/8/1930 at Custer, OK). This is a "quilt as you go" quilt. Each block is quilted as it is put together. The maker saw this pattern in Southern Living's Award Winning Quilts in the 1970's. "I didn't think I was accomplished enough for traditional quilting so I thought I would try this method."

**Foley, Alice King** (James D.)
Chickasaw Bluff Chapter
Ancestor: Abraham Seay, VA —
#747887
This "Cathedral Window" quilt was made in the 1970's at Meridian, MS by the owner.

**Foley, Alice King** (James D.)
Chickasaw Bluff Chapter
Ancestor: Abraham Seay, VA —
#747887
This "Nine Patch" quilt was started in the 1930's at Arapaho, OK by the owner's sister, Billie King (born 3/7/1925 at Custer, OK, married F. H. Whittemore). The owner finished the quilt in 1993 at Memphis, TN. "We lived on a farm in western OK in the 1930's, and when harvest or chores were done, we took to sewing. There was no such thing as TV or even radio, and trips to town were few and far between…after sixty years in the making, this old quilt became a finished family heirloom."

**Foley, Alice King** (James D.)
Chickasaw Bluff Chapter
Ancestor: Abraham Seay, VA —
#747887
This "Friendship/Family Album" quilt was pieced in 1988 at Memphis, TN by the owner for her mother, Lydia Dowler, on her 90th birthday. At her mother's death, the quilt came back to the owner. "My mother had a quilt like this given to her mother by a Sunday School group where her husband preached. I decided to copy the quilt and use my mother and father, all their children and grandchildren's names in the block. For my own children, I used fabric from their respective clothing. The pieced top was given to my mother on her 90th birthday. She had it quilted by Edith Sturgeon of Cordell, OK."

**Foley, Alice King** (James D.)
Chickasaw Bluff Chapter
Ancestor: Abraham Seay, VA—
#747887
This "Cathedral Window" quilt was begun in 1968 by the owner's mother, Lydia Lucile Dowler King. Her husband became ill so she had to put the quilt aside. Then when she had time, her health and eyesight had failed. The owner and her sister, Virginia Cleckley, finished the quilt on Christmas Eve, 1980. The owner inherited the quilt when her mother died in 1993.

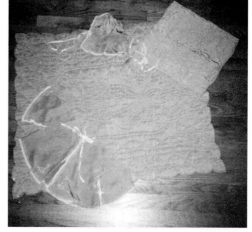

**Ford, Ann Sawyers**
(Buck, Jr.)
Robert Lewis Chapter
Ancestor: William Bingham, NC —#672494
This quilted baby comforter was made in 1939 at Lincoln County, TN by the owner's mother, Sarah Bigham Sawyers (born 10/7/1916 at Marshall County, TN, married Arthur M. Sawyers, died 10/8/1997 at Marshall County). The maker made the comforter while awaiting the owner's birth.

**Ford, Ann Sawyers**
(Buck, Jr.)
Robert Lewis Chapter
Ancestor: William Bingham, NC — #672494
This "Snow Crystals" quilt was made in 1944 at Lincoln County, TN by the owner's mother, Sarah Bigham Sawyers. As a child, the owner helped her mother cut the pieces for this and other quilts. She lost a cherished sapphire ring and was surprised to find it years later in the bag of quilt scraps.

**Foster, Katie Sue Pinkston**
(Robert)
Jane Knox Chapter
Ancestor: William Pinkston, NC —#650870
This "Double Wedding Ring" quilt was made circa 1935 at Maury County, TN by the owner's mother, Argie Virginia Grissom Pinkston (born 11/2/1886 at Columbia, TN, married Merritt Oliver Pinkston, died 4/3/1968 at Columbia). The owner was twelve years old when the quilt was made and she remembers having to be careful not to run into the quilt frame, which hung from the ceiling. The neighbors came and spent the day quilting, stopping only to eat lunch. Much of the maker's fabric for her quilts came from feed sacks and flour sacks, but she was eager to go to town each Saturday to choose complimentary materials and threads for her quilts.

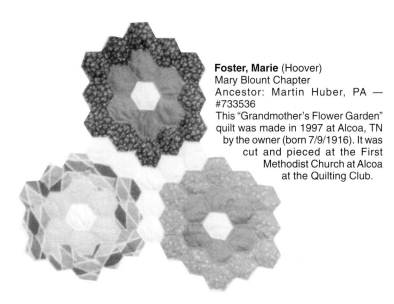

**Foster, Marie** (Hoover)
Mary Blount Chapter
Ancestor: Martin Huber, PA —#733536
This "Grandmother's Flower Garden" quilt was made in 1997 at Alcoa, TN by the owner (born 7/9/1916). It was cut and pieced at the First Methodist Church at Alcoa at the Quilting Club.

**Foster, Marie** (Hoover)
Mary Blount Chapter
Ancestor: Martin Huber, PA —#733536
This "Diamond" quilt was made circa the 1950's in Iowa by the owner's great aunt, Beulah Wygal McPherson (born 6/8/1878 at Lee County, VA, married Evan McPherson, died 6/8/1964 in IN). The maker gave the quilt to the owner.

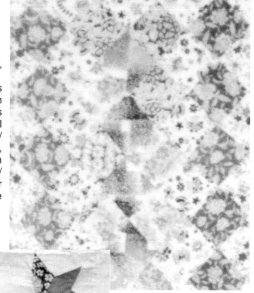

**Fowler, Ruth Ann Shepherd** (Paul A.)
Andrew Bogle Chapter
Ancestor: William Woodford, VA —#645017
This "Rising Star" quilt was made in 1976 in GA by the owner's mother-in-law, Hattie Fowler (born 1903 at Crabapple, GA, married J.D. Fowler). The quilt was made for the owner's son for the Bicentennial.

**Fowler, Ruth Ann Shepherd** (Paul A.)
Andrew Bogle Chapter
Ancestor: William Woodford, VA —#645017
This "Turkey Tracks" quilt was made in the 1930's in KY by the owner's mother, Virginia Woodford Sheperd (born 1/15/1907 at Clark County, KY, married Leslie T.). The maker gave it to the owner.

**Fowler, Ruth Ann Shepherd** (Paul A.)
Andrew Bogle Chapter
Ancestor: William Woodford, VA — #645017
This "Flower Basket" quilt was made in the 1930's in KY by the owner's aunt, Ruth Shepherd Cowan (born 1902 at Clark County, KY, married Dr. Glenn Cowan, died 1995 at Clark County). The quilt was made for the 1933 World's Fair, but was not submitted.

**Fox, Ann Moore** (Nathan)
Thomas McKisick Chapter
Ancestor: Roger Quarles, VA —#634782
This antique quilt was made circa 1895 at Putnam County, TN by Ms. Isabell (born and died in Putnam County). It was a gift to the owner's parents when they married in 1903. They passed it to the owner.

**Fox, Dixie Grier** (Donald)
Rhea-Craig Chapter
Ancestor: Moses Grier, GA & NC —#790084
This "Dresden Plate" friendship quilt was made in 1937 at Springfield, AR by the owner's mother, Georgia Jordan Grier (born 1/18/1901 at Springfield, married Perry A. Grier). The quilt has the names of the owner's mother, grandmother, and four aunts embroidered in the centers along with one center that says, "Springfield Ark 1937."

**Fox, Irene Dixon**
(Grady Bascom, Jr.)
Spencer Clack Chapter
Ancestor: Johann Martin Schultz, NC —#765492
This "Tennessee Trouble" coverlet was made circa 1910 in Sevier County, TN by the owner's husband's grandmother, Martha Lawson Fox (born 6/14/1849 at Sevier County, TN, married Tilman Grady Bascom Fox, died 2/21/1932 in the same county). The wool was raised on their farm. Tillman Fox sheared the sheep. Martha spun and died the wool and wove it into coverlets. Her daughter, Mattie Rawlings (married Fred Rawlings) owned the coverlet and gave it to the owner.

**Fox, Irene Dixon**
(Grady Bascom, Jr.)
Spencer Clack Chapter
Ancestor: Johann Martin Schultz, NC —
#765492
This "Crown of Thorns/New York Beauty/Rocky Mountain Road" quilt was made circa 1891 at Sevier County, TN by the owner's husband's grandmother, Martha Lawson Fox.. This is a very old pattern and has been named all three of the above names.

**Fox, Irene Dixon**
(Grady Bascom, Jr.)
Spencer Clack Chapter
Ancestor: Johann Martin Schultz, NC —
#765492
This "Tulip" quilt was made circa 1891-1900 at Sevier County, TN by the owner's husband's grandmother, Martha Lawson Fox.

**Frazier, Ann Edwards**
Gen Daniel Smith Rock Castle Chapter
Ancestor: James Draughon, NC —
#567038
This "Dutch Doll" quilt was made in 1932 at Robertson County, TN and was purchased by the owner's father at a raffle in 1932 for 25 cents.

**Freeland, Helen Vaughn**
(Robert D.)
Hatchie Chapter
Ancestor: Peter Perkins, VA —#586094
This "Grandmother's Flower Garden" quilt was pieced in 1945 at Bolivar, TN by the owner's grandmother, Priscilla Marsh Morrow (born 9/13/1871 at Toone, TN, married William D. Morrow, died 2/20/1967 at Bolivar, TN). The owner received the quilt when her mother died in 1986. The owner had the quilt quilted by a Mennonite lady, Fannie Helmuth, who lives near Whiteville, TN.

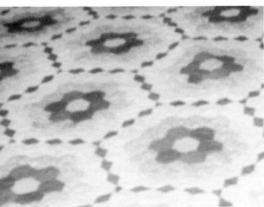

**Freeland, Helen Vaughn**
(Robert D.)
Hatchie Chapter
Ancestor: Peter Perkins, VA —#586094
This "Grandmother's Flower Garden" quilt was made in the early 1940's at Whiteville, TN by the owner's husband's grandmother, Ola Irby Seddens (born 7/21/1872 at Whiteville, married Johnson Saddens, died 1/28/1961 at Whiteville). The quilt was given to the owner as a wedding gift in July, 1945.

**Freeland, Helen Vaughn**
(Robert D.)
Hatchie Chapter
Ancestor: Peter Perkins, VA —#586094
This "Glorified Nine Patch" quilt was made circa 1940 at Whiteville, TN by the owner's husband's grandmother, Ola Irby Seddena.

**Freeze, Irene Jarrell**
Manchester Chapter
Ancestor: Capt. Josiah Hill Rogers, NC —
#782390
This "Double Wedding Ring" quilt was made in 1935 at Coffee County, TN by the owner's aunt, Cora Rogers Patrick (married Jodie Patrick). The quilt was given as a wedding gift to the owner in 1935.

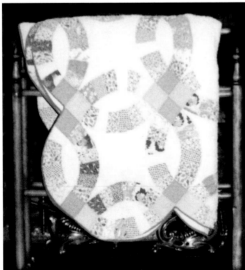

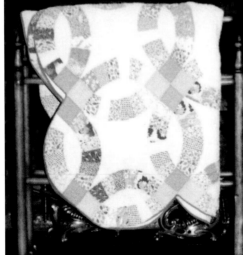

**Fritz, Dorothy Suter** (William J.)
Hiwassee Chapter
Ancestor: Nathan Seward, CT —#510769
This "Monkey Wrench/Churn Dash" quilt was made circa 1892 in OH by the owner's grandmother, May Avery Seward (born 5/4/1870 at Brecksville, OH, married Henry Baldwin Seward, died 6/18/1957 at Youngstown, OH). The quilt was inherited from the owner's mother.

**Fritz, Dorothy Suter** (William J.)
Hiwassee Chapter
Ancestor: Nathan Seward, CT —#510769
This original design "Flower Basket Variation" was appliqued in the early 1960's by the owner. She sent it to her sister, Alice Suter Zwanck (born 7/12/1918 at Youngstown, OH, married Arnold L. Zwanck, died 6/22/1976 at San Francisco, CA). Alice finished the quilt and sent it back to the owner.

**Fritz, Dorothy Suter** (William J.)
Hiwassee Chapter
Ancestor: Nathan Seward, CT —
#510769
This original design "Trellis" quilt was made in 1962 at San Francisco, CA by the owner's sister, Alice Suter Zwanck. This quilt was made for the owner's parents golden wedding anniversary. The maker taught quilting to school girls in the St. John's Presbyterian Church and in the neighborhood.

**Fritz, Dorothy Suter** (William J.)
Hiwassee Chapter
Ancestor: Nathan Seward, CT —
#510769
This original design "URSA Minor Constellation" quilt was made in 1972 at San Francisco, CA by the owner's sister, Alice Suter Zwanck. It was sent to the owner after the maker's death. This quilt and the pattern appears in a book by the maker, Color and Quilt.

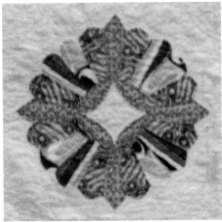

**Fry, Jean Lockhart** (William)
Glover's Trace Chapter
Ancestor:    Alexander McCorkle, NC —#532281
This "Dresden Plate" quilt was made in the 1950's perhaps at Conway, AR and was a gift from the owner's maternal aunt, Dr. Virginia Priestly Smith.

**Fry, Jean Lockhart**
(William)
Glover's Trace Chapter
Ancestor:    Alexander McCorkle,    NC    — #532281
This "Dresden Plate" quilt belonged to the owner's husband's mother, Mary McCullough Fry.

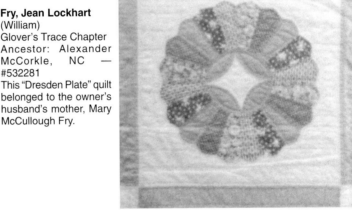

**Fry, Jean Lockhart**
(William)
Glover's Trace Chapter
Ancestor: Alexander McCorkle, NC — #532281
This "Dogwood" quilt was made in the 1980's at Camden, TN by Floye Markham.

**Fry, Jean Lockhart** (William)
Glover's Trace Chapter
Ancestor: Alexander McCorkle, NC —#532281
This "Schoolhouse" quilt was made in Camden, TN by the Retired Senior Volunteer Program. The quilt was made for the owner's daughter, Beth.

**Gallaway, Sandra Terry** (Jerry)
Old Reynoldsburgh Chapter
Ancestor: John Terry, VA — #518835
This "Shooting Stars" quilt was made circa 1920 in Van Wert, OH by the owner's grandmother, Flo Lucretia (Beck) Terry (born 6/18/1896 at Van Wert, OH, married Vernon A. Terry, died 12/14/1973 at Van Wert). The quilt was passed from W. Dale and Joan Terry to current owner. The owner (born in 1945) remembers using this quilt when staying at her grandparents' home.

**Gallaway, Sandra Terry** (Jerry)
Old Reynoldsburgh Chapter
Ancestor: John Terry, VA — #518835
This "Lone Star" quilt was made circa 1925 in Van Wert, OH by the owner's grandmother, Flo Lucretia (Beck) Terry. Yellow was a favorite color of the quiltmaker. To the owner's knowledge all o                      f

**Galyon, Helen LeVerne Summit** (Sam B.)
Rhea Craig Chapter
Ancestor: Francis Summitt, NC — #730925
This "Irish Chain" quilt was made circa 1843 in Madisonville, TN by the owner's great great grandmother, Mary Lowery (born circa 1828 in Madisonville, TN, married Hugh Kelso Lowery, died circa 1895 in Madisonville). The quilt was passed from maker, to owner's mother, to owner, and is over 150 years old.

**Galyon, Helen LeVerne Summit** (Sam B.)
Rhea Craig Chapter
Ancestor: Francis Summitt, NC — #730925
This "Hands All Around" quilt was made in the early 1900's in Sweetwater, TN by the owner's mother-in-law, Mrs. Sam B. Gaylon, Sr. (born 5/2/1879 in Roane County, TN, died in 1978 in Monroe County, TN). The owner received the quilt from her husband's family in 1982.

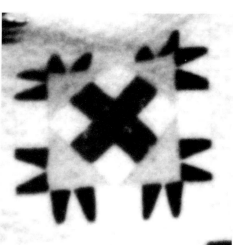

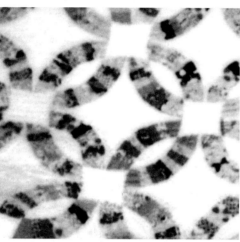

**Galyon, Helen LeVerne Summit** (Sam B.)
Rhea Craig Chapter
Ancestor: Francis Summitt, NC — #730925
This "Double Wedding Ring" quilt was made in 1927 in Sweetwater, TN by the owner's mother, Mrs. Murray Summitt (born 5/15/1891 at Madisonville, TN, died 2/16/1973 at Sweetwater, TN). The quilt was given to the owner by her mother.

**Galyon, Helen LeVerne Summit** (Sam B.)
Rhea Craig Chapter
Ancestor: Francis Summitt, NC — #730925
This "Ohio Star" quilt was made circa 1926 in Sweetwater, TN by the owner's mother, Mrs. Murray Summit, and passed from her to the owner.

**Galyon, Helen LeVerne Summit** (Sam B.)
Rhea Craig Chapter
Ancestor: Francis Summitt, NC — #730925
This "Double Irish Chain" quilt was made circa 1848 by a member of the owner's maternal great grandmother's family. It was given to the owner by her mother who received it from her mother.

**Galyon, Helen LeVerne Summit** (Sam B.)
Rhea Craig Chapter
Ancestor: Francis Summitt, NC — #730925
This "Double Wedding Ring" quilt was made circa 1925 in Sweetwater, TN by the owner's mother, Mrs. Murray Summitt, and given to the owner circa 1943.

**Gann, Janet**
Ancestor: Maj. Gilbert Christian —#769218
This cross stitch quilt was made in 1965 by the owner's mother, Jean Webb.

**Gann, Janet**
Ancestor: Maj. Gilbert Christian — #769218
This "Pink Dogwood" quilt was made in 1960 by the owner's mother, Jean Webb.

**Gann, Janet**
Ancestor: Maj. Gilbert Christian —#769218
This "Flowers" quilt was made in the early 1960's by by the owner's mother, Jean Webb.

**Gann, Janet**
Ancestor: Maj. Gilbert Christian —#769218
This "Sunbonnet Sue" quilt was made in the late 1950's by the owner's mother, Jean Webb. The maker used fabric from the owner's childhood clothes.

**Gann, Janet**
Ancestor: Maj. Gilbert Christian —#769218
This "Sunbonnet Sue" quilt was made in 1930 by "Mama" Pearl Stephens.

**Gann, Janet**
Ancestor: Maj. Gilbert Christian —#769218
This "Dogwood" quilt was made in the early 1960's by the owner's mother, Jean Webb.

**Gann, Janet**
Ancestor: Maj. Gilbert Christian —#769218
This "Pink Rose" quilt was made by the owner's mother, Jean Webb.

**Gant, Kitty Carney** (Paul)
Lt. James Sheppard Chapter
Ancestor: Captain William Lytle, NC —#439686
This "Tulip" quilt was pieced in 1927 in Warren County, TN by Katherine Gant and quilted by someone else in Warren County.

**Garbarino, Jackie Payne** (Dr. A. J.)
William Cocke Chapter
Ancestor: Robert Paine, VA —#509491
This appliqued "Tulip" quilt was made in 1840-50 in South Carolina. The owner obtained this quilt from Stevens and Turner Antiques in Charleston, SC.

**Garbarino, Jackie Payne** (Dr. A. J.)
William Cocke Chapter
Ancestor: Robert Paine, VA —#509491
This "Spider's Web" quilt was made in 1870 in Ohio. The owner found the quilt in a small shop in Germantown, TN in 1988. Under the top of this quilt is another quilt.

**Garbarino, Jackie Payne** (Dr. A. J.) William Cocke Chapter Ancestor: Robert Paine, VA —#509491 This "Cross and Crown/Blue Birds Flying" quilt was made in 1850 at Newport, TN by one of the Seehorn Sisters. It was purchased at Miller's Auction in Newport, TN by the owner.

**Garbarino, Jackie Payne** (Dr. A. J.) William Cocke Chapter Ancestor: Robert Paine, VA —#509491 This hand dyed "Drunkard's Path" quilt was made in 1840-50 in East TN. It was purchased by the owner from Sandy Arden in Knoxville, TN.

**Garbarino, Jackie Payne** (Dr. A. J.) William Cocke Chapter Ancestor: Robert Paine, VA —#509491 This "Log Cabin" quilt was made in 1840-50 at South Carolina and was purchased at Stevens and Turner Antiques in Charleston, SC in 1988.

**Garbarino, Jackie Payne** (Dr. A. J.) William Cocke Chapter Ancestor: Robert Paine, VA —#509491 This "Double Arrow" quilt was made in 1880-90 in East TN and was purchased at the Miller Auction in Newport, TN.

**Garbarino, Jackie Payne** (Dr. A. J.) William Cocke Chapter Ancestor: Robert Paine, VA —#509491 This original design quilt is similar to the "Courthouse Square." It was made in South Carolina in 1850. It was was purchased at Stevens and Turner Antiques in Charleston, SC.

**Garrett, Betty Jo Greer** (Joseph) Captain William Edmiston Chapter Ancestor: Anthony Bledsoe —#493644 This "Grandmother's Flower Garden" quilt was pieced in 1985 at Clarksville, TN by the owner (born 1932 at Goodlettsville, TN and quilted by a lady in Old Hickory, TN

**Garrett, Betty Jo Greer** (Joseph) Captain William Edmiston Chapter Ancestor: Anthony Bledsoe — #493644 This "Cathedral Window" quilt was made in 1960 at Nashville, TN by the owner's mother-in-law, Mrs. Julius Carey (born 1911 at Bethpage, TN, died in 1998 at Nashville).

**Garrett, Betty Jo Greer** (Joseph) Captain William Edmiston Chapter Ancestor: Anthony Bledsoe — #493644 This "Nursery Rhyme" quilt was made in 1930 at Goodlettsville, TN by the owner's mother, Mrs. Mitchum W. Greer (born 1910 at Nashville, died in 1990 at Hendersonville, TN).

**Garrett, Betty Jo Greer** (Joseph) Captain William Edmiston Chapter Ancestor: Anthony Bledsoe —#493644 This "Flying Geese" quilt was made in Ohio and purchased at an antique show in Nashville, TN.

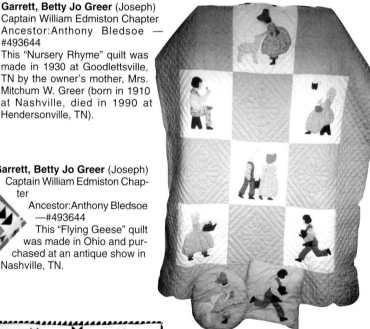

**Garrett, Betty Jo Greer** (Joseph) Captain William Edmiston Chapter Ancestor: Anthony Bledsoe — #493644 This "Log Cabin" quilt was made in 1985 at Paducah, KY and was a gift to the owner from her husband.

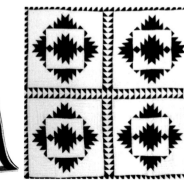

**Garrett, Lynn S.** (William) Old Glory Chapter Ancestor: Solomon Yeager, VA — #583113 This "Electric Mountain" quilt was made in 1987 in Franklin, TN by Mable Hood (born before 1920). It was purchased at a church auction for $900. It is made in tiny squares hardly larger than a postage stamp. It is quilted on every tiny piece. This quilt is signed "Mabel Hood for Cowles Chapple Methodist Church, June 1987."

Garrett, Lynn S. (William)
Old Glory Chapter
Ancestor: Solomon Yeager,
VA — #583113
This "Nine Patch" quilt was made in 1927 in Imboden, AR by ladies of Imbodden as a wedding gift for owner's parents. When the owner's mother, Esther L. Hendrix, was 21 years old, she left home against her father's wishes to attend the Sloan-Hendrix Academy in Imbodden, AR. While a student, she met Norman E. Smith and they planned to marry in 1927. The women of Imboden who had connections to the Academy gave a shower for the couple. Hostesses for the shower made up kits of quilt blocks and every woman at the shower pieced a block for the quilt. Before the festivities, they got together and finished the quilt. It was then presented to the couple at the shower.

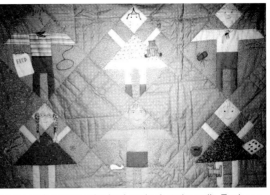

Garrett, Lynn S. (William)
Old Glory Chapter
Ancestor: Solomon Yeager, VA — #583113
This "Children of the World" quilt was made in 1986 in Franklin, TN by the members of the St. Paul Episcopal Church. The owner won this quilt at a church fund-raiser. It came with a little book with notes written by each person who had worked on the quilt. Each participant had received the basic pattern for the quilt and then individualized their blocks. Therefore, each child is different.

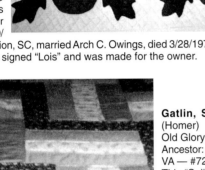

Garrison, Lois Owings (Claude R.)
Fort Nashborough Chapter
Ancestor: Solomon Langston, SC — #589541
This "Oak Leaf" quilt was made in 1920 at Gray Court, SC by the owner's mother, Evie Power Owings (born 10/20/1877 at Power Station, SC, married Arch C. Owings, died 3/28/1972 at Greenville, SC). The quilt was signed "Lois" and was made for the owner.

Gathman, Bertha Johnson (R.A.)
Old Glory Chapter
Ancestor: Hugh Montgomery, NC — #573162
This "Crazy" quilt was made in 1840 by Sophronia Dotson. The owner inherited the quilt from her grandmother, Mrs. Macon Bostick who had bought it from the quiltmaker.

Gatlin, Sue Smithson (Homer)
Old Glory Chapter
Ancestor: John Smithson, VA — #728349
This "Split Rail" quilt was made in 1988 in Franklin, TN by the owner.

Gatlin, Sue Smithson (Homer)
Old Glory Chapter
Ancestor: John Smithson, VA — #728349
This "Crazy" quilt was made in 1986 in Franklin. TN by the owner (born 4/13/1918 at Williamson County, TN).

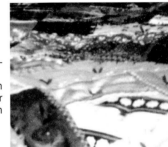

Gatlin, Sue Smithson (Homer)
Old Glory Chapter
Ancestor: John Smithson, VA — #728349
This "Crazy" quilt was made in 1988 in Williamson County, TN by the owner.

Giles, Martha Carothers (George B.)
Old Glory Chapter
Ancestor: William Jordan, VA — #636067
This "Wandering Foot/Turkey Tracks" quilt was made in 1870 in Williamson County, TN by the owner's grandmother, Martha Palmira Jordan Carthers (born 11/2/1846 in Williamson County, TN, married James Robert Carothers, died 2/9/1934). This quilt was passed to the owner by her grandmother.

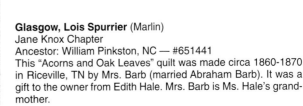

Glasgow, Lois Spurrier (Marlin)
Jane Knox Chapter
Ancestor: William Pinkston, NC — #651441
This "Acorns and Oak Leaves" quilt was made circa 1860-1870 in Riceville, TN by Mrs. Barb (married Abraham Barb). It was a gift to the owner from Edith Hale. Mrs. Barb is Ms. Hale's grandmother.

**Glover, Betty Shropshire** (William Lloyd)
Key Corner Chapter
Ancestor: Maximilian Conner, SC — #648600
This "Woolsey - Linsey" coverlet was made circa 1850 in Birchwood by the owner's great grandmother, Juda Carr Roark (married Joseph Roark, died at Birchwood, TN). It is made from wool and flax grown on the maker's farm. The Roark's gave it to their son, William Marion Roark, and his wife, Virginia Conner, who gave it to their daughter, Laura Roark Shropshire in 1936. She gave the coverlet to the current owner in 1970. According to the owner, there is a book in the Tennessee Archives that has pictures and a history of this coverlet and one belonging to her sister.

**Glover, Rita Lee Hankins** (Charles)
James Buckley Chapter
Ancestor: Mathias Harmon, VA — #665286
This "Dresden Plate" quilt was made in the 1930's in TN by the owner's special friend, Lois Johnson (born 12/10/1913, married Oscar B. Johnson). It was given to the owner by the maker.

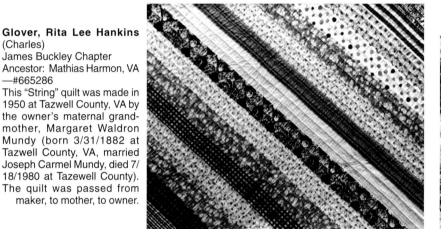

**Glover, Rita Lee Hankins** (Charles)
James Buckley Chapter
Ancestor: Mathias Harmon, VA —#665286
This "String" quilt was made in 1950 at Tazwell County, VA by the owner's maternal grandmother, Margaret Waldron Mundy (born 3/31/1882 at Tazwell County, VA, married Joseph Carmel Mundy, died 7/18/1980 at Tazewell County). The quilt was passed from maker, to mother, to owner.

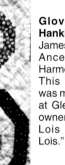

**Glover, Rita Lee Hankins** (Charles)
James Buckley Chapter
Ancestor: Mathias Harmon, VA —#665286
This "Umbrella" quilt was made in the 1930's at Gleason, TN by the owner's special friend, Lois Johnson "Aunt Lois."

**Goodman, Mary Gill** (William R.)
Charlotte Reeves Robertson Chapt.
Ancestor: Aaron Lockhart, SC — #550591
This "Crazy" quilt was made in Robertson County, TN by the owner's husband's grandmother, Minerva Murphy Head (born 3/25/1855 at Muhlenberg County, KY, married Hiram Jefferson Head, died 7/13/1930 at Springfield, TN). The owner's husband's aunt passed it down from his grandmother's belongings.

**Goodman, Mary Gill** (William R.)
Charlotte Reeves Robertson Chapt.
Ancestor: Aaron Lockhart, SC — #550591
This "Variation of a Blazing Star" quilt was made in Robertson County, TN. This quilt was found in the belongings of owner's great–grandmother, Hannah Lockert Bailey (born 2/24/1842 at Robertson County, TN, died 4/7/1952 in the same county).

**Googe, Luna Nell Morton** (George Walker)
Jackson-Madison Chapter
Ancestor: William McFerrin, VA — #739878
This "Old Triple Irish Chain" quilt was made in the 1830's at Booneville, MS. The quilt belonged to the owner's paternal great grandmother, Louisa Angeline Curlee Forbes. It was passed from Louisa to Laura Bettie Forbes Morton to the owner's father, Charles Cullen Morton, to the owner. Louisa was the daughter of Eleanor Duncan McFerrin, a Real Daughter, and a child of William McFerrin, the owner's Revolutionary War ancestor. Her DAR number was 32970

**Gordon, Evelyn Anderson** (Charles)
John Sevier Chapter
Ancestor: John McCluer, VA — #541217
This "Crazy" quilt was made in 1885 in Marion, VA by the owner's grandmother, Lucretia S. Lincoln (born 2/16/1862 at Marian, VA, married Reamon T. Lincoln, died 9/30/1945 at Marion). The quilt is dated "Feb 1885."

**Granstaff, Joanne**
French Lick Chapter
Ancestor: Dep QM General John Medearis, NC — #782924
This "Eight Pointed Star" quilt was made in the early 1900's in Wilson County by the owner's great grandmother, Emma Lanius Walker (born 1/12/1868 at Wilson County, TN, married William Bell Walker, died 11/30/1945 at Nashville, TN). It was passed from great grandmother, to grandmother, to mother, to owner.

**Granstaff, Mary Medearis** (John J.)
French Lick Chapter
Ancestor: Capt. John Medearis, NC — #776445
This "Lone Star" quilt was made in 1976 in Nashville, TN by Shelia Scott (born 3/1/1948 in Nashville) teacher at school where owner was principal. Owner received the quilt from Ms. Scott.

**Granstaff, Mary Medearis** (John J.)
French Lick Chapter
Ancestor: Capt. John Medearis, NC — #776445
This "Crazy" quilt was made in 1900 in Wilson County by the owner's grandmother, Emma Lanius Walker (born 1/12/1868 at Wilson County, TN, married William Bell Walker, died 11/30/1945 at Nashville, TN). It was passed from grandmother, to daughter, to her daughter, the current owner.

**Granstaff, Mary Medearis** (John J.)
French Lick Chapter
Ancestor: Capt. John Medearis, NC — #776445
This original applique quilt was made in 1985 in Nashville, TN by members of the Beta Upsilon Chapter of Delta Kappa Gamma sorority when the owner was president of this organization. It was made in celebration of the Golden Anniversary of Delta Kappa Gamma Society for Key Women Educators. It was displayed at this celebration in Sewanee, TN. Two squares were made by members of the French Lick DAR Chapter; Jane G. Dugger (4/1/1950, married Keith Dugger) and Joanne Granstaff (born 9/3/1953). Each piece has the initials of the person who made it.

**Graves, Jessie Wagner** (Henry)
Great Smokies Chapter
Ancestor: Zachariah Longley, MA— #765136
This "Arkansas Snow Flake" quilt was made circa 1940 in Oklahoma by a friend of the owner's parents, Amy Goetz, (married to Joseph Goetz). The owner received this quilt as a wedding gift in 1942.

**Graves, Jessie Wagner** (Henry)
Great Smokies Chapter
Ancestor: Zachariah Longley, MA — #765136
This "Cathedral Window" quilt was made in 1986 in Pigeon Forge, TN by the owner who says, "This is the first and last quilt I ever made."

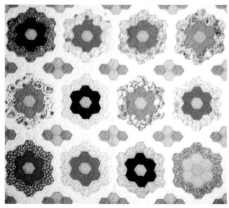

**Graves, Jessie Wagner** (Henry)
Great Smokies Chapter
Ancestor: Zachariah Longley, MA — #765136
This "Grandmother's Flower Garden" quilt was made in 1948 in Grant County, OK by the owner's husband's aunt, Tishie Graves Pierce (born 1/9/1891 at Blount County, TN, married Henry A. Pierce, died 7/22/1970 at Harper County, KS).

**Green, Jessie Sue Hutcheson** (Walter)
Cavett Station Chapter
Ancestor: John Carter, VA —#788939
This "Tulip" quilt was made in 1977 at Geraldine, AL by the owner's mother, Eva Mae Johnson Hutcheson (born 12/25/1917 at Marshall County, AL, married Bethel Boyd Hutcheson). The maker loved to make quilts for Chirstmas gifts. This one was made for the owner as a Christmas gift in 1977.

**Green, Jessie Sue Hutcheson** (Walter)
Cavett Station Chapter
Ancestor: John Carter, VA — #788939
This "Variation of an Eight Pointed Star/Christmas Star" quilt was made in 1986 at Geraldine, AL by the owner's mother, Eva Mae Johnson Hutcheson. This quilt was a Christmas gift to the owner in 1986.

**Green, Jessie Sue Hutcheson** (Walter)
Cavett Station Chapter
Ancestor: John Carter, VA —#788939
This "One Patch" quilt was made in 1965 at Jackson County, AL by the owner's grandmother, Ollie Mae Barnes Hutcheson (born 3/1896 at Jackson County, AL, married John Newton Hutcheson, died 8/1976 at DeKalb County, AL). When Ollie Mae died, she passed the quilt to the owner.

**Green, Jessie Sue Hutcheson** (Walter)
Cavett Station Chapter
Ancestor: John Carter, VA —#788939
This "50 States" quilt was made in 1996 at Geraldine, AL by the owner's mother, Eva Mae Johnson Hutcheson. The maker was 79 years old when she made this quilt.

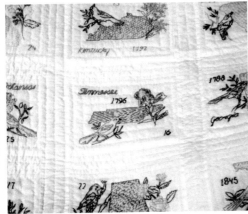

**Green, Jessie Sue Hutcheson** (Walter)
Cavett Station Chapter
Ancestor: John Carter, VA — #788939
This "Bicentennial" quilt was made in LaCrosse, VA by the owner's mother-in-law, Pink Irene Taylor Walker (born 11/18/1907 at Mecklenburg County, VA, married Clem Walker, died 10/1993 at Mecklenburg County). It was made to celebrate the Bicentennial of the United States and given as a gift to the owner.

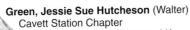

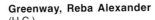

**Green, Jessie Sue Hutcheson** (Walter)
Cavett Station Chapter
Ancestor: John Carter, VA — #788939
This "Fan" quilt was made in 1935 at Marshall County, AL by the owner's mother, Eva Mae Johnson Hutcheson. It was made the year after the maker married. When the owner got married, her mother took the quilt from the cedar chest and gave it to her as a wedding gift.

**Greenway, Reba Alexander** (H.C.)
Gen. William Lenior Chapter
Ancestor: George Huffaker, VA — #583331
This "Sixteen Patch" quilt was made circa 1896-1900 in Loudon County, TN by owner's mother, Jennie Matlock Alexander (born 1/10/1880 at Loudon County, TN, married Joe Alexander, died 5/26/1965 at Loudon). The quilt was passed from Jennie Alexander to Reba Greenway. The owner received the quilt at the death of her mother.

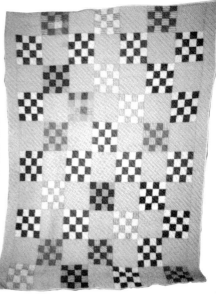

**Greenwood, Judy Gore** (Elmer A. "Tom")
Roaring River Chapter
Ancestor: John Gore, VA —#787788
This "Cathedral Window" quilt was made in 1995 at Overton County, TN by the owner's mother-in-law, Zelpha Bowman Greenwood (born 11/1921 at Overton County).

**Gregory, Ellen Hoge** (Bruce)
Charlotte Reeves Robertson Chapter
Ancestor: James Robertson, VA — #650213
This "Cross and Crown" quilt was made circa 1920's at Cross Plains, TN by the owner's great great aunt, Julie Ozella Roney Austin (born 1857 at Cross Plains, married Lon Austin, died circa 1935 at Cross Plains). Passed from maker, to owner's grandmother, to her mother, who gave it to current owner.

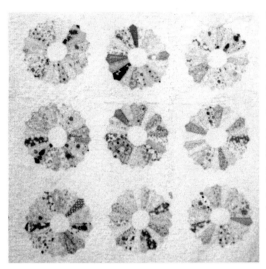

**Gregory, Ellen Hoge** (Bruce)
Charlotte Reeves Robertson Chapter
Ancestor: James Robertson, VA — #650213
This "Dresden Plate" quilt was made 1917-18 in Chattanooga, TN by owner's great grandmother, Hattie Wild (born in Hamilton County, TN, married Thomas Wild). The quilt was made for owner's grandmother, Irene Wild Hoge, as a wedding present.

**Griffin, Mary Jane Ragsdale** (Walter Wanzel)
Andrew Bogle Chapt.
Ancestor: Boston Graves, NC — #787356
This "Yo Yo" quilt was made in 1935-38 in Morgan, GA by the owner's mother-in-law, Trudie Rice Griffin (born 10/2/1905 at Morgan, GA, married Walter Wright Griffin, died 1/12/1997 at Edison, GA). It was used as a bedspread in the main and guest bedrooms. The quilt was passed from maker's estate, to the current owner. There are 2020 yo yo's in the quilt.

**Griffin, Mary Jane Ragsdale** (Walter Wanzel)
Andrew Bogle Chapt.
Ancestor: Boston Graves, NC — #787356
This embroidered "Nursery Animal" quilt was made in early 1927 in Knox County, TN by the owner's mother, Sophronia Burdetti Thompson Ragsdale ( born 10/5/1899 at Rockcastle County, KY, married Ira Vincent Ragsdale, a University of Tennessee Physics teacher, died 3/11/1975 at Knoxville, TN). Quiltmaker's husband made the frames used for quilting. Owner's children Walter Vincent (born 1952, Glenn Edwin (born 1954) and Edwin Wanzel (born 1964) used this quilt at their "Grammie's" house. Owner's grandchildren Travis Vincent Griffin (born 1977) and Sophronia Pear Griffin born 1998) now use this quilt when they visit their grandmother, Mary Jane.

**Griffin, Mary Jane Ragsdale** (Walter Wanzel)
Andrew Bogle Chapt.
Ancestor: Boston Graves, NC — #787356
There are two "Dresden Plate" quilts made exactly alike for twin beds. The quilts were made in Fountain City, TN in 1935 by the owner's mother, Sophronia Burdetti Thompson Ragsdale. These quilts were given to the owner after she married.

**Griffin, Mary Jane Ragsdale** (Walter Wanzel)
Andrew Bogle Chapt.
Ancestor: Boston Graves, NC — #787356
There are two "Dutch Doll/ Sunbonnet Sue" quilts made in 1935-36 at Fountain City, TN. They were made by the owner's mother, Sophronia Burdetti Thompson Ragsdale. These quilts were given to the owner after she married.

**Griffin, Mary Jane Ragsdale** (Walter Wanzel)
Andrew Bogle Chapt.
Ancestor: Boston Graves, NC — #787356
This original "University of Tennessee 1998 National Football Champions" quilt was made to order in 1999 at Knoxville, TN by the owner's dressmaker, Denice Weaver. In 1926 the owner's father, Ira Vincent Ragsdale, came with his bride, Sophronia Burdetti Thompson Ragsdale, to Knoxville, TN to join the University of Tennessee Physics faculty. The Ragsdales became avid football fans as are three generations of descendants. Ten UT graduate and undergraduate degrees have been earned by Ira Vincent and his descendants. This orange and white quilt is an appropriate family keepsake.

**Grimmer, Adelyn Summer** (Carl)
Watauga Chapter
Ancestor: Benjamin Mileham, VA—#609902
This "Wild Goose Chase" quilt was made circa 1875 in South Mississippi by the owner's great aunt, Maria. The owner inherited the quilt through her father's family in 1962. It hangs on a quilt rack in the owner's guest bedroom.

**Grimmer, Adelyn Summer** (Carl)
Watauga Chapter
Ancestor: Benjamin Mileham, VA—#609902
This "Wild Goose Chase" quilt was made circa 1875 by the owner's great aunt, Maria in Mississippi. This quilt is a part of the owner's memories as a child when the family would take it to the park for picnics, put food on it, sit on it, and use it for naps. The

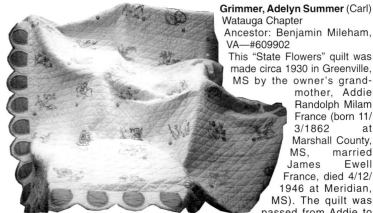

**Grimmer, Adelyn Summer** (Carl)
Watauga Chapter
Ancestor: Benjamin Mileham, VA—#609902
This "State Flowers" quilt was made circa 1930 in Greenville, MS by the owner's grandmother, Addie Randolph Milam France (born 11/3/1862 at Marshall County, MS, married James Ewell France, died 4/12/1946 at Meridian, MS). The quilt was passed from Addie to daughter, Aileen Summer to current owner.

family thought of it as so "ugly" it could not be of value. but since old quilts are "in" now, it has a new home hanging on a quilt rack for display and it is never used.

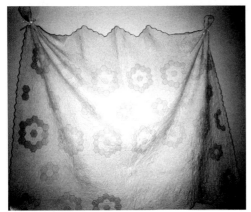

**Groves, Sue McFarland**
Robert Cooke Chapter
Ancestor: David Hale—#655861
This "Grandmother's Flower Garden" quilt was made circa 1948 at Springfield, MA by the owner's paternal grandmother, Virginia Hunt McFarland (born 1/18/1875 at Baltimore, MD, married William James Renwick MacFarland, died 6/25/1958 at Hornell, NY).

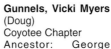

**Gunnels, Vicki Myers**
(Doug)
Coyotee Chapter
Ancestor: George Oliver, NC — #779559
This " Trip Around The World" quilt was made in 1954 in Greenback, TN by the owner's grandmother, Ella Long Hammontree (born 8/10/1900 at Greenback, TN, married Leon Hammontree, died 10/11/1992 at Greenback)

and great aunt, Julia Lois Thompson (born 4/17/1893 at Blount County, TN, married Charles Thompson, died 5/18/1978 in the same county). "Granny" and "Aunt Julie" made this quilt for the owner while they were "sitting" for the owner's great grandfather, John Long, during his illness.

**Gunnels, Vicki Myers**
(Doug)
Coyotee Chapter
Ancestor: George Oliver, NC — #779559
This "Starry Nights" quilt was made in 1968 at Greenback, TN by the owner's grandmother, Ella Long Hammontree. It was given to the owner by her grandmother when she graduated from high school. The quiltmaker gave each of her 10 grandchildren a quilt for their high school graduation. To insure that each one got a quilt, she made the ones for the younger grandchildren in advance.

**Gunnels, Vicki Myers**
(Doug)
Coyotee Chapter
Ancestor: George Oliver, NC — #779559
This "Cathedral Window" quilt was made in the 1960's in Greenback, TN by the owner's grandmother. The quiltmaker originally gave the quilt to the owner's mother, Johnnie Hammontree Myers and then it was passed to the current owner.

**Gustafson, Bettie Parker** (L. Gene)
River City Chapter
Ancestor: Abraham Bolt, Sr., VA—#708627
This "Sister's Choice" friendship quilt was pieced circa 1940 at Marshall County, MS by the ladies of the Marshall County Home Demonstration Club. The owner's aunt, Susie Parker Williams, was a home demonstration agent in that county. The owner had the quilt quilted by a group of ladies who quilt at the Bolton Community Center in Shelby County, TN. The owner plans to have this quilt displayed in Marshall County, so that descendants of the makers can see the finished quilt.

**Gustafson, Bettie Parker** (L. Gene)
River City Chapter
Ancestor: Abraham Bolt, Sr., VA—#708627
This second "Sister's Choice" friendship quilt was also pieced circa 1940 at Marshall County, MS by the Home Demonstration Club and quilted by the ladies at the Bolton Community Center.

**Gustafson, Bettie Parker** (L. Gene)
River City Chapter
Ancestor: Abraham Bolt, Sr., VA—#708627
This "Grandmother's Flower Garden" quilt was made circa the 1920's at Corinth, MS by the owner's step mother, Vivian Irene Prince Parker (born 1/22/1904 at Prentiss County, MS, married Homer William Parker). the owner acquired this quilt when her step mother entered the nursing home in 1996. The quilt was documented by the Quilt Search Project of the Mississippi Quilter's Association.

**Gustafson, Bettie Parker** (L. Gene)
River City Chapter
Ancestor: Abraham Bolt, Sr., VA—#708627
This "Dresden Plate" quilt was made circa 1985 at Prentiss County, MS by the owner's sister-in-law, Shirley Mae Holland Parker (born 8/2/1928 at Detriot, MI, married William Raymond Parker, died 2/11/1990 at Prentiss County). This quilt was pieced on the sewing machine.

**Gustafson, Bettie Parker** (L. Gene)
River City Chapter
Ancestor: Abraham Bolt, Sr., VA—#708627
This "Bow Tie" quilt was made circa 1890 at Randolph County, AL by the owner's great aunt, Nancy Ann "Tweet" Parker Norred (born 1/20/1863 at Bibb County, GA, married Larken S. Norred, died 11/14/1960 at Woodland, AL). The maker gave this quilt to the owner's step mother who gave it to the owner.

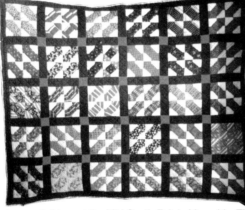

The quilt received a 2nd place red ribbon at the Mid-South Fair in Memphis, TN in the "Every Day Quilt" category. This quilt was documented by the Quilt Search Proejct of the Mississippi Quilter's Association.

**Gustafson, Bettie Parker** (L. Gene)
River City Chapter
Ancestor: Abraham Bolt, Sr., VA—#708627
This "Poppy" quilt was made circa 1980 at Panola County, MS by a friend of the owner's aunt who lived at Panola. The owner received the quilt from her aunt, Lena Pearl Parker Pope, who she cared for in her last years.

**Gustafson, Bettie Parker** (L. Gene)
River City Chapter
Ancestor: Abraham Bolt, Sr., VA—#708627
This "Colonial Lady" quilt was pieced circa 1935 at Prentiss County, MS by the owner's mother, Callie Bonds "Bonnie" Robertson Parker (born 8/9/1901, married Homer William Parker, died 7/27/1946 at Prentiss County). It was given to the owner when she married in 1957. The owner had the quilt quilted by Mrs. Johnnie Roach Pitts who lived near Shelby Forrest in Shelby County, TN.

**Gwaltney, Ann Miriam Shanks** (William)
French Lick Chapter
Ancestor: Capt. William Jared, VA —#776505
This coverlet was made circa 1823 in Tennessee by the owner's great grandmother, Dorcas Byrne (born 12/10/1803, married Joseph Jared 10/31/1829, died 12/20/1833 at Putnam County, TN). Photos and history of the coverlet are at the University of Maryland since 1997. The coverlet was passed from maker, to Carolyn Jared Kerr, to Kerr Boyd, to Dona Boyd Shanks, to current owner.

**Haas, Ann George** (William R.)
Hatchie Chapter
Ancestor: Jonathan Pickens, SC — #638496
This "Princess Feather" quilt was made by someone in the Jackson family (owner's great grandparents) around 1850. It was passed down from Armon O. Jackson, to Jesse C. Jackson, to Frances Jackson, to owner's husband William R. Haas.

**Haas, Ann George** (William R.)
Hatchie Chapter
Ancestor: Jonathan Pickens, SC — #638496
This "Whig's Defeat" quilt made around 1800 by someone in the Jackson family (owner's great grandparents). Passed down from Robert Jackson, to Armon O. Jackson, to Jesse C. Jackson, to Frances V. Jackson, to Blanche O. Barker, to owner's husband, William R. Haas.

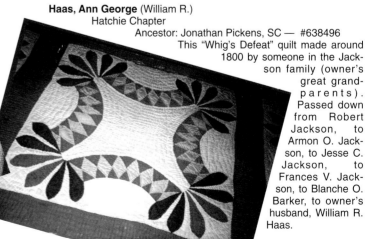

**Haas, Ann George** (William R.)
Hatchie Chapter
Ancestor: Jonathan Pickens, SC — #638496
This "Tulip" quilt made before 1857 by owner's great great grandmother, Lucinda (Honnow) Jackson in Hardeman or McNairy County, Tennessee. The quiltmaker was born around 1809 and died around 1844. It was given to the quiltmaker's son Jesse Cannon Jackson as a wedding gift in 1857. It was passed down from Armon Jackson, to Jessee Jackson, to Frances Barker, to Blanche O. Barker, to William Haas. His grandmother, Frances V. Jackson Barker, told the owner that the quilt was hidden in the smokehouse during the War Between the States. Her father, Jesse C. Jackson showed her where it was stained while it was hidden.

**Hackney, Virginia Scott** (Joseph)
Mary Blount Chapter
Ancestor: Robert Shields, VA — #756915
This "Dutch Doll/Sunbonnet Sue" quilt was made in 1994 in Blount County, TN by the owner's mother-in-law, Margaret Hackney (born 2/25/1919, married Hugh Mike Hackney, died 8/11/1994). It was a birthday gift to Megan Hackney on her 10th birthday. The quiltmaker died before the quilt was finished, but the family was able to get someone else to finish it.

**Haff, Lydia Moore** (R.W., Sr.)
Chucalissa Chapter
Ancestor: Captain Thomas Butler, PA — #756090
This "Hit and Miss" quilt is a tied quilt made in TX in the early 1900's. The quilt maker is unknown. The quilt was brought to Whitehaven, TN from Houston, TX in the 1960's by owner's uncle.

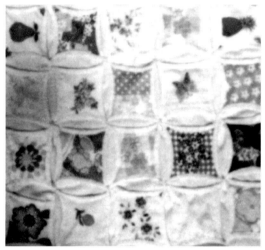

**Hagood, Beatrice Simpson** (A.C.)
John Sevier Chapter
Ancestor: William Worthington, SC — #402340
This "Cathedral Window" quilt was made in 1975-79 in Johnson City, TN by the owner (11/19/1906 in Fayette County, AL).

**Hale, Mary Virginia**
Samuel Doak Chapter
Ancestor: Capt. Landrum Younger, VA —#718056
This "Tree of Life" quilt was made by the owner's aunt, Mary Delilah Hale Hurley (born 9/24/1868 at Cocke County, TN, married James A. Hurley, died 9/17/1904 at Hamblen County, TN). Mary had a quilting party at her home. This was in honor of her brother, Jim's wife, Laura Inman Hale. They were married 11/2/1898. It was a cold November day when an unexpected guest came by to warm, and play a joke on the quilters. This was Laura's nephew, Ben A. Davis. His joke was to stitch his name and November 4, 1898 on the quilt. This joke proved to be important later on. It was Laura's request that this quilt remain in the Hale family.

**Hale, Mary Virginia**
Samuel Doak Chapter
Ancestor: Capt. Landrum Younger, VA —#718056
This "Rose of Sharon Variation" quilt was made in 1850-60 at Greene County, TN by the owner's grandmother, Catherine Ottinger (born 5/20/1835 at Greene County, TN, married Chadrack H. Inman, died 9/6/1917 at Cocke County, TN). This quilt was hidden in an ashhopper during the War Between the States on Peter Ottinger's farm in Caney Branch Community in Greene County, TN.

**Hall, Ella Merle**
Samuel Doak Chapter
Ancestor: John Helm, VA — #613343
This "Poppy" quilt was made by owner's great grandmother, Elizabeth Rodgers Helm (1808-1886) around 1820 in Jefferson County, TN. She made the quilt before her marriage in 1822 to William Boyd Helm. She gave the quilt to her son, William Dela Fletcher Helm and his wife, Margaret McNabb Helm, circa 1860's. When Margaret died the quilt was passed to her daughter, Virginia Helm Hall. When she died in September 1954, the quilt was passed to the current owner.

**Hall, Frances Capps** (Maynard)
Old Glory Chapter
Ancestor: John Neblett, VA — #418569
This "Strip" quilt was made by owner's mother-in-law, Kate Alice Davis Hall, in the 1940's in Wise County, VA. The quilt maker was born in Wise County, VA March 28, 1891 and died in the same county December 4, 1965. She was married to Fred Tharpe Hall.

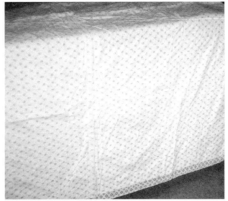

**Hall, Frances Capps**
(Maynard)
Old Glory Chapter
Ancestor: John Neblett,
VA — #418569
This whole cloth pattern was also made by the owner's mother-in-law, Kate Alice Davis Hall in Wise County, VA during the 1940's.

**Hall, Sarah Alexander**
(John R.)
Coytee Chapter
Ancestor: John Alexander, NC — # 646328
This "Double Wedding Ring" quilt was made by the owner's mother-in-law, Carrie Cleo Calloway Hall (1890-1940) in Greenback, TN in the 1930's. It was passed from Mrs. Carrie Hall to current owner. She was married to Dr. Joe Hall.

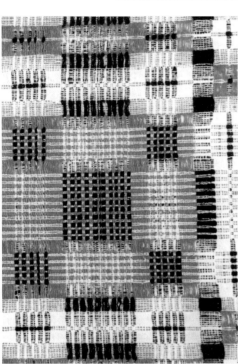

**Hall, Shirley Ridings**
(Ralph G.)
Coytee Chapter
Ancestor: James Taylor, NC — #598519
This woven coverlet was made in Blount County, TN circa 1852-60 by Elvira Howard Hall, the owner's husband's great grandmother, (born 3/3/1832 in Monroe County, TN, died 7/8/1902 in Blount County, TN). She was married to William S. Hall. The wool was from sheep raised by the family. The coverlet was acquired by the owner in 1953. It was passed down from the owner's husband's great grandmother, to his grandfather, to his father, to the owner.

**Hall, Shirley Ridings**
(Ralph G.)
Coytee Chapter
Ancestor: James Taylor, NC — #598519
This "Wild Rose Variation "quilt was given to the owner by her grandmother, Mrs. J.D. Hughes.

**Hamilton, Ann Mitchell**
(O.L., Jr.)
Volunteer Chapter
Ancestor: Thomas McCulloch, VA — #405744
This "Crazy" quilt was made in 1887-88 at Arlington, VA by the owner's grandmother, Mrs. A.C. Honaker (born 8/20/1864 at Chilhowie, VA, died 9/18/1953 at Bristol, VA).

**Hamilton, Ann Mitchell**
(O.L., Jr.)
Volunteer Chapter
Ancestor: Thomas McCulloch, VA — #405744
This "Crazy" quilt was made in 1905-06 at Arlington, VA by the owner's grandmother, Mrs. A.C. Honaker.

**Hamilton, Ann Mitchell**
(O.L., Jr.)
Volunteer Chapter
Ancestor: Thomas McCulloch, VA —#405744
This "Grandmother's Flower Garden" quilt was made in 1945 at Bristol, VA by the owner's grandmother, Mrs. A.C. Honaker.

**Hamilton, Ann Mitchell**
(O.L., Jr.)
Volunteer Chapter
Ancestor: Thomas McCulloch, VA —#405744
This "Dresden Plate" quilt was made in 1935-36 at Bristol, VA by the owner's mother, Mrs. Baker Mitchell (born 11/16/1886 at Chilhowe, VA, died 3/3/1971 at Bristol, TN).

**Hanks, Joan Hill** (George R.)
Moccasin Bend Chapter
Ancestor: Martin Shofner, NC — #656482
This "Crazy" quilt was made by the owner's aunt, Edith Gattis Gilmore (born 4/1895 at Shelbyville, TN, married William Gilmore, died 10/1975 at Rutherford County, TN).

**Hanks, Joan Hill** (George R.)
Moccasin Bend Chapter
Ancestor: Martin Shofner, NC — #656482
This "Patchwork String" quilt was made circa 1900-1910 at Rutherford County, TN by the owner's great grand-mother, Elvira Ann Williams Green (born 7/7/1841 at Bedford County, TN, married James Garrett Green, died 2/22/1929 at Rutherford County, TN).

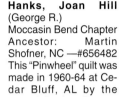
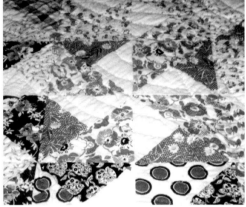

**Hanks, Joan Hill** (George R.)
Moccasin Bend Chapter
Ancestor: Martin Shofner, NC —#656482
This "Pinwheel" quilt was made in 1960-64 at Cedar Bluff, AL by the owner's husband's aunt, Effie Theodoria Watters (born 4/17/1902 at Cedar Bluff, died 5/1981 at Chattanooga, TN).

**Hanks, Joan Hill** (George R.)
Moccasin Bend Chapter
Ancestor: Martin Shofner, NC —#656482
This "Dresden Plate" quilt was made circa 1870's-80's at Bedford County, TN by the owner's great grand-mother, Julia B. Euless Gattis (born 8/12/1827 at Bedford County, married Thomas A. Gattis, died 7/5/1910 at Bedford County).

**Hansbrough, Maxine Sims** (Charles)
Glover's Trace Chapter
Ancestor: Alexander McCorkle, NC — #532281
The coverlet was made circa 1850 by the owner's great uncle, Robert Sims' mother-in-law, Harriet Bliss Higgins (born 1832 in Vermont, married to John Higgins, died 1895 in Lexington, KY). The coverlet was probably made in Vermont about 1850. Owner's father acquired it in 1941 at the death of his uncle. The coverlet was given to the owner by her father.

**Harris, Linda Lewis** (Donald)
Chickasaw Bluff Chapter
Ancestor: Henry Hastings, NC — #775789
This "Modified Nine Patch" quilt was pieced in 1938 at White County, AR by the owner's aunt, Faye E. Lewis (born 7/17/1921, died 7/31/1940 in White County, AR). The quilt top was passed down from Faye Lewis to Maggie Lewis to Linda Lewis Harris. The owner quilted the quilt in 1995.

**Harris, Linda Lewis** (Donald)
Chickasaw Bluff Chapter
Ancestor: Henry Hastings, NC — #775789
This "Courthouse Square" quilt was pieced by the owner's aunt in 1938. The top was passed from Faye Lewis to Maggie Lewis to Linda Lewis Harris. It was quilted by the owner in 1986.

**Harris, Lynne Stallings** (Roger R.)
Key Corner Chapter
Ancestor: John Perry, NC —#785767
This "Double Wedding Ring" quilt was made in the 1920's at Halls, TN by the owner's grandmother, Louisa Morris Stallings (born 10/1877 at Mayfield, KY, married John Frank Stallings, died 1/4/1937 at Halls, TN).

**Harris, Mary Frances Turner** (George)
Old Glory Chapter
Ancestor: William Turner, NC — #558753
This "Dresden Plate" quilt was made in 1930 in Henry County, TN by the owner's mother, Addie H. Turner (born in 1877, married William Claude Turner, died in 1943). The quilt was passed from mother to daughter.

**Harris, Mary Frances Turner** (George)
Old Glory Chapter
Ancestor: William Turner, NC — #558753
The maker of this "Grandmother's Flower Garden" quilt is unknown.

**Harris, Mary Frances Turner** (George)
Old Glory Chapter
Ancestor: William Turner, NC — #558753
This "Labyrinth" quilt was made by the owner's mother, Addie H. Turner, before 1943 in Paris, TN

**Harris, Mary Frances Turner** (George)
Old Glory Chapter
Ancestor: William Turner, NC — #558753
This "Double Wedding Ring" quilt was made in 1932 at Paris, TN by owner's mother, Addie H. Turner . It was passed from mother to daughter.

**Harris, Mary S. Gaylor** (Robert W.)
Clinch Bend Chapter
Ancestor: Jacob Moser, MD —#776367
This "Variation of Rose of Sharon" quilt was made by the owner's great great grandmother, Carmack Harris (died at Whitwell, TN, married Cowan Russell Harris). The quilt was given to the owner by her mother. Her father told her that it had been made in 1836 and was his mother's quilt.

**Harris, Mary S. Gaylor** (Robert W.)
Clinch Bend Chapter
Ancestor: Jacob Moser, MD —#776367
This "Variation of Rose of Sharon" quilt was made by the owner's great great grandmother, Carmack Harris.

**Harris, Mary S. Gaylor** (Robert W.)
Clinch Bend Chapter
Ancestor: Jacob Moser, MD — #776367
This "Double T" quilt was made by the owner's great great grandmother, Carmack Harris.

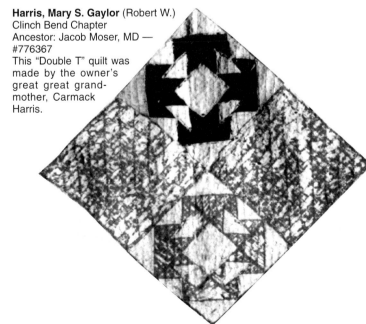

**Harris, Mildred Hale**
Travelers Rest Chapter
Ancestor: John Hale, NC — #591645
This "Princess Feather" quilt was made circa 1855 in Newberry, SC by the owner's grandmother, Mary Elizabeth Houselle Hentz (married David Julius Hentz, died in Newberry County, SC in 1936).

**Hartman, Deborah Looper** (Henry)
Jane Knox Chapter
Ancestor: Captain Robert Sevier, NC
— #769582
This "Churn Dash" quilt was made in the 1930's by owner's great grandmother Nancy Julie Ann Speck (born 5/16/1881, died 5/5/1956 in Overton County, TN). Her husband was William Horace Speck. The quilt was made in Overton County, TN and was passed from great grandmother, to grandmother, to owner.

**Hartman, Deborah Looper**
(Henry)
Jane Knox Chapter
Ancestor: Captain Robert Sevier, NC — #769582
This "Sunbonnet Sue" quilt was also made by the owner's great grandmother, Julie Ann Speck, in the 1930's in Overton County, TN.

**Hartman, Deborah Looper** (Henry)
Jane Knox Chapter
Ancestor: Captain Robert Sevier, NC — #769582
This "Chimney Sweep" quilt was made in the early 1900's by owner's great great grandmother, Delilah Narrod Qualls (born in 1861, died in 1934 in Overton County, TN). Her husband was Gatewood Qualls. This quilt was given to the owner by her grandmother who received it from her grandmother.

**Hartman, Deborah Looper** (Henry)
Jane Knox Chapter
Ancestor: Captain Robert Sevier, NC — #769582
This "Crazy Friendship" quilt was made in 1970 at Overton County, TN by the owner's grandmother, Mabel Looper (born 5/15/1903, married Roy Looper, died 12/26/1979). The quilt was signed by her friends. She gave the quilt to the current owner.

**Hatley, Joan Travis** (Elton)
Glover's Trace Chapter
Ancestor: William Robinson, NC — #634209
This "Prairie Star" quilt, made in 1998, was purchased by the owner at a craft shop in New Brunswick Canada in 1998.

**Hatley, Joan Travis** (Elton)
Glover's Trace Chapter
Ancestor: William Robinson, NC — #634209
This 'Modified Nine Patch' quilt was made by Vivian Bain Lewis (born circa 1902 at Benton County, TN, died circa 1996 in the same county).

**Hatley, Joan Travis** (Elton)
Glover's Trace Chapter
Ancestor: William Robinson, NC — #634209
This "Friendship Sampler" quilt was made by members of the Cedar Grove Church of Christ in 1994, and was purchased by the owner as part of a fundraiser for the Christian School. The center block is embroidered with the name of the church and the date.

**Haynes, Janie DeCourley**
Chickasaw Bluff Chapter
Ancestor: Francis Cypert, Jr., NC — #699334
This "Bow Tie" quilt was made in Hardin County, TN by owner's grandmother, Lillie Abel Tidwell (born 6/30/1895, married Joe A. Tidwell, died 7/1/1975 in Hardin County, TN).

**Haynes, Janie DeCourley**
Chickasaw Bluff Chapter
Ancestor: Francis Cypert, Jr., NC — #699334
This "Pansy" quilt was made by the owner's grandmother in Hardin County, TN in the 1960's and was given as a wedding gift to owner. Mrs. Tidwell gave each of her grandchildren two handmade quilts and two feather pillows for wedding gifts. She let each grandchild pick the quilt tops from her cedar chest. There were always many patterns to choose from. The owner's favorites were those that included the scraps of fabric from clothes her mother had made for her.

**Haynes, Janie DeCourley**
Chickasaw Bluff Chapter
Ancestor: Francis Cypert, Jr., NC — #699334
This "Lone Star" quilt was also made by Mrs. Tidwell in the 1960's.

**Haynes, Janie DeCourley**
Chickasaw Bluff Chapter
Ancestor: Francis Cypert, Jr., NC — #699334
This "Hands All Around" quilt was made by owner's ex-husband's grandmother who lived in Hardin County, TN.

**Haynes, Janie DeCourley**
Chickasaw Bluff Chapter
Ancestor: Francis Cypert, Jr., NC — #699334
This "Wheel of Fortune" quilt was made in the 1920's by the owner's great grandmother, Mary Elizabeth Clement Abel (born in Hardin County, TN 1/1865, married Andrew Jackson Abel, died there 4/3/1928). The calico fabric for this quilt was purchased at a store in Cerro Gordo, TN for as much as $.10 per yard. The unbleached muslin used for the back was died with walnuts. The quilt has three rounded corners. The cotton batting was grown on the farm and she carded the cotton to make the batts.

**Head, Mary Sue Corbin** (Bobby M.)
Charlotte Reeves Robertson Chapter
Ancestor: Captain John Miller, VA — #712941
This "Crazy" quilt was made circa 1902 by owner's husband's grandmother, Julia Huskey Head (born 12/28/1863 in Robertson County TN, married Miles Thurston Head, died in the same County 4/25/1962). This quilt was passed from Julia Head, to son Morris Head, to his son Bobby M. Head.

**Helton, Nancy Rogers** (William)
Mary Blount Chapter
Ancestor: Nicholas Gibbs, NC — #778724
This "Trip Around the World" quilt was made in the 1960's at Knoxville, TN by the owner's maternal grandmother, Dora Roley who married John Wesley. This quilt was made especially for the owner.

**Hemmrich, Nancy Garrison** (Geoffrey)
Ft. Nashborough Chapter
Ancestor: William Halbert, VA — #569720
This "Wind Blown Star" quilt was made circa 1900 at Gray Court, SC by Miss Allie Babb.

**Henderson, Rozetta Thompson**
Rhea-Craig Chapter
Ancestor: Richard Williams, NC — #782082
This "Crazy" quilt was made in 1995 at Spring City, TN by owner's daughter, Marcia Conner (born 1954 in Leoti, KS, married James Connors). This quilt was passed from daughter to mother. This quilt is made from antique linens such as dresser scarves, table cloths, dollies, lace collars, trim, armchair covers, pillow cases, and bread covers. The embroidery, or needlework parts, were cut away and sewn on to sixteen inch squares of backing made from a sheet. The quilt recycles old linens and preserves family heirlooms.

**Hendricks, Ruth Theile** (Hugh)
The Crab Orchard Chapter
Ancestor: Capt. James Jones, NC —#406796
This "Dresden Plate" quilt was made at Crossville, TN by Inez Wren. The owner bought this quilt from the maker.

**Hendrix, Katy McCrary** (J. Eason)
James Buckley Chapter
Ancestor: John Redden, VA —#742485
This tacked wool comforter was made in the 1890's at Trousdale County, TN by the Lauderdale Family, the owner's brother-in-law's family.

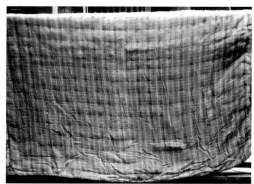

**Henry, Patsy Gooch** (E. Parman)
Old Glory Chapter
Ancestor: James Turner, NC — #601996
This is an original design quilt. The center was designed and made by Allison and Joe Arnold and features the Nolansville United Methodist Church. They made it for her mother, Dot Arnold as a Christmas gift in 1990 a week before she had a heart attack. When she recovered later in 1991, she and some friends at the church pieced the area that frames the picture. Dot finished the quilt and sold sections around the squares for people's names to be inscribed which she wrote on the quilt herself. The owner's mother's and father's names are on the quilt. The money was given to the Church's building fund. A year later the quilt was sold at auction during the church festival to Mrs. Boswell. Again the money went to the Church's building fund. In 1993, Mrs. Boswell donated the quilt back to the Church to be sold once more at auction. Owner purchased it and intends to pass it to future generations in the family.

**Henry, Patsy Gooch**
(E. Parman)
Old Glory Chapter
Ancestor:    James Turner, NC — #601996
This "Eight Pointed Star" quilt was made in the 1930's in Columbia, TN by the owner's maternal grandmother, Pattie Bellafant Akin (born 5/11/1863 in Culleoka, TN, married Melville Cox Akin, died 5/30/1941 in Columbia, TN). The quilt was passed from maker, to grandmother, to mother, to daughter.

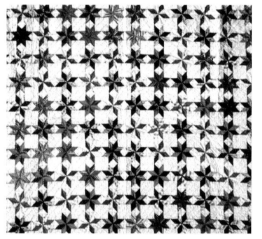

**Henson, Doris Owens**
(Flodie)
Glover's Trace Chapter
Ancestor:    Alexander Wheatley, NC — #459816
This "Dresden Plate" quilt was made in 1969 in Camden, TN by the owner's sister, Mildred Owens Reichard (born 11/17/1917 in Medina, TN, married Edgar Reichard, died 11/10/1979 in Camden, TN). The owner received the quilt from her niece, Dorris Arnold.

**Henson, Doris Owens**
(Flodie)
Glover's Trace Chapter
Ancestor:    Alexander Wheatley, NC — #459816
This "Grandmother's Flower Garden" quilt was made in 1970 in Camden, TN by the owner's sister.

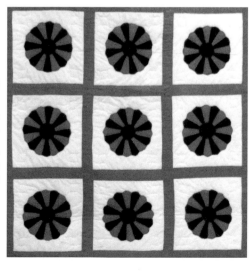

**Henson, Doris Owens**
(Flodie)
Glover's Trace Chapter
Ancestor: Alexander Wheatley, NC — #459816
This "Dresden Plate" quilt was made by owner's sister in Camden, TN in 1969.

**Henson, Doris Owens**
(Flodie)
Glover's Trace Chapter
Ancestor: Alexander Wheatley, NC — #459816
This "Blocks" quilt was made by owner in 1997 in Camden, TN.

**Henson, Doris Owens**
(Flodie)
Glover's Trace Chapter
Ancestor: Alexander
Wheatley, NC — #459816
This "Martha Star" quilt was
made in 1987 by the owner
in Palmetto, FL.

**Henson, Doris Owens**
(Flodie)
Glover's Trace Chapter
Ancestor: Alexander
Wheatley, NC — #459816
This "Sunbonnet Sue" quilt
was made in 1955 in
Westchester, IL by the
owner.

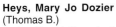

**Henson, Margaret Barnes** (Wallace)
Buffalo River Chapter
Ancestor: Conner Dowd, NC — #546513
This "Ohio Star" Amish quilt was made in 1983 in Etheridge, TN by Sarah L. Zook (born in Ohio, married Noah Zook, died 1992 in Etheridge, TN). The quilt was purchased by the owner and will be passed down to the owner's only daughter, Rosemary.

**Henson, Margaret Barnes** (Wallace)
Buffalo River Chapter
Ancestor: Conner Dowd, NC — #546513
This "Double Wedding Ring" quilt was made in Lawrenceberg, TN in the 1920's or 30's by Mrs. Elvis Mayberry. The quilt top was purchased in 1995 at a benefit auction for a sick grandchild. The uniqueness of this quilt is that it is made from flour and feed sacks. It was pieced by hand using the string that was raveled from the sack to open it. The Amish quilted the quilt in Etheridge, TN.

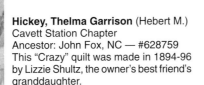

**Heys, Mary Jo Dozier**
(Thomas B.)
Judge David Campbell Chapter
Ancestor: Reuben Cook, GA — #746866
This "Crazy" quilt was made by Mrs. Rogers, the mother of the owner's close friend, Mrs. Hart who is over 100 years old. The quilt was made in the early 1900's in Iowa and then it was passed from the maker, to the owner's daughter, and then given to the owner as a gift.

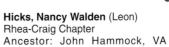

**Hickey, Thelma Garrison** (Hebert M.)
Cavett Station Chapter
Ancestor: John Fox, NC — #628759
This "Crazy" quilt was made in 1894-96 by Lizzie Shultz, the owner's best friend's granddaughter.

**Hickey, Thelma Garrison** (Hebert M.)
Cavett Station Chapter
Ancestor: John Fox, NC — #628759
This "Lone Star Quilt" was made circa 1900 in Knox County, TN by the owner's grandmother, Betty Calloway (born 1/17/1847 in Knox County, TN, married William Wright Calloway, died 6/2/1918 in the same county ) The name of each child is quilted around the border.

**Hicks, Nancy Walden** (Leon)
Rhea-Craig Chapter
Ancestor: John Hammock, VA — #774691
This cross stitch quilt was made in the early 1960's by the owner's mother-in-law, Lillian Hicks (born in Alabama 10/1/1900, married Robert T. Hicks, Sr., died in Chattanooga, TN 1/21/1967). The quilt was made from a kit the owner purchased in 1960 to give her mother-in-law something to keep her occupied while she was ill with terminal cancer. The cross stitch helped ease her pain, and she lived five years longer than expected.

**Hicks, Nancy Walden** (Leon)
Rhea-Craig Chapter
Ancestor: John Hammock, VA — #774691
This "Star Within A Star" quilt was made in the early 1900's in Stinking Creek, TN by the owner's great grandmother, Martha Bolton Walden (born 2/26/1845 in Campbell, TN, married Benjamin Franklin Walden, died 10/4/1926).

**Hightower, Anne Buchanon** (Frank C.)
Tullahoma Chapter
Ancestor: Brig. General William Russell, Sr., VA — #678799
This "Mosaic" quilt was made in Nashville, TN by Margaret Nichol Vaulx Crockett, the owner's husband's great grandmother (born 12/17/1845 in Lobelville, TN, married to George Bell Crockett 8/29/1871, died 10/16/1895 in Lobelville). It was given to the owner by her mother-in-law, the granddaughter of the quiltmaker. The quiltmaker used silk dresses and ribbons. Margaret Crockett was the granddaughter of General Robert Armstrong, General Andrew Jackson's aid-de-camp. General Armstrong married Margaret Dysart Nichol in General Andrew Jackson's living room at the Hermitage, against the wishes of her parents. President James Polk appointed General Armstrong as USC Consul to Liverpool, England. Margaret's father, Joseph Vaulx, apparently was present at the Hermitage when General Jackson passed away.

**Hill, Ruth Rhea Tubb** (Wyman)
Rock House Chapter
Ancestor: Charles Dibrell, VA — #581399
This "Contrary Wife" quilt was pieced in Sparta, TN by the owner's great grandmother, Mary Ann Rogers Bronson (born 1/11/1837 in Sparta, TN, married Robert Lucas Bronson, died 12/23/1923 in the same town). An aunt gave the owner the top and she had it quilted.

**Hill, Ruth Rhea Tubb** (Wyman)
Rock House Chapter
Ancestor: Charles Dibrell, VA — #581399
This "Caesar's Crown Variation" quilt was made in the 1930's or 40's in Beersheba Springs, TN by the owner's mother-in-law, Minnie Clendenon Hill (born 10/20/1882 in Hills Creek TN, married Benjamin Hill, died in Beersheba Springs, TN 2/10/1971). The quilt was a wedding gift to the owner and her husband.

**Hill, Ruth Rhea Tubb** (Wyman)
Rock House Chapter
Ancestor: Charles Dibrell, VA — #581399
This embroidered quilt was made by the owner's great grandmother or great great grandmother. It was given to the owner by her mother.

**Hill, Ruth Rhea Tubb** (Wyman)
Rock House Chapter
Ancestor: Charles Dibrell, VA — #581399
This "Crazy" quilt was made in 1930 in Sparta, TN by the owner's grandmother Narcissa Rhea Dibrell (born 10/4/1868 in Sparta, TN, married Sydney Stanton Dibrell, died (6/12/1948 in the same town). The owner received the quilt as a gift when she was a young girl.

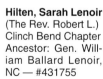

**Hill, Ruth Rhea Tubb** (Wyman)
Rock House Chapter
Ancestor: Charles Dibrell, VA — #581399
This Cross Stitch quilt mas made by the owner in Sparta, TN.

**Hilten, Sarah Lenoir** (The Rev. Robert L.)
Clinch Bend Chapter
Ancestor: Gen. William Ballard Lenoir, NC — #431755
This "North Carolina Lilly" quilt was made in the 1930's in Kentucky. The owner bought it at a "moving" sale.

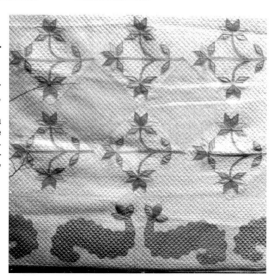

**Hinds, Lettie Connelly** (Carl E.)
Robert Lewis Chapter
Ancestor: William Murdock, NC —#376701
This "Wild Rose" quilt was made in 1875-80 at Marshall County, TN by the owner's great great aunt, Manerva Acuff (born 1840 at Marshall County, died 6/1/1897 at Cornersville, TN).

**Hinton, Nora Smith** (T. Earl)
Col. Hardy Murfree Chapter
Ancestor: Bartholomew Stovall, VA — #756958
This "Variation of a New York Star" quilt was passed down in the owner's family from her grandmother, Nora Lee Gardner Smith, wife of Willaim Fredrick Smith to the owner's father,

Alfred Gardner Smith. He gave it to the owner. Nora was one of seven children born to Alfred and Mary Ann Gardner, early settlers in Weakley County, TN and Dresden, TN. She married William Fredrick Smith in 1867. Their only child was Alfred Gardner, the owner's father. They spent part of their married life in Evansville, Indiana. Nora later returned to Dresden, TN and married John R. Thomason. She died there in 1924.

**Hinton, Nora Smith** (T. Earl)
Col. Hardy Murfree Chapter
Ancestor: Bartholomew Stovall, VA — #756958
This "Log Cabin" quilt was also passed down from Nora Lee Gardner, to the owner's father, to owner. This quilt was made from velvet, silk and satin.

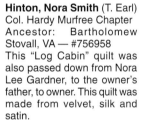

**Hinton, Nora Smith**
(T. Earl)
Col. Hardy Murfree Chapter
Ancestor: Bartholomew Stovall, VA — #756958
This "Princess Feather" quilt was also passed down from Nora Lee Gardner, to the owner's father, to owner.

**Hinton, Nora Smith**
(T. Earl)
Col. Hardy Murfree Chapter
Ancestor: Bartholomew Stovall, VA — #756958
This "Victorian Crazy" quilt was made in 1884 in Evansville, Indiana by owner's grandmother, Nora Lee Gardner Smith. The maker won an award for this quilt at a fair. There are two red and blue bows attached to the corners. The quiltmaker's calling card is attached with a small blue ribbon.

**Hixson, Kathleen Moody**
(C. Lynn)
Judge David Campbell Chapter.
Ancestor: William Polk, VA — #655506
This "Grandmother's Flower Garden" quilt was made in the 1970's in Chattanooga, TN by the owner's great aunt, Frances (Fannie) Stephens Scheffler (born 4/7/1892 in Manchester, TN, married Albert Scheffler, died 7/29/1976 in Chattanooga, TN).

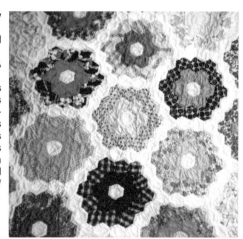

**Hixson, Kathleen Moody**
(C. Lynn)
Judge David Campbell Chapter.
Ancestor: William Polk, VA — #655506
This "Pickle Dish" pattern was made in 1915 in Manchester, TN by owner's great grandmother, Mary Purvis Gentry (born 1/29/1852 in Warren County, TN, married Joseph Houston Gentry, died 9/19/1937 in Rutherford County, TN).

**Hixson, Kathleen Moody**
(C. Lynn)
Judge David Campbell Chapter.
Ancestor: William Polk, VA — #655506
This "One Patch" quilt was made in 1975 in Chattanooga, TN by the owner's mother-in-law, Laura Ethel Barker Hixson (born 4/8/1904 in Hixson, TN, married Dewey G. Hixson, died 6/8/1996).

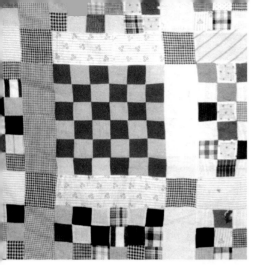

**Hobbs, Kristin Douthit** (Mark)
Clinch Bend Chapter
Ancestor: Arthur Sheffled —
#748364
This "Nine Patch" quilt was
made in the 1900's near
Blanche, TN by the first wife of
the owner's great grandfather,
Daniel Thomas Hardin.

**Hobbs, Kristin
Douthit** (Mark)
Clinch Bend Chapter
Ancestor: Arthur
Sheffled —#748364
This "Sugar Loaf"
quilt was made in the
1900's near Blanche,
TN by the first wife of
the owner's great
grandfather, Daniel
Thomas Hardin.

**Hofstetter, Gwendolyn
Robbins** (James)
Gen. Daniel Smith's Rock
Castle Chapter.
Ancestor: William Collins,
PA — #577583
This "Crazy" quilt was made
during the War Between the
States in Hermitage, TN by
the owner's mother-in-law,
Catherine Hofstetter (born
5/8/1827 at Beiern in
Keltenbrumm, Germany,
married Christian Hofstetter,
died 9/12/1914 at Hermit-
age, TN).

**Holbert, Mary Faye McMahon** (Stephen)
Spencer Clack Chapter
Ancestor: Christopher Myers,
VA — #762010
This "Grandmother's
Flower Garden" quilt
was made in 1930 in
Sevier County, TN
by the owner's
husband's grand-
mother, Hattie Murph
Wade (born 1881 in
Sevier County, mar-
ried Jerry Jackson
Wade, died in 1974
in same county). It
was passed to cur-
rent owner when her
m o t h e r - i n - l a w
passed away.

**Holland, Claris Mabry**
(David K.)
Campbell Chapter
Ancestor: Charles
Garrett, VA —#681863
This "Grandmother's
Flower Garden" quilt
was made in 1940 at
Cunningham, KY by the
owner's aunt, Ethel
Mabry Jones (born circa
1876 at Cunningham,
married Carl Jones, died
1947 at Cunningham,
KY).

**Holland, Claris Mabry**
(David K.)
Campbell Chapter
Ancestor: Charles
Garrett, VA —#681863
This "Double Wedding
Ring" quilt was made in
the 1930's at Hickman,
KY by the owner's
husband's grandmother,
Nancy Matilda Coffey
(born circa 1860 at
Linville, KY, married Wil-
liam Terry Coffee, died
1946 at Hickman, KY).

**Hoover, Margaret Denny**
(Walter K. )
Stones River Chapter
Ancestor: Timothy Riggs,
Jr., NC — #513902
This "Single Irish Chain"
quilt was made in 1913 in
Dickson County, TN by the
owner's great grand-
mother, Elizabeth
Edwards Grove (born 7/
18/1841 at Burns, TN,
married John Grove, died
in 1919 at Burns). The
quiltmaker made it as a
wedding present for her
granddaughter. It was
given to the current owner
by her mother.

**Horton, Betty Gillenwater** (Robert
Donald)
Coytee Chapter
Ancestor: James Hall, VA —
#701598
This "Ocean Waves"
quilt was made in
1900 in Hawkins
County, TN by
the owner's
grandmother,
Rachael M.
Gillenwater
(born 12/1/
1852 in
Hawkins County,
married Andrew
Campbell, died 12/28/
1945 in Blount County,
TN). It was passed from the
owner's aunt, Cora Gillenwater
Walker, to the current owner.

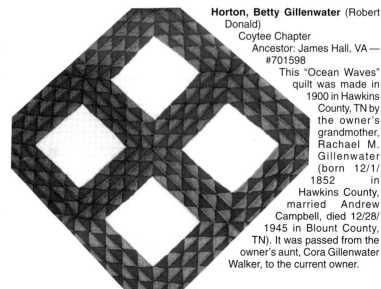

**House, Dinah Lee Howard** (Douglas)
Col. Hardy Murfree Chapter
Ancestor: Moses Field, MA —#754693
This "Mariner's Compass" quilt was made in DeKalb County, TN by Allie Ashburn, (born circa 1881 at DeKalb County, TN, married R. W. Ashburn, died at DeKalb County).

**House, Dinah Lee Howard** (Douglas)
Col. Hardy Murfree Chapter
Ancestor: Moses Field, MA — #754693
This "Crazy" quilt was made in 1912 at Liberty, TN by Alice Sadler Craddock (born 1879 at Liberty, married Willie J. Craddock, died 1948 at Liberty). Alice is the aunt of the owner's friend. The owner purchased the quilt at the estate sale of Mrs. Monice Lee Sadler Odom. The quilt is signed, "January 10, 1912. Monice and Alice."

**Huddleston, Bernice Hoge** (Tim Lee)
Chief John Ross Chapter
Ancestor: George William Walker, NC—#612600
This "Tulip" quilt was made in 1931 at Pikeville, TN by the owner who was born 11/10/1907. The quiltmaker's mother, Sallie Greer Hoge, gave her the pattern and helped her with the quilt. Her mother is a direct descendent of Captain George Walker of Faquier County, VA. She was born 7/2/1873 and died 7/28/1955. The quilt will be handed down to my only daughter, Sara H. Tidwell of Toronto, Canada.

**Hudson, Kathleen Bean** (Jack)
Adam Dale Chapter
Ancestor: Captain Jacob Kornegay, NC — #711399
This "Star Sampler" quilt was made in 1958 in Union, MS by the owner (born 7/10/1922 in Itta Bena, MS.

**Hudson, Kathleen Bean** (Jack)
Adam Dale Chapter
Ancestor: Captain Jacob Kornegay, NC — #711399
This "Sunflower Medallion" candlewicked quilt was made in 1992 in Memphis, TN by the owner. The owner is making heirlooms for each of her children.

**Hudson, Kathleen Bean** (Jack)
Adam Dale Chapter
Ancestor: Captain Jacob Kornegay, NC — #711399
This "Queen Ann Star" quilt was made in 1996 in Memphis, TN by the owner. It was made as an heirloom for her son.

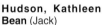

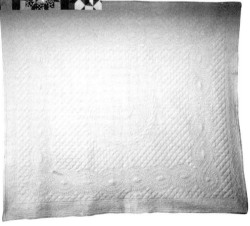

**Hughes, Mary LaRue McDonald** (Roy Demonbreum)
John Nolan Chapter
Ancestor: John Cooper, NC —#574477
This "Tulip" quilt was probably made in the early 1900's by the owner's mother, Amanda Lee Haley McDonald (born 1870, died 1951 at Nolensville, TN).

**Hughes, Mary LaRue McDonald**
(Roy Demonbreum)
John Nolan Chapter
Ancestor: John Cooper, NC —#574477
This "Fan" quilt was made in 1979 at Nolensville, TN by the owner to be sold at auction at the Nolensville United Methodist Church Festival. The owner's husband had the high bid of $1,100.

**Hughes, Mary LaRue McDonald**
(Roy Demonbreum)
John Nolan Chapter
Ancestor: John Cooper, NC —#574477
This "Rob Peter To Pay Paul" quilt was made in Nolensville, TN by the owner's great great aunt, Susie Haley. She started this quilt the same day her brother left home to fight in the Confederate Army in the War Between the States.

**Hughes, Pheribol Hutcheson** (Noah)
The Crab Orchard Chapter
Ancestor: Edward McDonald, VA —#605647
This embroidered quilt was made in the 1970's at Crossville, TN by the owner (born 1922 at Bledsoe County, TN).

**Hughes, Pheribol Hutcheson**
(Noah)
The Crab Orchard Chapter
Ancestor: Edward McDonald, VA —#605647
This "H" quilt was made prior to 1930 at Bledsoe County, TN by the owner's mother Verna Blevins Hutcheson (born 1897 at Rhea County, TN, married Raleigh Darius Hutcheson, died 1930 at Rhea County). The quiltmaker died when the owner was eight years old.

**Hunter, Nancy Foster**
(Michael)
Jane Knox Chapter
Ancestor: William Pinkston, NC — #649969
This "Neck Tie" quilt was made in 1930 in Maury County, TN by the owner's grandmother, Argie Virginia Grissom Pinkston (born 11/2/1886, married Merritt Oliver Pinkston, died 4/3/1968 in Columbia, TN). The quilt was passed from grandmother, to her daughter, Sue, and then to Sue's daughter, the current owner. The quiltmaker's ancestors, James and Margaret McKelvey, came from County Antrim, Ireland in 1767 and settled in Charleston, SC. They received a land grant and their sons fought in the Revolutionary War. Most were farmers and Methodist preachers. The Owner's grandmother's parents, Minnie McKelvey and Lee Grissom, settled in Maury County where owner's family still owns property. The owner remembers her grandmother piecing and quilting, canning, killing hogs, and sewing for the family.

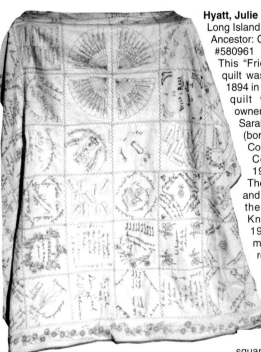

**Hyatt, Julie Sarnoff** (John)
Long Island Chapter
Ancestor: Christian Moser, PA — #580961
This "Friendship" embroidery quilt was finished March 31, 1894 in New Hartford, IA. The quilt was made by the owner's great grandmother, Sarah Adeline Bolton Knipe (born 4/18/1857 in Cedar County, IA, married Jesse Cox Knipe, died 2/1/1939 in Waverly, IA). The quiltmaker's sisters and friends assisted with the quilt. It was in the Knipe family until the 1990's. The owner's mother, Jane B. Sarnoff, received it from Vivian David Nicholson. She is writing a book about it as a genealogical record. Many families in New Hartford, IA embroidered squares. Groups contributing were: Knights of Pythia, Masons, Order of the Eastern Star, Odd Fellows, Robert Olmstead Women's Relief Corps, G.A.R., and the Finch Ford Band.

**Hyatt, Julie Sarnoff** (John)
Long Island Chapter
Ancestor: Christian Moser, PA — #580961
This "Drunkard's Path" quilt was made in 1948 in Jonesville, VA by the owner's husband's grandmother, Mary Hester Isenberg Hyatt (born 10/5/ 1876 at Rodgersville, TN, married Loren Bethel Hyatt and died 12/1963 in Jonesville, VA. The quilt was made for Marjorie Hyatt McCormick, but she told her grandmother it was too old fashioned. Granny Hyatt picked out the embroidered name and saved it for John A. Hyatt, her youngest grandson. There is a mistake in piecing a maroon square that may be intentional.

**Hyatt, Julie Sarnoff** (John)
Long Island Chapter
Ancestor: Christian Moser, PA — #580961
This "Pansy" quilt was made in 1926 in Blackwater, VA by the owner's mother-in-law, Nina Estelle Anderson Hyatt (born 3/2/1917 at Blackwater and married Onza Maroni Hyatt). Nina Hyatt gave quilt to current owner. The quiltmaker made this quilt when she was nine years old. Her mother helped quilt it.

**Hyatt, Julie Sarnoff** (John)
Long Island Chapter
Ancestor: Christian Moser, PA — #580961
This "Eight Pointed Star" quilt was made in 1976 in Blackwater, VA by the owner's husband's grandmother, Effie Mae Baker Anderson (born 7/5/1896, married Lloyd L. Anderson (born 10/21/1890, died 4/26/1970). Effie died 8/27/1978. It was given to current owner by her mother-in-law, Nina Hyatt.

**Hyatt, Julie Sarnoff** (John)
Long Island Chapter
Ancestor: Christian Moser, PA — #580961
This "Butterfly' quilt was made in 1986 by the owner's mother-in-law, Nina Estelle Anderson Hyatt in Jonesville, VA. It was given to the owner as an anniversary present.

**Hyatt, Julie Sarnoff** (John)
Long Island Chapter
Ancestor: Christian Moser, PA — #580961
This "Lone Star" quilt was made in 1934 in Morristown, TN by the owner's mother-in-law, Nina Hyatt. The quiltmaker made it when she spent a summer in Morristown, TN with her aunt.

**Hyatt, Julie Sarnoff** (John)
Long Island Chapter
Ancestor: Christian Moser, PA — #580961
This "Grandmother's Flower Garden" quilt was possibly made in the 1920's but certainly before 1941 in Mooresburg, TN. It was made by the owner's husband's grandmother, Mary Louisa Olinger Hyatt (born 3/18/1851 at Olinger, VA, died 10/4/1946, married Maroni Eldridge Hyatt (born 11/16/1845). This quilt was made as a wedding present for Onza Maroni Hyatt who was born in 1907. Although he didn't marry until 1941, the quilt was probably made in the 1920's. The Hyatts owned several small farms in Hancock County, TN and the Lee County, VA area. Some of their children were born in Mooresburg, TN.

**Hyatt, Julie Sarnoff** (John)
Long Island Chapter
Ancestor: Christian Moser, PA — #580961
This "Grandmother's Flower Garden" quilt was made in the 1920's in New Hartford, IA by the owner's great grandmother, Sarah Adeline Bolton Knipe. The quilt was passed from Sarah Knipe, to daughter, Lillian M. Berninghausen, to granddaughter, Jane B. Sarnoff, to great granddaughter, Julie S. Hyatt. As a child the current owner was allowed to use this quilt for special occasions and holidays. She still does especially in the spring.

**Hyatt, Julie Sarnoff** (John)
Long Island Chapter
Ancestor: Christian Moser, PA — #580961
This "Sunbonnet Girls" quilt was made in 1980 by the owner's mother-in-law, Nina Hyatt, in Jonesville, VA. Mrs. Hyatt gave the quilt to her granddaughter, Alice Hyatt Love.

**Hyatt, Julie Sarnoff** (John)
Long Island Chapter
Ancestor: Christian Moser, PA — #580961
This "Pinwheel/Daisy Chain" quilt was made in 1954 in Jonesville, VA by the owner's husband's grandmother, Mary Hester Isenberg Hyatt. The owner likes to use this quilt at Christmas.

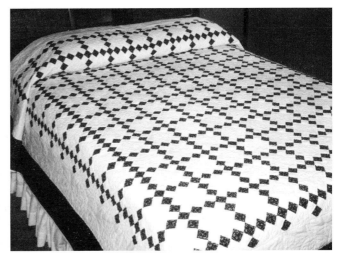

**Jackson, Annie Skelley** (C. Robert)
John Nolen Chapter
Ancestor: Joseph Potts, NC —#695511
This "Single Irish Chain" quilt was made in 1983 at Williamson County, TN by the owner (born 1/17/1921 in Williamson County).

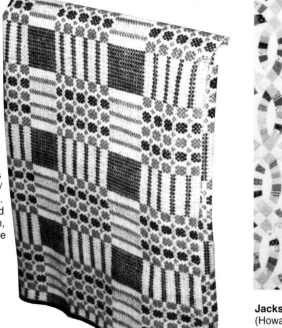

**Jackson, Annie Skelley**
(C. Robert)
John Nolen Chapter
Ancestor: Joseph Potts,
NC —#695511
This "Snowballs and
Table" coverlet was made
in 1856 at Williamson
County, TN by the owner's
grandmother, Sarah
Louise Skelley (born 2/24/
1836 at Williamson County,
TN, married James
Crawford Skelley, died 1/7/
1920 in the same county).
The coverlet was passed
from the maker, to her son,
Henry P. Skelley, to the
owner.

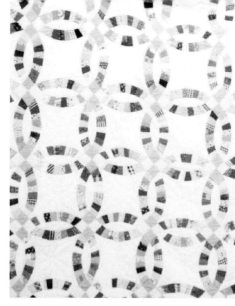

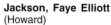

**Jackson, Faye Elliott**
(Howard)
Charlotte Reeves Robertson
Chapter
Ancestor: Capt. Joseph
Shinn, NC —#753975
This "Double Wedding Ring"
quilt was pieced in 1986 at
Columbia, TN by the
owner's mother, Louise Morrow Elliott (born 10/27/1914
at Maury County, TN, mar-
ried William Howell Elliott,
died 7/27/1987 at Colum-
bia). This quilt was pieced by
the owner's mother, while
she was suffering from cancer. After her death, the
owner's sister, Eleanor E.
Riddle, quilted it.

**Jackson, Faye
Elliott** (Howard)
Charlotte Reeves
Robertson Chapter
Ancestor: Capt. Jo-
seph Shinn, NC —
#753975
This "Bicentennial"
quilt was made in 1976
at Franklin, TN by the
owner's sister, Eleanor
Elliott Riddle (born at
Columbia, TN, married
Bobby Ray Riddle).

**Jackson, Faye Elliott**
(Howard)
Charlotte Reeves
Robertson Chapter
Ancestor: Capt. Joseph
Shinn, NC —#753975
This "Lone Star Strip"
quilt was made circa
1950 at Maury County,
TN by the owner's
husband's grand-
mother, Mary Margaret
Lumsden Jackson (born
12/18/1879 at Maury
County, TN, married
Robert Harris Jackson,
died 3/4/1963 at Colum-
bia). The "H" on the quilt
indicates the maker
made the quilt for her
son.

**Jackson, Linda Sue**
Manchester Chapter
Ancestor: Capt. Jonathan
Langdon, VA —#779653
This "Eastern Star" quilt
was made at Hillsboro, TN
by the owner's sister-in-
law, Martha Brothers
Duncan (born 1929 at
Coffee County, TN, mar-
ried Kenneth Duncan,
died 1977 at Nashville,
TN). This quilt was made
for the owner when she
was Worthy Matron for the
Eastern Star.

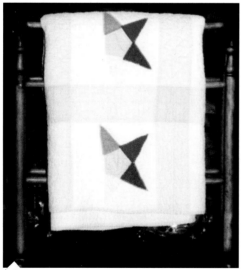

**James, Joan Knight** (Lee)
Charoltte Reeves Robertson
Chapter
Ancestor: Richard Nuckolls,
VA —#741140
This "Variation of a Nine
Patch" quilt was made in the
1920's at Robertson County,
TN by the owner's
husband's grandmother,
Lela O'Brien James (born 2/
20/1873 at Cheatham
County, TN, married
Solomon Lewis James, died
10/28/1932 at Robertson
County, TN).

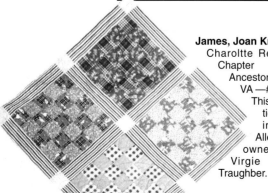

**James, Joan Knight** (Lee)
Charoltte Reeves Robertson
Chapter
Ancestor: Richard Nuckolls,
VA —#741140
This "Nine Patch Varia-
tion" quilt was made
in the 1920's at
Allensville, KY by the
owner's grandmother,
Virgie Lee Widick
Traughber.

**James, Joan Knight** (Lee)
Charoltte Reeves Robertson
Chapter
Ancestor: Richard Nuckolls,
VA —#741140
This coverlet was made in
1885-90 at Springfield, TN by
the owner's grandmother,
Virgie Lee Widick Traughber
(born 11/27/1867 at
Robertson County, married
Ed, died 1/12/1945 in the
same county). The maker
made this coverlet on a hand
loom before she married. It
was passed from grand-
mother, to daughter, to
granddaughter.

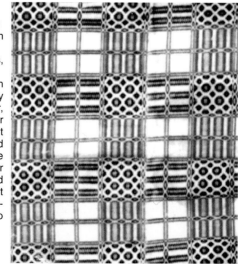

**James, Joan Knight** (Lee)
Charoltte Reeves Robertson Chapter
Ancestor: Richard Nuckolls, VA —#741140
This "Nine Patch" quilt was made in the 1950's at Springfield, TN by the owner's mother, Verna Lynn Traughber Knight (born 11/14/1896 in KY, married Preston, died 6/27/1973 at Davidson County, TN). The quilt was passed from mother to daughter.

**James, Joan Knight** (Lee)
Charoltte Reeves Robertson Chapter
Ancestor: Richard Nuckolls, VA —#741140
This "Variation of a Christmas Star/Winding Blades" quilt was made 1910-20 in KY by Virgie Lee Widick Traughber.

**James, Joan Knight** (Lee)
Charoltte Reeves Robertson Chapter
Ancestor: Richard Nuckolls, VA —#741140
These "20th Century Nine Patch" quilts were made in KY in the 1920's by the owner's grandmother, Virgie Lee Traughber.

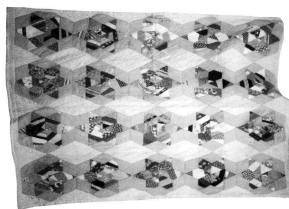

**James, Joan Knight** (Lee)
Charoltte Reeves Robertson Chapter
Ancestor: Richard Nuckolls, VA —#741140
This "Texas Star" quilt was made in the 1940's at Robertson County, TN by the owner's mother-in-law, Mabelle Rosson James (born 6/20/1896 at Robertson County, TN, married Frank James, died 11/23/1985 at Newberg, IN).

**James, Joan Knight** (Lee)
Charoltte Reeves Robertson Chapter
Ancestor: Richard Nuckolls, VA —#741140
This "Texas Star" quilt was made in the 1930's at Robertson County, TN by the owner's mother-in-law, Mabelle Rosson James.

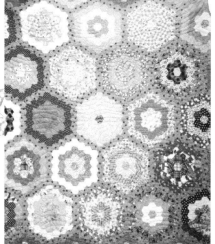

**James, Joan Knight** (Lee)
Charoltte Reeves Robertson Chapter
Ancestor: Richard Nuckolls, VA —#741140
This "Grandmother's Flower Garden" quilt was made in the 1920's at KY by the owner's grandmother, Virgie Lee Traughber.

**James, Joan Knight** (Lee)
Charoltte Reeves Robertson Chapter
Ancestor: Richard Nuckolls, VA —#741140
This "Sunbonnet Sue" quilt was made in the late 1930's at Robertson County, TN by the owner's grandmother, Virgie Lee Tranghber. She made it for the owner when she was a baby.

**James, Joan Knight** (Lee)
Charoltte Reeves Robertson Chapter
Ancestor: Richard Nuckolls, VA —#741140
This "Crown of Thorns" quilt was made 1920-30 in TN by the owner's grandmother, Virgie Lee Traughber.

**James, Joan Knight** (Lee)
Charoltte Reeves Robertson Chapter
Ancestor: Richard Nuckolls, VA —
#741140
This "Triple Irish Chain" quilt was made
1910-20 in KY by the owner's grand-
mother, Virgie Lee Traughber.

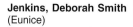

**Jenkins, Deborah Smith**
(Eunice)
Fort Prudhomme Chapter
Ancestor: David Craig, NC
741781
This "Blazing Star" quilt
was made 30 years ago at
Ripley, TN by the owner's
husband's grandmother,
Maude Jenkins (died at
Lauderdale County, TN).

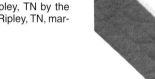

**Jenkins, Deborah
Smith** (Eunice)
Fort Prudhomme
Chapter
Ancestor: David Craig,
NC 741781
This "Snow Crystals" quilt was made in 1965-70 at Ripley, TN by the
owner's grandmother, Marie Minner Craig (born 1906 at Ripley, TN, mar-
ried Jarome, died 1980 at Ripley).

**Jenkins, Susan Napier**
(David)
Chief Piomingo Chapter
Ancestor: George
Murrell, NC —#759645
This "Whole Cloth" quilt
was made from
feedsack material by the
owner's grandmother,
Tennessee Jackson
Hartley (born 11/5/1888
at Webster County, MO,
married George Jesee
Hartley, died at Laramie,
WY). This feedsack fab-
ric covers an older quilt.

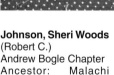

**Jenkins, Susan Napier** (David)
Chief Piomingo Chapter
Ancestor: George Murrell, NC
—#759645
This "Basket" quilt was
made circa 1920 at
Webster County, MO
by the owner's great
grandmother, Jane
Missouri Salina Murrell
Hartley (born 10/23/
1852 at Dallas County,
MO, married Robert
Hartley, died 1/7/1940
at Webster County,
MO). This quilt was made
for the owner's mother, Jane
Hartley, as a birthday gift.

**Johnson, Agnes Vincent**
(William Jeryl)
Hatchie Chapter
Ancestor: Joseph Shearin,
NC —#704048
This "Sunbonnet Sue/Dutch
Girl" quilt was made circa
1960 at Bolivar, TN by the
owner's mother, Rubye
Smalley Vincent (born 1910
at Fayette County, TN, married M.O. Vincent). Scraps
from the dresses of the
maker's first grandchild,
Jana Johnson, were used to
make the girls for this quilt,
providing the owner with
memories of her daughter's earliest garments. Later this quilt will be a cherished
keepsake for Jana because it was made by "MomMom."

**Johnson, Sheri Woods**
(Robert C.)
Andrew Bogle Chapter
Ancestor: Malachi
Hinton, NC —#646038
This "Drunkard's Path"
quilt was made at
Eagleville, TN by the
owner's husband's
grandmother, Selma
Cecilia Womack
Johnson (born 5/22/
1874 at Rutherford, TN,
married Joseph Albert
Johnson, died at
Eagleville, TN). The
owner received this quilt
as a wedding gift in No-
vember, 1965 from her
husband's aunt, Mary
Elizabeth Johnson
Grassman.

**Johnson, Sheri Woods**
(Robert C.)
Andrew Bogle Chapter
Ancestor: Malachi Hinton,
NC —#646038
This "Star of Bethlehem"
quilt was made at
Eagleville, TN by the
owner's husband's grand-
mother, Selma Cecilia
Womack Johnson. The
owner received this quilt
as a wedding gift in No-
vember, 1965 from her
husband's aunt, Mary
Elizabeth Johnson
Grassman.

**Joles, Paula Foley**
(Rocky)
Chickasaw Bluff Chapter
Ancestor: Abraham Seay, VA —#759890
This "Basket Weave" quilt was made in 1980 at Memphis, TN by the owner's mother, Alice King Foley (born 1930 at Custer, OK, married James Davis Foley). The maker gave the quilt to the owner.

**Joles, Paula Foley**
(Rocky)
Chickasaw Bluff Chapter
Ancestor: Abraham Seay, VA —#759890
This "Basket Weave" quilt was made in 1979 at Memphis, TN by the owner's mother, Alice King Foley. The maker gave the quilt to the owner's grandfather, and upon his death, she received the quilt.

**Joles, Paula Foley**
(Rocky)
Chickasaw Bluff Chapter
Ancestor: Abraham Seay, VA —#759890
This "Quint 5" quilt was made in 1978 at Lindsay, OK by the owner's grandmother, Susie Davis Foley (born 1896 at Shelby, TX, married Edgar William Foley, died 1988 at Garvin, OK). The maker gave the quilt to the owner.

**Joles, Paula Foley**
(Rocky)
Chickasaw Bluff Chapter
Ancestor: Abraham Seay, VA —#759890
This "Nine Patch Sampler" quilt was pieced in 1993 at Memphis, TN by the owner's mother, Alice King Foley. It was quilted by Clara Fullegrade of Cordell, OK. The maker gave the quilt to the owner.

**Jolley, "Mina" La Vonne Collins**
Moccasin Bend Chapter
Ancestor: John Wright, Sr., VA —#648750
This "Butterfly" quilt was made circa 1900-1910 near Chattanooga, TN by the grandmother, "Mama" Laurie Scott. The maker gave the quilt to her daughter, Grace Douglass, who gave it to the owner in the 1960's.

**Jolley, "Mina" La Vonne Collins**
Moccasin Bend Chapter
Ancestor: John Wright, Sr., VA —#648750
This "Washington Plume" quilt was made circa 1900-1910 near Chattanooga, TN by the grandmother of the owner's former husband Edgar M. Jolley, Sr. "Mama" Laurie Scott was born circa 1870-80 near Chattanooga, TN married Willima P. Scott, died in the 1960's at Winchester, TN). The maker gave the quilt to

her daughter, Grace Douglass (married W.H.) who gave it to the owner in the 1960's.

**Jones, Barbara Bigham**
(Wayne)
Robert Lewis Chapter
Ancestor: Tyree Harris, NC —#749527
This "Old Wild Goose Chase" quilt was purchased at an auction in the 1960's. It was given to the owner after her mother's death.

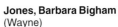

**Jones, Barbara Bigham** (Wayne)
Robert Lewis Chapter
Ancestor: Tyree Harris, NC —#749527
This "Dresden Plate" quilt was made circa 1970 at Lewisburg, TN by the owner's mother, Katherine Bigham (born 4/14/1915 at Giles County, TN, married David Bigham, died 9/8/1986 at Lewisburg, TN). It was given to the owner after her mother's death.

**Jones, Barbara Bigham**
(Wayne)
Robert Lewis Chapter
Ancestor: Tyree Harris, NC —#749527
This "Lemoyne Star/Eight Pointed Star" quilt was made in 1968 at Lewisburg, TN by the owner's mother, Katherine Bigham. The quilt was passed from maker to owner.

**Jones, Barbara Bigham**
(Wayne)
Robert Lewis Chapter
Ancestor: Tyree Harris, NC —#749527
This "Fan" quilt was made in 1970 at Lewisburg, TN by the owner's mother, Katherine Bigham.

**Jones, Fleda**
Coytee Chapter
Ancestor: James Matthews, SC — #716950
This "Crazy Flower" quilt was made in 1881 at Loudon County, TN by the owner's grand-mother, Elvira Tennessee Humphrey Jones (born 3/10/1862 at Blount County, TN, married William W. Jones, died 6/12/1905 at Loudon County, TN).
The quilt is signed "Forget Me Not Mama-1899. Willie J. 3 years old - 1888 Phila T." Wiilie J. is the owner's father, Willie Jones. Philia T. Stands for Philadelphia, TN. The quilt was passed from the maker, to her son, and then to the owner.

**Jones, Gloria Ferguson**
River City Chapter
Ancestor: Samuel Box, SC — #769149
This "Double Wedding Ring" quilt was made in 1930 at Memphis, TN by the owner's grand-mother, Nellie Elizabeth Box Goddard (born 10/6/1885 at Polk County, MO, married James J. Goddard at Springfield, MO, died 3/15/1956 at Mem-phis, TN). James and Elizabeth traveled to Memphis and spent the rest of their lives there. Elizabeth is the great great

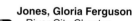

great great granddaughter of Samuel Box, a veteran of the Revolutionary War. He fought in the battles of Charleston and Sullivan Island in SC. He was taken a prisoner and confined for 22 days. He returned to fight in the battles of Ft. Stone and Camden, SC. The maker gave the quilt to the owner.

**Jones, Gloria Ferguson**
River City Chapter
Ancestor: Samuel Box, SC — #769149
This "Grandmother's Flower Garden" quilt was made in 1931 at Memphis, TN by the owner's grandmother, Nellie Elizabeth Box Goddard. The owner had the two quilts, made by her grandmother, stored carefully in her "hope chest." This was a custom where young girls would receive special gifts as they grew up. These gifts would be saved until the "proper" young man came along and she married him.

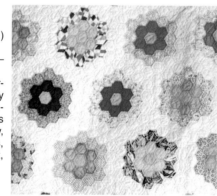

**Jones, Gloria Ferguson**
River City Chapter
Ancestor: Samuel Box, SC — #769149
This "Trip Around the World" quilt was made in 1933 at Shelby County, TN by the owner's pa-ternal grandmother, Eudorra Holland (born 10/22/1858 at Hardeman County, TN, mar-ried William Franklin Ferguson, died 11/10/1954 at Memphis). This quilt was passed to the owner's fa-ther and mother, and then to the owner.

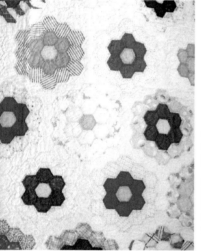

**Jones, Jean Walters** (Robert D.)
Jane Knox Chapter
Ancestor: Robert Walters, VA —#508018
This "Grandmother's Flower Garden " quilt was made in 1937 at Maury County, TN by the owner's great aunt, Tinie Walters Hawkins (married George Hawkins). The maker made the quilt for the owner to use on a youth bed when she was a small child.

**Jones, Jean Walters** (Robert D.)
Jane Knox Chapter
Ancestor: Robert Walters, VA — #508018
This "Grandmother's Flower Gar-den" quilt was made at Maury County by the owner's grand-mother, Pearl Oakley Walters (born 7/16/1887 at Maury County, TN, married Willie Irvin Walters, died 7/6/1948 at Mt. Pleasant, TN).

**Jones, Jean Walters** (Robert D.)
Jane Knox Chapter
Ancestor: Robert Walters, VA —#508018
This "Basket" quilt was made in the early 1930's at Mt. Pleasant, TN by the owner's mother, Evelyn Elizabeth Smith Walters (born 11/17/1908 at Columbia, TN, married Douglas Irvin Walters, died 6/24/1989 at Co-lumbia).

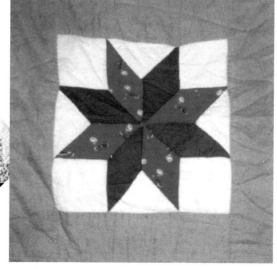

**Jones, Linda Sue Brown** (Loy Wesley)
Great Smokies Chapter
Ancestor: Samuel Wilson, NC — #737698
This "LeMoyne Star" quilt was made in 1948 at DeQuincy, LA by the owner's grandmother, Carrie Viola Bean Brown (born 4/25/1984 at Deweyville, TX, mar-ried Martin Brown, died 3/22/1975 at DeQuincy, LA).

**Jones, Shirley Farris** (Jerry L.)
Col. Hardy Murfree
Ancestor: Richard Faris, VA
—#744308
This "Strip and Patchwork" quilt was made circa 1912 at Hillsboro, TN by the owner's grandmother, Mary Neese Farris (born 6/11/1878 at Hillsboro, married Dr. John Kennerly Farris, Jr., died 1/18/1952 at Manchester, TN). "My father, Malcolm Robert Farris, was born 6/1/1912, the youngest of four children born to Mary and John Farris. According to my Aunt Ruth, my father's eldest sister (8/22/1901-12/22/1995), their mother made this quilt especially for him, as she had done with each of her previous children. Daddy was a sickly child and nearly died with pneumonia when he was five, despite his father being a doctor and every medical treatment possible being administered. My aunt said she could remember sitting beside her very sick baby brother for hours on end and continually covering him and re-arranging this quilt to keep him warm during the time that he was so ill. She said that the light from the bedside lantern cast a very interesting glow over the various colors and fabrics in the quilt. My father died on 9/17/1989 and my aunt gave the quilt to me the next year."

**Jordan, Margaret Allen** (James)
Robert Lewis Chapter
Ancestor: George Ewing, Sr., VA — #576691
This "Flowers" quilt was made in the 1930's at Marshall County, TN by the owner's mother, Pearl Harwell Allen (born 1/1/1887 at Giles County, TN, married Kennie A. Allen, died 3/3/1972 at Lewisburg, TN).

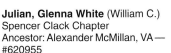

**Julian, Glenna White** (William C.)
Spencer Clack Chapter
Ancestor: Alexander McMillan, VA — #620955
This "One Patch" quilt was pieced 1930-40 at Knox County, TN by the owner's mother-in-law, Lola Mae Manes Julian (born 4/13/1906 at Sevier County, TN, married Louie Calloway Julian, died 3/1978 at Knox County, TN). It is made from feed sacks. Many women purchased the number of feedsacks of a particular design to get enough fabric for a sewing project. This quilt is machined quilted.

**Julian, Glenna White** (William C.)
Spencer Clack Chapter
Ancestor: Alexander McMillan, VA — #620955
This "ABC" quilt was made in 1934 at Knox County, TN by the owner's aunt, Helma Lee White (born 8/30/1909 at Knox County, married Artel Trent, died 10/15/1992 at Knox County). It was used with babies from 1934-64. George White was Helma Lee's oldest brother when she made the quilt for his children. It was kept and used when the 7 grandchildren came to visit. When Mrs. George M. White died, it was willed to the current owner.

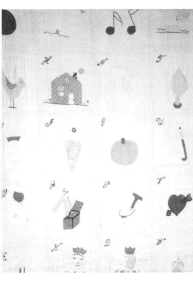

**Jones, Shirley Farris** (Jerry L.)
Col. Hardy Murfree
Ancestor: Richard Faris, VA
—#744308
This "Nine Patch/Four Patch" quilt was made in 1941-42 at Manchester, TN by the owner's grandmother, Mary Neese Farris. Dr. Farris suffered a stroke. When the maker made this quilt, she was caring for an invalid husband as well as raising a teenage son. Much of the fabric for this quilt came from Martha White Flour sacks. The 1930's brought much change to the Farris family.

**Julian, Glenna White** (William C.)
Spencer Clack Chapter
Ancestor: Alexander McMillan, VA —#620955
This "Ocean Waves" quilt was pieced in 1900 at Knox County, TN by the owner's great grandmother, Annie Elizabeth Drummer White (born 3/3/1855 at Knox County, married George M. White who was born 8/26/1851, died 5/14/1923 at Knox County). The quilt was quilted by other members of the family. Annie's ancestors were from Rhinstock Saxony, Germany. She made this quilt for her first grandchild who was named after the maker's husband. It was then willed to the current owner.

**Julian, Glenna White** (William C.)
Spencer Clack Chapter
Ancestor: Alexander McMillan, VA — #620955
This "Yo Yo" quilt was made in 1955 at Knox County, TN by the owner (born 2/16/1937 at Knox County). She made the quilt while her husband to be was doing his college homework. This was a way to be together while both were occupied doing different things.

**Julian, Glenna White** (William C.)
Spencer Clack Chapter
Ancestor: Alexander McMillan, VA — #620955
This "Wild Flowers" quilt was pieced in 1976-77 at Sevier County, TN by the owner, her husband and children, Dub Glenna, Guane, Jerome, Giner and Ian. The blocks were sewn together by the owner's mother, Bessie Huffstetler White. It was quilted by the "Wandering Widows," a group of Bessie's friends who often quilted together.

**Julian, Glenna White**
(William C.)
Spencer Clack Chapter
Ancestor: Alexander McMillan, VA — #620955
This "Tulip" quilt was made in the 1920's at Blount County, TN by the owner's great grandmother, Melissa Emmaline Saffell Huffstetler (born 11/2/1842 at Blount County, TN married George Washington Huffstetler, died 7/13/1938 at Blount County). Mellisa's youngest granddaughter, Bessie Violet Huffstetler was living with her in Nash-

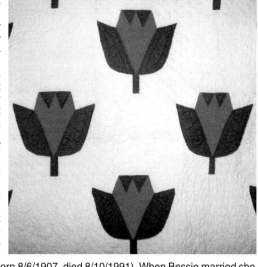

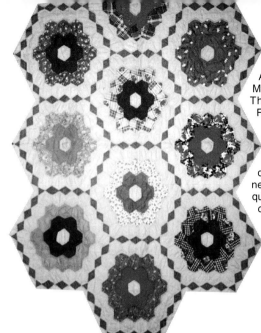

**Julian, Glenna White**
(William C.)
Spencer Clack Chapter
Ancestor: Alexander McMillan, VA —#620955
This "Grandmother's Flower Garden" quilt was pieced in 1942 at Knox County, TN by the owner's mother, Bessie Huffstetler White and quilted with help from neighboring women. This quilt was always kept in the cedar chest with the knowledge that it would someday belong to the owner.

ville, TN. Bessie was born 8/6/1907, died 8/10/1991). When Bessie married she made her this quilt. The quilt was never used for daily wear. It was stored carefully in a cedar chest made by George White in 1918. It was only taken out for special occasions. The quilt and chest are still together.

**Keene, Flora Mae Summitt**
(W.B. Keene)
Rhea-Craig Chapter
Ancestor: Johannes Francis Summitt, NC — #776911
This "Flower Basket" quilt was made circa 1925 at Loudon County, TN by the owner's mother-in-law, Mrs. Roy F. Keene (born 7/27/1891 at Burton Mill, TN, died 5/15/1970 at Knoxville, TN). It was given to the owner circa 1945.

**Keene, Flora Mae Summitt**
(W.B. Keene)
Rhea-Craig Chapter
Ancestor: Johannes Francis Summitt, NC — #776911
This "Flower Basket" quilt was made circa 1920 at Madisonville, TN by the owner's mother, Mrs. Murray Summitt (born 5/15/1891, 2/16/1973 at Monroe County, TN).

**Keene, Flora Mae Summitt**
(W.B. Keene)
Rhea-Craig Chapter
Ancestor: Johannes Francis Summitt, NC — #776911
This "Bow Tie" quilt was made over 155 years ago probably at Madisonville, TN.

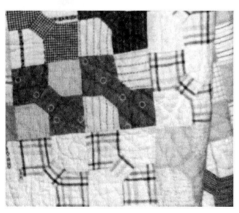

**Kelton, Claudette Durham** (Samuel)
Robert Cooke Chapter
Ancestor: Samuel Durham, VA —#623501
This "Variation of Sunrise" coverlet was made in KY by Cassie Jane Tucker Durham.

**Kelton, Claudette Durham**
(Samuel)
Robert Cooke Chapter
Ancestor: Samuel Durham, VA —#623501
This coverlet "Snail Trail and Cat Tracks" was made by Cassie Jane Tucker Durham (born 4/19/1884 at Taylor County, KY, married Frank Halsey Durham, died 12/25/1926 at Columbia, KY). The owner inherited the quilt.

**Kenna, Sylvia Dianne Burnette**
(Fenton Lee)
Great Smokies Chapter
Ancestor: Capt. George Doherty, NC —
#772894
This "Bow Tie" quilt was made before
1931 at Corinth, MS by the owner's great
grandmother, Rehaba Ellen Love
Vincent (born 12/9/1852 at Weakley
County, TN, married William Harley
Vincent, died 5/5/1941 at Corinth, MS).
"Grandma Vincent to Diane" is embroi-
dered on the edge.

**Kenna, Sylvia Dianne Burnette**
(Fenton Lee)
Great Smokies Chapter
Ancestor: Capt. George Doherty, NC
—#772894
This "Postage Stamp" quilt was made
in the 1950's at Corinth, MS by the
owner's step grandmother, Edna
Tirner Morris Barar ( born 1898 or 99
at Indian Territory, OK, married John
Morris, married 2nd Harold Barar, died
1989 at Denver, CO).

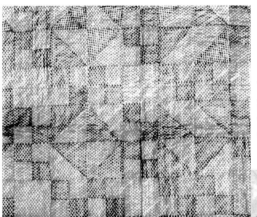

**Kilts, Craigie Powell**
(Ralph)
Tullahoma Chapter
Ancestor: William Dale,
VA 650378
This is a "Variation of
Jacob's Ladder" quilt.

**Kilts, Craigie Powell** (Ralph)
Tullahoma Chapter
Ancestor: William Dale, VA 650378
This "Butterfly" quilt was made by the owner's
mother, Ruth Rankin Samuel (born 6/7/1878
at Indian Territory, OK, married Lester
Samuel).

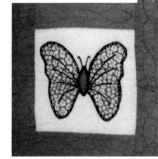

**King, Elizabeth Barber** (Joe D.)
Charlotte Reeves Robertson Chapter
Ancestor: James Carr, NC —#592162
This "Cathedral Window" quilt was
made in 1978 at Bradford, TN by the
owner's step grandmother, Elsie
Overton (born 11/25/1908 at Bradford,
TN, married Thomas Paul Overton).
This quilt was made with material from
the owner's clothes as a child. It was
given to the owner as a wedding
present.

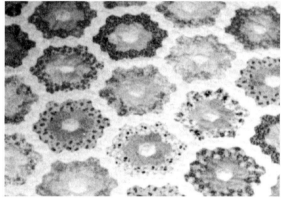

**King, Elizabeth Barber** (Joe D.)
Charlotte Reeves Robertson Chapter
Ancestor: James Carr, NC —#592162
This "Grandmother's Flower Garden" quilt was made in the
1970's at Springfield, TN by the owner's husband's paternal
grandmother, Floy King (born 8/7/1897 at Springfield, TN,
married Roy L. King). The owner received this quilt as a wedding present.

**King, Elizabeth Barber** (Joe D.)
Charlotte Reeves Robertson Chapter
Ancestor: James Carr, NC —#592162
This "Grandmother's Flower Garden" quilt was made at Russeville,
KY by the owner's maternal grandmother, Willie Berry (born 12/3/
1905 in KY, married Meade H. Berry).

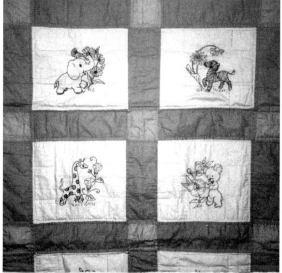

**King, Rebecca Bruch**
(Benjamin Fenner)
Zachariah Davies Chapter
Ancestor: Capt. William
Brockett, SC —#759122
This original "Animals and
Flowers" embroidered quilt
was made in 1948 at Pleas-
ant Shade, TN by the
owner's grandmother,
Tennie Hackett Ballard
(born 1/1902 at Pleasant
Shade, married A.F. Ballard,
died 6/1973 at Carthage,
TN). There are six panels
with animals and flowers.
The quilt was made for the
owner when she was born.

**King, Rebecca Bruch** (Benjamin Fenner)
Zachariah Davies Chapter
Ancestor: Capt. William Brockett, SC —#759122
This "Carolina Lilly" quilt was made in the 1870's at Douglasville, TX by the owner's husband's great aunt, Xaviera King (born at Douglasville, TX). The quilt was passed from the maker's brother, the Rev. Whitaker King to his son Vernon H. King to the maker's grandson, Benjamin F. King. The quilt was made for Whitaker to take to seminary in Louisville, KY. It has remained in the owner's husband's family along with the desk he took with him to school.

**King, Sarah McKelley** (Walter Hughey)
Col. Hardy Murphree Chapter
Ancestor Lt. David Jameson, VA —#481123
This "DAR" quilt was pieced and quilted by Mrs. Paul H. Long (Pamela), who was Historian General, National Society of the Daughters of the American Revolution. It was presented to the

owner when she was the President General, NSDAR. This presentation was made at the national board meeting held in Washington, D.C. The quilt features the signatures of every executive committee member, of each Vice-president General and of each State Regent. The evening event was called "This Is Your Life" and the presentation of the quilt, bearing the insignia of the NSDAR, was the highlight.

**King, Sarah McKelley** (Walter Hughey)
Col. Hardy Murphree Chapter
Ancestor Lt. David Jameson, VA —#481123
This "Crown of Thorns / New York Beauty" quilt was made by Amy Craddock of Jonesville, LA. The owner purchased the quilt from the Catahoula Chapter, Louisiana DAR, while she was in that state as a guest speaker at the 1993 State Conference. The owner had this beautiful quilt cleaned by a conservator in Washington, D.C.

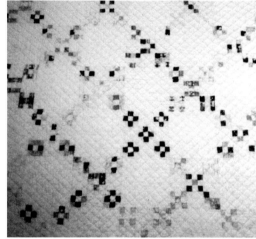

**Kittrell, Betty Brient** (William Henry)
General William Lenoir Chapter
Ancestor: James Matthews, NC —#649968
This "Postage Stamp and Diamond" quilt was made in the 1830's at Blount County, TN by the owner's husband's great grandmother, Sarah Bowerman Hoover (born 5/12/1802 at Blount County, married John Jefferson Hoover, died 5/1/1842 in the same county).

**Knight, Mabel L.**
Old Reynoldsburgh Chapter
Ancestor: James Hamilton, NC —#708705
This "Autumn Leaf" quilt was made in 1936 at Humphreys County, TN by the children and mothers of Halls Creek school as a gift for Louise Powers McDonald, a teacher. The Powers family gave the owner the quilt.

**Knight, Mabel L.**
Old Reynoldsburgh Chapter
Ancestor: James Hamilton, NC —#708705
This "Amish Lily" quilt was made in 1897 at Humphreys County, TN. The quilt was given to Mae Summers Knight (born 9/5/1897) as a baby gift from her aunt Harriet Summers.

**Knodel, Waldine Clark** (Howard)
General James Winchester Chapter
Ancestor: Charles Lee, VA —#755326
This "Jacob's Ladder" quilt was made in 1930 at Cyril, OK by the owner's grandmother, Annie Black (born in 1865 at Franklin County, TN, married Warner Black, died in 1947 at Cyril, OK). The following was written on the quilt: "Given to Waldine Feb. 2, 1930 for her 12th birthday. By grandmother, Annie Black." The quilt is made of linen.

**Knoll, Judith Peace** (Edward)
Mary Blount Chapter
Ancestor: Elisha Battle, VA —#349084
This "Carpenter's Square" quilt was made before 1900 in West TN. The owner's aunt, Sadie Hastings Boyd, brought the quilt to Madisonville in 1925 when she moved from Big Sandy, TN to live with the owner's parents, T.W. and Mary Hastings Peace. She had been left a young widow with an invalid daughter in the early 1900's. She had remade her home with her parents, John and Mary E. Greer Hastings in Big Sandy until her move to Madisonville. Because this quilt came from her husband's family, it has always been referred to as the "Boyd Quilt."

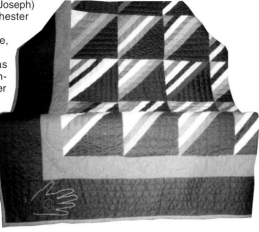

**Koltick, Lona Black** (Joseph)
General James Winchester Chapter
Ancestor: Charles Lee, VA —#662500
This "Amish" quilt was made in 1986 at Winchester, TN by the owner (born 3/24/1923 at Cyril, OK). The quilt is inscribed "With my heart in my hand LK 1986." The quilter's hand is traced on the quilt. This is an Amish tradition.

**Kristofferson, Frances Sain** (H.C.)
Campbell Chapter
Ancestor: Capt Hugh Innes —#716095
This "Rose Cross" quilt was acquired from Mrs. Mabel Mays Welsh, who was a niece of the maker, Mrs. Fannie M. Perry. Mabel is the owner's second cousin. The quilt was inherited from the owner's mother, Mrs. Wade Sain.

**Lackey, Rinehart Miller** (Carl)
Ocoee Chapter
Ancestor: Adam Wetzel, PA — #696797
This "Lone Star" quilt was made in Polk County, TN by the owner's husband's aunt, Martha Ann Lackey Carpenter (born 10/11/1877 at Old Fort, TN, married Jack Carpenter, died 4/28/1962 at same town). The quiltmaker was the sister of the owner's father, Sam. She had no children. The quilt was given to the current owner at Martha's death.

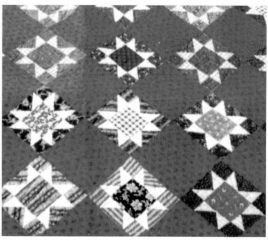

**Lackey, Rinehart Miller** (Carl)
Ocoee Chapter
Ancestor: Adam Wetzel, PA — #696797
This "Star" quilt was made 1912-1915 in Johnson County, TN by owner's mother, Lena Kate Wills Miller (married Leonidas D. Miller 1915, died "9/18/1923 in Johnson County, TN). The quilt was pieced before her marriage. Lena Kate was born and lived on the Valverda farm five miles north of Mountain City, TN. The fabric used for the quilt was left over scraps from family clothing. A particular favorite of the owner is a horseshoe design. The quilting was done in the 1950's by a Mrs. DeFriese in Cleveland, TN. The quilt was given directly to the owner by her mother who was a member of the Mountain City Chapter of the DAR.

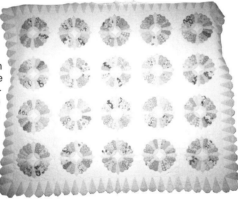

**Lamb, Mary Gilbert** (F. Michael)
Robert Cooke Chapter
Ancestor: Sgt. Daniel McKenney, NC — #677076
This "Variation of a Dresden Plate" quilt was made in the late 1920's by the owner's maternal grandmother, Maude Anna Kibler Edwards (born 1878 at Bradley County, TN, married Edgar Arthur Edwards, died in 1930 in the same county).

**Lamon, Elizabeth Patton** (Fred)
Chucalissa Chapter
Ancestor: Samuel Pointer, VA — #718207
This "Milky Way" quilt was made in 1950 by Mrs. Hamlin, a neighbor and friend of the owner. It was the prize ticket at the Tennessee Bicentennial Celebration at Boonehill, TN in 1996. Mrs. Hamlin said the quilt had been in her cedar chest unused. It was made from her clothing scraps, even some from her childhood.

**Lamon, Elizabeth Patton** (Fred)
Chucalissa Chapter
Ancestor: Samuel Pointer, VA — #718207
This "Double Wedding Ring" quilt was made prior to 1962 in Pennsylvania, and the owner inherited it from her maternal great aunt, Annie Mae Hitchens Sheffer (Phil A.), when she died 9/1962 in Berlin, PA.

**Lamon, Elizabeth Patton** (Fred)
Chucalissa Chapter
Ancestor: Samuel Pointer, VA — #718207
This "Sunbonnet Sue and Overall Bill" quilt was made in 1939 in Memphis, TN by the owner's aunt, Mildred Patton Farris (born 6/6/1912 at East lake, AL, married Hartle H. Farris, died 1/11/1993 at Memphis, TN). The quilt was made for Joanna Farris (1939 -1986).The owner inherited this quilt and uses it for grandchildren.

**Lamon, Elizabeth Patton** (Fred)
Chucalissa Chapter
Ancestor: Samuel Pointer, VA — #718207
This "Grandmother's Flower Garden" quilt was made in the mid 1930's in Memphis, TN by the owner's aunt, Mildred Patton Farris. She was assisted by her mother-in-law, Lela Carruthers Farris. They made the quilt not long after the marriage of Mildred and Hartle.

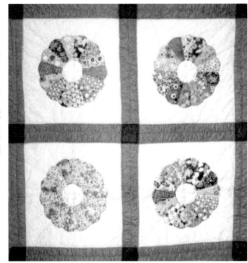

**Lamon, Elizabeth Patton** (Fred)
Chucalissa Chapter
Ancestor: Samuel Pointer, VA — #718207
This "Dresden Plate" quilt was made in the 1940's in Memphis, TN by the owner's aunt, Mildred Patton Farris.

**Lamon, Elizabeth Patton** (Fred)
Chucalissa Chapter
Ancestor: Samuel Pointer, VA — #718207
This "Block/Brick" quilt was made in 1940 in Memphis TN by the owner's aunt, Mildred Patton Farris.

**Lamon, Elizabeth Patton** (Fred)
Chucalissa Chapter
Ancestor: Samuel Pointer, VA — #718207
This "Crazy" quilt was made circa 1890, in Morgantown, WV. The quiltmaker is unknown. In the 1940's the owner's grandmother gave it to her to use as a bedspread. Two of the squares have initials — "K.H." and "G.H." The owner thinks that the "K.H." could be her great grandmother, Kate Hitchens. The quilt could have been a wedding gift (10/31/1898) or an early marriage gift to the owner's grandmother, Mary Elizabeth Hitchens Brady (married John). There is a practice strip on the quilt which has a ribbon from the Centennial at Morgantown, WV dated 1885. "At this time my grandmother was 14 years old and may have worked on this strip (or her baby sister who was five or six years old)."

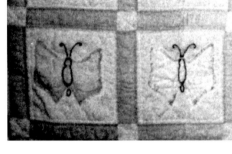

**Lamon, Elizabeth Patton** (Fred)
Chucalissa Chapter
Ancestor: Samuel Pointer, VA — #718207
This "Butterfly" quilt was made before 1950 in Lincoln County, TN by Mrs. Paul Shaw. Mr. and Mrs. Shaw were tenant farmers who gave the quilt to the owner's aunt and uncle, Lewis and Nina Brady, when they moved to the family farm in 1950. The quilt was "used hard" by the Brady's and by the current owner. The cotton is lumpy and the applique stitches are wearing out.

**Lamon, Elizabeth Patton** (Fred)
Chucalissa Chapter
Ancestor: Samuel Pointer, VA — #718207
This "Picnic" quilt was made in the early 1970's in Memphis, TN by the owner's life long friend, Cary Cartwright Pou (born in 1924 at Memphis, TN, married Dudley M. Pou).

**Lasley, Regina Mann** (John T.)
Jane Knox Chapter
Ancestor: John Pearson, Jr., VA — #630564
This "Fan" quilt was made in 1992 in Maury County, TN by Daphne Caruthers and Irene Sneed, friends of the owner.

**Lasslo-Meeks, Millicent** (Dennis)
Chickasaw Bluff Chapter
Ancestor: Price Key, VA — #662046
This "Jack-in-the Box" quilt was made in Tallahatchie County, MS several years ago by owner's husband's grandmother, Addie Rhew White (born 7/19/1907, married J.V. White, died 7/17/1995). The quiltmaker made a quilt for each of her grandchildren. She gave this one to owner's husband.

**Latham, Olive Atchley** (Earl)
Spencer Clack Chapter
Ancestor: Col. Samuel Wear, VA — #359985
This "Crazy" quilt was made in Sevierville, TN by owner's cousin, Miss Adah Mullendore (born 1882 at Sevierville, TN and died 1988 in the same county). The quilt was given to the owner at the death of her cousin.

**Latimore, Alice Walton** (William S., Jr.)
Judge David Campbell Chapter.
Ancestor: Thomas Boyd, PA — #564735
This "Feathered Star" quilt was made circa 1850 in Rhea County, TN by the owner's husband's great grandmother, Elizabeth Brabson Smith Roddy(e) (born 6/16/1822 in Rhea County, married David M. Roddy, died 1/26/1902 in the same county). This quilt was passed from quiltmaker, to daughter, Ann Preston Roddy Thomas (married Joseph Harry), to Mary Belle Thomas Latimore (married William S.), to son, William Spears Latimore Jr., to the present owner. The quilt was shown at the "Quilts of Tennessee" exhibit at the Hunter Museum in 1982 and was documented by Bets Ramsey and Merikay Waldvogel in 1984.

**Latimore, Alice Walton** (William S., Jr.)
Judge David Campbell Chapter.
Ancestor: Thomas Boyd, PA — #564735
This "Building Blocks" quilt was made in the early 1900's in Rhea County, TN by a member of the owner's husband's family. It was given to the current owner by her mother-in-law. In recent months, when the owner

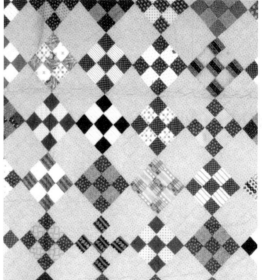

was moving, she found this quilt and noticed that the back was made of feed sacks. Words such as "lb." can be seen faintly on the back. The feed sacks were probably from the quiltmaker's farm in the country before she moved to Chattanooga, TN.

**Latimore, Alice Walton** (William S., Jr.)
Judge David Campbell Chapter.
Ancestor: Thomas Boyd, PA — #564735
This "Grandmother's Flower Garden" quilt was made in the early 1930's in Chattanooga, TN by the owner's aunt, Margaret Seagle Hackney (born 7/15/1898 at St. Elmo, TN, died 4/26/1989 at Lookout Mountain, TN). Margaret gave this quilt to the owner 15 or 20 years ago. Aunt Margaret told her that the quilt was made from scraps of fabric from hers and her sister's (owner's mother) dresses.
She said the green fabric was suppose to be a vine. The hexagons are very small, one inch on each side.

**Lauer, Jacquelyn Acord** (Rodney)
Tullahoma Chapter
Ancestor: Samuel Huckstep, VA — #727649
This "Diagonal Nine Patch" quilt was made in York County, PA by the owner's husband's great grandmother, Savannah Raffensberger Lauer (born 10/12/1835 at York County, PA, married Peter Ahl Lauer, died 1/14/1900 at York County). The quilt was passed from great grandmother, to her son, to his son.

**Lauer, Jacquelyn Acord** (Rodney)
Tullahoma Chapter
Ancestor: Samuel Huckstep, VA — #727649
This "Wild Goose Chase" quilt was made in 1938-39 in York, PA by husband's grandmother, Anna Rebecca Smyser Brunhouse (born 8/2/1874 at York, PA, married Fredrick W. Brunhouse, (died 8/20/1948 at York). The quilt was passed from grandmother to grandson.

**Lauer, Jacquelyn Acord** (Rodney)
Tullahoma Chapter
Ancestor: Samuel Huckstep, VA — #727649
This "Baby Blocks" quilt was made in 1939-40 in York, Pennsylvania by owner's husband's grandmother, Anna Rebecca Smyser Brunhouse. It was passed from grandmother, to daughter, to son ( husband of current owner).

**Lauer, Jacquelyn Acord**
(Rodney)
Tullahoma Chapter
Ancestor: Samuel Huckstep,
VA — #727649
This "Basket of Pansies" quilt
was made in York, PA by the
owner's husband's grand-
mother, Ellen Katherine
Copenhafer Lauer (born 1/8/
1865 at York, PA, married
Franklin P. Lauer, died 6/3/
1930 at York). The quilt was
passed from grandmother, to
son to son (husband of current owner).

**Lea, Lucinda Taylor**
(James W. Jr.)
Col. Hardy Murfree
Chapter
Ancestor: Thomas
Barnes, NC —
#763227
This "Dresden Plate"
quilt was made in
1982 at Cookeville,
TN by the owner's
mother, Edith Breed-
ing Taylor (born 3/30/
1917 at Putnam County,
TN, married Harris Tay-
lor, died 8/28/1997).

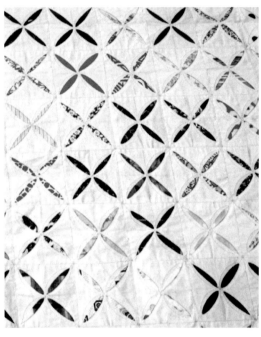

**Lea, Lucinda Taylor**
(James W. Jr.)
Col. Hardy Murfree
Chapter
Ancestor: Thomas
Barnes, NC —
#763227
This "Stained Glass
Window" quilt was
made in 1986 at
Cookeville, TN by the
owner's mother-in-
law, Ruth Hankins
Lea (born 9/8/1919 at
Wilson County, TN,
married James W.
Lea, Sr., died 2/25/
1990 at Putnam
County, TN).

**Lea, Lucinda Taylor**
(James W. Jr.)
Col. Hardy Murfree
Chapter
Ancestor: Thomas
Barnes, NC —
#763227
This "Bow Tie" quilt
was made in 1974 at
Cookeville, TN by the
owner's mother, Edith
Breeding Taylor. The
quilt was made as a
gift for the owner.

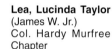

**Lea, Lucinda Taylor**
(James W. Jr.)
Col. Hardy Murfree
Chapter
Ancestor: Thomas
Barnes, NC —#763227
This "Star of Bethlehem"
quilt was made in 1985 at
Cookeville, TN by the
owner's mother-in-law,
Ruth Hankins Lea.

**Lea, Lucinda Taylor**
(James W. Jr.)
Col. Hardy Murfree Chapter
Ancestor: Thomas Barnes,
NC —#763227
This "Dresden Plate" quilt
was made in Cookeville, TN
by the owner's mother, Edith
Breeding Taylor.

**Lea, Lucinda Taylor**
(James W. Jr.)
Col. Hardy Murfree
Chapter
Ancestor: Thomas Barnes,
NC —#763227
This "Double Wedding Ring"
quilt was made in 1980 at
Cookeville, TN by the owner's
mother, Edith Breeding Taylor.

**Leftwich, Mary Lancaster**
(Ray)
Caney Fork Chapter
Ancestor: William Jared, VA
— #606344
This woven coverlet was
made in the 1850's or later
by someone on the paternal
side of the owner's family,
the Ira B. Cowan or Matthew
Hogan Family (early 1800's
to 1870's Lancaster, PA).
The current owner pur-
chased this coverlet at her
cousin, Goldie Cowan
Reynolds,' estate sale. Her
cousin had told her that this coverlet had come from the owner's grandmother,
Matilda Frances Cowan's family.

**Lemmon, Virginia Holland**
River City Chapter
Ancestor: Abraham Bolt, SC —
#710795
This "Appalachian Autumn
Maple Leaf" quilt was made
circa 1988 at Prentiss
County, MS by the
owner's aunt,
Shirley Mae Holland Parker
(born 8/2/1928 at
Detroit, MI, married
William Raymond
Parker, died 2/11/1990 at
Booneville, MS). "My aunt desired to make quilts for all her
nieces and nephews, but she died
making her third and fourth quilts. Her
daughter had these completed after she
died."

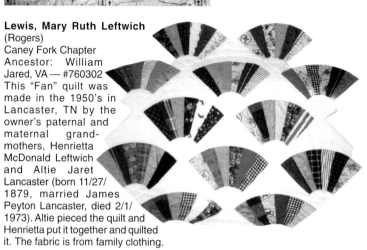

**Lemmon, Virginia Holland**
River City Chapter
Ancestor: Abraham Bolt, SC —
#710795
This original "Family" quilt was
made in 1997 at Shelby County,
TN by the wife of the owner's first
cousin, Jeanne Maureen Roberts Parker(born 4/22/1961, married David Walter Parker).

**Lewis, Mary Ruth Leftwich** (Rogers)
Caney Fork Chapter
Ancestor: William Jared,
VA — #760302
This "Dutch Doll/Sunbonnet Sue" quilt
was made in the 1950's
in Putnam County, TN
by the owner's paternal
grandmother, Henrietta
McDonald Leftwich
(born 10/28/1885 at
Putnam County, TN,
married Roscoe
Leftwich, died 8/30/1968
at Cookeville, TN). The
pieces of fabric are from
the owner's clothes and
those of other family members. The owner also has Henrietta's quilt frame.

**Lewis, Mary Ruth Leftwich**
(Rogers)
Caney Fork Chapter
Ancestor: William
Jared, VA — #760302
This "Fan" quilt was
made in the 1950's in
Lancaster, TN by the
owner's paternal and
maternal grandmothers, Henrietta
McDonald Leftwich
and Altie Jaret
Lancaster (born 11/27/
1879, married James
Peyton Lancaster, died 2/1/
1973). Altie pieced the quilt and
Henrietta put it together and quilted
it. The fabric is from family clothing.

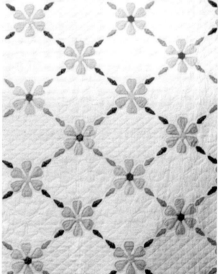

**Lines, Delores Colburn**
(Richard L.)
Cavett Station Chapter
Ancestor: John Ulmer,
MA —#758649
This "Texas Star/Lone
Star" quilt was made in
1937 at Valentine, NE by
the owner's grandmother,
Lizzie Jane Shepard
(born 3/11/1877 at Kent,
IN, married Ora Elbridge
Colburn, died 5/12/1968
at Valentine, NE). "My
grandmother and I had a
very close and special
relationship. Because I
was her first and favorite
granddaughter, she made
this quilt for me using
scraps from my clothes
made by mother. Her eyesight was failing, so this was likely her last quilt."

**Lingerfelt, Nancy Shilling**
(James William.)
William Cocke Chapter
Ancestor: Shilling — #533657
This "Flower" quilt was made
circa 1930 in Columbus, OH by
the owner's grandmother,
Desdemona Dixon Innis (born
6/28/1874 at Licking County,
OH, married Lewis Innis, died
12/29/1949 at Columbus, OH).
The quilt top was apparently a
kit popular in the 1930's. The
quiltmaker is a descendent of
Revolutionary War Soldier
Samuel Poppleton (Nancy
Elnora Warner, Nancy Jane
Poppleton, Daniel, Samuel II,
Samuel). The quilt was handed
down from maker to daughter,
Elnora Innis Shilling, and then
to Elnora's daughter, the current
owner, who quilted it in
1975.

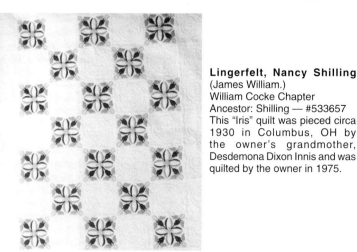

**Lingerfelt, Nancy Shilling**
(James William.)
William Cocke Chapter
Ancestor: Shilling — #533657
This "Iris" quilt was pieced circa
1930 in Columbus, OH by
the owner's grandmother,
Desdemona Dixon Innis and was
quilted by the owner in 1975.

**Lingerfelt, Nancy Shilling**
(James William.)
William Cocke Chapter
Ancestor: Shilling — #533657
This "Six Pointed Star" quilt
was made circa 1950 in Sevier
County, TN by a patient of the
owner's father, Dr. Ralph H.
Shilling. Dr. Shilling gave it to
his daughter as a wedding
present.

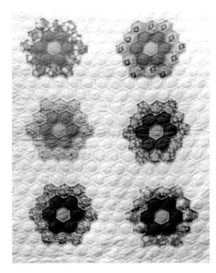

**Lingerfelt, Nancy Shilling (James William.)**
William Cocke Chapter
Ancestor: Shilling — #533657
This "Grandmother's Flower Garden" quilt was pieced circa 1930 in Columbus, OH by the owner's grandmother, Desdemona Innis. "Dess" always wore aprons and the fabric for this quilt was probably made from the wornout ones. It remained unquilted and was passed to the maker's daughter, Elnora Innis Shilling, when the maker died in 1949. The current owner learned to quilt in 1975 and was given several tops which "Dess" had pieced. This quilt was quilted by the owner (born 9/5/1942 in Columbia, SC) in 1976.

**Lingerfelt, Nancy Shilling (James William.)**
William Cocke Chapter
Ancestor: Shilling — #533657
This "Double Nine Patch" quilt was made circa 1876 in Ohio by the owner's great grandmother, Nancy Elnora Warner Dixon (born 9/18/1853 Licking County, OH, married Newton Dixon, died 10/10/ 1911 at Licking County). In one corner of the quilt is the outline of a tiny hand the size of a two year old's. Desdemona Dixon was born to Nancy and Newton Dixon in 1874 and under the little hand are the initials "D.D."

**Lingerfelt, Nancy Shilling (James William.)**
William Cocke Chapter
Ancestor: Shilling — #533657
This "One Patch" quilt was made circa 1800-1830 in Licking County, OH by either Nancy Wilbur Poppleton (wife of Daniel Poppleton, died 12/16/1879) or by her daughter, Nancy Jane Poppleton Warner (born 4/24/1823, married Daniel Warner, died 7/18/1907).

**Lingerfelt, Nancy Shilling (James William.)**
William Cocke Chapter
Ancestor: Shilling — #533657
This "Bow Tie/Spool" quilt was made circa 1800-1830 in Ohio probably by Nancy Wilbur Poppleton or her daughter, Nancy Jane Poppleton Warner.

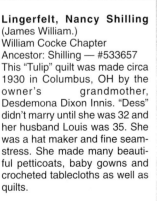

**Lingerfelt, Nancy Shilling (James William.)**
William Cocke Chapter
Ancestor: Shilling — #533657
This coverlet was made circa 1800 in either New York or Ohio by someone in the Daniel Poppleton family - either Rosannah Poppleton, wife of Samuel Poppleton I or Caroline Osborne Poppleton, wife of Samuel Poppleton II.

**Lingerfelt, Nancy Shilling (James William.)**
William Cocke Chapter
Ancestor: Shilling — #533657
This coverlet was made circa 1800 in either New York or Ohio by either Caroline Osborne Poppleton or Nancy Wilbur Poppleton (died 1879 at Overton, OH).

**Lingerfelt, Nancy Shilling (James William.)**
William Cocke Chapter
Ancestor: Shilling — #533657
This blanket was hand woven on the Poppleton farm in Licking County, OH circa 1800-1815. It is probably similar to what soldiers carried with them during the War Between the States.

**Lingerfelt, Nancy Shilling (James William.)**
William Cocke Chapter
Ancestor: Shilling — #533657
This "Tulip" quilt was made circa 1930 in Columbus, OH by the owner's grandmother, Desdemona Dixon Innis. "Dess" didn't marry until she was 32 and her husband Louis was 35. She was a hat maker and fine seamstress. She made many beautiful petticoats, baby gowns and crocheted tablecloths as well as quilts.

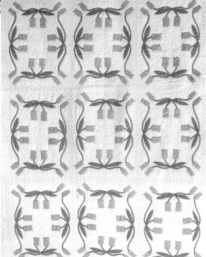

UNION
UNICOI
VAN BUREN
WARREN
WASHINGTON
WAYNE
WEAKLEY
WHITE
WILLIAMSON
WILSON
ANDERSON
BEDFORD
BENTON
BLEDSOE
BLOUNT
BRADLEY
CAMPBELL
CANNON
CARROLL
CARTER
CHEATHAM
CHESTER
CLAIBORNE
CLAY
COCKE
COFFEE
CROCKETT
CUMBERLAND
DAVIDSON
DECATUR
DEKALB
DICKSON
DYER
FAYETTE
FENTRESS
FRANKLIN
GIBSON
GILES
GRAINGER
GREENE
GRUNDY
HAMBLEN
HAMILTON
HANCOCK
HARDEMAN
HARDIN
HAWKINS
HAYWOOD
HENDERSON
HENRY
HICKMAN
HOUSTON
HUMPHREYS
JACKSON
JEFFERSON
JOHNSON
KNOX
LAKE
LAUDERDALE
LAWRENCE
LEWIS
LINCOLN
LOUDON
MACON
MADISON
MARION
MARSHALL
MAURY
McMINN
McNAIRY
MEIGS
MONROE
MONTGOMERY
MOORE
MORGAN
OBION
OVERTON
PERRY
PICKETT
POLK
PUTNAM
RHEA
ROANE
ROBERTSON
RUTHERFORD
SCOTT
SEVIER
SEQUATCHIE
SHELBY
SMITH
STEWART
SULLIVAN
SUMNER
TIPTON
TROUSDALE
our smoky mountains
Sevier Station
Col. John Montgomery
TENNESSEE
200
LAST BATTLE OF REVOLUTIONARY WAR
LOOKOUT MOUNTAIN CHATTANOOGA
CANEY FORK CHAPTER
King's Mountain Messenger Chapter
ROCK HOUSE
SPARTA, TN
CAMPBELL CHAPTER
Presidential Fanfare
1796
TENNESSEE
1996
MARBLE SPRINGS-HOME OF JOHN SEVIER -- FIRST GOVERNOR OF TENNESSEE
THE HERMITAGE
JOHN NEEL CHAPTER
MURFREESBORO
GEOGRAPHICAL
FORT NASHBOROUGH
FORT BLOUNT
CUMBERLAND RIVER
AVERY
TRACE
200
CHUCALISSA
Long Island Chapter
STATE HISTORIC AREA

*Jamie Clifton*

*Carolee McKinstry*

Janet Gann

Helen Stephens

Laura Reagan

Jamie Clifton

Nancy Lingerfelt

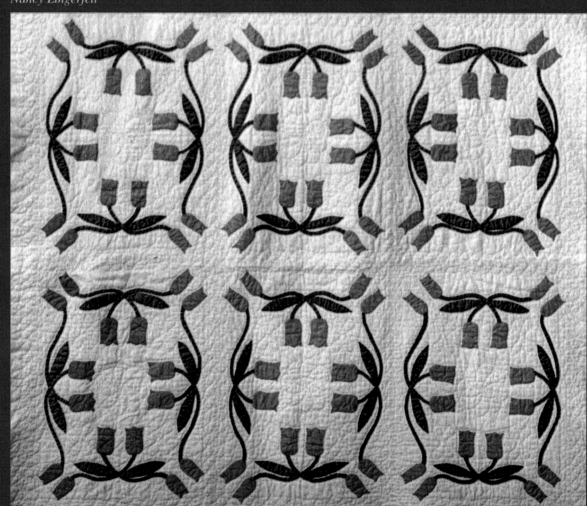

*Lee Petry*

*Juanita Crosby*

*Alice Mitchum Fitts*

*Dinah House*

JAN·10·1913

*Barbara Sliger*

*Nina Sutton*

Suzanne Field

Suzanne Burow

Juanita Crosby

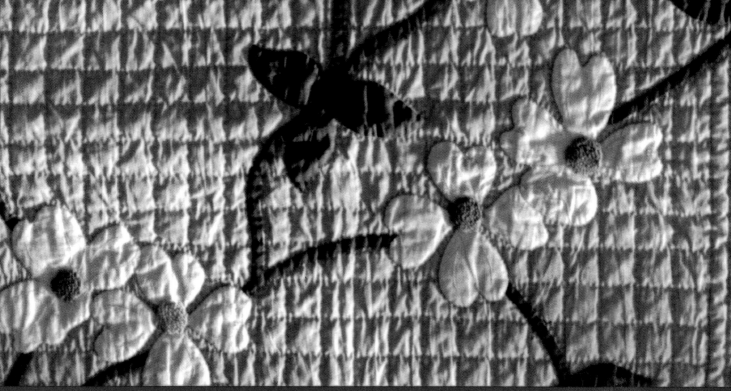

*Betty Pope*

*Julia Bawcum*

Sandra T. Gallaway

Anne Hightower

Judith Chaffin

*Elizabeth Stevens*

*Charlotte Reynolds*

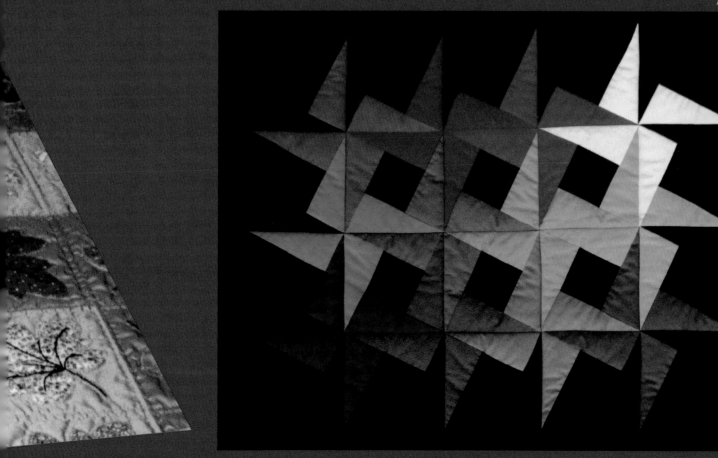

Lee Petry

*Heritage in Quilts* **125**

Ila Mae Morton

Betty Ruth Davis

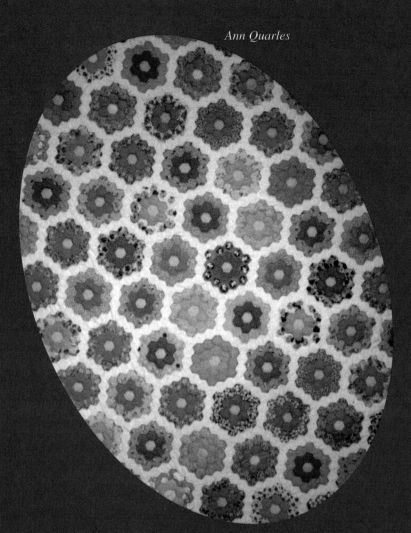

Ann Quarles

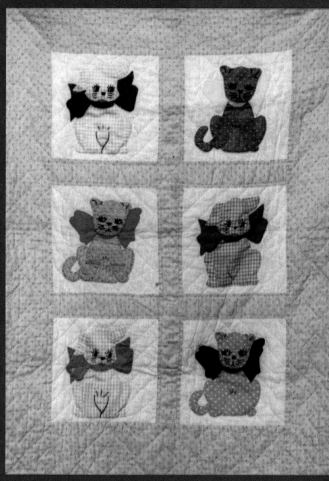

Bridget Ciaramitaro

Jamie Clifton

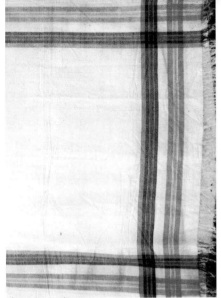

**Lingerfelt, Nancy Shilling**
(James William.)
William Cocke Chapter
Ancestor: Shilling — #533657
This hand woven, woolen coverlet was made by, according to family history, Rosannah Whaley, wife of Samuel Poppleton I. He was the the father of Revolutionary War Soldier Samuel Poppleton II (born 12/25/1751).

**Lingerfelt, Nancy Shilling**
(James William.)
William Cocke Chapter
Ancestor: Shilling — #533657
This "Virginia Snowball/Ohio Star/Hummingbird" quilt was pieced circa 1943-45 in Columbus, OH by the owner's grandmother, Desdemona Dixon Innis. It is composed of scraps of baby clothing made for the owner and piece's from the owner's mother's only maternity dress. The quiltmaker was 68-70 years old when she made this top. It was in the possession of the quiltmaker's daughter Elnora until the 1970's when it was given to the current owner to quilt and keep.

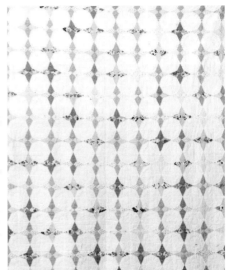

**Lingerfelt, Nancy Shilling**
(James William.)
William Cocke Chapter
Ancestor: Shilling — #533657
This coverlet was made circa 1800 in either New York or Ohio by either Rosannah Poppleton or Caroline Osborne Poppleton.

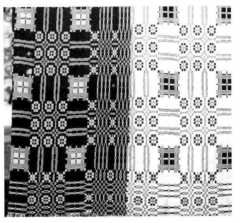

**Lingerfelt, Nancy Shilling**
(James William.)
William Cocke Chapter
Ancestor: Shilling — #533657
This woolen coverlet was made circa 1800 in either New York or Ohio by either Rosannah Poppleton or Caroline Osborne Poppleton.

**Lingerfelt, Nancy Shilling**
(James William.)
William Cocke Chapter
Ancestor: Shilling — #533657
This "Drunkard's Path" quilt was made in either Ohio or Maryland by the owner's great great paternal grandmother. This quilt has embroidered in one corner, "Feb 1898 to B.A. Wilkinson from Granma Hagar." These quilts were made for sisters, Effie and Blanche Wilkinson, by their maternal grandmother Hagar. Effie died from unknown causes at age sixteen and Blanche was given her sister's quilt. Blanche was the paternal grandmother of the current owner.

**Little, Edith Burns**
(Eugene)
Mary Blount Chapter
Ancestor: James Taylor, NC — #381536
This "Wild Rose" quilt was made in the 1930's at Maryville College in Maryville, TN by the current owner who was 90 years old in 1998. In the 1930's, this college had a maidshop where students could learn sewing. This quilt was made from one of the first "quilt kits" by Edith Little in whose possession it has been since then. Then hundreds of this "Wild Rose" pattern were made and sold during the depression.

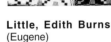

**Litton, Hermena Dickerson**
(Bill)
Chief John Ross Chapter
Ancestor: James Landrum, VA — #556190
This "Butterfly" quilt was made in the 1930's in Morristown, TN by the owner's paternal grandmother, Sara Thomas Dickerson (born 1882 in Iowa, married R. Dickerson, died 1960 at Morristown). As a small child the owner loved the butterflies on the quilt and called the quilt "Mena's" butterflies. When the owner married, her grandmother gave the quilt to her.

**Litton, Hermena Dickerson**
(Bill)
Chief John Ross Chapter
Ancestor: James Landrum, VA — #556190
This "Crazy" quilt was made in the 1930's in Morristown, TN by the owner's grandmother, Sara Thomas Dickerson, who gave the quilt to her.

**Long, Lucye Maxwell**
(Max)
Caney Fork Chapter
Ancestor: Joseph Morgan, NC — #602813
This "Poppy" quilt was made in Gainsboro, TN by Thelma Rodgers Page. The owner bought the quilt kit and had the quiltmaker applique and quilt it. It won first prize in its category at the "Polk Salat" Festival in Gainsboro, TN in 1998.

**Long, Lucye Maxwell**
(Max)
Caney Fork Chapter
Ancestor: Joseph Morgan, NC — #602813
This "Grandmother's Flower Garden" quilt was made in 1938-1950 in Gainsboro, TN by the owner (born 1/18/22 at Gainsboro). She started piecing this quilt when she was a teenager. She finished the quilt long after she married. This cherished quilt contains pieces of fabric from the quiltmaker's mother's, sisters' and her own dresses. Two favorites are fabric from a dress made by the owner in her first year of Home Ec and one of a housecoat made to wear at boarding school. It won second place in its category at the "Polk Salat" festival in Gainsville, TN in 1998.

**Long, Marcia Maxwell**
(William C)
Rhea Craig Chapter
Ancestor: Nathan Deane, MA — #754011
This "Chevron" quilt was made in 1929 in Athens, OH by the owner's grandmother, Alma Jane Everett Maxwell (born 1/17/1898 at Athens, OH, married Robert Dean, died 3/12/1966 at Athens). It was passed from grandmother to granddaughter.

**Long, Marcia Maxwell**
(William C)
Rhea Craig Chapter
Ancestor: Nathan Deane, MA — #754011
This "Wild Rose" quilt was made in 1908 in Shelby, IA by the owner's great aunt, Ida Delilah Dean Watkins (born 4/19/1876 at Athens, OH, married George E. Watkins, died at Shelby, IA). Passed from maker to current owner. This quilt won first place at the McMinn County Quilt Show at the Hermitage Museum in Athens, TN.

**Long, Marcia Maxwell** (William C)
Rhea Craig Chapter
Ancestor: Nathan Deane, MA — #754011
This "Broken Star" quilt was made in 1927 in Sandusky, OH by the owner's aunt, Jennie Maxwell Bowman (Born 2/1/1906 at Athens, OH, married Harry Bowman, died 4/18/1979 at Sandusky, OH). This quilt received an honorable mention at the McMinn County Quilt Show at the Hermitage Museum in Athens, TN.

**Long, Marcia Maxwell**
(William C)
Rhea Craig Chapter
Ancestor: Nathan Deane, MA — #754011
This "Blazing Star" quilt was made in 1924 in Athens, OH by owner's great aunt, Jeannie Maxwell Bowman.

**Long, Marcia Maxwell**
(William C)
Rhea Craig Chapter
Ancestor: Nathan Deane, MA — #754011
This "Ocean Wave" quilt was made in 1930 in Sandusky, OH by the owner's great aunt, Jennie Maxwell Bowman

**Long, Marcia Maxwell**
(William C)
Rhea Craig Chapter
Ancestor: Nathan Deane, MA — #754011
This "Double Pyramids" quilt was made circa 1879 in Athens, OH by the owner's great great grandmother, Mary Lucinda Dean Stimson (born 9/2/1826 at Athens, OH, married John Hubbard Stimson, died 5/6/1881 at Athens). This quilt won first place in the Smoky Mountain Quilt Show at Oak Ridge, TN in 1987.

**Long, Marcia Maxwell**
(William C)
Rhea Craig Chapter
Ancestor: Nathan Deane, MA — #754011
This "Log Cabin" quilt was made circa 1870 in New England. The owner took care of an elderly lady and she gave her the quilt. She said it was made by her great grandmother.

**Long, Marcia Maxwell**
(William C)
Rhea Craig Chapter
Ancestor: Nathan Deane, MA — #754011
This "Crazy" quilt was made circa the 1890's and was purchased by the owner at an auction.

**Long, Marcia Maxwell**
(William C)
Rhea Craig Chapter
Ancestor: Nathan Deane, MA — #754011
This "Nine Patch" quilt was made circa 1920 in Madisonville, TN where it was purchased by the owner at an antique shop in 1990.

**Lotz, Roberta Moore**
(Gilbert M.)
Chucalissa Chapter
Ancestor: Joseph Manchester, RI — #512181
This "Crazy" quilt was made in 1898 in Carroll County, Ohio by the owner's paternal aunt, Mary Annetta Moore (born 10/19/1873 at Carroll Co., Ohio, died 2/5/1922 at Canton, Stark County, OH). The date is embroidered on it, as well as the initials of a fa-

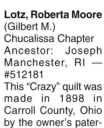

vorite cousin "J.A.M." (John Moore). The owner's father was a brother to the quiltmaker. It has been a Blue Ribbon Winner at Ohio County Fairs.

**Lotz, Roberta Moore**
(Gilbert M.)
Chucalissa Chapter
Ancestor: Joseph Manchester, RI — #512181
This "White on White" quilt was made circa 1858-1865 in Carroll County, OH by the owner's paternal grandmother, Caroline M. McCaskey Moore (born 9/28/1834 at Jefferson County, OH, married John Hunter Moore, died 3/27/1903 at Carroll County, OH). The quilt won Blue Ribbons at Ohio County

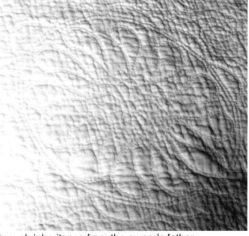

Fairs and was obtained through inheritance from the owner's father.

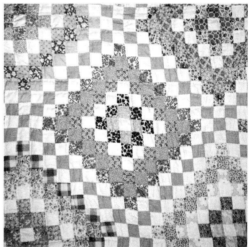

**Lovell, Mary Margaret Erwin** (Monroe)
Jane Knox Chapter
Ancestor: Samuel Moore, VA —#630549
This "Postage Stamp" quilt was made in 1900 at Maury County, TN by the owner's mother, Elizabeth Moore Erwin and her grandmother, Bessie Frank Owen Moore. Elizabeth was born 9/14/1842 and died 10/8/1980. Bessie was born 7/31/1870 and died 9/24/1944).

**Lovell, Mary Margaret Erwin** (Monroe)
Jane Knox Chapter
Ancestor: Samuel Moore, VA —#630549
This "Missouri Puzzle Friendship" quilt was made circa 1930 at McCains, TN by the owners mother, Elizabeth Moore Erwin, and the members of the McCain Cumberland Presbyterian Church Missionary Society. Anyone could have their name on the quilt by donating ten cents. There are 459 names on the quilt.

**Lovell, Mary Margaret Erwin**
(Monroe)
Jane Knox Chapter
Ancestor: Samuel Moore, VA — #630549
This "Winning Ribbons" quilt was made circa 1930 at Columbia, TN by the owner's mother, Elizabeth Moore Erwin. It is made from ribbons she won at the Tennessee State and County Fairs for canning, baking, sewing, flowers, poultry, etc.

**Lowe, Jennifer Johnson** (Todd N.)
Hatchie Chapter
Ancestor: Edgecomb Suggett, VA — #762774
This original design "Double Heart and Squares" quilt was made circa 1900 in Mississippi by the owners great great grandmother, Mary F. Edwards (born 1842 at SC, married L.F. Edwards, died 1912 at Mississippi). This quilt happens to have the heart motif of the current NSDAR President General's administration.

**Lowe, Jennifer Johnson** (Todd N.)
Hatchie Chapter
Ancestor: Edgecomb Suggett, VA —#762774
This "Butterfly" quilt was made in 1948 at Cardwell, MO by the owner's grandmother, Mary Amelia Griffin Johnson (born 1907 at LaGrange, TN, married William Carey Johnson, died 1987 at Bolivar, TN). Amelia went to college in Jonesboro, AR where she met her husband. She taught in Missouri and in Memphis, TN.

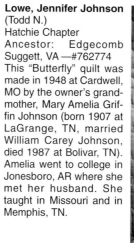

**Lowe, Jennifer Johnson** (Todd N.)
Hatchie Chapter
Ancestor: Edgecomb Suggett, VA —#762774
This "Double Wedding Ring" quilt was made in the 1950's by the owner's grandmother, Mary Amelia Griffin Johnson,

**Lowry, Susan Shore** (William)
James Buckley Chapter
Ancestor: John Redden, VA —#743256
This "Chi Omega Owls" quilt was made in 1983 at Weakley County, TN by the owner's mother, Emily H. Shore (born 4/11/1940 at Humphreys County, TN, married James William Shore). The quilt was made for the owner when she was in college.

**Lowry, Susan Shore** (William)
James Buckley Chapter
Ancestor: John Redden, VA —#743256
This "Doing Little Boy Things" quilt was made in 1998 at Gleason, TN by Audrey Crossett, the aunt of the owner's nurse. It was given to the owner at the birth of her son, Kyle.

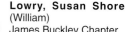

**Lowry, Susan Shore** (William)
James Buckley Chapter
Ancestor: John Redden, VA —#743256
This "25 Squares" quilt was made in 1992 at Madison County, TN by the owner (born 6/19/1964 at Chattanooga, TN).

**Lucas, Francine Estes** (Porter)
Chickasaw Bluff Chapter
Ancestor: Alexander McCollough, GA — #730268
This "Improved Nine Patch/Nine Patch Variation" quilt was made in 1930-1940 in Newbern, TN by the owner's mother-in-law, Effie Porter Lucas (born 12/19/1892 at Cisco, TX, married Joseph Bennett, died 2/5/1963 at Newbern, TN).

**Lucas, Francine Estes** (Porter)
Chickasaw Bluff Chapter
Ancestor: Alexander McCollough, GA — #730268
This "Wild Goose Chase" quilt was made 1930-1940's in Newbern, TN by owner's mother-in-law, Effie Porter Lucas.

**Lucas, Francine Estes** (Porter)
Chickasaw Bluff Chapter
Ancestor: Alexander McCollough, GA — #730268
This "Sunbonnet Sue" quilt was made 1930-1940's in Newbern, TN by the owner's mother-in-law, Effie Porter Lucas

**Lyles, Mary Smith** (Henry)
Thomas McKissick Chapter
Ancestor: James Armstrong, SC
— #401109
This "Windmill" quilt was made before 1869 by Susan Cochran (Born 2/22/1834 at Columbia, TN, married J.L.T. Cochran (born 1828, died 1900), died 6/20/1869 at Columbia). This quilt was given to the owner by her mother in 1960. The quilt originally belonged to the owner's father's first wife, Susan. "My grandfather gave it to my mother when he married the second time" (Queen Cochran).

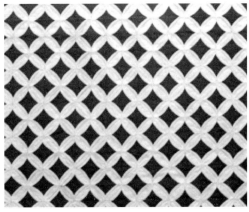

**Lynch, Mildred Ousley** (W. Ted)
Samuel Frazier Chapter
Ancestor: Capt. John Miller, NC — #576120
This "Cathedral Window" quilt was made circa 1968 in Knox County, TN by the owner's mother, Mossie Needham Ousley (born 1898 at Claiborne County, TN, married Charles Lafayette Ousley, died in 1993 in Knox County, TN).

**Lynch, Mildred Ousley** (W. Ted)
Samuel Frazier Chapter
Ancestor: Capt. John Miller, NC — #576120
This "Variation of Double Wedding Ring" quilt was made in 1930 in Claiborne County, TN by the owner's grandmother, Virginia DeBusk Needham (born 1874 at Claiborne County, TN, married George Brock Needham, died 1957 at Union County, TN). The quilt was passed from quiltmaker, to son (owner's uncle), to the owner.

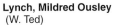

**Lynch, Mildred Ousley** (W. Ted)
Samuel Frazier Chapter
Ancestor: Capt. John Miller, NC — #576120
This "Pinwheel" quilt was made circa 1848 in Claiborne County, TN by owner's great grandmother, Nancy Butcher DeBusk (born circa 1834 at Claiborne County, TN, married Martin DeBusk, died 1907 at Claiborne, County). The quilt was passed from quiltmaker, to the current owner through daughters.

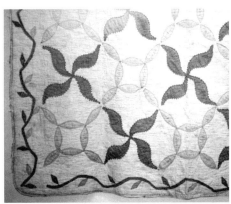

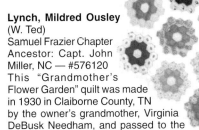

**Lynch, Mildred Ousley** (W. Ted)
Samuel Frazier Chapter
Ancestor: Capt. John Miller, NC — #576120
This "Grandmother's Flower Garden" quilt was made in 1930 in Claiborne County, TN by the owner's grandmother, Virginia DeBusk Needham, and passed to the current owner through her mother.

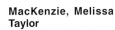

**MacKenzie, Melissa Taylor**
David Craig Chapter
Ancestor: Lt. David Meriwether — #352056
This "Dresden Plate" quilt was made in 1930 at Chicago, IL by the owner's great aunt, Rose Eleanor Hewette Turner (born circa 1854 at Centralia, IL, married 1st Dr. John W. Turner, died in 1940 at Chicago). The quiltmaker was an accomplished artist. The owner has her oil paintings that were painted in New Zealand and Australia circa 1880-90. She also studied lace making in Brussels.

**MacKenzie, Melissa Taylor**
David Craig Chapter
Ancestor: Lt. David Meriwether —#352056
This "Eight Pointed Star" quilt was made in the 1870's by the owner's maternal great grandmother, Mary Russell Hewette (born 10/1/1834 at Centralia, IL, married R.E.M. Hewette, died 1916 at Trenton, TN).

**MacKenzie, Melissa Taylor**
David Craig Chapter
Ancestor: Lt. David Meriwether —#352056
This "Crazy" quilt was made circa 1893 at Chicago, IL by the owner's great aunt, Rose Eleanor Hewette Turner. This quilt is dated with several silk patches from the Chicago Exposition of 1893.

**MacKenzie, Melissa Taylor**
David Craig Chapter
Ancestor: Lt. David Meriwether — #352056
This wool "Crazy" quilt was made circa the 1880's at Centralia, IL by the owner's maternal great grandmother, Mary Russell Hewette.

**MacKenzie, Melissa Taylor**
David Craig Chapter
Ancestor: Lt. David Meriwether — #352056
This wool "Crazy" quilt was made circa 1895 at Chicago, IL by the owner's great aunt, Rose Eleanor Hewette Turner.

**MacKenzie, Melissa Taylor**
David Craig Chapter
Ancestor: Lt. David Meriwether —#352056
This "Friendship Crazy" quilt was made in 1886 at Brownsville, TN by the owner's paternal grandmother, Helen Bond Taylor (born 5/31/1858 at Brownsville, TN, married Dr. William David Taylor, died 4/20/1916 at Brownsville). Dr. Taylor was born 9/1/1850 and died 3/15/1900. The maker told the owner that the quilt has received awards.

**Maddox, Claudia Garrison**
(Sidney)
Fort Nashborough Chapter
Ancestor: William Halbert, VA —#559820
This "Tulip" quilt was made in 1933 at Lauerns, SC by the owner's great aunt, Eulake Power (born 1879 at Laurens County, SC, died 1937 in the same county).

**Maggart-Petty, Sue Woodard**
(Gordon)
Caney Fork Chapter
Ancestor: Edward Lawrence, VA — #606516
This "Star" quilt was made circa 1900 in Smith County, TN by the owner's great grandmother, Delilah Lawrence Vantrease (born 1842 at Wilson County, TN, married Nicholas Vantrease, died 1905 at Smith County, TN). It was passed from quiltmaker, to her son, to his daughter, to the current owner. In 1909, this quilt won a second place red ribbon at the State Fair.

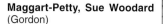

**Maggart-Petty, Sue Woodard** (Gordon)
Caney Fork Chapter
Ancestor: Edward Lawrence, VA — #606516
This "Lone Star" quilt was made in 1940 in Smith County, TN by the owner's mother-in-law, Edna McDonald Maggart (born 1895 at Smith County, TN, married Orville M. Maggart, Sr., died 1988 at Carthage, TN). This quilt was passed from maker, to her son, to the current owner.

**Maggart-Petty, Sue Woodard**
(Gordon)
Caney Fork Chapter
Ancestor: Edward Lawrence, VA — #606516
This "Princess Feather" quilt was made in 1940 by the owner's mother-in-law, Edna McDonald Maggart. She made it for her son, the owner's husband.

**Major, Lula Fain Moran**
(Herman)
Old Glory Chapter
Ancestor: James Brown, NC #591209
This "Sugar Loaf" quilt was made before July 23, 1887 by owner's great great aunt, Mary Louise Pearre Hamilton (born 7/27/ 1838 at Williamson County, TN, married John Hall Hamilton, died 12/24/1913 at Memphis, TN). She made this quilt for her niece, Mary E. Sawyer (1866-1887) who died July 23, 1887. At her death, Mary's mother gave the quilt to Mary's brother, Robert B. Sawyer, the owner's great grandfather. He passed the quilt to his daughter, Mary Elizabeth Sawyer Robinson (Mrs. William Litton) who gave it to the current owner.

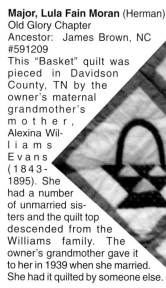

**Major, Lula Fain Moran** (Herman)
Old Glory Chapter
Ancestor: James Brown, NC #591209
This "Basket" quilt was pieced in Davidson County, TN by the owner's maternal grandmother's mother, Alexina Williams Evans (1843-1895). She had a number of unmarried sisters and the quilt top descended from the Williams family. The owner's grandmother gave it to her in 1939 when she married. She had it quilted by someone else.

**Major, Lula Fain Moran**
(Herman)
Old Glory Chapter
Ancestor: James Brown, NC #591209
This "Little School House" quilt was made in 1916 at Williamson County, TN by the owner's maternal grandmother, Lillie Evans Sawyer (born 3/2/1867 at Davidson County, TN, married Robert Brown Sawyer, died 1/27/1943 at Williamson County, TN). The owner's grandmother pieced the quilt for her when she was two years old. She had it quilted in 1939 when she married.

**Major, Lula Fain Moran** (Herman)
Old Glory Chapter
Ancestor: James Brown, NC #591209
This "Star" quilt was made in Rutherford County, TN by the owner's husband's grandmother, Dora Cawthon Burnett (born 1/11/1861 at Wilson County, TN, married Turner Perry Burnett, died 4/4/1947 at Rutherford County, TN). The maker of the quilt left it to her youngest daughter, the owner's husband's aunt, and she gave it to the current owner.

**Manley, Francis Watson**
Elizabeth Marshall Martin Chapter
Ancestor: —#372938
This "Tulip Baskets" quilt was made in 1935 at Whitehaven, TN by the owner's mother, Frank Sharpe Patton Watson (born 7/29/1882 at Trenton, TN, died 6/29/1970 at Memphis, TN).

**Manley, Francis Watson**
Elizabeth Marshall Martin Chapter
Ancestor: —#372938
This "Variation of Rose of Sharon" quilt was made in 1820 at Paris, TN by the owner's great great grandmother, Harriet Adaline Craige Cowan (born 5/23/1795 at Philadelphia, PA, married James Agustus Cowan, died 8/21/1867 at Trenton, TN). This quilt is inscribed with the following, "This quilt belongs to Mrs. E. L. Ewing - made in 1820 by Mrs. James Cowan, grandmother of Mrs. Ewing, 112 years old. " The message is signed, "Mrs. Ewing 1932."

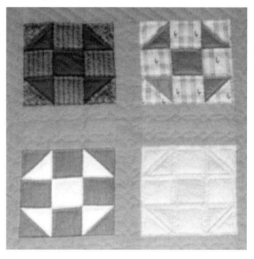

**Manley, Francis Watson**
Elizabeth Marshall Martin Chapter
Ancestor: —#372938
This "Crazy" quilt was made 1885-90 at Trenton, TN by the owner's grandmother, Hallie Cowan Sharp Patton (born 11/29/1855 at Henry County, TN, married Charles William Patton (1856-1936), died 6/26/1920 at Memphis, TN). Lining from Charles' wedding hat and a piece of Hallie's wedding dress are included in the quilt.

**Marshall, Joyce Kizer** (Joseph M.)
Clinch Bend Chapter
Ancestor: James Henry, VA—#783215
This "Wheels" quilt was made in 1912 at Meadow, TN by the owner's grandmother, Carrie Henry, and others in the community. Carrie was born circa 1880 at Meadow, TN, married John Martin Henry, died 3/9/1925 at Knoxville, TN. This quilt was a community fundraising project. Each individual or group had to make a donation to get their name on the quilt. The quilt has 335 names listed.

**Martin, Allison Leigh**
Chickasaw Bluff Chapter
Ancestor: John King, NC — #791381
This "Shoo-fly" quilt was made in 1992 in Memphis, TN by the owner's grandmother, Alice King Foley (born 11/8/1930 at Butler, Custer, OK, married James Davis Foley). This quilt is made from fabric left over from ten years of the owner's dresses. It was quilted by Clara Fullegrabe at Cordell, OK.

**Martin, Carolyn Christian** (Chester)
Robert Cooke Chapter
Ancestor: James Mayfield, NC — #780062
This "Double Wedding Ring" quilt was pieced in 1970 in Vienna, VA by the owner's husband's grandmother, Florrie Thomas Martin (born 10/27/1894 at Chesterfield County, SC, married Joel Daniel Martin, died 5/1/1979 at Fairfax County, VA). This quilt was passed from quiltmaker to her grandson, the owner's husband. In the ten years before her death, the quiltmaker made tops for all her grandchildren. She used materials saved from sewing she did for her children and grandchildren. This quilt top was stored in the owner's cedar chest for 25 years. One day she noticed the hand stitching was starting to pull apart. She took it to a shop and had it machine quilted. She gave it to her husband for Christmas in 1995. He was so touched to see the quilt again, he had tears in his eyes. It hangs on the wall as a cherished reminder of his grandmother.

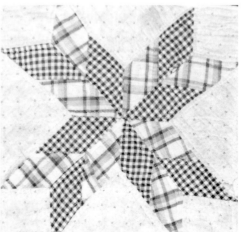

**Massie, Sandra Beeler** (Ira)
Coytee Chapter
Ancestor: Joseph Beeler, NC — #709675
This "Star" quilt was made in 1892 in Wasburn, TN by the owner's great grandmother, Suffie Wolfenbarger Beeler (born 9/29/1869 at Grainger County, TN, married William Isaac Beeler, died 4/2/1959 at Washburn, TN). This quilt was passed from the owner's great grandmother, to grandmother, to father, then to the owner.

**Masters, Donna Jean Priddy** (John A)
Gen. William Lenoir Chapter.
Ancestor: Edward Burns, CT — #678364
This "Broken Star" quilt was made in 1948 in Hilham, TN by the owner's mother-in-law, Clora Alice Masters (born 8/13/1877 at Timothy, TN, married John Riley Masters, died 12/28/58 at Hilham, TN).

**Matherne, Betty Graham** (Kirby)
David Craig Chapter
Ancestor: Martin Luther Roller, VA —#751645
This "Cathedral Window" quilt was made in 1984 at Brownsville, TN by the owner (born 4/30/1918). The maker gave the quilt to her husband on their 40th wedding anniversary.

**Matherne, Betty Graham** (Kirby)
David Craig Chapter
Ancestor: Martin Luther Roller, VA —#751645
This "Six Pointed Star" quilt was pieced in 1942 by the owner's mother and quilted in 1975 at Haywood County, TN by the owner. The quilt is made of pieces of dresses from the owner's students in the home economics classes she taught at Blountville High School in Sullivan County in 1941-44.

**Matherne, Betty Graham** (Kirby)
David Craig Chapter
Ancestor: Martin Luther Roller, VA — #751645
This "Drunkard Path" quilt was made in 1989 at Haywood County, TN by the owner.

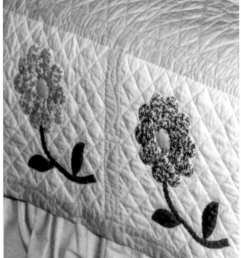

**Matherne, Betty Graham** (Kirby)
David Craig Chapter
Ancestor: Martin Luther Roller, VA —#751645
This "Rose" quilt was made in 1984 at Haywood County, TN by the owner. It won a first prize blue ribbon at the Haywood County Peach Festival in 1985.

**Mays, Adelyn Sumner** (Glenn H., Sr.)
Lydia Russell Bean Chapter
Ancestor: Ephraim Randall, MA —#774381
This "Dresden Plate" quilt was made in the early 1930's at Caryville, TN by the owner's grandmother, Bessie Condry Gleason (born 1874 at Campbell County, TN, married Michael Dolan Gleason, died 1942 at Caryville, TN). She made the quilt for the owner's mother using scraps from her dresses.

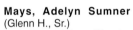

**Mays, Anna Odell** (John E.)
Admiral David Farragut Chapter
Ancestor: Shadrack Hale, NC — #573516
This "Amish Diamond" quilt was made circa 1900 in Washington County, TN by the owner's great grandmother, Nancy Ann Ferguson Hale (born 10/4/1844 at Washington County, married James Ellis Hale, died 4/5/1932 in the same county). The quiltmaker gave the quilt to her grandson Eugene Hale Odell, the owner's father, and he gave it to the current owner. The quiltmaker gave each grandchild a quilt. Eugene got to pick first and this is the one he picked.

**Mays, Anna Odell** (John E.)
Admiral David Farragut Chapter
Ancestor: Shadrack Hale, NC — #573516
This "Friendship Crazy" quilt was made circa 1920-25 in Washington County, TN by the owner's grandmother, Mary Tennessee Hale, and approximately twenty other women. It was made for her sister, Martha Hale, when she married and moved to North Carolina. She had no grandchildren, so the owner's father inherited it, and then passed it to the current owner.

**Mays, Anna Odell** (John E.)
Admiral David Farragut Chapter
Ancestor: Shadrack Hale, NC — #573516
This "Cockscomb and Currants" quilt was made circa 1930-40 by the owner's cousin, Willie Ferguson (born 11/29/1893, married H. Oakie Ferguson, died June 27, 1952). Anna Mays purchased it from Willie Ferguson.

**Mays, Anna Odell** (John E.)
Admiral David Farragut Chapter
Ancestor: Shadrack Hale, NC — #573516
This "Double Irish Chain" quilt was made circa 1910-15 in Washington, County, TN. The owner purchased it from the quiltmaker's daughter-in-law, Willie Ferguson.

**Mays, Anna Odell** (John E.)
Admiral David Farragut Chapter
Ancestor: Shadrack Hale, NC — #573516
This "LeMoyne Star" quilt was made circa 1940 in Washington County, TN by the owner's mother, Rowena Watkins Odell (born 5/24/1910 in Hawkins County, TN, married Eugene Hale Odell). The quiltmaker stopped in Greenville, TN on the way home from a University of Tennessee Football game and purchased the blue and yellow fabric for the quilt.

**Mays, Anna Odell** (John E.)
Admiral David Farragut Chapter
Ancestor: Shadrack Hale, NC — #573516
This "Feathered Star" quilt was made circa 1890-1900 in Pulaski County, VA by the owner's great grandmother, Sarah Jane Jenkins Odell (born 3/29/1844 in Nolaney County, VA, married James Riley Odell, died 8/2/1915 in Pulaski County, VA). The quiltmaker made it for her son, Albert, when he married Mary T. Hale and moved to Tennessee. Their son, Eugene, inherited the quilt and the owner inherited it from Eugene.

**McCallen, Elizabeth Griffith** (James Francis)
Chucalissa Chapter
Ancestor: Ens. John Russell, CT — #732331
This "Grandmother's Flower Garden" quilt was made in the late 1930's in Memphis, TN by the owner's husband's grandmother, Laura Frances Smith Buchanan (born 12/5/1877 at Crockett County, TN, married Greer Berry Buchanan, died 9/12/1957 at Humboldt, TN).

**McDaniel, Estelle Sloan** (James M.)
Adam Dale Chapter
Ancestor: Capt. Fredrick Gray — #621828
This "Dresden Plate" quilt was made in 1940 at Memphis, TN by the owner's mother, Estelle L. Gray Sloan (born 9/14/1891 at Octibbeha County, MS, married William Sloan, died 11/29/1986 at Memphis, TN).

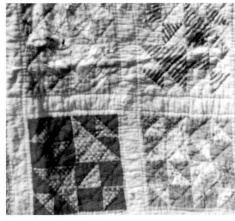

**McDaniel, Estelle Sloan** (James M.)
Adam Dale Chapter
Ancestor: Capt. Fredrick Gray —#621828
This "Crosses and Losses" quilt was made in 1940 at Memphis, TN by the owner's mother, Estelle L. Gray Sloan.

**McDaniel, Estelle Sloan** (James M.)
Adam Dale Chapter
Ancestor: Capt. Fredrick Gray — #621828
This "Double Wedding Ring" quilt was made in 1980 at Memphis, TN by the owner's mother, Estelle L. Gray Sloan.

**McDaniel, Estelle Sloan** (James M.)
Adam Dale Chapter
Ancestor: Capt. Fredrick Gray —#621828
This "Snowball" quilt was made in Memphis, TN by the owner's mother, Estelle L. Gray Sloan.

**McDaniel, Estelle Sloan** (James M.)
Adam Dale Chapter
Ancestor: Capt. Fredrick Gray —
#621828
This "Crazy" quilt was made in Memphis, TN by the owner's mother, Estelle Gray Sloan.

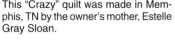

**McDaniel, Estelle Sloan** (James M.)
Adam Dale Chapter
Ancestor: Capt. Fredrick Gray —#621828
This "Bow Tie" quilt was made in 1938 at Memphis, TN by the owner's grandmother, Margaret J. Wooten Sloan (born 8/19/1861 at Independence, MS married Mark E. Sloan, died 5/14/1941 at Memphis, TN).

**McDaniel, Estelle Sloan** (James M.)
Adam Dale Chapter
Ancestor: Capt. Fredrick Gray —#621828
This "Pants/Bar" quilt was made in 1970 by the owner's mother, Estelle L. Gray Sloan.

**McDaniel, Estelle Sloan** (James M.)
Adam Dale Chapter
Ancestor: Capt. Fredrick Gray —#621828
This "Fan" quilt was made in Memphis, TN in the late 1970's by the owner's mother, Estelle L. Gray Sloan.

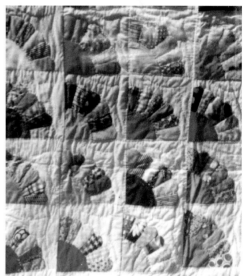

**McDaniel, Estelle Sloan** (James M.)
Adam Dale Chapter
Ancestor: Capt. Fredrick Gray —#621828
This "Grandmother's Flower Garden" quilt was made in 1940 at Memphis, TN by the owner's mother, Estelle L. Gray Sloan.

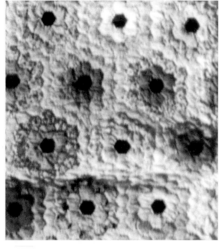

**McFalls, Rowena Henderson** (Ben)
Spencer Clack Chapter
Ancestor: Benjamin Seaton, PA —#647374
This "Fan" quilt was made in the 1970's in Puerto Rico and Tennessee by a friend of the owner who is a native of Puerto Rico.

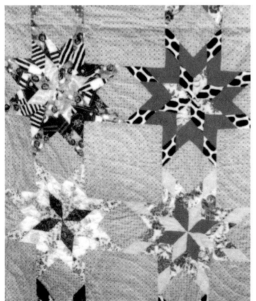

**McFalls, Rowena Henderson** (Ben)
Spencer Clack Chapter
Ancestor: Benjamin Seaton, PA —#647374
This "Blazing Star" quilt was made in 1975 at Sevier County, TN and was purchased by the owner at a public auction.

**McGoldrick, Jane Ellen St. Clair** (William J.)
Chucalissa Chapter
Ancestor: Francis McCraw, VA — #594349
This "Flying Geese" quilt was inherited from the owner's grandmother, Cora Morris St. Clair.

**McGoldrick, Jane Ellen St. Clair** (William J.)
Chucalissa Chapter
Ancestor: Francis McCraw, VA — #594349
This "Sugar Loaf" quilt was made circa 1845-55 in Moorefield, WV by the owner's great grandmother, Ann Rebecca Harness Kuykendall (born 12/2/1825 at Moorefield VA, married James Kuykendall, died 1/4/1890 at Moorefield WV). The quilt was passed from the maker, to Jane Clark Gilkerson Kuykendall, to Maude (Mrs. Edwin) Kuykendall (born 1866, died 1947), to Mollelle Kuykendall (born 1892, died 1980), to Lucy Lee Kuykendall St. Clair (born 1910), to current owner.

**McGoldrick, Jane Ellen St. Clair** (William J.)
Chucalissa Chapter
Ancestor: Francis McCraw, VA — #594349
This "Saw Tooth" silk quilt was made circa 1845-55 in Moorefield, WV by the owner's great grandmother, Ann Rebecca Harness Kuykendall. The descent is the same as owner's "Sugar Loaf" quilt.

**McGoldrick, Jane Ellen St. Clair** (William J.)
Chucalissa Chapter
Ancestor: Francis McCraw, VA — #594349
This "Jacquard" coverlet was made in 1837. The coverlet was passed from Mollelle Kuykendall (born 1892, died 1980), to Lucy Lee Kuykendall, to the owner's mother, to owner.

**McGoldrick, Jane Ellen St. Clair** (William J.)
Chucalissa Chapter
Ancestor: Francis McCraw, VA — #594349
This "Carolina Lilly" quilt was made circa 1845-55 in Moorefield, WV by the great grandmother, Ann Rebecca Harness Kuykendall. The descent is the same as owner's "Sugar Loaf" quilt.

**McGoldrick, Jane Ellen St. Clair** (William J.)
Chucalissa Chapter
Ancestor: Francis McCraw, VA — #594349
This "Flying Geese" quilt was made circa 1845-55_ in Moorefield, WV by the owner's great grandmother, Ann Rebecca Harness Kuykendall. The descent is the same as owner's "Sugar Loaf" quilt.

**McIlvain, Helen Gore** (Franklin)
Roaring River Chapter
Ancestor: John Gore, VA —#787787
This "Maple Leaf" quilt was made in 1981 at Overton County, TN by the owner's sister, Gladys Gore Davis (born 9/16/1931 at Overton County, TN, married Fred Davis).

**McIlvain, Helen Gore** (Franklin)
Roaring River Chapter
Ancestor: John Gore, VA — #787787
This "Butterfly" quilt was pieced at Ohio by the owner's sister, Lena Bell Gore Carmack Halcomb (born 1/7/1921 at Overton County, married 1st A.B. Cormack, married 2nd Bergie Halcomb). After her death 7/15/1982 in Dayton, OH, the owner's niece, Janie C. Carmack Copeland (born in 1941 at Overton County, TN, married R.V. Copeland), finished the quilt.

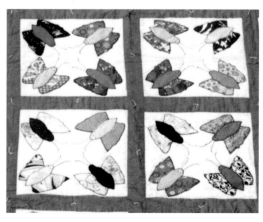

**McIlvain, Helen Gore** (Franklin)
Roaring River Chapter
Ancestor: John Gore, VA — #787787
This "Cathedral Window" baby quilt was made in 1998 at Overton County, TN by the owner (born 10/17/1934 at Overton County).

**McIlvain, Helen Gore** (Franklin)
Roaring River Chapter
Ancestor: John Gore, VA —#787787
This "Nine Patch" quilt was made in New Market, OH by the owner.

**McIlvain, Helen Gore** (Franklin)
Roaring River Chapter
Ancestor: John Gore, VA —#787787
This "Compass" quilt was started prior to 1931 at Overton County, TN by the owner's aunts, Sarah Martelia Gore (1847-1923), Eliza Jane Gore (1865-1931). The top was passed down to Lena Gore Carmack Halcomb, the owner's niece. She finished the quilt in Dayton, OH in 1974.

**McIlvain, Helen Gore** (Franklin)
Roaring River Chapter
Ancestor: John Gore, VA —#787787
This "Cathedral Window" baby quilt was made in 1990 in Ohio by the owner's niece, Janie C. Carmack Copeland.

**McIlvain, Helen Gore** (Franklin)
Roaring River Chapter
Ancestor: John Gore, VA —#787787
This "Cathedral Window" quilt was made in 1990 in Livingston, TN by the owner.

**McIlvain, Helen Gore** (Franklin)
Roaring River Chapter
Ancestor: John Gore, VA —#787787
This "Grandmother's Flower Garden" quilt was made in 1976 in Dayton, OH by the owner's sister, Lena Bell Gore Carmack Halcomb.

**McIlvain, Helen Gore** (Franklin)
Roaring River Chapter
Ancestor: John Gore, VA —#787787
This "Maple Leaf" quilt was made prior to 1982 at Dayton, OH by the owner's sister, Lena Bell Gore Carmack Halcomb

**McIlvain, Helen Gore** (Franklin)
Roaring River Chapter
Ancestor: John Gore, VA —#787787
This "Eight Pointed Star" quilt was made in the late 1930's at Overton County, TN by the owner's grandmother, Sarah Belle Swallows Gore (born 2/18/1869 at Overton County, TN, married Jefferson Davis Gore, died 10/26/1944 in the same county). Sarah was widowed in 1936. She maintained her independence by making quilts

**McKee, E. Caroline Ferguson** (James)
Hatchie Chapter
Ancestor: John Macon, NC — #775053
This "Jacobean Garden" quilt was made from Bucilla Kit #49232 in 1987 in Bolivar, TN by the owner's mother, Bernice Hazlegrove Ferguson (born 5/25/1919, married Thomas Boyd Ferguson). The quilt was a birthday gift to the owner on March 18, 1987. The quilt is signed, "Jacobean Garden— Happy Birthday Caroline McKee, from Bernice Ferguson 3/18/1987."

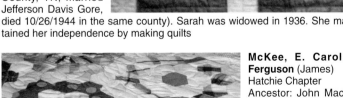

**McKee, E. Caroline Ferguson** (James)
Hatchie Chapter
Ancestor: John Macon, NC — #775053
This "Grandmother's Flower Garden" quilt was purchased at a charity auction held by the Communication Workers of America in November, 1992.

**McKee, E. Caroline Ferguson** (James)
Hatchie Chapter
Ancestor: John Macon, NC — #775053
This "One Patch Random Square" quilt was made in 1977 in Bolivar, TN by the owner's grandmother, Bernice Hazlegrove Ferguson (born 5/14/1919 at Hardeman County, TN, married Thomas Boyd Ferguson). The quiltmaker made it for the owner and signed it, "Beese, 1977."

**McKee, E. Caroline Ferguson** (James)
Hatchie Chapter
Ancestor: John Macon, NC — #775053
This "Cathedral Window" quilt was made in 1982 in Bolivar, TN by the owner's mother, Bernice Hazlegrove Ferguson. It was a birthday gift from the maker to the owner and is signed, "B. Ferguson to C. McKee 3/18/1982."

**McKee, E. Caroline Ferguson** (James)
Hatchie Chapter
Ancestor: John Macon, NC — #775053
This "Cathedral Spire" quilt was made in 1996 in Bolivar, TN by the owner's mother, Bernice Hazlegrove Ferguson. It was a Christmas gift from the maker to the owner and is signed, "Bernice H. Ferguson 12/25/1996.

**McKee, E. Caroline Ferguson** (James)
Hatchie Chapter
Ancestor: John Macon, NC — #775053
This "Applique Animals" quilt was made in 1946 in Whiteville, TN by the owner's mother, Bernice Hazlegrove Ferguson. The baby quilt was made by the quiltmaker before the owner was born.

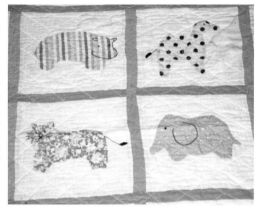

**McKee, E. Caroline Ferguson** (James)
Hatchie Chapter
Ancestor: John Macon, NC — #775053
This "Broken Dishes" quilt was made before 1950 at Bolivar, TN by the owner's grandmother, Laura Cleo Carter Hazlegrove (born 8/25/1876 at Hardeman County, TN, married Walter A. Hazlegrove, died 11/9/1957 in the same county). The owner received this quilt from the estate of the quiltmaker.

**McKelvy, Dana Lynch** (William R.)
Chucalissa Chapter
Ancestor: Andrew Weeks, NY — #580282
This "Nine Patch" quilt was made circa 1932-36 in New York City by the owner's maternal grandmother, Florence Weeks Heckle (born 12/17/1885, married John Archer Heckle, died 11/27/1978). The owner inherited the quilt through her mother.

**McKelvy, Dana Lynch** (William R.)
Chucalissa Chapter
Ancestor: Andrew Weeks, NY — #580282
This "Dresden Plate" quilt was made 1932-36 in New York City by the owner's maternal grandmother, Florence Weeks Heckle. The owner inherited the quilt through her mother.

**McKelvy, Dana Lynch** (William R.)
Chucalissa Chapter
Ancestor: Andrew Weeks, NY — #580282
This "Dresden Plate" quilt was made circa 1932-36 in New York City by the owner's maternal grandmother, Florence Weeks Heckle. The owner inherited the quilt through her mother.

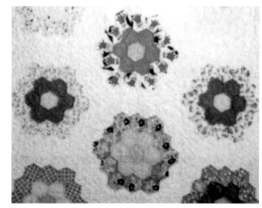

**McKinstry, Carolee Porter** (Sam W.)
Ann Robertson Chapter
Ancestor: Col. Robert Levers, PA —#503670
This "Grandmothers Flower Garden" quilt was made in 1939 at Blackwell, MO by the owner's husband's grandmother, Flora Bookstaver McKinstry (born 8/20/1883 at DuQuoin, IL, married Samuel McKinstry, died 11/18/1973 at Potosi, MO). It was given to the owner's husband's parents as a wedding gift in 1939 and then passed to the current owner.

**McKinstry, Carolee Porter** (Sam W.)
Ann Robertson Chapter
Ancestor: Col. Robert Levers, PA —#503670
This "Eight Pointed Star" quilt was made in 1947 at Cape Girardeau, MO by the owner's husband's grandmother, Laura Haw Wescoat (born 4/18/1877 at Charleston, MO, married Dr. William Henry Wescoat, died 2/3/1962 at Cape Girardeau).

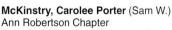

**McKinstry, Carolee Porter** (Sam W.)
Ann Robertson Chapter
Ancestor: Col. Robert Levers, PA — #503670
This "Double Wedding Ring" quilt was made in 1939 at Blackwell, MO by the owner's husband's grandmother, Flora Bookstaver McKinstry. It was given to the owner as a wedding gift in 1964.

**McKinstry, Carolee Porter**
(Sam W.)
Ann Robertson Chapter
Ancestor: Col. Robert Levers, PA —#503670
This "Poppy" quilt was made in 1947 at Cape Girardeau, MO by the owner's husband's grandmother, Laura Haw Wescoat.

**McMahan, Margaret Wilkins** (Richard)
Chickasaw Bluff Chapter
Ancestor: Henry Bonner, VA —#741776
This "Pomegranate Variation" quilt was started in Memphis, TN by the owner's great grandmother, Nancy Cate (born 1837 at Upson County, GA, married 1st George Rushin, married 2nd John Washington Halley, died at Collierville, TN). It was finished by the sewing circle of Buntyn Presbyterian Church in Memphis, TN sometime between 1925-30.

**McReynolds, Willie Mae**
Ocoee Chapter
Ancestor: Lt. Isaac Lane, NC — #692128
This "Double Wedding Ring" quilt was made in the 1930's in Bradley County, TN by the owner's grandmother, Merilda Jane Brown Cartwright (born circa 1860 at Bradley County, married William Carroll Cartwright, died May 1957 in the same county). Before the quiltmaker died, she gave the quilt to the owner. This is one of nine quilts she made for each of her grandchildren. She not only pieced the quilts, but she also made the cotton batts to go between the top and back of the quilt. Her wooden quilt frame was always up. She and her friends spent many pleasant hours visiting and quilting. The quiltmaker's husband was the Tax Assessor for Bradley County.

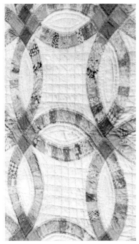

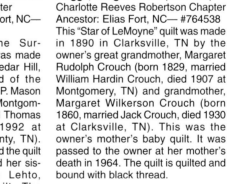

**Medford, Delores Freeze** (Riley)
Manchester Chapter
Ancestor: John Roach, VA —#786474
This "Grandmother's Flower Garden" quilt was made at Coffee County, TN by the owner's grandmother, Ettie Cumi Gentry Freeze (born 12/15/1898 at Coffee County, TN, married Manuel Freeze, died 1/24/1961 in the same county). The quilt is made from the owner's childhood dresses and was a gift from the quiltmaker.

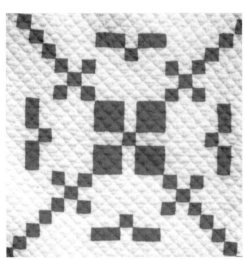

**Meggs, Margaret Fort**
(Emerson)
Charlotte Reeves Robertson Chapter
Ancestor: Elias Fort, NC—#764538
This "Burgoyne Surrounded" quilt was made circa 1960 in Cedar Hill, TN by a friend of the owner, Madeline P. Mason (born 1910 at Montgomery, TN, married Thomas Mason, died 1992 at Robertson County, TN). This friend pieced the quilt top and she and her sister, Ernestine Lehto, quilted the quilt. The owner and her husband bought the quilt in Adams,
TN at the Adams Quilt Festival about 1980. According to the owner, the name of the quilt refers to the Battle of Saratoga in the American Revolution. The Americans surrounded British General John Burgoyne in October, 1777. According to the Encyclopedia Britannica this was a turning point in our fight for independence.

**Meggs, Margaret Fort** (Emerson)
Charlotte Reeves Robertson Chapter
Ancestor: Elias Fort, NC— #764538
This "Star of LeMoyne" quilt was made in 1890 in Clarksville, TN by the owner's great grandmother, Margaret Rudolph Crouch (born 1829, married William Hardin Crouch, died 1907 at Montgomery, TN) and grandmother, Margaret Wilkerson Crouch (born 1860, married Jack Crouch, died 1930 at Clarksville, TN). This was the owner's mother's baby quilt. It was passed to the owner at her mother's death in 1964. The quilt is quilted and bound with black thread.

**Meggs, Margaret Fort**
(Emerson)
Charlotte Reeves Robertson Chapter
Ancestor: Elias Fort, NC—#764538
This "Monkey Wrench" quilt was made circa 1970 in Adams, TN by the owner (born 1925 at Clarksville, TN). It was made for a handmade doll bed. It was one of her first quilting projects to see if she could make a miniature pattern and quilt it. The owner's grandchildren now enjoy playing with the quilt.

**Meisenheimer, Eleanor Hedges** (Stephen)
Andrew Bogle Chapter
Ancestor: Benjamin Chapin, VA — #769225
This embroidered quilt was made in 1972 at Ownesboro, KY by the owner's mother-in-law, Lovina Loring Meisenheimer (born 4/25/1922 at Cody, Wyoming, married Edward George Meisenheimer). The quiltmaker made the quilt for the owner and her husband as a wedding gift. It was quilted by Edyth Feldhaus.

**Michener, Kathryn Crowell** (Lawrence) Southwest Point Chapter Ancestor: Lt. Col. Thomas Jansen, NY —#753419 This "Blue Irish Chain" quilt was completed April 23, 1871 at Kings Hill, NY by the owner's grandmother, Catherine Garrison (born 10/16/1848 at Orange County, NY, married Robert Burns Crowell, died 11/8/1908 at Ulster County, NY). It was given to the quiltmaker's daughter, Mary Anna Crowell, and then given to the owner as a wedding gift November 9, 1940.

**Miller, Carla Sanders** (Lee R.) Sarah Hawkins Chapter Ancestor: Ninian Beall— #641075 This "Friendship" quilt was made circa late 1930's by friends of the owner.

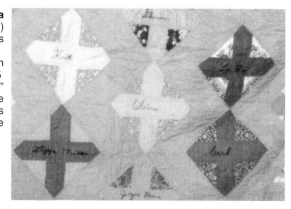

**Miller, Carla Sanders** (Lee R.) Sarah Hawkins Chapter Ancestor: Ninian Beall— #641075 This "Four Patch" quilt was made circa 1890's by the owner's great grandmother, Mary Snider Miley (born 1842, died 1924).

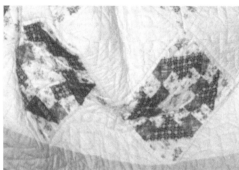

**Miller, Carla Sanders** (Lee R.) Sarah Hawkins Chapter Ancestor: Ninian Beall— #641075 This "Crow's Nest" quilt was made circa the 1980's by owner's mother, Thelma Bell Sanders (born 1901, died 1998).

**Miller, Carla Sanders** (Lee R.) Sarah Hawkins Chapter Ancestor: Ninian Beall— #641075 This "Daisy" quilt was made circa 1960's by the owner.

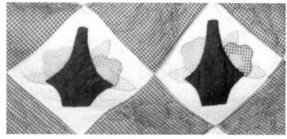

**Miller, Carla Sanders** (Lee R.) Sarah Hawkins Chapter Ancestor: Ninian Beall— #641075 This "Flower Basket" quilt was made circa 1960's by the owner.

**Miller, Carla Sanders** (Lee R.) Sarah Hawkins Chapter Ancestor: Ninian Beall— #641075 This wool" One Patch" quilt was made in the 1970's by the owner. Each square is sown on three sides, turned, stuffed with nylon hose, and whipped closed. It is hand quilted diagonally corner to corner. All squares are hand whipped together, then all seams are feather stitched on both sides, making the quilt reversible.

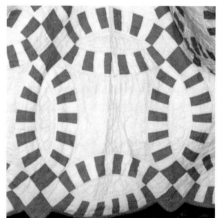

**Miller, Carla Sanders** (Lee R.) Sarah Hawkins Chapter Ancestor: Ninian Beall— #641075 This "Double Wedding Ring" quilt was made in the 1930's by the owner's husband's grandmother, Mary Catherine Skaggs Miller, (born in 1866, died in 1938). It was quilted by Eunice Davis Miller, the owner's husband's mother.

**Miller, Carla Sanders** (Lee R.) Sarah Hawkins Chapter Ancestor: Ninian Beall— #641075 This "Double Wedding Ring" quilt was made in the early 1930's by the owner's mother, Thelma Bell Sanders.

**Miller, Carla Sanders** (Lee R.) Sarah Hawkins Chapter Ancestor: Ninian Beall— #641075 This "Grandmother's Flower Garden" quilt was made in the 1930's by the owner's mother, Thelma Bell Sanders. The quilt is made of scraps from dresses the owner wore as a little girl.

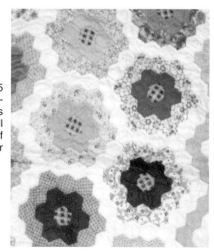

**Miller, Carla Sanders** (Lee R.)
Sarah Hawkins Chapter
Ancestor: Ninian Beall— #641075
This "Double Wedding Ring" quilt was made in the early 1940's by the owner's grandmother, Martha Houston Bell (born 1873, died 1962).

**Miller, Carla Sanders** (Lee R.)
Sarah Hawkins Chapter
Ancestor: Ninian Beall— #641075
This "Nine Patch and Double X" quilt was made in the early 1990's by the owner's mother, Thelma Bell Sanders (born 1901, died 1998).

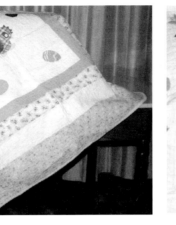

**Miller, Carla Sanders** (Lee R.)
Sarah Hawkins Chapter
Ancestor: Ninian Beall— #641075
This baby quilt was made in 1959 by the owner's mother, Thelma Bell Sanders.

**Miller, Carla Sanders** (Lee R.)
Sarah Hawkins Chapter
Ancestor: Ninian Beall— #641075
This "Flower Applique Sampler" quilt was made in 1962 by the owner and her mother, Thelma Bell Sanders. It was designed by Mrs. Sanders.

**Miller, Carla Sanders** (Lee R.)
Sarah Hawkins Chapter
Ancestor: Ninian Beall— #641075
This "Double X" quilt was made in the late 1980's by the owner's mother, Thelma Bell Sanders.

**Miller, Carla Sanders** (Lee R.)
Sarah Hawkins Chapter
Ancestor: Ninian Beall— #641075
This "Nine Patch" baby quilt was made in 1949 by the owner's grandmother, Martha Houston Bell, and quilted by Leora Minnie Thompson.

**Miller, Elizabeth Winter** (Darius)
William Cocke Chapter
Ancestor: Michael Nehs, Jr., VA — #657773
This coverlet was made in the early 1900's at Cocke County, TN by the owner's grandmother, Florence Huff Winter (born 12/25/1867 at Greene County, TN, married Issaac N., died 7/14/1942 at Cocke County, TN). It was passed from maker to son, to owner.

**Miller, Elizabeth Winter** (Darius)
William Cocke Chapter
Ancestor: Michael Nehs, Jr., VA — #657773
This "Cactus and Rose" quilt was made in 1884 at Cocke County, TN by the owner's great grandmother, Nancy Blanchard Brooks (born 1/28/1825 at Cocke County, TN, married David D., died 4/1/1912 in Washington State). She made the quilt as a wedding present for her son, Joel. Joel passed it to his son, Harold. The quilt was then passed to his cousin, the current owner.

The quilt won first place in the "Applique Before 1900" category at the Newport-Cocke County Quilt Show in 1997.

**Miller, Elizabeth Winter** (Darius)
William Cocke Chapter
Ancestor: Michael Nehs, Jr., VA — #657773
This "Maple Leaf Friendship" quilt was started by the owner's mother, Vera B. Winter, and finished by her friends in the early 1930's after she died. Vera Winter was born 7/6/1902 at Cocke County, TN, married Cecil, died 8/10/1934 in the same county. Mrs. Winter died when her daughter, the owner, was only six years old. Her friends completed two quilts started by the owner's mother, one for the owner and one for her sister.

**Miller, Elizabeth Winter** (Darius)
William Cocke Chapter
Ancestor: Michael Nehs, Jr., VA — #657773
This woven geometric coverlet was made in 1884 at Cocke County, TN by the owner's great grandmother, Nancy Wright Click (born 9/28/1833 at Cocke County, TN, married William, died 2/23/1906 in the same county). The quilt was made as a wedding gift for Nancy Click's daughter, Mary Elizabeth Click Brooks. The owner inherited it from Mary Elizabeth and has willed it to her daughter Beth, and then to her granddaughter Brittany.

**Miller, Laura Tyer** (William)
Old Glory Chapter
Ancestor: Lt. William Russwurm, PA — #444530
This "Crazy" quilt was made in the 1950's by Mrs. Jesse Bourne, the owner's neighbor.

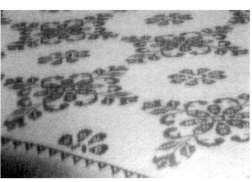

**Miller, Laura Tyer** (William)
Old Glory Chapter
Ancestor: Lt. William Russwurm, PA — #444530
This cross stitch quilt was made in the 1940's at Davidson County, TN by Mrs. Joe Brent (born 1890 at Davidson County, TN, died in the 1940's in the same county).

**Mills, Mary Alice Clift** (Ted)
Judge David Campbell Chapter
Ancestor: John Brooks, VA — #672072
This "Dogwood" quilt was made at Fallingwater, TN by Mrs. Louise Pitts.

**Mills, Mary Alice Clift** (Ted)
Judge David Campbell Chapter
Ancestor: John Brooks, VA — #672072
This "Lone Star" quilt was made in 1978 in an Amish Community. It was purchased by the owner in an antique quilt shop in Pensacola, FL in 1978.

**Mills, Mary Alice Clift** (Ted)
Judge David Campbell Chapter
Ancestor: John Brooks, VA — #672072
This "Centennial" quilt was pieced in the late 1970's. A lady walked into a business in Chattanooga wanting to sell the quilt top for $20. The owner purchased the top and Mrs. Penney at Soddy, TN quilted and bound the quilt for $65.

**Mills, Mary Alice Clift** (Ted)
Judge David Campbell Chapter
Ancestor: John Brooks, VA — #672072
This "Heavenly Roses" quilt was made in the 1970's in an Amish community. It was purchased by the owner in an antique quilt shop in Pensacola, FL in 1978.

**Mills, Mary Alice Clift** (Ted)
Judge David Campbell Chapter
Ancestor: John Brooks, VA — #672072
This "Dresden Plate" quilt was made in 1980 at Telford, TN by Mrs. Coy Williams. The owner sent the quiltmaker a piece of wallpaper asking her to select quilt materials that would coordinate.

**Mills, Mary Alice Clift** (Ted)
Judge David Campbell Chapter
Ancestor: John Brooks, VA — #672072
This "Double Wedding Ring" quilt was made over 25 years ago in Telford, TN by Mrs. Coy Williams. This quilt is pictured on page 158 of Progressive Farmer Award Winning Quilts by Effie Chalmers, copyright 1974 by Oxmoor House. Library of Congress catalog number 74-80235.

**Mills, Mary Alice Clift** (Ted)
Judge David Campbell Chapter
Ancestor: John Brooks, VA — #672072
This "Garden Poppy" quilt was made in the late 1970's in an Amish community and purchased by the owner in an antique quilt shop in Pensacola, FL in 1978.

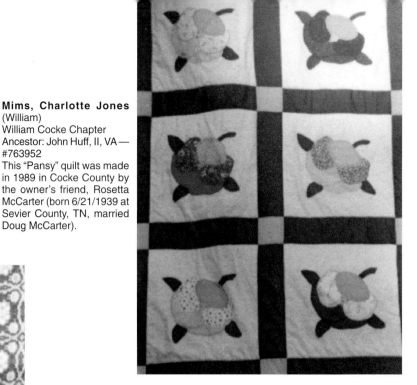

**Mims, Charlotte Jones**
(William)
William Cocke Chapter
Ancestor: John Huff, II, VA
— #763952
This "Poppy" quilt has been handed down from Charlotte Boyd Hampton, to Margaret Hampton Stokley, to Elizabeth Stokley Jones, to the current owner.

**Mims, Charlotte Jones**
(William)
William Cocke Chapter
Ancestor: John Huff, II, VA —
#763952
This "Pansy" quilt was made in 1989 in Cocke County by the owner's friend, Rosetta McCarter (born 6/21/1939 at Sevier County, TN, married Doug McCarter).

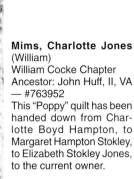

**Mims, Charlotte Jones** (William)
William Cocke Chapter
Ancestor: John Huff, II, VA — #763952
This Jacquard coverlet was handed down from Charlotte Boyd Hampton, to Margaret Hampton Stokley, to Elizabeth Stokley Jones, to the current owner.

**Mims, Charlotte Jones**
(William)
William Cocke Chapter
Ancestor: John Huff, II, VA — #763952
This geometric coverlet was handed down from Charlotte Boyd Hampton, to Margaret Hampton Stokley, to Elizabeth Stokley Jones, to the current owner.

**Mims, Charlotte Jones**
(William)
William Cocke Chapter
Ancestor: John Huff, II, VA — #763952
This coverlet was handed down from Elizabeth Garret Boyd to Charlotte Boyd Hampton, to Margaret Hampton Stokley, to Elizabeth Stokley Jones, to the current owner.

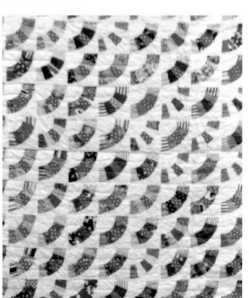

**Mims, Charlotte Jones** (William)
William Cocke Chapter
Ancestor: John Huff, II, VA — #763952
This "Church" quilt was made in 1981 at Newport, TN by the owner's friend, Rosetta McCarter.

**Mingle, Carol Anne Galyon** (William M.)
Rhea-Craig Chapter
Ancestor: Joannes Francis Summitt, NC — #778794
This "Dutch Doll" quilt was made circa 1930 at Sweetwater, TN by the owner's grandmother, Mrs. Murray D. Summitt (born 5/15/1891 at Monroe County, TN, married Murray D. Summitt, died 2/16/1973 in the same county). The quilt was given to the owner by her mother.

**Mitchell, Bessie Lowry** (Harold)
Glover's Trace Chapter
Ancestor: John Lowery, NC — #778361
This "Nine Patch" double knit quilt was made in 1970 at Benton County, TN by the owner (born 11/5/1919).

**Mitchell, Bessie Lowry**
(Harold)
Glover's Trace Chapter
Ancestor: John Lowery, NC — #778361
This "Small Fan" quilt was made in 1945 at Benton County, TN by the owner's mother, Ollie Lowry (born 2/11/1885 at Benton County, TN, married Henry Lowry, died 5/2/1968 in the same county). The quilt was passed from the maker to the owner.

**Mitchell, Bessie Lowry**
(Harold)
Glover's Trace Chapter
Ancestor: John Lowery,
NC — #778361
This "Dove at the Window" quilt was made in
1948 at Benton County,
TN by the owner's
mother, Ollie Lowry.

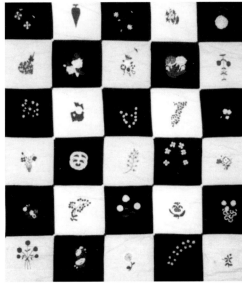

**Mitchell, Joanne E.**
Ancestor: #657026
This original "Seed Catalog" quilt was made in
the 1870's-80's at Dixon,
TN by the owner's great
grandmother, Amanda
Lucinda Dudley
Dunnegan (born at
Dixon, TN). The maker
designed the quilt using
pictures of flowers from
the seed catalog.

**Mitchell, Julia Caldwell**
(Thomas E.)
Great Smokies Chapter
Ancestor: Isreal
Greenleaf, MA — #329297
This "Fan Variation" quilt
was made in the early
1900's in Lawrence, MI by
the owner's step great
grandmother, Mrs. H. S.
Wallace.

**Mook, Myrna Jane**
Mary Blount Chapter
Ancestor: Marshall Galloway, MD — #771065
This "Triple Irish Chain"
quilt was given to the owner
by a friend, Ms. Webb. The
friend said that during the
depression the quilt was
given to her great grandfather, Granville Lequire, who
was a doctor, as payment
for services. Ms. Webb's
mother, Mrs. Faye Kenst, a
long time DAR member, inherited it. After Mrs. Kenst
died, Ms. Webb, her daughter, gave the quilt to the current owner.

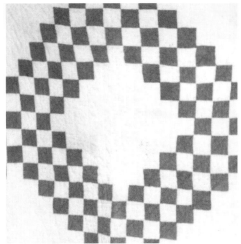

**Moore, Daryl Williams**
(Charles W. III.)
Buffalo River Chapter
Ancestor: David Wood, VA
— #651406
This "Log Cabin" quilt was
made 1980-82 in
Lawrenceburg, TN by the
owner, (born 6/18/1930 at
Indianapolis, IN).

**Moore, Jane Douglas**
(Glen R.)
King's Mountain Messenger Chapter
Ancestor: William Douglas, VA —#568058
This "Crazy" quilt was
made by the owner's
great grandmother, Jane
McCabe Terrett (born 6/
25/1832 at Leesburg, VA,
married Nathaniel H.
Terrett, died 7/9/1924 at
Nashville, TN). The
maker's father was John
M Cabe, the mayor of
Leesburg. He welcomed
Lafayette, who was accompanied by Presidents
Madison and Monroe, when he visited America after the Revolutionary War. This
quilt was brought to Nashville, TN when the family moved there after the War
Between the States. Margaret brought it to her home in Fayetteville, TN. When
Margaret's daughter-in-law died, she helped her son, Byrd, raise four children.
When she died in 1944, the quilt was passed to Byrd. When he died in 1958, the
quilt was passed to the owner's sister, Sarah Douglas Byrd Posey. When she
died in 1999, the quilt was passed to the current owner.

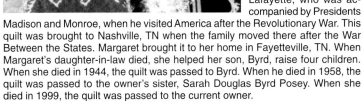

**Moore, Joanne Cullom**
(Samuel S.)
Watauga Chapter
Ancestor: Robert Wilson, NC — #663640
This embroidery quilt
was made in 1963 by
the owner's mother,
Katherine Virginia Jones
Cullom (born 10/4/1917
at Osceola, AR, married
Joseph Ransom
Cullom, Jr.). The quilt
was passed from maker
to owner.

**Moore, Joanne Cullom** (Samuel S.)
Watauga Chapter
Ancestor: Robert Wilson, NC — #663640
This "Buttercup" quilt was made in the 1930's
in Mississippi County, AR by the owner's
great grandmother, Kate Oury Cox (born 9/
2/1877 at Haywood County, TN, married Byrd
Anderson Cox, died 8/27/1958 at Mississippi
County, AR). The quilt was passed from the
maker, to her daughter, Katherine, and then
to the current owner.

**Moore, Joanne Cullom** (Samuel S.)
Watauga Chapter
  Ancestor: Robert Wilson, NC —
#663640
    This "Poppy" quilt was made in
the 1920's at Osceola, AR by
the owner's great grand-
mother, Kate Oury Cox .

**Moore, Sarah Hunt**
Tenn-at-large Chapter
  Ancestor: Robert
Moore, NC —#618628
    This "Tulip" quilt was
made in the 1900's at
Huntsville, AL by a
friend of the owner's
mother, Miss Margaret
Keith (born 1872 at
Franklin County, TN,
died at Scottsboro, AL).

**Moore, Sarah Hunt**
Tenn-at-large Chapter
Ancestor: Robert Moore,
NC —#618628
This "Log Cabin" quilt
was made at Hatland, TN
by the owner's grand-
mother, Tappie Lipscomb
Hunt (born 10/27/1822 at
Louisa County, VA, died
11/9/1907).

**Moore, Sara Pauline
Powel** (James O.)
Nancy Ward Chapter
Ancestor:     Archibald
McLean, Jr., PA —#740176
This "Christmas Rose" quilt
was made in 1983 in
Fayetteville, TN by the
owner's mother-in-law, Nell
Commons Moore (born 7/
20/1911 at Fayetteville, TN,
married Harry F. Moore, died
5/11/1995 at Nashville, TN).
The quiltmaker gave it to her
son, James, the owner's
husband, as a keepsake.
The quiltmaker was an artist in quiltmaking, and every
stitch is by hand. She loved
making "designer" quilts.

**Moore, Sara Pauline Powel** (James O.)
Nancy Ward Chapter
  Ancestor: Archibald McLean, Jr.,
PA —#740176
    This "Briar Rose" quilt was
made in 1937-38 by the
owner's mother, Fannie
Maud Hall Powel (born 10/
30/1908 at Crossville, TN,
married John C. Powel).
The maker began the quilt
in the fall of 1937 when
she became aware that
she was expecting her
second child (the owner)
. The quilt was finished in
February and her baby
was born in March. The
quiltmaker told her daughter that the quilt was "a celebration of springtime and
a new little bird in the nest!"
This quilt was given to the
owner as a wedding gift.

**Moran, Patsy Neblett**
(George)
Old Glory Chapter
Ancestor:     William
Neblett, VA —#710149
This "Double Wedding
Ring" quilt was made in
the 1920's at Henry
County, KY by the
owner's grandmother,
Neblett.

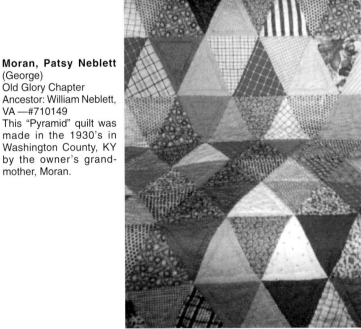

**Moran, Patsy Neblett**
(George)
Old Glory Chapter
Ancestor: William Neblett,
VA —#710149
This "Pyramid" quilt was
made in the 1930's in
Washington County, KY
by the owner's grand-
mother, Moran.

**Morgan,     Joyce
Amos** (Gillis)
General William
Lenior Chapter
Ancestor:     David
Campbell, NC —
#742660
This "Sunbonnet
Sue" quilt was made
in the 1930's in
McMinn County, TN
by the owner's
grandmother, Viola
Forrester Large
(born 9/16/1899 at
McMinn County,
TN, married Charlie
Large, died 6/25/
1980 at Leonoir
City, TN). Viola
made this quilt for
her son, Ross
Louis, who died at
age seven in 1937
from a wound to his
foot while swimming. The name "Ross" is embroidered on the quilt. Viola's other
son, Wayburn, died seven years later in WWII. The quilt was passed from grandmother to current owner.

**Morgan, Joyce Amos (Gillis)**
General William Lenior Chapter
Ancestor: David Campbell, NC — #742660
This "Wagon Wheels" quilt was made in the 1930's by the owner's grandmother, Viola Forrester Large. Viola made this quilt for her son Charles Wayburn Large, who died at twenty years of age in WWII while serving in Italy. The initials "C.W.L." are embroidered on the quilt.

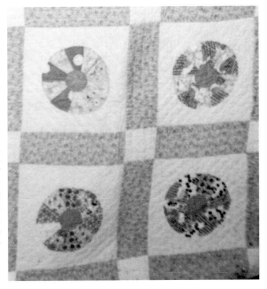

**Morgan, Joyce Amos (Gillis)**
General William Lenior Chapter
Ancestor: David Campbell, NC — #742660
This "Poinsettia" quilt was made in the 1960's in Lenoir City, TN by the owner's grandmother, Viola Forrester Large. Viola made each of her grandchildren a special quilt. This quilt has a special place in the owner's heart because the maker made it with especially her in mind. The owner has quite a few quilts made by her grandmother and she cherishes each of them.

**Morgan, Mary Cox (Thomas C.)**
Colonel Hardy Murfree Chapter
Ancestor: Isaac Allen, VA — #550205.
This "Dutch Doll/Sunbonnet Sue" quilt was made in 1933 at Cornersville, TN by the owner's mother, Mary Lou Cox (born 4/11/1906 at Giles County, TN, married Jesse Will, died 3/4/1972 at Murfreesboro, TN). This was a "baby" quilt made for the owner when she was born.

**Morgan, Mary Cox (Thomas C.)**
Colonel Hardy Murfree Chapter
Ancestor: Isaac Allen, VA — #550205.
This "Texas Star" quilt was made circa 1850 in Cocke County, TN by the owner's great great grandmother, Nancy Kelly Allen (born 1/1/1831 at Cosby, TN, married John Allen, died 7/7/1906 at Cornersville, TN). It was made for a wedding gift for a member of the family. The maker decided it wasn't "nice enough" and kept the quilt and made another one for the gift. The quilt was passed from maker, to owner's grandmother, to her parents, and then finally to the current owner. In 1952, the quilt won first place in the "most unusual gift" category at the Giles County Fair.

**Morgan, Mary Cox (Thomas C.)**
Colonel Hardy Murfree Chapter
Ancestor: Isaac Allen, VA — #550205.
This silk "Crazy" quilt was made circa 1939 at Cornersville, TN by the owner's grandmother, Ada Allen Cox (born 7/4/1878 at Cornersville, TN, married Floyd Cox, died 9/26/1941 in the same town). The quilt was made, in part, using the maker's husband's ties.

**Morgan, Mary Cox (Thomas C.)**
Colonel Hardy Murfree Chapter
Ancestor: Isaac Allen, VA — #550205.
This "Bow Tie" quilt was made in 1933 by friends and family members as a "Friendship" quilt for the owner at her birth.

**Morgan, Mary Cox**
(Thomas C.)
Colonel Hardy Murfree Chapter
Ancestor: Isaac Allen, VA — #550205.
This "Rose" quilt was made circa 1920 at Cornersville, TN by the owner's grandmother, Ada Allen Cox.

**Morgan, Mary Cox**
(Thomas C.)
Colonel Hardy Murfree Chapter
Ancestor: Isaac Allen, VA — #550205.
This "Martha Washington Flower Garden" quilt was made circa 1935 at Cornersville, TN by the owner's grandmother, Ada Allen Cox. The quilt top is silk, the lining is cotton, and the quilt is filled with goose down which the quiltmaker picked herself.

**Morgan, Mary Cox**
(Thomas C.)
Colonel Hardy Murfree Chapter
Ancestor: Isaac Allen, VA — #550205.
This "Vase, Flowers, and Birds" quilt was made circa 1930 at Cornersville, TN by the owner's grandmother, Ada Allen Cox.

**Morris, Leanne James** (Richard)
Charlotte Reeves Robertson Chapter.
Ancestor: Sgt. Richard James, SC — #781456
This "Double Wedding Ring" quilt was made in 1976 at Robertson County, TN by the owner's grandmother, Mabelle Rosson James (born 6/20/1896 at Robertson County, TN, married Frank James, died 11/23/1985 at Newbury, IN). The quilt was passed from the quiltmaker, to her son, to his daughter, the current owner.

**Morris, Leanne James** (Richard)
Charlotte Reeves Robertson Chapter.
Ancestor: Sgt. Richard James, SC — #781456
This "Eight Pointed Star" quilt was made in the 1930's in Robertson County, TN by the owner's great grandmother, Virgie Lee Widick Traughber (born 11/27/1867 at Robertson County, TN, married Ed Traughber, died 1/12/1945 in that county). The quilt was passed from the maker, to the owner's grandmother, then to her mother who passed it to the current owner.

**Morris, Leanne James**
(Richard)
Charlotte Reeves Robertson Chapter.
Ancestor: Sgt. Richard James, SC — #781456
This "Sunbonnet Kids" quilt was made in the 1950's at Robertson County, TN by the owner's grandmother, Verna Lynn Traughber Knight (born 11/14/1896 in Kentucky, married Preston Knight, died 6/27/1973 at Davidson County, TN. The quilt was passed from grandmother, to mother, to daughter.

**Morris, Leanne James**
(Richard)
Charlotte Reeves Robertson Chapter.
Ancestor: Sgt. Richard James, SC — #781456
This "Crazy" quilt was made in the 1890's at Robertson County, TN by the owner's great grandmother, Lela O'Brien James (born 2/20/1873 at Cheatham County, TN, married Solomon Lewis James, died 10/28/1932 at Robertson County, TN). The dress in two corners of the quilt belonged to the quiltmaker's son who died at the age of three. The quilt was passed from great grandmother, to grandfather, to father, to daughter.

**Morris, Leanne James**
(Richard)
Charlotte Reeves Robertson Chapter.
Ancestor: Sgt. Richard James, SC — #781456
This "Log Cabin" quilt was made in 1900-1910 in Kentucky by Virgie Lee Widick Traughber. The quilt was passed from great grandmother, to grandmother, to owner.

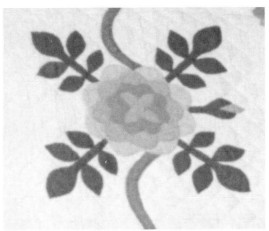

**Morrison, Margaret Elizabeth Young** (Roger Herbert) Campbell Chapter Ancestor: 2nd Lt. Thomas Sayre, NY —#749433 This "Pink Roses" quilt was made circa the 1920's at IN by the owner's great aunt, Minnie Shaver Teed.

**Morrison, Margaret Elizabeth Young** (Roger Herbert) Campbell Chapter Ancestor: 2nd Lt. Thomas Sayre, NY —#749433 This "Double Wedding Ring" quilt was made circa 1916 at Indiana by the owner's great aunt, Minnie Shaver Teed (born 8/5/1868 at Elkhart, IN, married Charles Teed, died at age 104 in 1972 at Denver, CO).

**Morrison, Margaret Elizabeth Young** (Roger Herbert) Campbell Chapter Ancestor: 2nd Lt. Thomas Sayre, NY —#749433 This "Four Patch" quilt was made circa 1900 in Indiana by the owner's grandmother, Cora Shaver Brodrick (born 5/13/1870 at Elkhart, IN, married Frank D. Brodrick, died 2/1/1968 at Denver, CO).

**Morrison, Margaret Elizabeth Young** (Roger Herbert) Campbell Chapter Ancestor: 2nd Lt. Thomas Sayre, NY —#749433 This "Red Poppies" quilt was made in the 1920's in Indiana by the owner's great aunt, Minnie Shaver Teed.

**Morrison, Francis Sue G.** (Thomas A.) Zachariah Davies Chapter Ancestor: Elijah Griffin, VA —#646961 This "Colonial America" quilt was made in 1980 at Braden, TN by the owner's mother-in-law, Annie Elizabeth Burrows Morrison (married Floyd Odell Morrison on 12/28/1944). The quilt was made as a wedding gift for the owner.

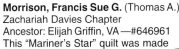

**Morrison, Francis Sue G.** (Thomas A.) Zachariah Davies Chapter Ancestor: Elijah Griffin, VA —#646961 This "Mariner's Star" quilt was made in 1985 at Braden, TN by the owner's mother-in-law, Annie Elizabeth Burrows Morrison. The "ship" quilting design in this quilt is copied from a petticoat at the National Museum of the Daughters of the American Revolution.

**Morrison, Francis Sue G.** (Thomas A.) Zachariah Davies Chapter Ancestor: Elijah Griffin, VA —#646961 This "Baltimore Album" wall hanging was made in 1997 at Braden, TN by the owner's mother-in-law, Annie Elizabeth Burrows Morrison.

**Morrison, Francis Sue G.** (Thomas A.) Zachariah Davies Chapter Ancestor: Elijah Griffin, VA — #646961

This "Eagle" quilt was made circa1862 at Mt. Pleasant, MS by the owner's great aunt, Sarah Morton (born 1852 at Mt. Pleasant, died in 1930). Sarah made this quilt for her hope chest during the War Between the States.

**Morrison, Francis Sue G.**
(Thomas A.)
Zachariah Davies Chapter
Ancestor: Elijah Griffin, VA
—#646961
This "Double Wedding Ring Variation" quilt was made in 1994 at Braden, TN by the owner's mother-in-law, Annie Elizabeth Burrows Morrison. Annie made this quilt in honor of her 50th wedding anniversary.

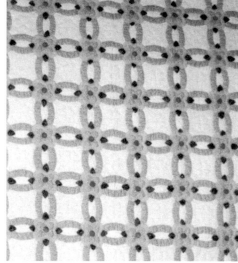

**Morton, Ila Mae Acton** (Bob)
Mary Blount Chapter
Ancestor: Bartlett Sisk, VA—#740992
This original "Houses Habitat" quilt was made in 1997-98 in Maryville, TN by the owner and members of the Foothills Quilters Guild. The quilt was sold at auction and the owner had the highest bid.

**Morton, Ila Mae Acton** (Bob)
Mary Blount Chapter
Ancestor: Bartlett Sisk, VA — #740992
This "Sampler" quilt was made in 1996 in Maryville, TN by the owner (born 3/1/1931 at Madisonville, TN). The quilt won 2nd place 4/19/1997 at the Dogwood Arts Quilt Show, and Viewer's Choice and cash award of $125 at the Mountain Quiltfest, Pigeon Forge, TN, 3/27/1998.

**Moss, Carol Garrett**
(William Todd)
Old Glory Chapter
Ancestor: Edward Garrett, SC — #663426
This "Drunkard's Path" quilt was made circa 1997 by the Amish women of Lancaster, PA. The owner purchased the quilt to enhance her collection and commemorate her 5th wedding anniversary.

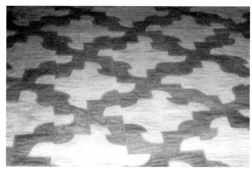

**Moss, Lorene Alsobrooks**
(Eugene D.)
Robert Cooke Chapter
Ancestor: William Alsobrooks, NC — #752536
This "Butterfly" quilt was made circa 1943 in Erin, TN by the owner's mother, Retha Ann Alsobrooks (born 7//4/1905 at Erin, TN, married James Isham Alsobrooks, died 2/29/1975 in the same town). The quilt was passed from mother to daughter.

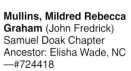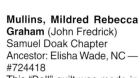

**Moss, Carol Garrett**
(William Todd)
Old Glory Chapter
Ancestor: Edward Garrett, SC — #663426
This "Mill Wheel" quilt was made between 1895-1900 in Arkansas by the owner's great grandmother, Lois Powers Parrish Smith (born 1/4/1881 at Izard County, AR, married Lee Smith, died in 1962 at Imboden, AR). The quilt was passed from great grandmother, to grandmother, to owner.

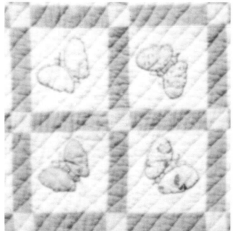

**Mullins, Mildred Rebecca Graham** (John Fredrick)
Samuel Doak Chapter
Ancestor: Elisha Wade, NC —#724418
This "Butterfly" quilt was made in 1958 at Charlotte, NC by the owner's mother, Mildred Rebecca Lowe Graham (born 7/17/1903 at Banner Elk, NC, married William Alexander Graham, Jr., died 12/10/1993 at Charlotte).

**Mullins, Mildred Rebecca Graham** (John Fredrick)
Samuel Doak Chapter
Ancestor: Elisha Wade, NC — #724418
This "Doll" quilt was made in 1958 at Charlotte, NC by the owner's mother, Mildred Rebecca Lowe Graham. There was a formal request from the Charlotte Mint Museum to display this quilt in their doll exhibit circa 1962.

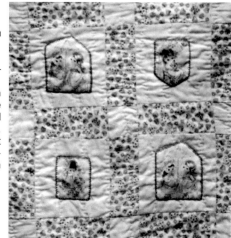

**Mullins, Mildred Rebecca Graham** (John Fredrick)
Samuel Doak Chapter
Ancestor: Elisha Wade, NC —#724418
This "Patchwork" doll quilt was made in 1879 at Banner Elk, NC by the owner's maternal grandmother, Nancy Blanche Voncanon (born 11/1869 at Banner Elk, married Robert Lee Lowe, died 2/16/1945 at Banner Elk).

**Murphy, Virginia Jernigan** (Fred R.)
Tullahoma Chapter
Ancestor: Cary Jernigan, SC — #562476
This "Dresden Plate" quilt made the owner's great great aunt, Sallie Myers Turner Seitz (born in 1859 at McMinnville, TN, married 2nd Dr. Albert Seitz, died in 1944 in the same town). Sallie Seitz was first married to Alexander G. Turner, a wholesale grocer in Nashville, TN. After his death she married Dr. Seitz, a graduate of the Vanderbilt Medical School and Polyclinic in New York. Sallie was very active in the Methodist Episcopal Church South. In addition to this quilt, she gave the owner many of her exquisite needlework pieces.

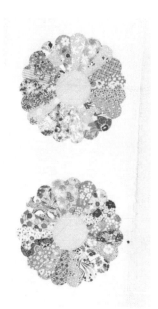

**Murr, Betty Blankenship** (Aubrey)
Coytee Chapter
Ancestor John Alexander, NC —#652732
This "Handkerchief" quilt was made in 1985 at Greenback, TN by the owner for her friend, Fleda Jones. Fleda asked Betty to make this quilt using the handkerchiefs she had received as gifts over 42 years of teaching in the Loudon County, TN schools. When it was finished Fleda gave the quilt to Betty.

**Murr, Betty Blankenship** (Aubrey)
Coytee Chapter
Ancestor John Alexander, NC —#652732
This "Crazy" quilt was made in 1970 at Greenback, TN by the owner (born 6/26/1934 at Greenback).

**Murr, Betty Blankenship** (Aubrey)
Coytee Chapter
Ancestor John Alexander, NC —#652732
This "Improved Nine Patch" quilt was made in 1965 by the owner.

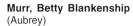

**Murr, Betty Blankenship** (Aubrey)
Coytee Chapter
Ancestor John Alexander, NC —#652732
This "Crazy" quilt with feed sack lining was finished in February 1952 at Greenback, TN by the owner. It is tacked with embroidery thread.

**Murr, Sarah**
Coytee Chapter
Ancestor: John Alexander, NC — #657624
This "Grandmother's Flower Garden" quilt was made in 1940 at Greenback, TN by the owner's great grandmother, Pearl Blankenship (born 8/11/1886 at Greenback, TN, married Charles Edgar Blankenship, died 1/8/1967 at Greenback). It was passed from the maker, to the owner's grandmother, to her mother, and finally to the owner.

**Murr, Sarah**
Coytee Chapter
Ancestor: John Alexander, NC — #657624
This "Yo Yo" quilt was made in 1984 at Greenback, TN by the owner's mother, Betty Murr.

**Murray, (Polly) Mary Pauline**
Andrew Bogle Chapter
Ancestor: William Mims, SC — # 762588
This "Ocean Waves" quilt was made circa 1880 in Cocke County, TN by the owner's great grandmother, Elizabeth Manning Murray (born 9/3/1829 at Cocke County, TN, married James Cannon Murray, died 9/9/1914 at Cocke County). The quilt was passed down through the family.

**Murray, (Polly) Mary Pauline**
Andrew Bogle Chapter
Ancestor: William Mims, SC — # 762588
This "Sampler" quilt was made in 1997 at Knoxville, TN by the owner (born 10/1/1928 at Knoxville, TN).

**Myers, Elizabeth Boyd**
(Andrew)
Lt. James Sheppard Chapter
Ancestor: David Barton, VA — #542692
This "Feathered Star" quilt was made in the 1800's in White County, TN. It was purchased from an antique dealer in the early 1980's.

**Murray, (Polly) Mary Pauline**
Andrew Bogle Chapter
Ancestor: William Mims, SC — # 762588
This "Dresden Plate" quilt was made in the early 1930's at Newport, TN by the owners grandmother, Lucia Rhea Mims (born 2/21/1864 at Newport, TN, married Charles Beauregard Mims, died 3/26/1936 at Newport).

**Myers, Elizabeth Boyd**
(Andrew)
Lt. James Sheppard Chapter
Ancestor: David Barton, VA—#542692
This "Grandmother's Flower Garden" quilt was made in the early 1900's at Myers Cove, Warren County, TN by the owners husband's grandmother, Octal Hill Myers (born 1860 at Warren Co., TN, married Andrew C. Myers, died 1941 at Coffee Co., TN). She made a quilt by this pattern for each of her children. This particular quilt came to the owner through the maker's youngest daughter.

**Nave, Jane Murphy**
Spencer Clack Chapter
Ancestor: First Lt. Spencer Clack, VA—#756419
This "Cats Meow" quilt was made circa 1940 as a gift for the owner.

**Neal, Roberta Conditt**
(Sam K.)
Caney Fork Chapter
Ancestor: James Thackston, VA — #606385
This "Rose of Sharon Variation" quilt was inherited from the owner's grandparents. It was made circa 1870.

**Neal, Roberta Conditt** (Sam K.)
Caney Fork Chapter
Ancestor: James Thackston, VA —#606385
This "Double Irish Chain" quilt was made at Elmwood, TN by the owner's mother, Mrs. Etta Allgier Conditt (born 6/24/1879 at Elmwood, TN, died 1/13/1931 at Elmwood). The quilt was begun over a summer vacation. "My daughter and I are the third and fourth generations (with our husbands) to live in the home my grandfather built sometime around 1865. Each generation has improved, remodeled and added on to the house until it is now quite comfortable nestled in the hills of Smith County, TN. I am the only child of the youngest of six daughters, so there are several quilts that I have no idea the origin or age. I always say, it came with the house."

**Neal, Roberta Conditt** (Sam K.)
Caney Fork Chapter
Ancestor: James Thackston, VA —#606385
This trapunto whole cloth quilt was inherited by the owner from her grandparents. "It came with the house." The owner's mother entered this quilt in the County Fair at Carthage, TN in the early 1920's and it received first prize. This quilt was used as a bed spread and is now framed and hanging in the owner's home.

**Neiman, Evagene Cowles** (Robert E.)
Chickasaw Bluff Chapter
Ancestor: John Cowles, Sr., MA —#769471
This "Double Wedding Ring" quilt was made in 1932 at Waterloo, IA by the owner's mother, Luella Cowles (born 9/29/1895 at Hudson, IA, married Ethan Perry Cowles, died 8/11/1948 at Waterloo, IA). The quilt is signed "Evagene from mother, 1932." There were three girls in the family and each received a quilt from their mother.

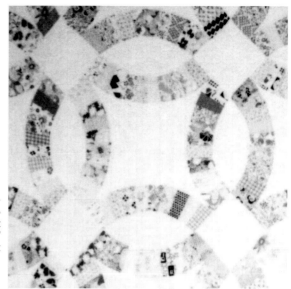

**Neil, "Laddie" Harton** (A.B., Jr.)
Campbell Chapter
Ancestor: Jonathon Foster —#399448
This "Memory" quilt was made in 1983 at Lebannon, TN by the owner's niece Mary Alice Ratcliff Bradley (married Tim Bradley). This quilt was made in honor of the owner's mother, Mrs. John W. Harton, on her 90th birthday on 6/22. She was a member of the DAR for over 50 years. The honoree's four children and nine grandchildren participated in making this quilt. Each participant made an original block that expressed their love for Mrs. Harton.

**Neil, "Laddie" Harton** (A.B., Jr.)
Campbell Chapter
Ancestor: Jonathon Foster —#399448
This "Dogwood" quilt was made in 1975 at Tullahoma, TN by the owner's mother, Frances Lewis Harton (born 6/22/1893 at New Hartford, NY, married John W. Harton, died 11/27/1989). "Mother was going to make three of these quilts, but only two were finished. She did these while watching the Watergate Hearings on TV." The maker lived to be 96 years of age.

**Nelson, Ann Amick** (Michael)
William Cocke Chapter
Ancestor: Maj. John Harding, Sr., VA —#681145
This "Whig Rose" quilt was made at Fort Ashby, WV by the owner's great aunt, Ella Blue Ansell Millar (born at Springfield, WV, married Charles Andrew Millar, died at Fort Ashby, WV). Aunt Ella gave the quilt to the owner's grandmother, Sarah Jemina Millar Amick. The owner inherited the quilt after her grandmother's death.

**Nelson, Terry Downs** (Lloyd E.)
Hermitage Chapter
Ancestor: Capt. Anthony Winston, Jr., VA —#658203
This "Sunbonnet Sue" quilt was made in the 1920's at Birmingham, AL by the owner's grandmother, Irene Jordan Sherrod (born 3/26/1877 at Clay County, MS, married Edmund Sherrod, died 1/31/1943 at Jefferson County, AL). The maker made the quilt for her Downs granddaughters. The material came from the maker's house dresses.

**Nelson, Terry Downs** (Lloyd E.)
Hermitage Chapter
Ancestor: Capt. Anthony Winston, Jr., VA —#658203
This "Hole in the Barn Door" quilt was made in the 1930's at Birmingham, AL by the owner's grandmother, Irene Jordan Sherrod. The quilt was made from clothes from the adult men in the family.

**Nevels, Patricia Zinser** (Travis)
Sarah Hawkins Chapter
Ancestor: Adam Brown, PA — #610245
This "Crazy" quilt was made in 1897 by Mary Wright Bradle who was born in Washington, IL.

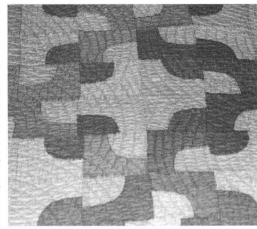

**Nevels, Patricia Zinser** (Travis)
Sarah Hawkins Chapter
Ancestor: Adam Brown, PA — #610245
This "Pineapple" quilt was made in the early 1900's by the owner's mother, Mrs. Eugene Zinser. It was made on a sewing machine when they were a new luxury and very scarce.

**Newman, Cindy Murr** (Samuel)
Coytee Chapter
Ancestor: John Alexander, NC — #657625
This "String Star" quilt was made in 1930 at Greenback, TN by the owner's great great aunt, Emma Blankenship (born 5/15/1881 at Blount County, TN, married Gilbert James Blankenship, died 4/10/1965 at Greenback). It was passed from the maker to the owner's mother, to the owner.

**Newman, Jacqueline Tipton** (James A.)
Cavett Station Chapter
Ancestor: Benjamin Tipton, VA —#646308
This "Drunkard's Path" quilt was made in the 1920's at Maryville, TN by the owner's grandmother, Emily Erwin Reed (born in 1874 at Monroe County, TN, married Wallace Benjamin Reed, died 2/2/1934 at Maryville, TN). Although the quiltmaker made many quilts, this is the only one that survived. When Wallace

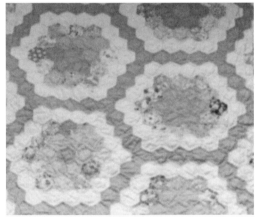

came to Tennessee as an engineer to construct roads in Monroe County, he met and married the quiltmaker. At Maryville, he owned and operated a prosperous machine shop. He traveled to Cuba for about six months every two years to build roads, leaving Emily to handle his business.

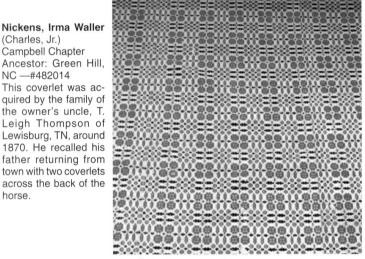

**Nickens, Irma Waller** (Charles, Jr.)
Campbell Chapter
Ancestor: Green Hill, NC —#482014
This coverlet was acquired by the family of the owner's uncle, T. Leigh Thompson of Lewisburg, TN, around 1870. He recalled his father returning from town with two coverlets across the back of the horse.

**Nickens, Irma Waller** (Charles, Jr.)
Campbell Chapter
Ancestor: Green Hill, NC —#482014
This "Grandmother's Flower Garden" quilt was made in early 1900 at Brentwood, TN by the owner's grandmother, Susannah Sneed Williams Wallace (born 9/17/1849 at Brentwood, married John Rains Waller, died 11/3/1941 at Nashville).

**Nickens, Irma Waller** (Charles, Jr.)
Campbell Chapter
Ancestor: Green Hill, NC —#482014
This silk comforter was made in 1930 at Brentwood, TN by the owner's grandmother, Susannah Sneed Williams Wallace. She made the blocks from men's ties and other clothing from the family.

**Noblitt, Anne Gammill** (H. L.)
Tullahoma Chapter
Ancestor: Lt. John Motlow, SC —#463387
This "Triple Irish Chain" quilt was given to the owner by her aunt, Susan Bird Hix Logan (1878-1962).

**Noblitt, Anne Gammill**
(H. L.)
Tullahoma Chapter
Ancestor: Lt. John Motlow,
SC —#463387
This "Variation of a Love
Apple" quilt was given to
the owner by her mother,
Fannie Hix Gammill.

**Noblitt, Anne Gammill** (H. L.)
Tullahoma Chapter
Ancestor: Lt. John Motlow, SC
—#463387
This "Rose" quilt was made
circa 1890 at Bedford County,
TN by the owner's grandmother,
Elizabeth Catherine Parkes Hix
(born 8/28/1853, married Benjamin
Franklin Hix, died 1/5/
1921 at Bedford County, TN).
The quilt was passed from the
maker, to the owner's mother,
to the owner.

**Norwood, Margaret Love** (Hoyt)
Alexander Keith Chapter
Ancestor: Lt. Robert Love, VA —#706506
This "Spinning Ball" quilt was made circa 1850-
60 at McMinn County, TN by the owner's great
grandmother, Myra Lenoir Reagan (born 4/2/
1810 at Lenoir City, TN, married Gen James
Hayes Reagan, died 3/8/1879 at Sweetwater,
TN). The owner inherited the quilt from her father
in 1959. It is thought to have been made at
Reagan Station in McMinn County as documented
by Bets Ramsey and M. Waldvogel.
This quilt won first place in the "Antique Pieced
Quilts" category at the McMinn Heritage Museum
Quilt Show in 1987.

**Nottingham, June Crabtree** (P.T., Jr.)
Long Island Chapter
Ancestor: James Crabtree, VA—#577532
This "Indian Sign' quilt was made in Kansas by the owner's mother-in-law, Lela Nottingham (born
6/20/1903 at Everest, KS, married P.T. Nottingham Sr.). Because the sign looks like a Swastika,
the quilt was put away during World War II.

**Nottingham, June Crabtree**
(P.T., Jr.)
Long Island Chapter
Ancestor: James Crabtree,
VA—#577532
This "Dresden Plate" quilt was
made in the 1970's by the
owner's mother, Elsie Crabtree
(born 1911 at Tazewill, VA,
married Garland Roosevelt
Crabtree).

**Nottingham, June Crabtree**
(P.T., Jr.)
Long Island Chapter
Ancestor: James Crabtree,
VA—#577532
This "Kaleidoscope" quilt was
made in 1970 at Huntsville, AL
by the owner's mother, Elsie
Crabtree. The quilt was made
in quilt class at the Church of
Christ in Huntsville.

**Nottingham, June Crabtree**
(P.T., Jr.)
Long Island Chapter
Ancestor: James Crabtree,
VA—#577532
This "Grandmother's Flower
Garden" quilt was made in
the 1970's by the owner's
mother, Elsie Crabtree.

**Nottingham, June Crabtree**
(P.T., Jr.)
Long Island Chapter
Ancestor: James Crabtree,
VA—#577532
This "Double Wedding
Ring"quilt was made in the
1970's by the owner's mother,
Elsie Crabtree.

**Nottingham, June Crabtree** (P.T., Jr.)
Long Island Chapter
Ancestor: James Crabtree, VA—#577532
This "Fan" quilt was made in the 1920's at Huntsville, AL by the owner's mother, Elsie Crabtree.

**Nottingham, June Crabtree** (P.T., Jr.)
Long Island Chapter
Ancestor: James Crabtree, VA—#577532
This "Lone Star" quilt was made by the owner's mother, Elsie Crabtree.

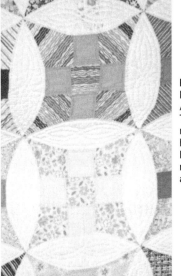

**Nottingham, June Crabtree** (P.T., Jr.)
Long Island Chapter
Ancestor: James Crabtree, VA—#577532
This "Four Leaf" quilt was made in the 1980's at Huntsville, AL by the owner's mother Elsie Crabtree.

**Nottingham, June Crabtree** (P.T., Jr.)
Long Island Chapter
Ancestor: James Crabtree, VA—#577532
This "Nine Patch Variation" quilt was made in Kansas by the owner's husband's grandmother, Emilia Geiser Bollinger (born 3/15/1868 at Kansas, married Grant Bollinger, died 8/12/1940 at Everest, KS).

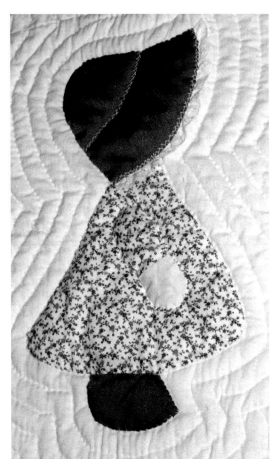

**Nottingham, June Crabtree** (P.T., Jr.)
Long Island Chapter
Ancestor: James Crabtree, VA—#577532
This "Dutch Girl/Sunbonnet Sue" quilt was made in the 1980's at Huntsville, AL by the owner's mother, Elsie Brown Crabtree.

**Owens, Fae Jacobs** (Robert S.)
Hatchie Chapter
Ancestor: Alexander Keith, VA —#546331
This "Crazy" quilt was made in 1913 at Tippah County, MS by the owner's great grandmother, Mary Elizabeth Richardson Keith (born 6/26/1835 in Tennessee, married John Alexander Keith, died 11/8/1922 at Tippah County, MS). The maker was 78 years old when she made the quilt.

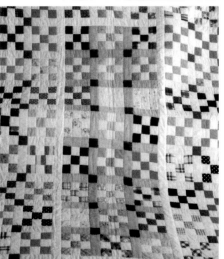

**Owens, Mary Estell New** (Garry W.)
Margaret Gaston Chapter
Ancestor: John Rutledge, SC —#630709
This "Nine Patch" quilt was begun in 1945 by the owner's great grandmother, Ida Clara Wooten Rutledge (born 12/7/1866 Rat Perkins County, GA, married Rollie Noscoe Rutledge, died 4/2/1950 at Brown County, TX) The quilt was finished in 1986 by the owner (born 7/25/1933 at Sipe Springs, TX).

**Owens, Mary Estell New**
(Garry W.)
Margaret Gaston Chapter
Ancestor: John Rutledge,
SC —#630709
This embroidered quilt
was made circa 1983 at
Odessa, TX by the
owner's mother, Lena
Rutledge New (born 11/
19/1908 at Brownwood,
TX, married John Edward
New, died 5/29/1992 at
Lebanon, TN).

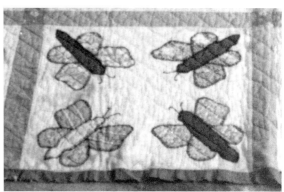

**Owens, Mary Estell New**
(Garry W.)
Margaret Gaston Chapter
Ancestor: John Rutledge,
SC —#630709
This "Tulip" quilt was pur-
chased by the owner in
August 1996.

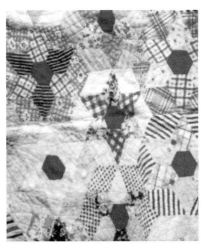

**Owens, Mary Estell New** (Garry W.)
Margaret Gaston Chapter
Ancestor: John Rutledge, SC —
#630709
This "Six Pointed Star" quilt was
made circa 1956 at Brownwood, TX
by the owner's mother, Lena
Rutledge New.

**Owens, Mary Estell New** (Garry W.)
Margaret Gaston Chapter
Ancestor: John Rutledge, SC —#630709
This "Butterfly" quilt was pieced by the
owner's great aunt Mary and finished in
1947 at Brownwood, TX by the owner's
mother, Lena Rutledge New.

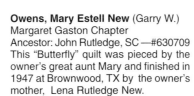

**Owens, Mary Estell
New** (Garry W.)
Margaret Gaston
Chapter
Ancestor: John
Rutledge, SC —
#630709
This "Lone Star"
quilt was pieced by
a member of the
quilting club in
Morristown, TN and
quilted by the owner
circa 1982.

**Paessler, Jane Park** (Charles F.)
Chickasaw Bluff Chapter
Ancestor: Moses Park, NC —#755109
This "Improved Nine Patch" quilt was
made at Obion County, TN by the
owner's husband's great grandmother,
Sarah Frances "Sallie" Isbell (born 6/
13/1851 at Germantown, TN, married
Calvin Clay Naylor, died 9/2/1940 at
Union City, TN).

**Paessler, Jane Park**
(Charles F.)
Chickasaw Bluff Chapter
Ancestor: Moses Park,
NC —#755109
This "Patchwork" quilt
was made in the 1970's
at Memphis, TN by the
owner (born 5/24/1934).

**Paessler, Jane Park** (Charles F.)
Chickasaw Bluff Chapter
Ancestor: Moses Park, NC —#755109
This "Texas Lone Star" quilt was made in the late 1930's at Union City, TN by the
owner's mother, Lovie Joyner Park (born 10/11/1908 at Obion County, married
David H. "Dick" Park, died 9/10/1992 at Obion County, TN).

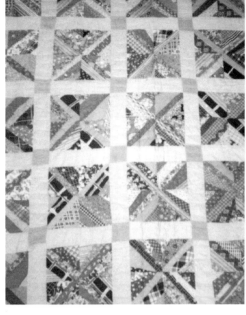

**Paessler, Jane Park**
(Charles F.)
Chickasaw Bluff Chapter
Ancestor: Moses Park,
NC —#755109
This "Paper" quilt was
pieced at Obion County,
TN by the owner's grand-
mother, Ludie Bittick
Joyner (born 4/29/1873
at Obion County, TN,
married John Thomas
Joyner, died 8/6/1950 in
the same county). A pa-
per quilt is equal squares
of paper covered with
scraps of fabric, then
trimmed to the size of the
paper. The paper is re-
moved before the blocks
are sewn together. This
quilt was quilted by the
owner

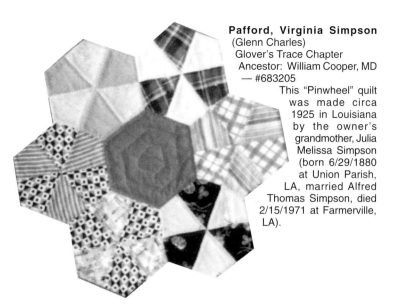

**Pafford, Virginia Simpson**
(Glenn Charles)
Glover's Trace Chapter
Ancestor: William Cooper, MD
— #683205
This "Pinwheel" quilt
was made circa
1925 in Louisiana
by the owner's
grandmother, Julia
Melissa Simpson
(born 6/29/1880
at Union Parish,
LA, married Alfred
Thomas Simpson, died
2/15/1971 at Farmerville,
LA).

**Pafford, Virginia Simpson**
(Glenn Charles)
Glover's Trace Chapter
Ancestor: William Cooper,
MD — #683205
This "Snowball" quilt was
pieced circa 1950 by
owner's husband's aunt,
Eva McKelvy Kennon (born
12/22/1883 at Benton
County, TN, married
Clarence Kennon, died in
1962 at Benton) It was
quilted by the owner in
1995.

**Painter, Frances Mitchell**
(Auburn)
Tullahoma Chapter
Ancestor: 1st Lt. John
Motlow, SC —#701651
This "Crazy" quilt is re-
ferred to by the owner as a
"Friendship" quilt.

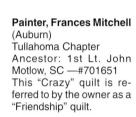

**Painter, Frances Mitchell**
(Auburn)
Tullahoma Chapter
Ancestor: 1st Lt. John
Motlow, SC —#701651
This is a "Double Wedding
Ring" quilt.

**Palladino, Wanda Whitaker** (Joseph)
Andrew Bogle Chapter
Ancestor: William Hargis, NC — #646019
This "Mill Wheel" quilt was made in
Putnam County, TN by the owner's
grandmother, Pearlie Lee Finley Clouse
(born 12/10/1887 at Overton County, TN,
married Rollis Bevie Clouse, died 5/20/
1967 at Putnam County, TN). The quilt
is pieced from fabric from the maker's
dresses. The quilt was passed from
maker, to daughter, Nellie Clouse
Whitaker, to her daughter, the current
owner. Like many of her other quilts, she
will pass it on to her sons, Joseph Kenneth and Leonard Peyton Paladino.

**Palladino, Wanda Whitaker**
(Joseph)
Andrew Bogle Chapter
Ancestor: William Hargis, NC
— #646019
This "Sunbonnet Sue" quilt
was made in Cookeville, TN
by the owner's mother, Nellie
Clouse Whitaker (born 5/22/
1910 at Putnam County, TN,
married Henry Peyton
Whitaker, died 3/7/1997 at
Jefferson County, KY). Because she loved dolls so
much, the owner's mother always made her doll quilts.

**Palladino, Wanda Whitaker**
(Joseph)
Andrew Bogle Chapter
Ancestor: William Hargis, NC
— #646019
This "Starlight" quilt, made in
red, white and blue, was
made in Putnam County, TN
by the owner's mother, Nellie
Clouse Whitaker. She passed
the quilt to her daughter, the
current owner.

**Palladino, Wanda Whitaker** (Joseph)
Andrew Bogle Chapter
Ancestor: William Hargis, NC — #646019
This "Gussie Groat's Bonnet/Sunbonnet Sue" quilt was made in Putnam County, TN by the owner's mother, Nellie Clouse Whitaker.

**Palladino, Wanda Whitaker** (Joseph)
Andrew Bogle Chapter
Ancestor: William Hargis, NC — #646019
This "Starlight" quilt, in shades of blue and white, was also made by Nellie Clouse Whitaker, the owner's mother.

**Palladino, Wanda Whitaker** (Joseph)
Andrew Bogle Chapter
Ancestor: William Hargis, NC — #646019
This "Little Bo Peep/Colonial Girl" quilt was made in Putnam County, TN by the owner's mother, Nellie Clouse Whitaker.

**Palladino, Wanda Whitaker** (Joseph)
Andrew Bogle Chapter
Ancestor: William Hargis, NC — #646019
This "Hole in the Barn Door" quilt was made in Putnam County, TN by the owner's grandmother, Pearlie Lee Finley Clouse. The quilt was passed from maker, to daughter, Nellie Clouse Whitaker, to her daughter, the current owner. She will pass it on to her sons, Joseph Kenneth and Leonard Peyton Palladino. The quilt is made from the grandmother's dresses.

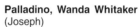

**Palladino, Wanda Whitaker** (Joseph)
Andrew Bogle Chapter
Ancestor: William Hargis, NC — #646019
This "Eight Pointed Star" quilt was made in Putnam County, TN by the owner's mother, Nellie Clouse Whitaker. She passed the quilt to her daughter, the current owner.

**Palladino, Wanda Whitaker** (Joseph)
Andrew Bogle Chapter
Ancestor: William Hargis, NC — #646019
This "Spools" quilt was made in Putnam County, TN by the owner's mother, Nellie Clouse Whitaker. She passed the quilt to her daughter, the current owner.

**Palladino, Wanda Whitaker** (Joseph)
Andrew Bogle Chapter
Ancestor: William Hargis, NC — #646019
This "Double Wedding Ring" quilt was made at Cookeville, TN by the owner's mother, Nellie Clouse Whitaker, or her grandmother, Pearlie Lee Clouse. The owner used this quilt as a small girl.

**Palladino, Wanda Whitaker** (Joseph)
Andrew Bogle Chapter
Ancestor: William Hargis, NC — #646019
This "Bow Tie" quilt was a made at Cookeville, TN by the owner's mother, Nellie Clouse Whitaker. Materials in this quilt are pieces of the owners play clothes from childhood.

**Palladino, Wanda Whitaker** (Joseph)
Andrew Bogle Chapter
Ancestor: William Hargis, NC — #646019
This "Fan" quilt was made at Cookeville, TN by the owner's mother, Nellie Clouse Whitaker.

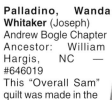

**Palladino, Wanda Whitaker** (Joseph)
Andrew Bogle Chapter
Ancestor: William Hargis, NC — #646019
This "Overall Sam" quilt was made in the 1960's at Cookeville, TN by the owner's mother, Nellie Clouse Whitaker.

**Palladino, Wanda Whitaker** (Joseph)
Andrew Bogle Chapter
Ancestor: William Hargis, NC — #646019
This "Sunbonnet Sue" quilt was made at Cookeville, TN by the owner when she was in college.

**Palladino, Wanda Whitaker** (Joseph)
Andrew Bogle Chapter
Ancestor: William Hargis, NC — #646019
This "Lady From Petticoat Row" quilt was made at Cookeville, TN by the owner's mother, Nellie Clouse Whitaker.

**Palladino, Wanda Whitaker** (Joseph)
Andrew Bogle Chapter
Ancestor: William Hargis, NC — #646019
This "Double Wedding Ring" quilt was made at Cookeville, TN by the owner's mother, Nellie Clouse Whitaker.

**Palladino, Wanda Whitaker** (Joseph)
Andrew Bogle Chapter
Ancestor: William Hargis, NC — #646019
This "Butterfly" quilt was made at Cookeville, TN by the owner's mother, Nellie Clouse Whitaker.

**Palladino, Wanda Whitaker** (Joseph)
Andrew Bogle Chapter
Ancestor: William Hargis, NC — #646019
This "Hands All Around" quilt was made at Cookeville, TN by the owner's mother, Nellie Clouse Whitaker.

**Palladino, Wanda Whitaker** (Joseph)
Andrew Bogle Chapter
Ancestor: William Hargis, NC — #646019
This "Bow Tie" quilt was made at Cookeville, TN by the owner's mother, Nellie Clouse Whitaker.

**Palladino, Wanda Whitaker** (Joseph)
Andrew Bogle Chapter
Ancestor: William Hargis, NC — #646019
This "World Without End" quilt was made at Cookeville, TN by the owner's mother, Nellie Clouse Whitaker. This quilt may have been made by Pearlie Lee Clouse, the owner's grandmother.

**Parker, Elizabeth Ingram** (James)
Glover's Trace Chapter
Ancestor: James Ingraham, VA — # 706036
This "Double Irish Chain" quilt was made in 1996 in Glencoe, AR and purchased by the owner at the "Quilt Place." While traveling in northern Arkansas on vacation in 1996 the owner stopped at this quaint quilt shop, "just to look". The shop is owned by Willie Ann Garner. It is located eight miles south of Salem, AR. The quilts displayed in the shop are made by women in the community and were so beautiful that the current owner of this quilt did more than just look.

**Parker, Elizabeth Ingram** (James)
Glover's Trace Chapter
Ancestor: James Ingraham, VA — # 706036
This "Alphabet With Pictures" quilt was made in 1996 at Camden, TN by volunteers in the Retired Senior Volunteer Program. The owner's mother, Guyneth was a part of the group. She was born 3/12/1909 at Huntington, TN, and died 2/2/1998 at Camden, TN).

**Parker, Elizabeth Ingram** (James)
Glover's Trace Chapter
Ancestor: James Ingraham, VA — # 706036
This "Pinwheel" quilt was made in 1954 at Logan County, AR by the women of the church. It was given to the owner and her husband as a Christmas gift the first year of their marriage. Each woman pieced a block. In the center block is stitched "PIONEER MEMORIAL, 1954." Services in this very small rural church were held only two

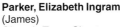

times a month, once on Sunday and once on Saturday night." In her 44 years as a clergy spouse, the owner has never known of another church with regular Saturday night services.

**Parker, Nola Goode** (Stewart J.)
Nancy Ward Chapter
Ancestor: Richard Goode, NC — #640558
This variation of an old 1800's pattern, "Oak Leaves and Acorns," quilt was made in 1874 at Brooklyn, AL by the owner's husband's grandmother, Dorcus Stucky Yancy (born 1859 at Brooklyn, AL, married R.B. Yancy, died 1/2/1931 at Brooklyn). This quilt was made by a young girl for her Hope Chest.

**Parks, Pauline Moredock** (Robert E.)
Robert Cooke Chapter
Ancestor: James Officer, VA —#948827
This "Star" quilt was made circa 1970 at Johnstown, PA by Emma Buksa, who made the quilt as a gift to the owner.

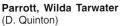

**Parrott, Wilda Tarwater** (D. Quinton)
William Cocke Chapter
Ancestor: William Kebble, VA — #602690
This "Crazy" quilt was made circa 1932 at Sevier County, TN by the owner's aunt, Theo Mashburn Tarwater, and members of the Tarwater family. Theo was born 5/25/1912 at Sevier County, TN, married Freeman Tarwater, and died 6/16/1995 in the same county.

**Parrott, Wilda Tarwater** (D. Quinton)
William Cocke Chapter
Ancestor: William Kebble, VA — #602690
This overshot linen and wool coverlet was made before 1900 at Jefferson County, TN. The owner received it from the estate of her mother-in-law, Audrey Poe Parrott.

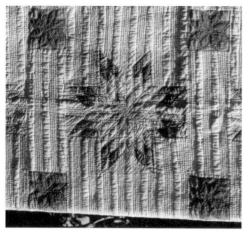

**Parrott, Wilda Tarwater**
(D. Quinton)
William Cocke Chapter
Ancestor: William Kebble,
VA — #602690
This "Star" quilt was made
circa 1900 in Jefferson
County, TN. The owner re-
ceived it from the estate
of her mother-in-law,
Audrey Poe Parrott.

**Parrott, Wilda Tarwater**
(D. Quinton)
William Cocke Chapter
Ancestor: William
Kebble, VA — #602690
This "Crazy" quilt was
made in the early 1900's
at Sevier County, TN by
the owner's mother, Ella
Floyd Tarwater (born 12/
3/1894 at Sevier County,
TN, married Millard E.
Tarwater, died 5/9/1980
at Sevier County). This
quilt was made from wool
scraps and lined in wool
for warmth.

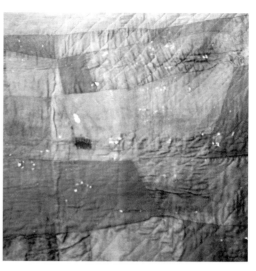

**Parrott, Wilda Tarwater** (D. Quinton)
William Cocke Chapter
Ancestor: William Kebble, VA —
#602690
This "Bow Tie" quilt was made before
the 1900's at Sevier County, TN by the
owner's grandmother, Nannie Rule
Tarwater (born 2/16/1870 at Sevier
County, TN, married Adam Tarwater,
died 6/3/1942 in the same county). The
owner received the quilt from
Mashburn Tarwater who received it
from the maker.

**Parrott, Wilda Tarwater**
(D. Quinton)
William Cocke Chapter
Ancestor: William Kebble,
VA — #602690
This "Grandmother's Flower
Garden" quilt was pieced in
the 1930's in Cocke County,
TN by the owner's mother-
in-law, Audrey Poe Parrott
(born 9/13/1906 at Jefferson
County, TN, married Cecil
Parrott, died 8/9/1993 at
Cocke County, TN). The
quilt was quilted in 1996 by
Willie Carlisle. It was passed
from the maker to the owner.

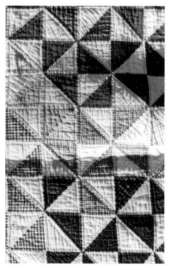

**Parrott, Wilda Tarwater** (D. Quinton)
William Cocke Chapter
Ancestor: William Kebble, VA — #602690
This "Pinwheel" quilt was made circa 1900 at Jefferson County,
TN by the owner's mother-in-law, Audrey Poe Parrott. The
owner received it from the maker's estate.

**Parrott, Wilda Tarwater** (D. Quinton)
William Cocke Chapter
Ancestor: William Kebble, VA — #602690
This "Trip Around the World" quilt was made before 1900 at
Jefferson County, TN. The owner received it from the estate
of Audrey Poe Parrott.

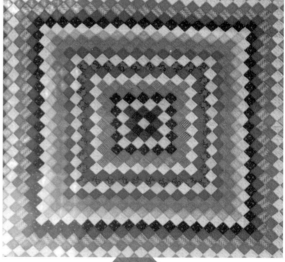

**Parsons, Barbara Buchanan** (Eugene)
The Crab Orchard Chapter
Ancestor: William Smith, GA —#586249
This "Dutch Doll and Tulip" quilt was made in
1939-40 by the owner's husband's grandmother, Savannah Hamby Ford (born 1882
at Crossville, TN, married Thomas Young Ford,
died 1967 at Crossville). The quilt was made for
the owner's husband, Eugene, when he was about
4-5 years old. He watched every stitch his grandmother
made and told her every color to make the dolls. When
she finished, Eugene told her he wanted something in the
empty squares. She asked him what he wanted and he selected
the tulip. She then went back and put a tulip in all the squares between the dolls. "Talk about a spoiled little Grandson!"

**Parsons, Thelma Ford** (Alma T.)
The Crab Orchard Chapter
Ancestor: John Ford, Sr., VA —
#505844
This "Double T" quilt was made in 1939-40 by the owner's mother, Savannah Hamby Ford.

**Patterson, Barbara Mynatt** (John David)
Mary Blount Chapter
Ancestor: Richard Mynatt, VA — #773095
This "Lone Star/Star of Texas" quilt was made in the 1940's in TN by the owner's grandmother, Rissa Mynatt (born 1884 at Grainger County, TN, married Arthur Allen Mynatt, died 1960 at Rockford, TN).

**Patton, Joyce Messer** (Barney Brooks)
Mary Blount Chapter
Ancestor: James Houston, VA —#320733
This "Quilt of Many Colors" was made in the 1930's at Hartwood, VA by the owner's mother-in-law, Sadie Cawley Patton (born 10/14/1886 in WV, married Dr. H.W. Patton, died 8/25/1970 at Fredricksburg, VA).

**Patton, Joyce Messer** (Barney Brooks)
Mary Blount Chapter
Ancestor: James Houston, VA —#320733
This "Cedar of Lebanon/Tree of Life" quilt was made in the 1930's at Maryville, TN by the owner's aunt, Bess Cowan McCall (born 12/19/1876 at Maryville, married H.B. McCall, Sr., died 1/26/1967).

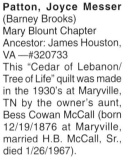

**Perryman, Shari Mims** (David)
William Cocke Chapter
Ancestor: John Huff, VA — #773571
This "Dinner Plate" quilt has been handed down for generations in the owner's family. Charlotte Boyd Hampton passed it to Maggie Hampton Stokley, who passed it to Elizabeth Stokely Jones, who passed it to Charlotte Jones Mims, who passed it to the current owner.

**Perryman, Shari Mims** (David)
William Cocke Chapter
Ancestor: John Huff, VA — #773571
This "Double Wedding Ring" quilt was made in 1980 at Cocke County, TN by the owner's friend, Rosetta McCarter (born 6/21/1939 at Sevier County, TN, married Doug McCarter). The quilt is made from fabric from the clothing of the owner, Charlotte Jones Mims, Shari Mims Perryman, and Annalisa Mims Cope.

**Perryman, Shari Mims** (David)
William Cocke Chapter
Ancestor: John Huff, VA — #773571
This "Democrat" quilt was made in 1985 by the owner's friend, Rosetta McCarter, who gave it to the owner.

**Peters, Millie Sims** (Duane A.)
Mary Blount Chapter
Ancestor: Burrell Bass, NC —#626088
This "Lilly of the Valley" quilt was made circa 1900 at Lee County, AL by the owner's grandmother, Emily Hester Codenhead Jones (born 5/23/1874 at Lee County, AL, married William Seaborn Jones, died 4/7/1966 at Alexander City, AL).

**Petry, Lee Jewett**
James White Chapter
Ancestor: Corporal
Ezra Smith, MA —
#774981
This "Flying Flags"
quilt was made in
1997 at Knoxville, TN
by the owner (born 9/
15/1935 at Denver,
CO).

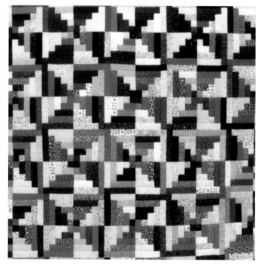

**Petry, Lee Jewett**
James White Chapter
Ancestor: Corporal
Ezra Smith, MA —
#774981
This "Postage Stamp"
quilt was made in
1966 in Chicago, IL by
the owner.

**Petry, Lee Jewett**
James White Chapter
Ancestor: Corporal
Ezra Smith, MA —
#774981
This "Small Pines"
quilted wall hanging
was made in 1996 at
Knoxville, TN by the
owner.

**Petry, Lee Jewett**
James White Chapter
Ancestor: Corporal Ezra
Smith, MA — #774981
This "Half Log Cabin"
quilt was made in 1994
in Knoxville, TN by the
owner.

**Petry, Lee Jewett**
James White Chapter
Ancestor: Corporal
Ezra Smith, MA —
#774981
This "Half Square Tri-
angle" quilt was made
in 1993 in Northbrook,
IL by the owner.

**Petry, Lee Jewett**
James White Chapter
Ancestor: Corporal
Ezra Smith, MA —
#774981
This "Birds in the Air"
quilt was made in
1996 in Knoxville, TN
by the owner.

**Petry, Lee Jewett**
James White Chapter
Ancestor: Corporal Ezra
Smith, MA — #774981
This "Log Cabin" quilt
was made in 1983 in
Northbrook, IL by the
owner.

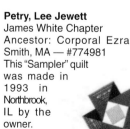

**Petry, Lee Jewett**
James White Chapter
Ancestor: Corporal Ezra
Smith, MA — #774981
This "Sampler" quilt
was made in
1993 in
Northbrook,
IL by the
owner.

**Petry, Lee Jewett**
James White Chapter
Ancestor: Corporal
Ezra Smith, MA —
#774981
This "Bear Paw"
quilted wall hanging
was made in 1988 at
Northbrook, IL by the
owner.

**Petry, Lee Jewett**
James White Chapter
Ancestor: Corporal Ezra
Smith, MA — #774981
This "Bargello" quilt was
made in 1998 at Knoxville,
TN by the owner.

**Petry, Lee Jewett**
James White Chapter
Ancestor: Corporal Ezra Smith,
MA — #774981
This "Bear Paw" quilt was made
in 1994 at Knoxville, TN by the
owner.

**Petry, Lee Jewett**
James White Chapter
Ancestor: Corporal Ezra Smith, MA —
#774981
This "Pinwheel" quilt was made in 1967
in Chicago, IL by the owner.

**Petry, Lee Jewett**
James White Chapter
Ancestor: Corporal Ezra
Smith, MA — #774981
This "Snowball/Star" quilt
was made in 1993 at
Northbrook, IL by
the owner.

**Petry, Lee Jewett**
James White Chapter
Ancestor: Corporal Ezra
Smith, MA — #774981
This "Folk Star" quilt was
made in 1998 in Grand Rap-
ids, ND by Cathy Tuslink. The
owner purchased the quilt at
the "Country Sampler" store in
Knoxville, TN.

**Petry, Lee Jewett**
James White Chapter
Ancestor: Corporal Ezra Smith,
MA — #774981
This combination "Ohio Star/
Irish Chain" quilt was made in
1997 in Knoxville, TN by the
owner.

**Petry, Lee Jewett**
James White Chapter
Ancestor: Corporal
Ezra Smith, MA —
#774981
This "Folk Art" appli-
que wall hanging was
made in 1998 at
Knoxville, TN by the
owner.

**Petry, Lee Jewett**
James White Chapter
Ancestor: Corporal Ezra
Smith, MA — #774981
This "Tessellated Star"
quilt was made in 1997
at Knoxville, TN by the
owner.

**Petry, Lee Jewett**
James White Chapter
Ancestor: Corporal Ezra Smith, MA — #774981
This "Heart in Hand/ Schoolhouse" quilt was made in 1996 at Knoxville, TN by the owner.

**Petry, Lee Jewett**
James White Chapter
Ancestor: Corporal Ezra Smith, MA — #774981
This "Sunflower" quilt was made in 1996 at Knoxville, TN by the owner.

**Petry, Lee Jewett**
James White Chapter
Ancestor: Corporal Ezra Smith, MA — #774981
This "Underground Railroad" quilt was made in 1998 at Knoxville, TN by the owner. It was made in memory of the owner's great great grandfather, Charles Jewett, whose farm in Milbury, MA, was reported to be a stop on the underground railroad before the end of slavery.

**Petty, Tenne Eleazer**
(James R., Jr.)
Hermitage Chapter
Ancestor: Col. George Waller, VA —#566352
This "Parasol Lady" quilt was made before the owner was born by her aunt, Dorothy Estelle Jamison Mitchell (born 11/13/1926 at Tiptonville, TN, married Lawson D., died 4/2/1990 at Memphis, TN).

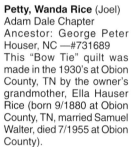

**Petty, Wanda Rice** (Joel)
Adam Dale Chapter
Ancestor: George Peter Houser, NC —#731689
This "Bow Tie" quilt was made in the 1930's at Obion County, TN by the owner's grandmother, Ella Hauser Rice (born 9/1880 at Obion County, TN, married Samuel Walter, died 7/1955 at Obion County).

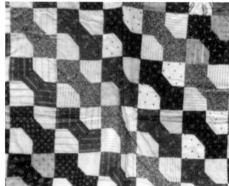

**Petty, Wanda Rice** (Joel)
Adam Dale Chapter
Ancestor: George Peter Houser, NC —#731689
This "Grandmother's Flower Garden" quilt was made in the 1930's at Obion County, TN by the owner's grandmother, Ella Hauser Rice.

**Petty, Wanda Rice** (Joel)
Adam Dale Chapter
Ancestor: George Peter Houser, NC —#731689
These "Six Pointed Star" quilts were made in the 1930's at Obion County, TN by the owner's grandmother, Ella Hauser Rice.

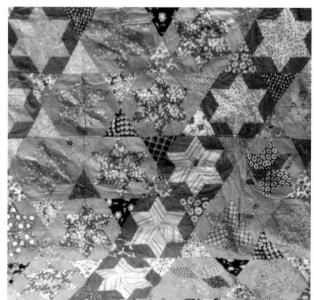

**Petty, Wanda Rice**
(Joel)
Adam Dale Chapter
Ancestor: George
Peter Houser, NC —
#731689
This "Double Wedding Ring" quilt was made in the 1920's-30's at Obion County, TN by the owners grandmother, Ella Hauser Rice, and her aunt, Gladys Rice

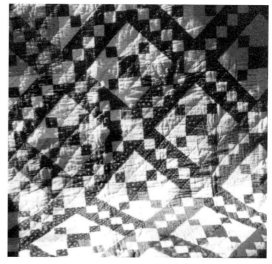

**Petty, Wanda Rice**
(Joel)
Adam Dale Chapter
Ancestor: George
Peter Houser, NC —
#731689
This "Jacob's Ladder" quilt was made in the 1920's -30's at Obion County, TN by the owners grandmother, Ella Hauser Rice.

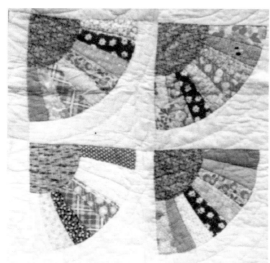

**Petty, Wanda Rice**
(Joel)
Adam Dale Chapter
Ancestor: George
Peter Houser, NC —
#731689
This "Fan" quilt was made in 1906 at Obion County, TN by the owners grandmother, Ella Hauser Rice.

**Petty, Wanda Rice**
(Joel)
Adam Dale Chapter
Ancestor: George Peter Houser, NC —
#731689
This "Nine Patch" quilt was made in 1870-80 at Obion County, TN by one of the owner's great grandmothers, either Matlida McCoy Hauser or Catherine Taylor Rice.

**Petty, Wanda Rice** (Joel)
Adam Dale Chapter
Ancestor: George Peter Houser, NC —#731689
This "Double Wedding Ring" quilt was made in the 1920's-30's at Obion County, TN by the owners grandmother, Ella Hauser Rice and her aunt, Gladys Rice.

**Petty, Wanda Rice**
(Joel)
Adam Dale Chapter
Ancestor: George Peter Houser, NC —
#731689
This "Dresden Plate" quilt was made in 1901-1930 at Obion County, TN by the owners grandmother, Ella Hauser Rice.

**Petty, Wanda Rice** (Joel)
Adam Dale Chapter
Ancestor: George Peter Houser, NC —#731689
This "Parasol Lady" quilt was made in the 1930's at Obion County, TN by the owner's mother, Jessie Fitz Rice (born 10/28/1907 at Waverley, TN, married Walter Glenn Rice).

**Petty, Wanda Rice** (Joel)
Adam Dale Chapter
Ancestor: George Peter Houser, NC —#731689
This "Sister's Choice" quilt was inherited from the owner's grandmother, Ella Hauser Rice, and was made by one of her great grandmothers.

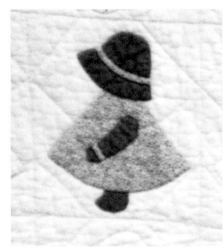

**Petty, Wanda Rice**
(Joel)
Adam Dale Chapter
Ancestor: George Peter Houser, NC —#731689
This "Dutch Doll/ Sunbonnet Sue" quilt was made in the 1930's at Obion County, TN by the owner's mother, Jessie Fitz Rice.

**Petty, Wanda Rice**
(Joel)
Adam Dale Chapter
Ancestor: George Peter Houser, NC —#731689
This "Grandmother's Flower Garden" quilt was made in 1990 at Old Hickory, TN by the owner's mother-in-law, Jean Jones Petty (born 2/6/1915 at Byrdstown, TN, married Glen Edward Petty).

**Phelps, Doris Tarwater**
Spencer Clack Chapter
Ancestor: Jacob Tarwater, PA —#571763
This "Nine Patch Variation" quilt was made circa 1840 at Sevier County, TN by the owner's paternal grandmother, Nannie Tarwater (born 1868 at Sevier County, married Adam H.Tarwater, died 1943 in the same county).

**Phelps, Doris Tarwater**
Spencer Clack Chapter
Ancestor: Jacob Tarwater, PA —#571763
This "Double T" quilt was made circa 1890 at Sevier County, TN by the owner's paternal grandmother, Nannie Tarwater.

**Phillips, Florentine Holmes**
Manchester Chapter
Ancestor: William Murchey, SC —#532183
This "Crazy" quilt was made circa 1882 in South Carolina by the owner's great aunt, Julie C. Shuler (born 8/27/ 1842, died 1/4/1917 at Orangeburg, SC).

**Phillips, Jo Allen Rogers** (Jack)
Manchester Chapter
Ancestor: Alexander McLarty, VA — #783551
This "Dutch Doll/ Sunbonnet Sue" quilt was made in 1949 at Manchester, TN by the owner's mother, Mabel Bruce Rogers (married Homer Rogers). "My mother had a quilt made for each of her four children as they graduated high school."

**Podell, Louise Smith** (Barry)
Capt. William Edmiston Chapter
Ancestor: Capt. John Catlett —#459183
This "Mosaic Star" quilt was made prior to 1900 at Montgomery County, TN by the women of the Barbee family — the mother, Rollow Barbee, and her daughters, Lucy, Mary and Becky. These sisters had no children. Their brother, John Rollow Barbee, and his wife, Allene Belford Smith, inherited the quilt. Allene was the current owner's father's sister. When Allene moved to the farm home in Clarksville in the late 1960's, she gave the quilt to the owner.

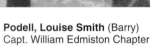

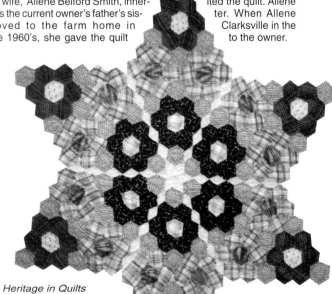

**Podell, Louise Smith** (Barry)
Capt. William Edmiston Chapter
Ancestor: Capt. John Catlett —#459183
This "Blazing Star and Eight Pointed Star" quilt was made circa 1875 at Montgomery County, TN by the women of the Barbee family.

**Pope, Betty Branham**
Col Hardy Murfree Chapter
Ancestor: Jesse Vawter, VA —#445185
This "Elizabeth's October" quilt was made in 1993 at Nolensville, TN by the owner's daughter, Kathy Elizabeth Pope (born 2/14/1958 at Fort Knox, KY). This quilt was never exhibited because it was made especially for the current owner, the maker's mother.

**Pope, Betty Branham**
Col Hardy Murfree Chapter
Ancestor: Jesse Vawter, VA —#445185
This "Grandmother's Flower Garden" quilt was found at the owner's aunt's house after she died. Katherine Coppage was born in 1897.

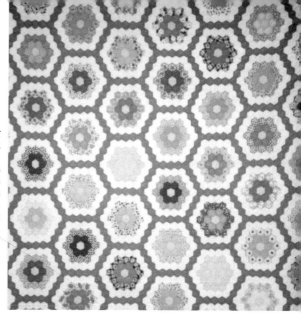

**Pope, Betty Branham**
Col Hardy Murfree Chapter
Ancestor: Jesse Vawter, VA —#445185
This "Make New Friends and Keep the Old" quilt was made in 1992 at Nolensville, TN by the owner's daughter, Kathy Elizabeth Pope. It has won the following awards: Second Place at the Kentucky Quilt show in 1992, "Best of Show" at the McKendree Quilt Show in 1992, exhibited in the "Quilts: An American Craft Legacy" at the Cheekwood Museum of Art in Nashville, TN in 1993, Third Place at the 1993 American Quilt Show, First Place at the 1993 McKendree Quilt Show, 1994 Best of Tennessee Crafts Biennial Exhibit, shown at the Carroll Reese Museum of Art at Johnson City, TN in 1994, and it was included in the Invitational Quilt Show at Nashville in 1995. It was published in Words and Quilts: A Selection of Quilt Poems by Felicia Mitchell in 1995 and Isometric Perspective by Katie Pasquini in 1992.

**Porch, Marie Stone**
(Davis Scott)
Old Reynoldsburgh Chapter
Ancestor: Robert Cowden, SC —#563023
This "Double Wedding Ring" quilt was made circa 1968 at Humphreys County, TN. The owner bought a chance for this quilt at the University Women's Club and won.

**Porch, Marie Stone**
(Davis Scott)
Old Reynoldsburgh Chapter
Ancestor: Robert Cowden, SC —#563023
This "Nine Patch" quilt was made circa 1940 at Humphreys County by the owner's friend, Pearl Cannon (born 9/6/1895, married Tom, died 10/6/1982).

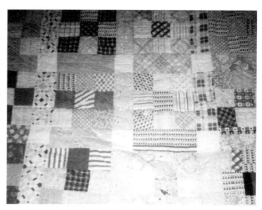

**Porter, Janet Rhodes**
(J. Kenneth)
William Cocke Chapter
Ancestor: Jacob Costner —#605614
This "Brides Knot/Monkey Wrench/Churn Dash" quilt was made circa 1913 at Dallas, NC by the owner's great grandmother, Sarah Alice Hoffman Rhodes (born 6/1/1864 at Dallas, NC, married Christian Oliver Peterson Rhodes, died 9/29/1946 at Dallas). The maker made a quilt for each of her grandchildren. This quilt was made for the owner's father, Earl Edward Rhodes.

**Porter, Janet Rhodes**
(J. Kenneth)
William Cocke Chapter
Ancestor: Jacob Costner —#605614
This "Double Irish Chain" quilt was made at Dallas, NC by the owner's great grandmother, Sarah Alice Hoffman Rhodes. The fabric came from Korea. It was given to the owner's great aunt, Caroline Jane Rhodes Deal, sister to the owner's grandfather, Alfred Rhodes. Aunt Callie was a Lutheran missionary to Korea along with her husband, Dr. Carl Deal. The cloth was woven by the people and called "character cloth."

**Porter, Martha Humber**
(Edwin James)
Mary Blount Chapter
Ancestor: John Bradford
—#351429
This "Star" quilt was made between 1880 and the early 1900's by the owner's maternal grandmother, Ann Persons Stallings (born 9/22/1861 in GA, married Lewis Day Richards, died 1/12/1933 at Hurtsboro, AL) and her great grandmother, Mary Elizabeth Cottingham Stallings (born 12/21/1838, died 1/26/1917)

**P'Pool, Evelyn Harris**
(Edwin)
French Lick Chapter
Ancestor: Henry Bibb, VA — #774560
This applique sampler quilt was made in 1939 at White Bluff, TN by the owner's aunts, Nora Spann (born 9/3/1911 at White Bluff, TN, married Earl Houser), Rosabella Spann Gray (born 6/11/1908 at White Bluff, married William Gray), and Ruth Martin Spann (born 7/2/1910 at White Bluff, married Coleman Spann, died 6/17/1977 at White Bluff). The aunts made the quilt as a Christmas gift for the owner in 1939.

**P'Pool, Evelyn Harris**
(Edwin)
French Lick Chapter
Ancestor: Henry Bibb, VA — #774560
This "Lone Star" quilt was made in 1943 at White Bluff, TN by the owner's grandmother, Pinnie Spann (born 9/15/1882, married James C. Spann, died 6/6/1960 at White Bluff) and great aunt, Minnie Stapleton (born 7/13/1879 at White Bluff, married F.L. Stapleton, died 4/1965 at White Bluff). This quilt was a wedding gift to the owner 9/17/1943.

**P'Pool, Evelyn Harris**
(Edwin)
French Lick Chapter
Ancestor: Henry Bibb, VA — #774560
This "Butterfly" quilt was made in 1945 at Dickson County, TN by the owner's great aunt, Minnie Stapleton.

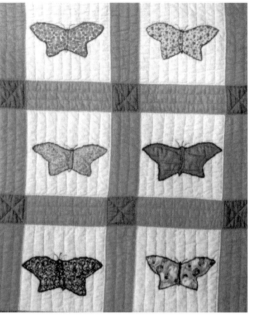

**P'Pool, Evelyn Harris**
(Edwin)
French Lick Chapter
Ancestor: Henry Bibb, VA — #774560
This "Dresden Plate" quilt was made 1940-45 at Dickson County, TN by the owner's great aunt, Minnie Stapleton and grandmother, Pinnie Spann.

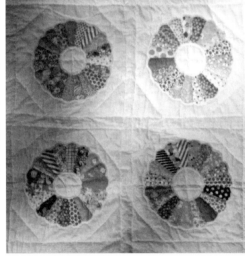

**P'Pool, Evelyn Harris** (Edwin)
French Lick Chapter
Ancestor: Henry Bibb, VA — #774560
This "Dutch Doll/Sunbonnet Sue" quilt was made in 1930 at Maury County, TN by the owner's mother, Maymie Harris (born 7/14/1905 at Dickson County, TN, married Burton Harris, died 6/26/1990 at Nashville, TN).

**P'Pool, Evelyn Harris** (Edwin)
French Lick Chapter
Ancestor: Henry Bibb, VA — #774560
This "Feathered Star" quilt was made in the early 1920's in Nashville, TN by the owner's husband's grandmother, Mildred P'Pool (Pettypool). Mildred was born 2/6/1858 at Trigg County, KY, married Edward Calvin Pettypool, and died 2/1/1940 at Davidson County, TN). It was a gift to the owner's husband.

**Posner, Barbara Duggan**
(James A.)
Chucalissa Chapter
Ancestor: Thomas Benjamin Blanton, VA — #700706
This "Crazy" quilt was made by the owner's grandmother, Barbara Ellen Duggan (born 2/9/1869 at Elkton, KY, married Benjamin Oscar Duggan).

**Potts, Elizabeth (Betty) Hall** (Glenn)
William Cocke Chapter
Ancestor: John Helm, NC — #612547
This "Martha Washington's Flower Garden" quilt was pieced circa 1930's at Jefferson County, TN by the owner's mother, Edna Griffin Hall (born 3/23/1901 at Cocke County, TN, married Stone Hall, died 3/28/1939 at Jefferson County). It was quilted circa 1966 by someone else.

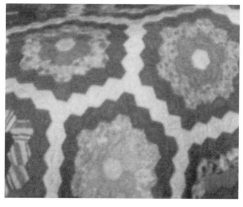

**Pouder, Dorothy Dorris** (R. Keith)
French Lick Chapter
Ancestor: Ludwell Grymes, VA —790135
This "Trumphet" quilt was made before 1844 and was in a trunk for about 60 years.

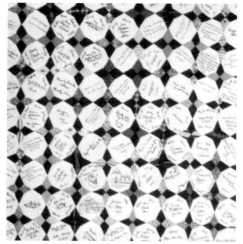

**Poyner, Roberta Plant** (Knox)
Old Reynoldsburgh Chapter
Ancestor: James Cooley, NC —#645541
This "Snow Ball/Friendship" quilt was made in 1959 by members of the Pisgah Methodist Church for a fundraiser. The owner and her husband bought this quilt at high bid for $100.

**Poyner, Roberta Plant** (Knox)
Old Reynoldsburgh Chapter
Ancestor: James Cooley, NC —#645541
This "Nine Patch Friendship" quilt was made by members of the Pisgah Methodist Church for a fundraiser. There are 140 names on this quilt of persons who made donations to the church.

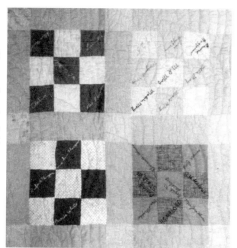

**Poyner, Roberta Plant** (Knox)
Old Reynoldsburgh Chapter
Ancestor: James Cooley, NC —#645541
This "Postage Stamp" quilt was made at Nashville, TN by the owner's great grandmother, Margaret Josephine Warren Goodwin (born 10/7/1856 at Humphreys County, TN, married Christopher Columbus Goodwin, died 5/30/1939 at Nashville, TN). Margaret was born at the old home place which is now owned by Roberta and Knox. "The only way I remember my great grandmother is sitting by her window, piecing quilts."

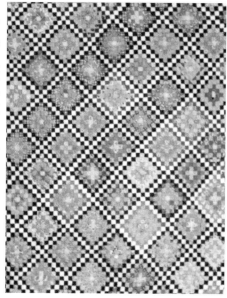

**Poyner, Roberta Plant** (Knox)
Old Reynoldsburgh Chapter
Ancestor: James Cooley, NC — #645541
This "Iris " quilt was finished in 1974 at the Plant community by the owner (born 10/30/1925). "I bought this stamped top and my mother-in-law said, 'You won't finish this.' You know that bothered me and after she died, I was even more determined to finish this. She died in 1974 and by the end of that year, I had the quilt finished. I was so proud to have a quilt with our state flower. I loved my mother-in-law. She was a good Christian lady. We lived together in the old Poyner family home for 23 years."

**Poyner, Roberta Plant** (Knox)
Old Reynoldsburgh Chapter
Ancestor: James Cooley, NC —#645541
This "Double Wedding Ring" quilt was pieced in 1953 by the owner's mother-in-law, Pearl Totty Poyner (married Alden Dorsey Poyner). It was quilted by the ladies of Pisgah Methodist Church. "When it was time to quilt the quilt, ladies from the church were invited to come and spend the day and quilt. They each brought a dish and had lunch together."

**Price, Christine Marsh** (R. W.)
King's Mountain Messenger
Ancestor: Joseph McAdams, NC —#689281
This "Star of Bethlehem" quilt was made at Mulberry, TN by the owner's husband's great aunt, Willie A. Renegar (born 1857 at Mulberry, TN, married Rufus, died 1936 at Mulberry, TN).

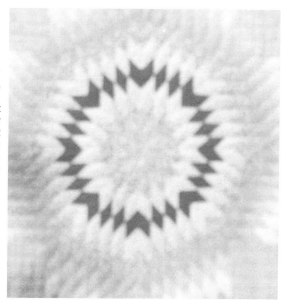

**Price, Christine Marsh**
(R. W.)
King's Mountain Messenger
Ancestor: Joseph McAdams,
NC —#689281
This "Star Within a Star" quilt
was made in 1930 at Mul-
berry, TN by the owner's
husband's great aunt, Willie
A. Renegar. She made the
quilt for the owner's husband
when he was a baby.

**Prince, Catherine Nelson**
(Glen)
Robert Cooke Chapter
Ancestor: Maj. John Nelson,
NC —#718427
This "Trip Around the World"
quilt was made in the 1930's
in TN by the owner's
husband's great grand-
mother, Ida Davis Gregory
(born 1867 at Lincoln County,
TN, married Moses Fenton
Gregory, died 1944 at
Franklin County, TN).

**Prince, Catherine Nelson**
(Glen)
Robert Cooke Chapter
Ancestor: Maj. John
Nelson, NC —#718427
This "Nine Patch Variation"
quilt was made in 1988 at
Nashville, TN by the owner
(born 1934 at Nashville).

**Prince, Catherine Nelson**
(Glen)
Robert Cooke Chapter
Ancestor: Maj. John Nelson, NC
—#718427
This "Log House Variation" quilt
was made in 1984 at Nashville,
TN by the owner.

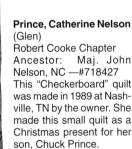

**Prince, Catherine Nelson**
(Glen)
Robert Cooke Chapter
Ancestor: Maj. John
Nelson, NC —#718427
This "Checkerboard" quilt
was made in 1989 at Nash-
ville, TN by the owner. She
made this small quilt as a
Christmas present for her
son, Chuck Prince.

**Prince, Catherine Nelson**
(Glen)
Robert Cooke Chapter
Ancestor: Maj. John Nelson,
NC —#718427
This "Double Irish Chain" quilt
was made in 1990 at Nash-
ville, TN by the owner.

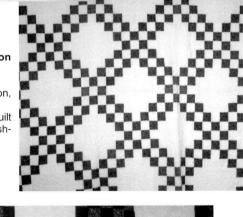

**Prince, Catherine Nelson** (Glen)
Robert Cooke Chapter
Ancestor: Maj. John Nelson, NC —#718427
This "Irish Chain Variation" quilt was made in
1987 at Nashville, TN by the owner.

**Puckett, Betty High**
(James A.)
Lt. James Sheppard
Chapter
Ancestor: Ebenezer
Webb, Jr., CT –
#614256
This "Tulip" quilt was
made in TN by the
owner's great grand-
mother, Liza High.

**Puckett, Jane Greer** (James B.)
Tullahoma Chapter
Ancestor: David Halliburton,
Jr., NC —#512367
This trapunto quilt was
made circa 1825 at
Clarksville, TN by the
owner's great grand-
mother, Jane Vernon Hamp-
ton Fort Turner (born 9/11/1811
at Clarksville, married John
Thomas Turner, died 8/6/
1856 at Winona, MS).
This quilt was given to
the owner by her aunt
who wanted her to
have it because she has
the same name — Jane.

**Puckett, Jane Greer**
(James B.)
Tullahoma Chapter
Ancestor: David
Halliburton, Jr., NC —
#512367
This "Star and Log Cabin"
quilt were made circa
1865 by the owner's great
aunt, Virginia Phillippi
Turner (born 3/16/1836 at
Clarksville, died 11/29/
1912 in Mississippi). The
quilt was given to the
owner in 1965 by her ma-
ternal aunt, Virginia
Hampton Newell Elgin.

**Puckett, Jane Greer**
(James B.)
Tullahoma Chapter
Ancestor: David
Halliburton, Jr., NC —
#512367
This "Eight Pointed Star"
quilt was made circa 1850
at Paris, TN by the owner's
great great grandmother,
Elizabeth A. Wells
Fitzgerald (born 2/17/1806
at Dover, TN, married William Fitzgerald, died 11/1/
1886). William defeated
Davy Crockett for congress
in 1830 and served in the
22nd congress.

**Purvis, Marjorie
Devine** (Harry)
Old Glory Chapter
Ancestor: William
Hardin, VA —
#577124
This "Dresden
Plate" quilt was
made in Kentucky
about 1969 by the
owner's mother-in-
law, Catherine
Coleman.

**Quarles, Ann Draper**
(James R.)
Charlotte Reeves
Robertson Chapter
Ancestor: Fitzgerald
Garrett, NC —#399431
This "Delectable Moun-
tain Variation" quilt was
made in 1930 at Jack-
son County, TN by the
owner's maternal grand-
mother, Mattie Alice
Chillcutt Darwin (born 8/
17/1865 at
Elizabethtown, KY, mar-
ried George Cowan Dar-
win III, died 3/7/1933 at
Jackson County, TN).
This quilt was made for
the owner's aunt who
gave it to the owner.

**Quarles, Ann Draper**
(James R.)
Charlotte Reeves
Robertson Chapter
Ancestor: Fitzgerald
Garrett, NC —
#399431
This "Delectable
Mountain Variation"
quilt was made in
1930 at Jackson
County, TN by the
owner's maternal
grandmother, Mattie
Alice Chillcutt Darwin.
The maker made this
quilt for the owner.

**Quarles, Ann Draper**
(James R.)
Charlotte Reeves
Robertson Chapter
Ancestor: Fitzgerald
Garrett, NC —#399431
This "Basket of Flowers"
quilt was made in 1925
at Jackson County, TN
by the owner's maternal
grandmother, Mattie
Alice Chillcutt Darwin.
The maker made this
quilt for the owner.

**Quarles, Ann Draper** (James R.)
Charlotte Reeves Robertson Chapter
Ancestor: Fitzgerald Garrett, NC —
#399431
This "Double Wedding Ring" quilt was
made 1932-33 at Jackson County, TN
by the owner's maternal grandmother,
Mattie Alice Chillcutt Darwin. It was
made for the owner.

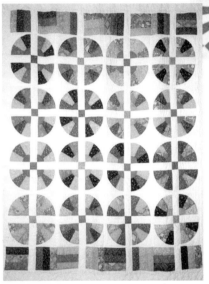

**Quarles, Ann Draper**
(James R.)
Charlotte Reeves
Robertson Chapter
Ancestor: Fitzgerald
Garrett, NC —#399431
This "Lone Star/Star of
Bethlehem" quilt was
passed to the owner from
her mother-in-law, Lucile
Saldler Quarles.

**Ragon, Natalie Cockroft** (James
Hugh)
Hatchie Chapter
Ancestor: Alexander McCorkle,
NC —#749730
This "Color Wheels" quilt was
made in 1994 at Memphis, TN by
the owner's daughter-in-law, Mimi
Jones Ragon (born 5/8/1957 at
Memphis, TN, married James Roy
Ragon).

**Ragsdale, Betty Buchanan**
(James S.)
Travelers Rest Chapter
Ancestor: John Raines, NC —
#631647
This "Irish Chain" quilt was made
circa 1935-40 at Davidson County,
TN by the owner's mother, Anne
Warren Buchanan (born 5/15/1899
at Williamson County, TN, married
John Burr Buchanan, died 2/4/
1977 at Nashville, TN). The quilt
was passed from maker to owner.
The owner says that "it is fun to look
at old family quilts and pick out who
had a dress made of that material,
my first grade supply bag, neighbors in the afternoon quilting in
mother's dining room."

**Ragsdale, Betty
Buchanan** (James S.)
Travelers Rest Chapter
Ancestor: John Raines,
NC — #631647
This "Butterfly" quilt was
made circa 1920 at
Williamson County, TN
by the owner's grand-
mother, Frances Anne
Hyde Warren (born 2/1/
1863, married Hardy
Thomas Warren, died 8/
15/1942 at Nashville,
TN).

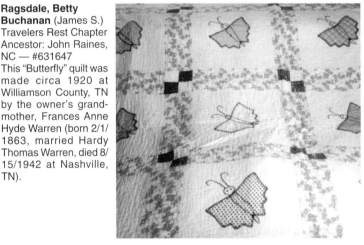

**Ragsdale, Betty
Buchanan** (James S.)
Travelers Rest Chapter
Ancestor: John Raines,
NC — #631647
This "Double Wedding
Ring" quilt was made
circa 1940 at Nashville,
TN by the owner's
mother, Anne Warren
Buchanan. The quilt
was passed from
mother to daughter.

**Ragsdale, Betty
Buchanan** (James S.)
Travelers Rest Chapter
Ancestor: John Raines,
NC — #631647
This "Butterfly" quilt
was made circa 1940 at
Davidson County, TN
by the owner's
mother, Anne Warren
Buchanan. The quilt
was passed from
mother to daughter.

**Ragsdale, Betty
Buchanan** (James S.)
Travelers Rest Chapter
Ancestor: John Raines, NC
— #631647
This "Rob Peter To Pay
Paul" strip quilt was made
in 1975 at Williamson
County, TN by the owner's
mother, Anne Warren
Buchanan. The quilt was
passed from mother to
daughter.

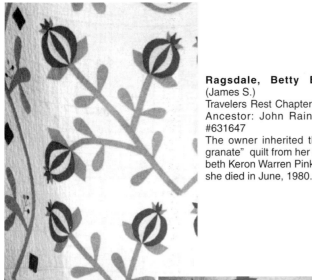

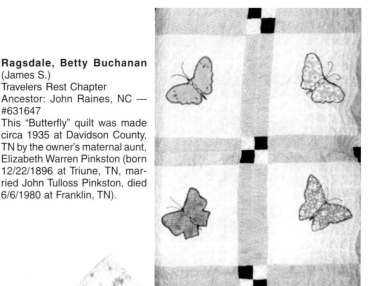

**Ragsdale, Betty Buchanan**
(James S.)
Travelers Rest Chapter
Ancestor: John Raines, NC —
#631647
The owner inherited this "Pome-granate" quilt from her aunt, Eliza-beth Keron Warren Pinkston, when she died in June, 1980.

**Ragsdale, Betty Buchanan**
(James S.)
Travelers Rest Chapter
Ancestor: John Raines, NC —
#631647
This "Butterfly" quilt was made circa 1935 at Davidson County, TN by the owner's maternal aunt, Elizabeth Warren Pinkston (born 12/22/1896 at Triune, TN, mar-ried John Tulloss Pinkston, died 6/6/1980 at Franklin, TN).

**Ragsdale, Betty Buchanan**
(James S.)
Travelers Rest Chapter
Ancestor: John Raines, NC —
#631647
This "Double Tulip" quilt was made in 1852 at Williamson County, TN by the owner's great grandmother, Hypasia Anne Nolen (born 8/27/1827 at Williamson County, TN, married Harvey Henderson Hyde 3/3/ 1853, died 4/18/1898 in the same county). The quilt was passed from the maker, to her daughter, then to Frances Hyde Warren, to Anne Warren Buchanan, and fi-nally to the owner. All the flowers on this quilt are red except for one which is yellow. Making a delib-erate mistake was said to be popular in the era.

**Ragsdale, Betty Buchanan** (James S.)
Travelers Rest Chapter
Ancestor: John Raines, NC —
#631647
This "Fan" quilt was made 1949-50 at Williamson County, TN by the owner's husband's grandmother, Lallna Fly Ragsdale (born 10/23/1874 at Williamson County, TN, married James Matthew Ragsdale, died 8/19/1955 in the same county).

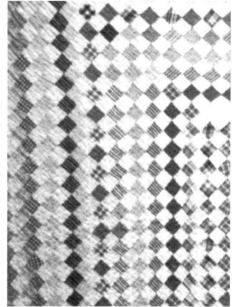

**Ramsey, Sandra Burkett**
(Samuel L.)
Charlotte Reeves Robertson Chapter
Ancestor: William Lenoir, NC — #645351
This "Tea Leaves" quilt was made in the mid 1920's at Lenoir City, TN by the owner's maternal grand-mother, Neta Glass Lowrie (born 8/15/1892 at Lenoir City, married Lerrander Arrance Lowrie, died 10/6/ 1970 in the same town). In this quilt are fabric scraps of dresses made for the owner's mother and grand-mother. The quilt was passed from grandmother, to mother, to owner.

**Ramsey, Sandra Burkett**
(Samuel L.)
Charlotte Reeves Robertson Chapter
Ancestor: William Lenoir, NC — #645351
This "Trip Around The World" quilt was made in the late 1920's or early 1930's at Lenoir City, TN by the owner's maternal grandmother, Neta Glass Lowrie.

**Randall, Judy Carr** (Charles)
Manchester Chapter
Ancestor: John Gore, VA —#782293
This "Lone Star" quilt was pieced in the 1920's at Overton County, TN by the owner's paternal grandmother, Mary Emma Loucreta Ann Gentry Carr (born 2/ 18/1881 at Overton County, TN, married Millard Cleveland Carr, died 7/4/1962 in the same county). It was given to the owner soon after she married in 1939. The owner carded the cotton for the batts and she and her sister quilted the quilt.

**Ramsey, Sandra Burkett** (Samuel L.)
Charlotte Reeves Robertson Chapter
Ancestor: William Lenoir, NC — #645351
This "Grandmother's Flower Garden" quilt was made prior to 1940 at Lenoir City, TN by the owner's paternal grand-mother, Elizabeth McGaughby Burdett (born 5/29/1878 at Cebitta, GA, married James Avery Buckett, died 7/15/1965 at Lenoir City, TN). The quilt was passed from the owner's grandparents, to her parents, to her. "Whoever looks at this quilt always comments on the tiny, me-ticulous, expert stitches."

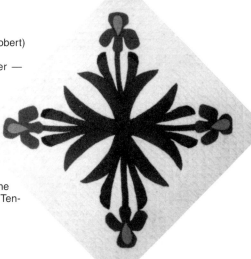

**Raper, Jean Simpson** (William Elmer)
Mary Blount Chapter
Ancestor: Amos Marney, VA — #591462
This "Rose of Sharon Variation" quilt was made in Loudon County, TN by the owner's great great grandmother, Elderidge. The owner's grandmother, Emma Wilson Simpson, gave it to the owner when she was sixteen years old in 1936.

**Ratcliffe, Alice Harton** (Robert)
Tullahoma Chapter
Ancestor: Jonathan Foster — #341426
This "Iris" quilt was made in the 1920's or 30's at Tullahoma by the owner's husband's grandmother, Della Wilson Clayton (born 7/21/1872 at Tullahoma, married James Clayton, died 10/31/1958 in the same town). This pattern is the Tennessee state flower.

**Ray, Elizabeth Parrish** (Jonothan)
Old Glory Chapter
Ancestor: Col. William Shute, NJ — #686546
This "Lone Star" quilt was made in 1991 at Fayette, AL by the owner's grandmother, Willeary Shute Stewart (born 7/16/1908 at Brownsville, AL, married Bruce B. Stewart).

**Ray, Elizabeth Parrish** (Jonothan)
Old Glory Chapter
Ancestor: Col. William Shute, NJ — #686546
This "Sampler" quilt was made in 1980 at Fayette, AL by the owner's grandmother, Willeary Shute Stewart. The owner says her family calls this a "crazy" quilt because it has so many different patterns.

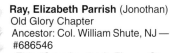

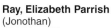

**Ray, Elizabeth Parrish** (Jonothan)
Old Glory Chapter
Ancestor: Col. William Shute, NJ — #686546
This "Grandmother's Flower Garden" quilt was made in 1995 at Fayette, AL by the owner's grandmother, Willeary Shute Stewart.

**Ray, Elizabeth Parrish** (Jonothan)
Old Glory Chapter
Ancestor: Col. William Shute, NJ — #686546
This "Lone Star" quilt was made in 1985 at Fayette, AL by the owner's grandmother, Willeary Shute Stewart.

**Reagan, Laura Sears** (Lawrence)
Glover's Trace Chapter
Ancestor: Asden Sears, MA — #598447
This "Sampler" wall hanging was made in 1993 at Rockford, IL by the owner (born 8/25/36 at Belviderre, IL). It was machine pieced by the owner in a quilting class. She quilted it by hand after she retired and moved to Tennessee.

**Reagan, Laura Sears** (Lawrence)
Glover's Trace Chapter
Ancestor: Asden Sears, MA — #598447
This "Thanksgiving" wall hanging was made in 1998 at Big Sandy, TN by the owner. This is part of a series of wall hangings she made for her home in Tennessee.

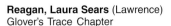

**Reagan, Laura Sears** (Lawrence)
Glover's Trace Chapter
Ancestor: Asden Sears, MA — #598447
This "Family Reunion" heirloom quilt was made for the Reagan Family Reunion held September 3, 1995 at the Orebank Community Center at Mosheim, TN. The quilt was made by the owner. By the day of the reunion, she had pieced the squares. Every family member signed on the white part of a square. Later she then hand tied the quilt.

**Reagan, Laura Sears** (Lawrence)
Glover's Trace Chapter
Ancestor: Asden Sears, MA — #598447
This "Sampler" quilt was pieced by machine in the 1980's at Belvidere, IL by the owner. She made this quilt in the first quilt class she took. It was machine quiltcd by a lady in Missouri.

**Reagan, Laura Sears** (Lawrence)
Glover's Trace Chapter
Ancestor: Asden Sears, MA — #598447
This "Trip Around the World" wall hanging was made in 1998 at Benton County, TN by the owner.

**Reagan, Laura Sears** (Lawrence)
Glover's Trace Chapter
Ancestor: Asden Sears, MA — #598447
This "Christmas Cube" wall hanging was made in 1997 at Big Sandy, TN by the owner.

**Reagan, Laura Sears** (Lawrence)
Glover's Trace Chapter
Ancestor: Asden Sears, MA — #598447
This "Lone Star of Texas" quilt was made in the 1970's by the owner's husband's aunt, Lady Ruth Reagan Inscore (born 11/22/1912 at Midway, TN, married Albert Inscore, died 2/24/1993 at Greenville, TN). The quilt was given to the owner by the maker shortly after the owner's marriage in 1954.

**Reagan, Laura Sears** (Lawrence)
Glover's Trace Chapter
Ancestor: Asden Sears, MA — #598447
This "State Birds and Flowers" quilt was made circa 1920 in North Carolina by the owner's husband's great aunt's sister, Miss Ada Lucas. The top won first place at the fair in Waynesville, NC. The top was embroidered in the early 1900's. Miss Ada gave the quilt top to Lady Ruth Reagan Inscore, the owner's husband's aunt. She finished putting the quilt together and hand quilted it. The owner believes that Miss Ada moved from Unicorn, TN to North Carolina to be closer to her sister, Cora Lucas Beach. Harvey Beach, Cora's husband, was the brother to the owner's husband's grandmother. It was passed from the grandmother to the owner.

**Reagan, Laura Sears** (Lawrence)
Glover's Trace Chapter
Ancestor: Asden Sears, MA — #598447
This "Grandmother's Flower Garden" quilt was made in the 1970's at Greene County, TN by the owner's husband's aunt, Lady Ruth Reagan Inscore. The quilt was given to the owner by the maker and is made of polyester scrap fabric given to the maker by the owner.

**Reagan, Laura Sears** (Lawrence)
Glover's Trace Chapter
Ancestor: Asden Sears, MA — #598447
This "Flower Basket" quilt was made in the 1970's at Greene County, TN by the owner's husband's aunt, Lady Ruth Reagan Inscore. The quilt is made of the polyester scrap fabric given to the maker by the owner. It is hand tied.

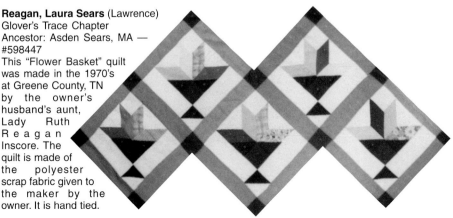

**Reisentz, Ellie Bowden** (Joseph)
John Babb Chapter
Ancestor: Elias Bowdoin, VA — #651348
This "Nine Patch" quilt was made between 1825-1850, possibly in Indiana. The quilt was purchased by the owner at an antique shop in Hazel, KY. The edging of this quilt is woven on a hand loom.

**Reynolds, Charlotte Stout** (Joe)
The Crab Orchard Chapter
Ancestor: Thomas Carleton, NC — #622175
This "Steeple Chase" quilt was made in the 1930's at Greenfield, TN by the owner's grandmother, Edna Baker Lipscomb (born 8/1881 at Giles County, TN, married William Franklin

Lipscomb, died 12/1963 at Martin, TN). This quilt was used on the owner's bed when she was a child.

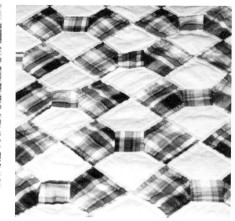

**Reynolds, Charlotte Stout** (Joe)
The Crab Orchard Chapter
Ancestor: Thomas Carleton, NC —#622175
This "Bow Tie" quilt was made in 1980 at Parsons, TN by the owner's mother-in-law, Hattie Sue Wheat Reynolds (born 1913 at Decatur County, TN, married William H. Reynolds). This quilt was given to the owner's husband on his 40th birthday.

**Reynolds, Charlotte Stout** (Joe)
The Crab Orchard Chapter
Ancestor: Thomas Carleton, NC — #622175
This "Maple Leaf" quilt was made in 1978 at Parsons, TN by the owner's mother-in-law, Hattie Sue Wheat Reynolds. Fabric is from remnants of the owner's daughters' clothes when they were small children.

**Rhodes, Evelyn Lillard** (Earl E.)
William Cocke Chapter
Ancestor: Bartlett Sisk, NC — #607154
This "Nine Patch Variation" quilt was made circa 1870's at Cocke County, TN by the owner's great aunt, Harriet Sisk (born 10/1842 at Newport, TN, died 11/20/1918 at Newport). The owner inherited the quilt through her mother, Elizabeth McNabb Lillard (married to Erastas Howell Lillard). The maker of this quilt was the daughter of Polly Gray and Bartlett Sisk, Jr. Her sister was Sarah Syche Sisk who was married to D. John McNabb. Sarah and John were the owner's grandparents.

**Rhoton, Patricia King** (Dr. Alex)
Chief John Ross Chapter
Ancestor: Isaac Hull, Sr., NJ — #495511
This "Pinwheel" quilt was made in the early 1890's in Ohio by the owner's maternal great grandmother, Althea Della Chase Hale (born 5/15/1863 at Hancock County, OH, married Lorenzo Douglas Hale, died 4/21/1922 in the same county).

**Rhoton, Patricia King** (Dr. Alex)
Chief John Ross Chapter
Ancestor: Isaac Hull, Sr., NJ — #495511
Ohio by the owner's paternal greatgrandmother, Ruth Ann Archer Thomas (born 1/31/1842 at Mt. Blanchard, OH, married Henry Benton Thomas, died 2/27/1892 at Mt. Blanchard). The quilt was passed from the maker, to the owner's grandmother, to her mother, and finally to the current owner.

**Richards, Betty Taylor** (Stanley)
Fort Nashborough Chapter
Ancestor: John Cunningham, VA — #774760
This "Fan" quilt was made in 1940 at Warren County, TN by the owner's mother, Augusta Taylor (born 4/8/1903 at Walling, TN, married Herman B. Taylor, died 11/6/1981 at McMinnville, TN). The owner received the quilt at the death of the maker.

**Richards, Betty Taylor** (Stanley)
Fort Nashborough Chapter
Ancestor: John Cunningham, VA — #774760
This "Double Wedding Ring" quilt was made in Warren County, TN in the 1940's by the owner's grandmother, Sara Katherine Goolsby Taylor (born 8/22/1873 at Coffee County, TN, married Andrew Jackson Taylor, died 9/3/1955 in MI while visiting there).

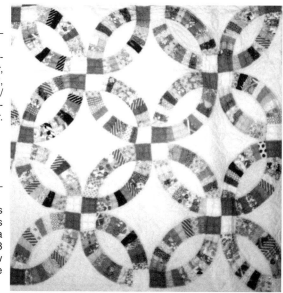

**Richardson, Alice Mayo** (Eldred)
Chickasaw Bluff Chapter
Ancestor: Jonathan Montgomery, NC —#780513
This "Dresden Plate" quilt was made in the 1930's at Carroll County, TN by the owner's grandmother, Rena Lee Dill Black (born 9/25/1888 at Carroll County, married William Filmore Black, died 4/9/1979 in the same county).

**Richardson, Thelma Hampton** (E.M.)
Old Glory Chapter
Ancestor: William Crutcher, VA — #662646
This "Dresden Plate" quilt was made in the 1930's at Nashville, TN by the owner's mother, Josephine Crutcher Hampton (born 10/23/1877 at Williamson County, TN, married F. Marion Hampton, died 10/22/1949). Marion was born 8/2/1879 at Maury County, TN.

**Richardson, Thelma Hampton** (E.M.)
Old Glory Chapter
Ancestor: William Crutcher, VA — #662646
This "Rose Tree" quilt was made over 150 years ago in Maury County, TN by a member of the Hampton family.

**Richardson, Thelma Hampton** (E.M.)
Old Glory Chapter
Ancestor: William Crutcher, VA — #662646
This "Dutch Girl" quilt was made circa 1939 at Nashville, TN by the owner's mother, Josephine Crutcher Hampton.

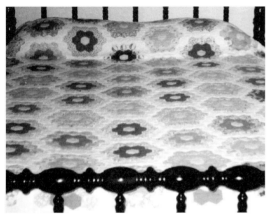

**Richardson, Thelma Hampton** (E.M.)
Old Glory Chapter
Ancestor: William Crutcher, VA — #662646
This "Grandmother's Flower Garden" quilt was made circa 1930's at Nashville, TN by the owner's mother, Josephine Crutcher Hampton.

**Richmond, Rebekah Noah** (Joseph)
Ocoee Chapter
Ancestor: John Hubbard, VA —#759154
This "Dutch Girl/Sunbonnet Sue" quilt was made in the 1950's by the owner's great grandmother, Hallie Dessie Thompson Robinson (born 3/27/1989 at Jonesville, VA, married Emmett Robinson, died 4/7/1970). The quilt was passed from maker, to the owner's father's sister, to the owner.

**Ricker, Isabelle K.** (Richard)
Campbell Chapter
Ancestor: Capt. James Ezra Ames, MA — #726645
This "Sampler" quilt was made in 1924 at Bath, NC by the owner's grandmother, Elizabeth Poor King (born at Boothbay Harbor, NC, married John King, died in 1940 at Bath, NC).

**Ricker, Isabelle K.** (Richard)
Campbell Chapter
Ancestor: Capt. James Ezra Ames, MA — #726645
This "Windmill" quilt was made in 1924 at Bath, NC by the owner's grandmother, Elizabeth Poor King.

**Riley, Betty Robertson** (Donald)
Andrew Bogle Chapter
Ancestor: William Gooch, NC — #596212
This "Crazy" quilt was made 1884-85 at Cannon County, TN by the owner's great great grandmother, Amanda Ann Kimbro Rushing (born 6/12/1821 at Rutherford County, TN, married Abel Rushing, died 8/29/1898 at Wilson County, TN). Amanda passed the quilt to her son, W. A. Rushing. He passed it to his daughter, Josephine Eaton Rushing, Robertson. Josephine passed it to her daughter, Kathleen Ogilvie Robertson. She passed it to her niece, the current owner.

**Rimer, Teresa Webb** (Thomas)
Chief John Ross Chapter
Ancestor: Jesse Webb, NC — #751419
This "Sampler" quilt was made in 1980 at Rector, AR by the owner's paternal grandmother, Grace Webb (born 11/3/1906 at Conway, AR, married Don Webb, died 3/9/1987 at Rector, AR).

**Rimer, Teresa Webb** (Thomas)
Chief John Ross Chapter
Ancestor: Jesse Webb, NC —
#751419
This "Friendship" quilt was made in 1950 at Rector, AR by the owner's great grandmother, Mary Elizabeth Bryant (born 3/5/1884 at Conway, AR, married Archie Parham, died 5/3/1977 at Rector, AR). Each circle contains the name of the maker's parents, brothers, sisters, and children. The owner inherited the quilt through her father.

**Roberts, Aline W. Gray** (James G.)
James Buckley Chapter
Ancestor: Moses White, VA —#604656
This "Nursery Rhyme" baby quilt was made in 1961 at Sharon, TN by the owner's mother-in-law, Martha Jim Roberts (born 9/16/1918 at Sharon, TN, married Malcolm Roberts). This quilt was made for the owner's first son born 7/25/1961.

**Roberts, Bettie Finney**
General James Winchester Chapter
Ancestor: Archibald Woods, VA — #555286
This "Crazy" quilt was made in 1863 at Bedford county, TN by the owner's great grandmother, Nancy Ward Crick (born 9/14/1849 at Bedford, County, married Alfred Pope Crick, died 6/15/1929 at Tullahoma, TN). The maker was a seamstress for a very wealthy lady in Shelbyville, TN who allowed Nancy to keep the scraps from the dresses she made. Nancy gave the quilt to the owner's father in 1915. She told him

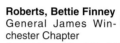

**Roberts, Bettie Finney**
General James Winchester Chapter
Ancestor: Archibald Woods, VA — #555286
This "Dresden Plate" quilt was made in 1964 at Estill Springs, TN by the owner's mother, Oleda Weaver Finney (born 8/26/1902 at Franklin, TN, married Doyle Finney, died 10/7/1980 at Estill Springs). The maker used fabric saved

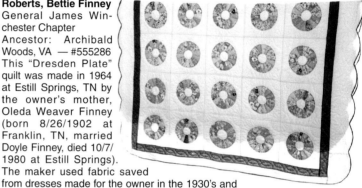

from dresses made for the owner in the 1930's and 40's. She can remember each one when she looks at the quilt. She says, "This quilt is truly a special tribute to my mother and a wonderful memory quilt for me."

to save the quilt to give to his daughter. The owner is the oldest daughter and the oldest granddaughter in the Finney family. The quilt was passed from the maker, to Doyle Finney, to the current owner. The owner plans to pass the quilt to her daughter, Judy Roberts Brower, who is a home economics teacher in Illinois. This quilt won a blue ribbon in the "oldest quilt" category at the Will County Fair in Protone, IL.

**Roberts, Mary Ann Tyree**
(Charles Edward)
Robert Lewis Chapter
Ancestor: Arthur Sheffield, NC —#545555
This "Drunkard's Path" quilt was made in 1980 at Lewisburg, TN by the owner's mother-in-law, Ethel Roberts (born 9/26/1903 at Lewisburg, married Clyde Roberts, died 11/22/1986 at Lewisburg). The quilt was made as a gift for the owner.

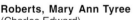

**Roberts, Mary Ann Tyree** (Charles Edward)
Robert Lewis Chapter
Ancestor: Arthur Sheffield, NC —#545555
This "Iris" quilt was made circa 1983 at Lewisburg by the owner's mother, Salle Dennis Tyree (born 11/16/1907 at Lewisburg, married Thomas Frank, died 9/13/1995 at Lewisburg). The quilt was a gift for the owner.

**Robinson, Barbara Manchester**
(William C.)
Tullahoma Chapter
Ancestor: Matthew Degarmd, NC —#362031
This "Pinwheel" quilt was pieced circa 1880 at Holly, NY by the owner's great grandmother, Marial Smith Hill (born 1822, married Loren Hill, died 1908 at Holly, NY). The quilt was passed from maker, to the owner's father, to the owner.

**Robertson, Gloria Tolmie** (Jack)
Andrew Bogle Chapter
Ancestor: Col John Sevier, NC —#755077
This wool and linen coverlet was made circa 1880 at Claiborne County, TN by the owner's great great grandmother, Mary Ann Carr Sharp (born 11/28/1856 at Claiborne County, married John G. Sharp, died 5/14/1943 in the same county).

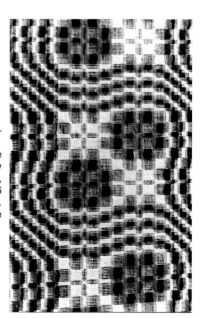

**Robinson, Debra Ann**
Adam Dale Chapter
Ancestor: Thomas Mercer, GA —#660106
This "Patch" quilt was made in 1982 at Memphis, TN by Elizabeth Bowie, an employee of the owner. Elizabeth was born 6/17/1919 and died in Memphis, TN. The quilt was made as a gift for the owner.

**Robinson, Debra Ann**
Adam Dale Chapter
Ancestor: Thomas Mercer, GA —#660106
This "Double Wedding Ring" quilt was made in 1952 at West Helena, AR by the owner's grandmother, Mary Rose S. E. Robinson (born 10/23/1900 at Brookhaven, MS, married William David Robinson, died 9/30/1993 at West Helena, AR).

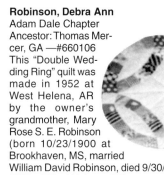
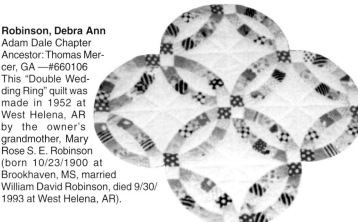

**Robinson, Debra Ann**
Adam Dale Chapter
Ancestor: Thomas Mercer, GA —#660106
This "Bird in the Bush" quilt was made in 1974 at Memphis, TN by Elizabeth Bowie, an employee of the owner.

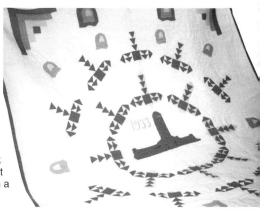

**Robinson, Debra Ann**
Adam Dale Chapter
Ancestor: Thomas Mercer, GA —#660106
This "Hit and Miss" quilt was made in 1940 at West Helena, AR by the owner's grandmother, Iva Gertrude Hinds Brown (born 6/13/1902 at Brinkley, AR, married Harry Kembrew Brown, died 7/9/1990 at West Helena). The quilt is made from wool pants and scraps of wool fabric.

**Robnett, Elizabeth Parham**
The Crab Orchard Chapter
Ancestor: Greenberry Wilson, NC —#627559
This "Starburst" quilt was made in the 1880's at Sequatchie Valley, TN by the owner's great grandmother, Elizabeth Brown Parham (born 1815 at Bledsoe County, TN, married John Parham, died 1913 in the same county).

**Robnett, Frances Sue**
The Crab Orchard Chapter
Ancestor: Greenberry Wilson, NC —#630803
This original design quilt was made in 1933 at Pikeville, TN by the owner's mother, Addie Swafford Robnett (born 2/28/1888 at Pikeville, TN, married James Robnett, died 1/1/1991 at Pikeville). This quilt was entered in the Sears Roebuck "Century of Progress " contest at the World's Fair and it won a "Merit Award."

**Rogers, Erma Henson** (Cecil V.)
Tullahoma Chapter
Ancestor: George Webb, NC — #705873
This "Double Wedding Ring" quilt was made prior to 1950 at Sullivan County, TN by the owner's aunt, Faye Webb Feathers (born 8/7/1889 at Sullivan County, TN, married Samuel Feathers, died in the same county).

**Rogers, Erma Henson** (Cecil V.)
Tullahoma Chapter
Ancestor: George Webb, NC — #705873
This "Log Cabin" quilt was made in 1997 at Hillsboro, TN by the owner (born 2/8/1932 at Bluff City, IO).

**Roggli, Ruby Clark** (Thomas)
General James Winchester Chapter
Ancestor: Charles Lee, VA — #741933
This "The Way of the Cross" quilt was made in 1928 at Cyril, OK by the owner's grandmother, Annie Black (born in 1865 at Franklin County, TN, married Warner Black, died in 1947 at Cyril, OK). The quilt was passed from maker to owner.

**Roggli, Ruby Clark** (Thomas)
General James Winchester Chapter
Ancestor: Charles Lee, VA — #741933
This "Tumbling Blocks" quilt was made in 1960 at Cyril, OK by the owner's mother, Eilene Clark (born 12/18/1896 at Dichord, TN, married Arthur Clark, died 5/7/1973 at Cyril, OK).

**Roggli, Ruby Clark**
(Thomas)
General James Winchester Chapter
Ancestor: Charles Lee, VA — #741933
This "Log Cabin" quilt was made in 1986 at Winchester, TN by the owner (born 2/18/1920 at Cyril, OK)

**Rollins, Judy Rogers** (Wayne)
Mary Blount Chapter
Ancestor: Henry Shreffler, PA — # 674541
This "Iris" embroidery quilt was made in 1994 in Florida by the owner's mother, Bernice Shreffler Rogers (born 11/28/1904, married John Clinton Rogers). The maker began the quilt with the intention of keeping it for herself since she loves blue irises. However, when she realized that the iris is the Tennessee State Flower, she decided to give the quilt to her daughter who lives in Tennessee. The handwork took 10 months to complete and she finished it at age 90 in 1994. Today, she is still busy making afghans for her grandchildren and great–grandchildren. She celebrated her 94th birthday last November!

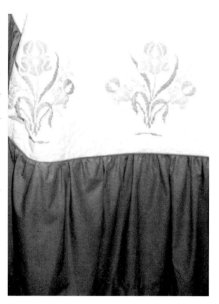

**Ross, Sharon Louisa**
Zachariah Davies Chapter
Ancestor: John Malone, VA —#603089
This "Eccentric Star" quilt was made by the owner's grandmother, Louise Malone Ross (born 7/22/1897 at Saulsbury, TN, married Jones Wesley Ross, Sr., died 5/24/1973 at Memphis, TN).

**Routzone, Donna Deem** (Jack)
Great Smokies Chapter
Ancestor: Michael Spencer — #783337
This "Nine Patch" quilt was purchased by the owner at an auction at Arcanum, OH in 1980.

**Routzone, Donna Deem** (Jack)
Great Smokies Chapter
Ancestor: Michael Spencer — #783337
This "Pinwheel" quilt was purchased at Arcanum, OH in 1985 by the owner.

**Routzone, Donna Deem** (Jack)
Great Smokies Chapter
Ancestor: Michael Spencer — #783337
This "Red Cross" quilt was purchased at Arcanum, OH in 1985 by the owner.

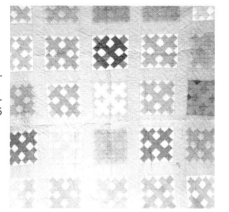

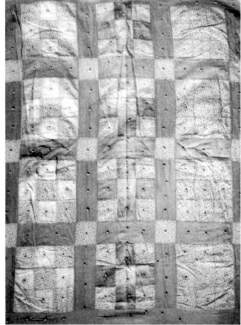

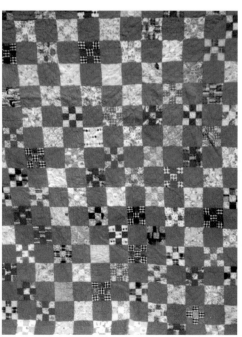

**Routzone, Donna Deem** (Jack)
Great Smokies Chapter
Ancestor: Michael Spencer — #783337
This "Nine Patch" quilt was given to the owner by her mother in 1955.

**Routzone, Donna Deem** (Jack)
Great Smokies Chapter
Ancestor: Michael Spencer — #783337
This "Nine Patch" quilt was made in 1955 at Greenville, OH by the owner's mother, Bessie E. Deem (born 11/6/1899 at Darke County, OH, married Fred, died 3/12/1985 at Montgomery, OH).

**Routzone, Donna Deem**
(Jack)
Great Smokies Chapter
Ancestor: Michael Spencer
— #783337
This "Dresden Plate" quilt
was purchased at Arcanum,
OH in 1985 by the owner.

**Routzone, Donna Deem**
(Jack)
Great Smokies Chapter
Ancestor: Michael Spencer
— #783337
This "Grandmother's Flower
Garden" quilt was purchased
at Arcanum, OH in 1985 by
the owner.

**Routzone, Donna Deem**
(Jack)
Great Smokies Chapter
Ancestor: Michael Spencer
— #783337
This "Nine patch" quilt was
made in 1956 at Greenville,
OH by the owner's mother,
Bessie E. Deem.

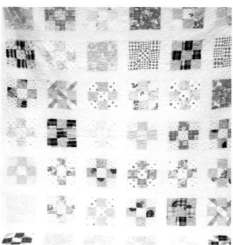

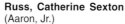

**Routzone, Donna Deem**
(Jack)
Great Smokies Chapter
Ancestor: Michael Spencer
— #783337
This "Cathedral Window"
quilt was made in 1979 at
Arcanum, OH by the owner
(born 6/20/1928 at
Eldorado, OH).

**Routzone, Donna Deem**
(Jack)
Great Smokies Chapter
Ancestor: Michael Spencer
— #783337
This "American Eagle"
quilt was made in 1975 at
Arcanum, OH by the
owner.

**Russ, Catherine Sexton**
(Aaron, Jr.)
Sarah Hawkins Chapter
Ancestor: John Chapman,
VA — #532731
This "Grandmother's
Flower Garden" quilt was
made in the 1940's.

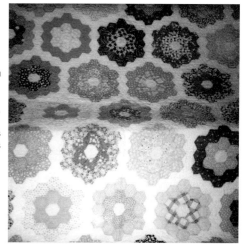

**Rowlett, Beth**
Chucalissa Chapter
Ancestor: John An-
thony, VA —#754993
This "Grape Vine"
quilt was made in
Jackson, TN by a
family friend, Miss
Reid, who gave the
quilt to the owner's
mother.

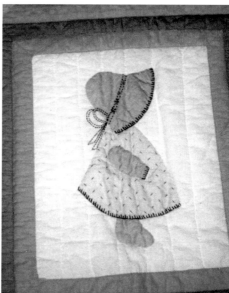

**Rowlett, Beth**
Chucalissa Chapter
Ancestor: John Anthony,
VA —#754993
This "Sunbonnet Baby"
quilt was made in 1947 by
the owner's aunt, Annie
Haynes Rowlett (born
1907 at Brownsville, TN,
married Herbert Rowlett,
died 1997 at Jackson,
TN).

**Sanders, Helen Landrum**
(Lionel J., Jr.)
General William Lenoir Chapter
Ancestor: Maj. Valentine Sevier, VA — #781261
This "Crazy" quilt was made in the 1920's at Scottsville, KY by the owner's husband's grandmother, Letha Susan Claiborne Sanders (born 11/16/1884 at Macon County, TN, married Clarence Albert Sanders, died in 1945 at Scottsville, KY). The quilt is pieced with fabric from wool clothing worn by the maker's family. The back is made from two colors of

flannel. The maker's daughter-in-law, Bertha E. Reagan Sanders, wife of the maker's only child, Lionel J. Sanders, Jr. used the quilt for warmth until her death in 1960. The quilt was then passed to Lionel J. Sanders, Jr., the only son and youngest of four children, and the owner's husband. The quilt has been with the current owner and her husband since their marriage in 1963.

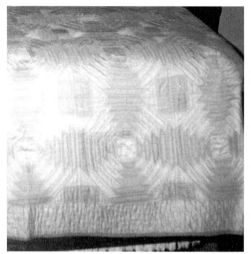

**Sanders, Kathryn Brown**
(David Paige)
Old Glory Chapter
Ancestor: Gideon Carr, VA — #749740
This "Pineapple" quilt was made in the 1940's at Dickson County, TN by Mrs. Ben Thompson. Mrs. Thompson made and sold quilts because her husband was on strike from the Nashville Bridge Company. The quilt won a blue ribbon at the Dickson County Fair. The owner received the quilt from her aunt, Mrs. Milton Daniel.

**Sanders, Kathryn Brown**
(David Paige)
Old Glory Chapter
Ancestor: Gideon Carr, VA — #749740
This "Windmill" quilt was made in 1940 at Nashville, TN by the owner's husband's grandmother, Annie Eliza Paige Sanders (born 1/17/1863 at Rutherford County, TN, married John Smith Sanders, died 2/26/1952 at Nashville, TN). The quilt was made as a wedding gift for the owner and her husband.

**Savage, Audrey Downer**
(Woodson, Jr.)
Hatchie Chapter
Ancestor: Steven Stephenhix, NC — #452582
This wool coverlet was made in 1985 at Bolivar, TN by the owner's husband (born 12/13/1915 at Bolivar, TN).

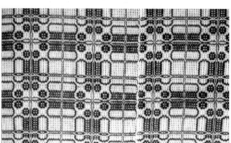

**Savage, Audrey Downer**
(Woodson, Jr.)
Hatchie Chapter
Ancestor: Steven Stephenhix, NC — #452582
This "Birds in the Air/Flying Geese/Double Pyramids" quilt was pieced in 1864 by the owner's great great aunt, Hattie Hicks Maples. It was quilted by her sisters, Ursula Hicks Downer and Jeannie Hicks Smith, during the War Between the States. Ursula was the owner's great grandmother.

**Savage, Janet DeVaul**
(Woodson)
Hatchie Chapter
Ancestor: William Enyeart, PA – #744820
This "Pineapple" quilt was made 8/30-9/22/1945 at Orbisconia, PA by the owner's great grandmother, Belle Grove (born 5/13/1854 at Blacklog, PA, married William Grove, died 9/22/1945 at Mt. Union, PA). This quilt was made from silk scraps from the factory in France (some have bolt markings still on them). The silk was brought to Pennsylvania by Belle's grandfather, John Gilliland, sometime before the War Between the

States. John was born 2/20/1764 and died 10/1/1861. The quilt top was started on the owner's birthday and was finished twenty four days later on the day the quiltmaker died. It was quilted by the Lou-Le-Wal Sunday School Class of Homestead Park United Methodist Church in 1960.

**Savage, Janet DeVaul**
(Woodson)
Hatchie Chapter
Ancestor: William Enyeart, PA 744820
This "Parasol Girl" quilt was made 1950-53 at Pittsburgh, PA by the owner and her neighbor, Grammy Collins, who died in 1955 at Pittsburgh. The parasol girls were embroidered by the owner as a teaching project over three summers. The printed material is from old house dresses and aprons. As they finished a panel, Grammy and the owner would sit on the porch swing and sing hymns, while Grammy quilted the panel. The owner received the finished quilt for Christmas in 1953.

**Savage, Janet DeVaul** (Woodson)
Hatchie Chapter
Ancestor: William Enyeart, PA 744820
This "Grandmother's Flower Garden" quilt was found in the bottom of a cupboard when the owner was first married in 1972.

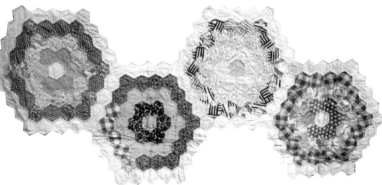

**Savage, Janet DeVaul** (Woodson) Hatchie Chapter Ancestor: William Enyeart, PA 744820

This woven coverlet was made in 1978 at Bolivar, TN by the owner's father-in-law, Woodson J. Savage, Jr. (born 12/1915 at Bolivar, TN, married Audrey Downer Savage). The coverlet was a gift from grandfather to grandson Jay.

**Savage, Janet DeVaul** (Woodson) Hatchie Chapter Ancestor: William Enyeart, PA 744820

This "Log Cabin" quilt was made in 1975 at Plain City, OH by an aquaintance of the owner, Mrs. Perry Yoder "Mable." This quilt was made by an Amish woman. It is machine pleced on a gasollne powered sewing machine and hand quilted.

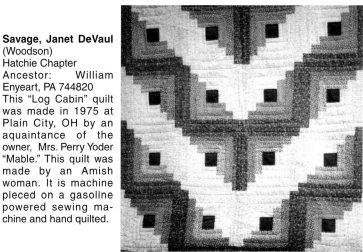

**Schonhoff, Patricia Cummings** (Clem Cook) Chickamauga Chapter Ancestor: Robert Cartwright, NC — #601476

This "Yellow Rose" quilt was made circa 1950 at Blytheville, AR by the owner's aunt by marriage, Myrtrous Cook (born circa 1913, died circa 1993 at Blytheville.

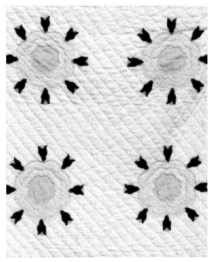

**Schonhoff, Patricia Cummings** (Clem Cook) Chickamauga Chapter Ancestor: Robert Cartwright, NC — #601476

This "Octagonal Star/Dutch Rose" quilt was made circa 1950 at Nashville, TN by the switch board operator at the Nashville Courthouse as a Christmas gift to the owner's father, Thomas L. Cummings, who was then mayor of Nashville.

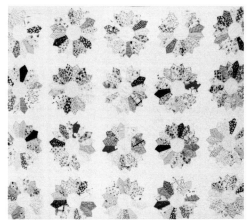

**Schonhoff, Patricia Cummings** (Clem Cook) Chickamauga Chapter Ancestor: Robert Cartwright, NC — #601476

This "Dresden Plate" quilt was made in the 1930's or 40's at Blytheville, AR by Myrtrous Cook.

**Schonhoff, Patricia Cummings** (Clem Cook) Chickamauga Chapter Ancestor: Robert Cartwright, NC — #601476

This "Nine Patch Variation " quilt was made circa 1940 at Blytheville, AR by Myrtrous Cook.

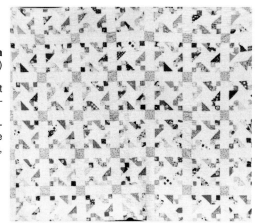

**Schonhoff, Patricia Cummings** (Clem Cook) Chickamauga Chapter Ancestor: Robert Cartwright, NC — #601476

This "Colonial Lady" quilt was made circa 1940 at Blytheville, AR by Myrtrous Cook.

**Schonhoff, Patricia Cummings** (Clem Cook) Chickamauga Chapter Ancestor: Robert Cartwright, NC — #601476

This "Windpower of the Osages/ Indian Symbol" quilt was made circa 1940 at Blytheville, AR by Myrtrous Cook.

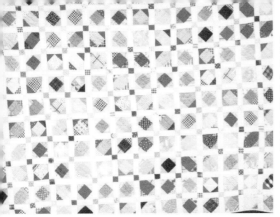

**Schonhoff, Patricia Cummings** (Clem Cook)
Chickamauga Chapter
Ancestor: Robert Cartwright, NC — #601476
This "Square in a Square" quilt was made at Blytheville, AR by Myrtrous Cook.

**Schumacher, Effie Vines** (Edward M.)
Travelers Rest Chapter
Ancestor: Benjamin May, NC — #560794
This "Variation of a Dresden Plate" quilt was made by the owner's husband's aunt, Irma Schumacher (born 6/19/1896 at St. Louis, MO, died 3/23/1971 at St.

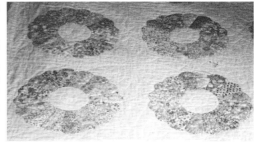

Louis). This quilt was started by the owner's husband's mother who died when he was just five years old. His maiden aunt, Irma, moved in to raise Ed and his 18 month old sister. Irma finished the quilt.

**Schumacher, Effie Vines** (Edward M.)
Travelers Rest Chapter
Ancestor: Benjamin May, NC — #560794
This "Pinwheel" quilt was made at St. Louis by the owner's husband's aunt, Norma Schumacher (born 5/19/1905 at St. Louis, died 3/4/1978 in the same city). This is one of a pair given to the owner's husband.

**Schweitzer, Betty Olson** (Thomas)
Kings Mountain Messenger Chapter
Ancestor: Samuel Hamilton, MA — #639807
This "Tumbling Blocks" crib quilt was made in the 1980's at Fayetteville, TN by the owner. Betty became interested in quiltmaking when she moved to Tennessee. All of her friends were making them and displaying their family quilts. After many lessons, she joined the fun and pleasure of quilt making.

**Schweitzer, Betty Olson** (Thomas)
Kings Mountain Messenger Chapter
Ancestor: Samuel Hamilton, MA — #639807
This "Sampler" quilt was made in 1980 at Fayetteville, TN by the owner. The owner's greatest pride was to make a block selected to be included in the Tennessee Bicentennial Quilt.

**Scribney, Jane Brady** (Michael)
James Sheppard Chapter
Ancestor: David Duff, NC — #545891
This "Dutch Girl/Sunbonnet Sue" quilt was made in 1933-34 at Van Buren County, TN by the owner's great aunt, Ella Boulder Worthington (born 1883 at Van Buren County, married John Worthington, died 1962). The owner received the quilt from Bessie Duff Brady, a 50 year member of the DAR, who she lovingly calls "Mother."

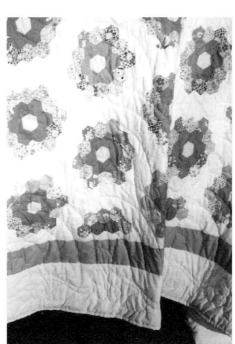

**Seeger, Ann Massengill** (Charles)
Long Island Chapter
Ancestor: Henry Massengill, Jr., NC — #594262
This "Indian Trails" quilt was made in the 1890's at Bluff City, TN by the owner's paternal grandmother, Maynard Massengill (born circa 1890's at Bluff City, TN, married Walter Massengill, died in the 1950's at Bluff City).

**Seeger, Ann Massengill** (Charles)
Long Island Chapter
Ancestor: Henry Massengill, Jr., NC — #594262
This "Grandmother's Flower Garden" made in the 1920's at Bluff City, TN by the owner's paternal grandmother, Maynard Massengill.

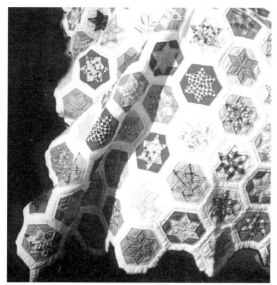

**Seeger, Ann Massengill**
(Charles)
Long Island Chapter
Ancestor: Henry Massengill, Jr., NC — #594262
This "Hexagon Star" quilt was made in the 1920's at Piney Flats, TN by the owner's maternal grandmother, Martha McKenry St. John (married George St. John).

**Seeger, Ann Massengill**
(Charles)
Long Island Chapter
Ancestor: Henry Massengill, Jr., NC — #594262
This "Pineapple" quilt was made in the 1920's at New Haven, CT by the owner's husband's grandmother, Ernestine Seeger (born circa 1880 in Germany, married Fredrick Seeger, died in 1940 at New Haven, CT).

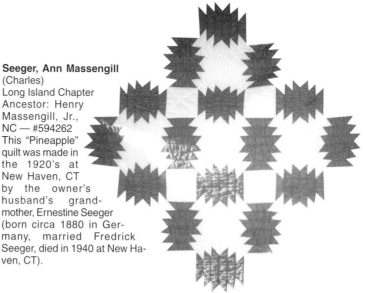

**Seeger, Ann Massengill**
(Charles)
Long Island Chapter
Ancestor: Henry Massengill, Jr., NC — #594262
This "Dresden Plate" quilt was made in the 1920's at New Haven, CT by the owner's husband's grandmother, Ernestine Seeger.

**Sellers-Young, Brenda Prater** (Ed)
Mary Blount Chapter
Ancestor:Gideon Stebbins, MA —#763493
This "Chimney Sweep/ Courthouse Square" quilt was made by Irene White Prater, the owner's grandmother. The blocks in this quilt are autographed in embroidery.

**Sellers, Donette Clark** (Terrell M.)
Buffalo River Chapter
Ancestor: Lt. Thomas Fortson, Jr., VA — #782710
This "Friendship Star" quilt was made circa 1933-34 at Gibson County, TN by the owner's mother-in-law, Ruby Mae Marshall Sellers (born 5/7/1912 at Gibson County, married Dennis A. Sellers, died 6/6/1996 at Lawerenceburg, TN). Nineteen of Ruby's friends helped with this quilt and their names appear in the squares along with Ruby's. The owner inherited this quilt from the maker.

**Senter, Sue Bolling**
Robert Cooke Chapter
Ancestor: Phillp Fulcher, VA — #571762
This "Variation of a Lover's Knot" coverlet was made in the Smoky Mountains circa 100 years ago. It was given to the owner's grandmother in the early 1900's and she gave it to the owner.

**Senter, Sue Bolling**
Robert Cooke Chapter
Ancestor: Phillp Fulcher, VA — #571762
This "Crazy" quilt was made in 1884 at Nashville, TN by the owner's great grandmother, Darthula Fulcher (born 8/4/1832 at Spotsylvania County, VA, married John Coleman Fulcher, died 1/18/1894). Some of the fabrics have been hand painted with oils. The quilt was passed from maker, to grandmother, to mother, to owner.

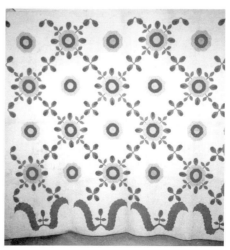

**Senter, Sue Bolling**
Robert Cooke Chapter
Ancestor: Phillp Fulcher, VA — #571762
This "Rose of Sharon Variation" quilt was made circa 1835 in Tennessee. The quilt was given to the owner's grandmother, Mary Fulcher Bolling (1862-1953). The quilt has sborder only on two sides which indicates that it was special and was used for a bed in the front room.

**Shearer, Nelly Galloway** (James O.)
Chickasaw Bluff Chapter
Ancestor: Nicholas Hale, MD —
#478142
This "Monkey Wrench" quilt was made in 1992 in Memphis, TN by Bessie Davis, the care giver of the owner's aunt, Mary Louise Hale. The pattern involves some of the slave signs used during the War Between the States. The quiltmaker explained the arrows and other significant directives on the quilt were the results of stories her grandmother and mother shared with her about the passage ways of the slaves to freedom during the war between the states.

**Shearer, Nelly Galloway** (James O.)
Chickasaw Bluff Chapter
Ancestor: Nicholas Hale, MD —
#478142
This "Cactus Basket/Desert Rose" quilt was made in1992 at Memphis, TN by Bessie Davis, the care giver of the owner's aunt, Mary Louise Hale. The quiltmaker was raised by a grandmother who had been a slave. As a young girl, she received her freedom and passage to Illinois. The symbols depict the ways slaves used quilts to communicate with other slaves about the path to freedom.

**Shearer, Nelly Galloway** (James O.)
Chickasaw Bluff Chapter
Ancestor: Nicholas Hale, MD —#478142
This embroidered "Roses" quilt was made in the 1970's at Oklahoma City, OK by the owner's aunt, Mae Hale Dean (married to Jackson Hale, died in 1977 at OK). The quilt was given to the owner's mother, Mildred Hale Galloway, at the death of her sister-in-law. The quilt was then passed to the owner at her mother's death. The owner has a special attachment to this quilt and remembers flying home after her aunt's funeral carefully holding the quilt.

**Shearer, Nelly Galloway** (James O.)
Chickasaw Bluff Chapter
Ancestor: Nicholas Hale, MD —#478142
This embroidered quilt was made in 1971-72 at Memphis by the owners friend, Betty Coe Cruzen (born in Centralia, IL, married Warren B.) The owner received the quilt from the maker as a wedding gift May, 1972.

**Shipley, Helen Wilburn** (Ralph)
General William Lenoir Chapter
Ancestor: Simeon Eldredge, NC —#661604
This "Dresden Plate" quilt was made in 1938 at Loudon County, TN by the owner's grandmother, Mary Kate Eblen Kollock (born 2/2/1880 at Loudon County, TN, married Floyd Kollock, died 1/4/1975 at Loudon County). When the owner graduated from Lenoir City High School in 1938, she received this quilt as a gift.

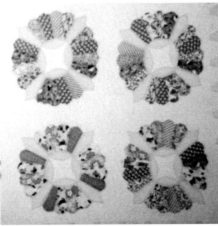

**Shinault, Irma Joyce**
Hatchie Chapter
Ancestor: Michael Robinson, NC — #771802
This "Butterfly" quilt was made in the 1930's or 40's at Tipton County, TN by the owner's grandmother, Mary Ophilia Clifton Shinault (born 12/2/1863 at Fayette County, TN, married Joseph Hamilton Shinault, died 4/14/1949 at Tipton County). Mary was the widow of John Marshall before she married Joseph in 1892. Her mother, Hannah Youree Shinault, was the first European woman to cross the Hatchie River into West TN. This is inscribed on her tombstone in Words Cemetery at Hickory Valley, TN. Joseph served in the War Between the States on the Confederate side, in Hood's Army. In 1890, he was elected state senator representing Tipton and Fayette Counties. The quiltmaker lived to be 86 years old, and was loved and respected by all who knew her.

**Shipley, Helen Wilburn** (Ralph)
General William Lenoir Chapter
Ancestor: Simeon Eldredge, NC —#661604
This "Trip Around the World" quilt was made in 1895 in Roane County, TN by the owner's great grandmother, Mary Jane Mourfield Kollock (born 3/17/1839 in Ohio, married Alexander Kollock, died 10/29/1910 at Loudon County). It was made from remnants of fabric from shirts worn by the owner's grandfather, Floyd Kollock.

**Shore, Emily Hendrix** (James William)
James Buckley Chapter
Ancestor: John Redden, VA —#647728
This "Tennessee Football" quilt was made in 1970 at Weakley County, TN by a patient of the owner's husband, Mrs. Robb (born 1880's in Holland, died in Weakley County, TN). She made it for the owner's husband who is a University of Tennessee Football fan.

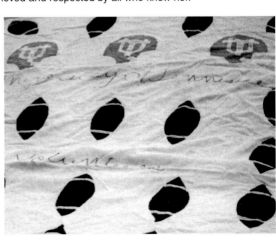

**Shore, Emily Hendrix**
(James William)
James Buckley Chapter
Ancestor: John Redden,
VA —#647728
This "Double Wedding
Ring" quilt was made in
1948 at Hartsville, TN by
the owner's aunt, Mary
McCrary Lauderdale
(born 1907 at Humphreys
County, TN, married
Brevard Lauderdale, died
1972 in the same
county). The quilt was
given to the owner as a
child and is made of her
dress scraps.

**Silvey, Bettye Moredock**
(Ancil)
Kings Mountain Messenger
Chapter
Ancestor: James Officer, VA
— #759453
This "Oak Leaf" quilt was
made in 1888 at Livingston,
TN by the owner's grand-
mother, Zilla Officer
Moredock (born 2/3/1856 at
Overton County, TN, married
George Lafayette Moredock,
died 9/21/1891 at Livingston,
TN). The maker originally
gave the quilt to her first born
daughter, Willie Moredock.
The owner received the quilt
from her sister, Pauline
Parks, in 1991.

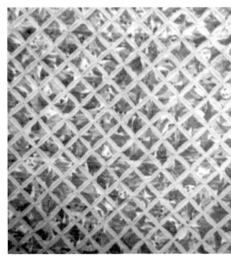

**Sims, Emma Saunders**
(Ernest J.)
Glover's Trace Chapter
Ancestor: Christopher Taylor
—#532282
This "Cathedral Window"
quilt was made circa 1955 at
Camden, TN by the owner's
mother, Maude Saunders
(born 8/5/1895 at Camden,
married Fred H. Saunders,
died 8/14/1977 at Camden).
The owner received the quilt
at her mother's death. This
quilt won first prize at a
Benton County, Tennessee
Fair.

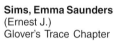

**Sims, Emma Saunders**
(Ernest J.)
Glover's Trace Chapter
Ancestor: Christopher
Taylor —#532282
This "Colonial Girl" quilt
was made in 1934 at
Camden, TN by the
owner's mother, Maude
Saunders. This quilt won
first prize at a Benton
County, Tennessee Fair.

**Sinder, Audrey Ackerman**
(Nicholas)
Mary Blount Chapter
Ancestor: Adrian Onderdonk,
NY —#723538
This "Irish Chain" quilt was
made in the 1920's in New
York. The quilt was found in
an attic in upstate New York.
It had been pieced by a farm
wife. It was quilted by the
owner's mother and the
United Methodist Women in
Huntington, NY.

**Sliger, Barbara Faye
DeLay** (Robert Lee)
Rhea-Craig Chapter
Ancestor: Lt. James De-
lay, NC —#687514
This "Spools" quilt was
made circa 1900 at
McMinn County, TN by a
relative of the owner's
mother-in-law, Mrs. Viola
Kyker Sliger (born 9/17/
1904 at McMinn County,
married Joe Wheeler
Sliger, died 4/1986 at
Chattanooga, TN). She
gave the quilt to the
owner.

**Sliger, Barbara Faye
DeLay** (Robert Lee)
Rhea-Craig Chapter
Ancestor: Lt. James
Delay, NC —#687514
This "Sunburst Varia-
tion" quilt was made
prior to 1900 at McMinn
County, TN. The quilt
was quilted by the
owner's mother-in-law,
Mrs. Viola Kyker Sliger.
There is a "V" embroi-
dered on the back cor-
ner. Viola gave the quilt
to the owner. This quilt
pattern was said to
have fallen off a home-
steaders wagon that
was going by Signal
Mountain in the 1850's.

**Sliger, Barbara Faye
DeLay** (Robert Lee)
Rhea-Craig Chapter
Ancestor: Lt. James De-
lay, NC —#687514
This "Tumblers" quilt was
made circa 1900 at
McMinn County, TN by
the owners husband's
grandmother, Mary
Louisa Stanton Kyker
(born 1884 at McMinn
County, TN, married J.L.
Kyker, died 4/30/1975 at
Athens, TN). The quilt
descended from maker,
to her daughter, to owner.

**Sliger, Barbara Faye DeLay** (Robert Lee)
Rhea-Craig Chapter
Ancestor: Lt. James Delay, NC —#687514
This "State Bird" quilt was hand painted in the early 1980's at Ten Mile, TN by Betty Jean Sliger and quilted by the owner's husband's mother, Mrs. Viola Kyker Sliger.

**Sliger, Barbara Faye DeLay** (Robert Lee)
Rhea-Craig Chapter
Ancestor: Lt. James Delay, NC —#687514
This "Shattered Star" quilt was pieced in the late 1980's at Chattanooga, TN by the owner's mother, Erelene DeLay (born 5/25/1915 at Cannon County, TN, married Samuel Ayers DeLay). The quilt was quilted in Milton, TN. Erelene gave the owner the quilt.

**Sliger, Barbara Faye DeLay** (Robert Lee)
Rhea-Craig Chapter
Ancestor: Lt. James Delay, NC —#687514
This "Maple Leaf" quilt was made in the 1950's at Milton, TN by the owner's grandmother, Erssie Beulah Jones DeLay (born 2/21/1890 at Cannon County, TN, married Jesse Miller DeLay, died 10/7/1978 at Rutherford County, TN). The quilt was passed from maker to owner.

**Sliger, Barbara Faye DeLay** (Robert Lee)
Rhea-Craig Chapter
Ancestor: Lt. James Delay, NC —#687514
This cross stitched quilt was made in the early 1980's at Ten Mile, TN by the owner, her mother-in-law, Mrs. Viola Kyker Sliger, and her sister-in-law, Betty Sliger. The owner embroidered the quilt and all helped to quilt it.

**Sliger, Barbara Faye DeLay** (Robert Lee)
Rhea-Craig Chapter
Ancestor: Lt. James Delay, NC —#687514
This "Now I Lay Me Down To Sleep" quilt was hand embroidered by the owner in the summer of 1976 at Madisonville, TN and later commercially quilted.

**Smith, Delene Craig** (Rufus)
Fort Prudhomme Chapter
Ancestor: David Craig, NC —#728936
This "Friendship" quilt was embroidered 1970-75 at Ripley, TN by friends in the Home Demonstration Club. Each of the twenty four blocks has a name of a member. They drew to see who would get the quilt blocks. The owner drew the first batch of blocks. The ladies at the Community Center, under Ms.

Maude Jenkins, bought the lining and quilted the quilt. Some of the members have moved away or died. This quilt is not just a "Friendship" quilt, it is a "Memory"quilt.

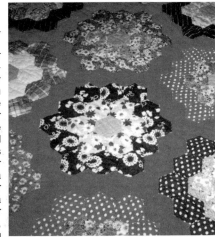

**Smith, Delene Craig** (Rufus)
Fort Prudhomme Chapter
Ancestor: David Craig, NC — #728936
This "Grandmother's Flower Garden" quilt was made in 1941-42 at Lauderdale County, TN by the owner's grandmother, Lou Baker Minner and by the owner's mother, Marie Minner Craig (born 1906 at Lauderdale County, married Jarome, died 1980 in the same county). It was passed to the owner by her mother. When the owner was a child and spent the night with her grandparents, she slept on a featherbed under three or four quilts. The quilts were so heavy, she would have trouble turning over. She remembers that in the morning she would awake to the smell of sausage and coffee and knew that there would be good biscuits, butter, and preserves too. She says, "These are precious memories. I'm 70 years old, but I can almost taste those good biscuits."

**Smith, Delene Craig** (Rufus)
Fort Prudhomme Chapter
Ancestor: David Craig, NC —#728936
This "Old Fashioned Quilt, An All Over Design" was pieced 50 or 60 years ago at Lauderdale County, TN by the owner's mother, Marie Minner Craig. It was quilted by the owner's grandmother, Lou Baker Minner. "When I was a child, quilt frames were up all winter, and there was usually a quilt in the making."

**Smith, Karen Fusselman** (John W.)
Zachariah Davies Chapter
Ancestor: James Garrison, NC —
#711346
This "Dutch Doll" quilt was made in the 1960's at Rockford, IL by the owner's great aunt, Edith Belle Dawdy Friend Roen (born 12/27/1897 at Greene County, IL, married Lewis Lloyd Friend, married 2nd John Roen, died 12/11/1985 at Rockford). Edith was the only sister of the owner's grandmother, Mary Eunice Dawdy Fussleman. This is one of the few quilt's for which Edith had to purchase fabric to finish. Aunt Edith was the youngest of five children born to James Monroe Dawdy and Laura Vermelia King Dawdy, all born near Patterson, IL. Edith's father died when she was eleven years old, and the family moved across the hill to Hillview, on the bluffs of the Pearl River. Both the owner's grandmother and Aunt Edith learned to do fine needlework from their mother. Aunt Edith married Lewis Lloyd Friend and moved to Scott County, IL and then to Rockford. When Uncle Lee died at an early age, Aunt Edith was faced with medical and funeral expenses. She went to work making locks. After dinner, she picked up needlework. Selling her handmade quilts supplemented her income. After being a widow for 25 years, she married John Roen of Norwegian descent. A gifted wood worker, he made a quilt frame which remained set up in the dining room. Even after her 80th birthday, she shoveled the snow in winter, mowed the grass in summer with a push mower, and raked the leaves in the fall.

**Smith, Karen Fusselman**
(John W.)
Zachariah Davies Chapter
Ancestor: James Garrison, NC —#711346
This "Drunkard's Path" quilt was made in the 1970's at Rockford, IL by the owner's great aunt, Edith Belle Dawdy Friend Roen, when she was 80 years old. The maker gave the quilt to the owner.

**Smith, Karen Fusselman**
(John W.)
Zachariah Davies Chapter
Ancestor: James Garrison, NC —#711346
This "Double Wedding Ring" quilt was made in the early 1980's at Rockford, IL by the owner's great aunt, Edith Belle Dawdy Friend Roen, who lived to be 88 years old.

**Smith, Karen Fusselman**
(John W.)
Zachariah Davies Chapter
Ancestor: James Garrison, NC —
#711346
This "Butterfly" quilt was made in the 1960's - 70's at Rockford, IL by the owner's great aunt, Edith Belle Dawdy Friend Roen. As a high school student, the owner received the quilt from her aunt.

**Smith, Karen Fusselman** (John W.)
Zachariah Davies Chapter
Ancestor: James Garrison, NC —#711346
This "Bow Tie" quilt was made in the 1960's at Rockford, IL by the owner's great aunt, Edith Belle Dawdy Friend Roen.

**Smith, Karen Fusselman** (John W.)
Zachariah Davies Chapter
Ancestor: James Garrison, NC —#711346
This "Airplane" quilt was pieced in 1912-20 at Hillview, IL by the owner's great grandmother, Laura Vermelia King Dawdy Stauffer (born 7/18/1870 at Greene County, IL, married James Monroe Dawdy, married 2nd Frank Stauffer, died 9/20/1949 at Hillview, IL). The owner finished the quilt.

**Smith, Karen Fusselman**
(John W.)
Zachariah Davies Chapter
Ancestor: James Garrison, NC —#711346
This "Tumbling Blocks" quilt was made in the 1970's at Rockford, IL by the owner's great aunt, Edith Belle Dawdy Friend Roen.

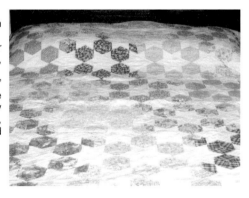

**Smith, Karen Fusselman** (John W.)
Zachariah Davies Chapter
Ancestor: James Garrison, NC —#711346
This "Sunbonnet Sue and Overall Sam" quilt was made in 1978 at Memphis, TN by the Deborah Sunday School Class at Audubon Park Baptist Church. They gave the quilt to the owner as a baby present for her third child, Jonathan.

**Smith, Karen Fusselman**
(John W.)
Zachariah Davies Chapter
Ancestor: James Garrison, NC —#711346
This "Sampler" wall hanging was made in 1996 at Cordova, TN by the owner (born at St. Louis, MO).

**Smith, Karen Fusselman**
(John W.)
Zachariah Davies Chapter
Ancestor: James Garrison, NC
—#711346
This "Pinwheel" crib quilt was
made in 1996 at Cordova, TN
by the owner for her first
grandchild.

**Smith, Karen Fusselman**
(John W.)
Zachariah Davies Chapter
Ancestor: James Garrison,
NC —#711346
This "Ohio Star" quilt was
made in 1976 at
Germantown, TN by the
owner. This was her first
quiltmaking effort. She took
a class at a local needle-
work shop.

**Smith, Karen Fusselman**
(John W.)
Zachariah Davies Chapter
Ancestor: James Garrison,
NC —#711346
This original "Meagan's" quilt
was made in 1995 at Cordova,
TN by the owner.

**Smith, Karen Fusselman**
(John W.)
Zachariah Davies Chapter
Ancestor: James Garrison, NC
—#711346
This "Lone Star" quilt was
made in the 1970's at Rockford, IL by the owner's great
aunt, Edith Belle Dawdy
Friend Roen. This quilt is only
used for special occasions.

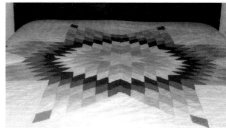

**Smith, Karen Fusselman** (John W.)
Zachariah Davies Chapter
Ancestor: James Garrison, NC —#711346
This "Bow Tie" quilt was made in 1998 at
Cordova, TN by the owner. She used the latest
techniques including the rotary cutter and machine quilting. This quilt will be soaked in tan fabric die to give it an aged, antique appearance,
and it will be used in the owner's new log house.

**Smith, Karen Fusselman** (John W.)
Zachariah Davies Chapter
Ancestor: James Garrison,
NC —#711346
This embroidered "John's Animal" quilt was made in 1943
at De Soto, MO by the owner's
mother-in-law, Rose Anne
Sansoucie Smith (born 10/28/
1916 at Klondike, MO, married Eldon John Smith, died 2/
6/1999 at De Soto, MO). The
quilt was made for the owner's
husband before he was born.
The owner received the quilt
at the death of her mother-in-
law in 1999.

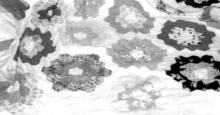

**Smith, Karen Fusselman** (John W.)
Zachariah Davies Chapter
Ancestor: James Garrison, NC —#711346
This "Grandmother's Flower Garden"
quilt was made in 1977 at De Soto,
MO by the owner's mother-in-
law, Rose Anne Sansoucie
Smith. This quilt was in
the maker's bedroom
when she died.

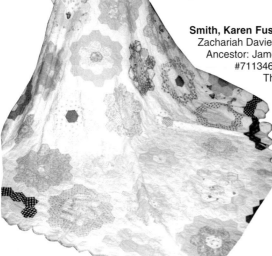

**Smith, Karen Fusselman** (John W.)
Zachariah Davies Chapter
Ancestor: James Garrison, NC —
#711346
This "Grandmother's
Flower Garden"
quilt was made
in the 1970's at
Rockford, IL by
the owner's
great aunt, Edith
Belle Dawdy
Friend Roen.

**Smith, Mary King**
(Walter)
Charlotte Reeves
Robertson Chapter
Ancestor: Sgt. David
Henry, VA —#714751
This "Dutch Doll" quilt
was made in 1936 at
Springfield, TN by the
owner's aunt, Elizabeth
Porter Perkins (born 9/
25/1887 at Springfield,
died 9/21/1950 at
Springfield). The maker
gave the quilt to the
owner.

**Smith, Mary Willie Tubb** (Leighton)
Rock House Chapter
Ancestor: Charles Dibrell, VA —#581401
This "Crazy" quilt was made after 1927 at Sparta, TN by the owner's grandmother, Narcissa Rhea Dibrell (born 4/10/1864 at Sparta, married Sydney Stanton Dibrell, died 12/16/1948 at Sparta).

**Smith, Mary Willie Tubb** (Leighton)
Rock House Chapter
Ancestor: Charles Dibrell, VA —#581401
This "Dutch Boy/Overall Bill" quilt was made in 1974 at Sparta, TN by Lourenia Davis (married Taylor Davis). The owner bought the quilt from the maker.

**Smith, Mary Willie Tubb** (Leighton)
Rock House Chapter
Ancestor: Charles Dibrell, VA —#581401
This "Dutch Girl/Sunbonnet Sue" quilt was made by the owner's husband's grandmother, Lucinda Lynch Bledsoe (born at Sherwood, TN, married Leon Bledsoe, died at Nashville, TN). The quilt was given to Maibelle Bledsoe Smith who gave it to the owner.

**Smith, Mary Willie Tubb** (Leighton)
Rock House Chapter
Ancestor: Charles Dibrell, VA —#581401
This "Dutch Girl/Sunbonnet Sue" quilt was made in1975 at Sparta, TN by Lourenia Davis. The owner bought the quilt from the maker.

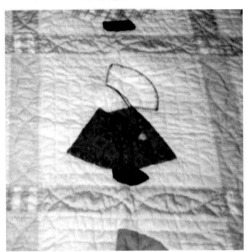

**Smith, Mary Willie Tubb** (Leighton)
Rock House Chapter
Ancestor: Charles Dibrell, VA — #581401
This "Combination Star" quilt was made at Sparta, TN by the owner's great grandmother, Amanda England Rhea (born 5/4/1840 at Sparta, married John Rhea, died 3/17/1916 at Sparta).

**Smith, Mary Willie Tubb** (Leighton)
Rock House Chapter
Ancestor: Charles Dibrell, VA —#581401
This "Tulip" quilt was made in the 1920's at Sherwood, TN by the owner's husband's grandmother, Lucinda Lynch Bledsoe.

**Smith, Patricia Williams** (Paul)
Tullahoma Chapter
Ancestor: Henry Haynes, PA —#686394
This "Crazy Patch" quilt was made before 1900 in Virginia by the owner's great grandmother.

**Smith, Patricia Williams** (Paul)
Tullahoma Chapter
Ancestor: Henry Haynes, PA —#686394
This "Cross and Crown" quilt was made by a woman named, McIntyre, who died in Washington, DC.

**Smothers, Ida Garrett Herod** (Fount Tillman, Jr.)
Jane Knox Chapter
Ancestor: William Herod, VA —#771603
This "Mexican Rose" quilt was made in the early 19th century by Mrs. Franklin Mayfield. The owner bought it from the estate of Mary Felice Ferrell in 1978 in Gallatin, TN.

**Smothers, Ida Garrett Herod** (Fount Tillman, Jr.)
Jane Knox Chapter
Ancestor: William Herod, VA — #771603
This "Baby/Building Blocks" woolen quilt was made in 1976 at Baton Rouge, LA by the owner (born 6/26/1932 at Hartsville, TN). Her family liked this quilt so well that she made another one for her son when he received his Ph.D. from the University of California in 1981.

**Smothers, Ida Garrett Herod** (Fount Tillman, Jr.)
Jane Knox Chapter
Ancestor: William Herod, VA —#771603
This "Double Star" quilt was made circa 1900 at Hartsville, TN by the owner's paternal grandmother, Victoria Isabella Garrett Herod (born 5/29/1861 at Dixon Springs, TN, married Wade Preston Herod, died 7/16/1943 at Hartsville). The quilt was passed from grandmother, to father, to owner.

**Smothers, Ida Garrett Herod** (Fount Tillman, Jr.)
Jane Knox Chapter
Ancestor: William Herod, VA — #771603
This "Star Burst" quilt was made in the mid 1800s or before. The quilt was passed down from the owner's husband's mother's family and passed to the owner at his mother's death in 1994.

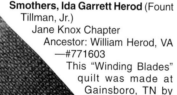

**Smothers, Ida Garrett Herod** (Fount Tillman, Jr.)
Jane Knox Chapter
Ancestor: William Herod, VA —#771603
This "Winding Blades" quilt was made at Gainsboro, TN by the owner's maternal Grandmother, Ida Johnson Johnson (born 8/17/1880 at Gainsboro, TN, married Norman Johnson, died 10/20/1962 at Gallatin, TN). The quilt was passed from the maker, to her daughter, to the owner.

**Smothers, Ida Garrett Herod** (Fount Tillman, Jr.)
Jane Knox Chapter
Ancestor: William Herod, VA —#771603
This "Broken Star" quilt was made in the 1930's at Nashville, TN by the owner's husband's mother, Ruth Moore Paschall Smothers (born 5/5/1901 in Arlington, TN, married Fount T. Smothers, Sr., died 9/13/1994 at Baton Rouge, LA). The maker gave the quilt to the owner.

**Smothers, Ida Garrett Herod** (Fount Tillman, Jr.)
Jane Knox Chapter
Ancestor: William Herod, VA —#771603
This "Crosses and Losses" quilt was made in 1977 at Baton Rouge, LA by the owner.

**Smothers, Ida Garrett Herod** (Fount Tillman, Jr.)
Jane Knox Chapter
Ancestor: William Herod, VA —#771603
This "Whig Rose" cross stitch quilt was made 1968-70 at Gallatin, TN by the owner's mother, Sammye Irene Johnson Herod (born 10/30/1903 at Gainsboro, TN, married Julius Edward Herod, died 6/30/1985 at Gallatin, TN). The maker gave the quilt to the owner.

**Smothers, Ida Garrett Herod**
(Fount Tillman, Jr.)
Jane Knox Chapter
Ancestor: William Herod, VA —
#771603
This "Elongated Hexagon" quilt
was made in 1940 at Hartsville,
TN by the owner's mother,
Sammye Irene Johnson Herod.
The maker gave the quilt to the
owner. The quilt is filled with wool
batting from sheep on the
maker's farm.

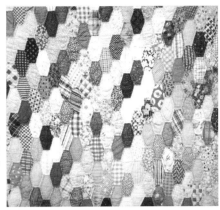

**Smothers, Ida Garrett
Herod** (Fount Tillman, Jr.)
Jane Knox Chapter
Ancestor: William Herod, VA
—#771603
This "Crazy" quilt was made
in the mid 1800's in Kentucky
by Mrs. M.L. Beddar (born
12/3/1806 at KY, died 9/17/
1895 at KY). The owner purchased the quilt in Dallas,
TX. Information about the
maker is embroidered on the
quilt.

**Snapp, Nancy J.**
French Lick Chapter
Ancestor: Lawrence
Snapp, Jr., VA —#784138
This "Grandmother's
Flower Garden" quilt was
made by the owner's
great–grandmother, Mary
Jane Howerth Young
(born 1860 at Zanesville,
OH, married Jesse B.
Young, died 1946 at Nash-
ville, TN). The owner re-
ceived the quilt from her
mother.

**Snapp, Nancy J.**
French Lick Chapter
Ancestor: Lawrence
Snapp, Jr., VA —#784138
This "Double Wedding
Ring" quilt was made in
1917 at Sumner County,
TN by the owner's great
aunt, Maude Daughtry
Keen (born 12/1/1897 at
Gallatin, TN, married Elzie
B. Keen, died 8/10/1974 at
Nashville, TN). This quilt
was passed from maker to
owner.

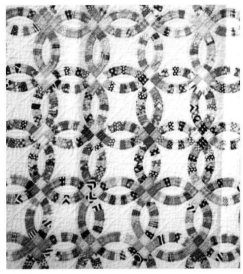

**Sorrels, Sherry Dryden**
(John)
Robert Lewis Chapter
Ancestor: Daniel McKissick,
NC —#777322
This "Cathedral Window"
quilt was made in 1966 at
Shelbyville, TN by the
owner's grandmother,
Emma Mae White Dryden
(born 10/26/1885, married
Thomas Floyd Dryden, died
2/9/1971 at Bedford County,
TN). This quilt was suppose
to have been completed by
the fall of 1966 where it was
to be entered in the State
Fair. But a good thing it was not, because that was the year the Tennessee State
Fair caught on fire."

**Sowell, Anne Cato** (Robert)
French Lick Chapter
Ancestor: John Medearis,
NC —#790408
This "T (Tallman)" quilt was
made around 1900 at Nash-
ville, TN by the owner's great
grandmother Anna Jones
Tallman (born 10/11/1852 at
Nashville, TN, married Ro-
maine Tallman, died 8/28/
1928 at Little Rock, AR). It
won second place in the "old
quilts" category at a quilt
show in Goodlettsville, TN.

**Speich, Lynn Reynolds** (Michael)
The Crab Orchard Chapter
Ancestor: Thomas Carlton, NC —
#718210
This "Georgetown Circle" quilt was
made in 1997 at Parsons, TN by the
owner's grandmother, Hattie Sue
Wheat Reynolds (born 1913 at Decatur
County, TN, married William Holland
Reynolds). The maker gave the quilt
to the owner as a wedding gift.

**Speich, Lynn Reynolds** (Michael)
The Crab Orchard Chapter
Ancestor: Thomas Carlton, NC —
#718210
This cross stitch embroidered "Tulip"
quilt was made in 1975 by the owner's
mother and grandmother, Hattie Sue
Wheat Reynolds. They embroidered
the pattern and then Hattie put the quilt
together and quilted it.

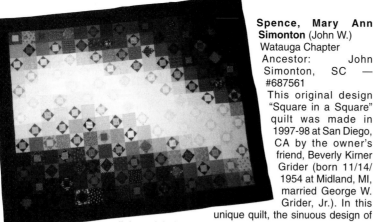

**Spence, Mary Ann Simonton** (John W.)
Watauga Chapter
Ancestor: John Simonton, SC — #687561
This original design "Square in a Square" quilt was made in 1997-98 at San Diego, CA by the owner's friend, Beverly Kirner Grider (born 11/14/1954 at Midland, MI, married George W. Grider, Jr.). In this unique quilt, the sinuous design of light and dark represent the Mississippi River, near which the owner and her husband have enjoyed their 53 year marriage. Quilted swirls represent the turbulent eddies such as those commonly found in swift moving currents.

**Spencer, Georgia Ann Giles** (W. Walter)
Old Glory Chapter
Ancestor: William Jordan, VA — #602167
This "Monkey Wrench" quilt was made in 1964 at Cheatham County, TN by the owner's mother-in-law, Ava Spencer (born 1/21/1922 at Clay County, TN, married Grady Spencer). The maker gave the quilt to the owner as a wedding present.

**Spencer, Sarah Head** (Cecil)
Robert Lewis Chapter
Ancestor: Sherwood Fowler, VA —#641853
This "Double Wedding Ring" quilt was made in 1935 at Marshall County by the owner's great aunt, Sarah Fowler (born 1836 at Marshall County, died 1939 at Marshall County). The owner requested the maker to take quilt scraps she provided and make a quilt.

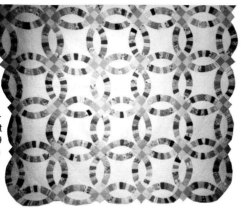

**Springer, Mary**
Andrew Bogle Chapter
Ancestor: Isaac Dawson-Rachael Dobbin, NC — #774183
**Springer, Rachael**
Andrew Bogle Chapter
Ancestor: Isaac Dawson-Rachael Dobbin, NC — #781351
**Springer, Julia Wright** (John)
Andrew Bogle Chapter
Ancestor: Isaac Dawson-Rachael Dobbin, NC — #728819

This "Double Wedding Ring" quilt was begun in 1984 at Martin, TN by the owner's mother, Mary Nell Lee Wright (born 1/5/1916 at Dresden, TN, married Harold Wright, died 11/5/1984 at Martin, TN). Mary Nell died suddenly with only the quilt top pieced. Her sister-in-law, Blanche Dunn and Annie Mae Wright, completed the quilt in memory of Mary Nell and in honor of Julia Springer and her daughters, Rachael, Mary and Esther.

**Stammer, Sara Harwell** (James)
Robert Lewis Chapter
Ancestor: James Merritt —#633612
This "Dresden Plate" quilt was made at Petersburg, TN and purchased circa 1939 from the maker.

**Stammer, Sara Harwell** (James)
Robert Lewis Chapter
Ancestor: James Merritt — #633612
This "Sunburst" quilt was made in 1937 at Ardmore, TN by the owner's good friend, Evelyn Smith Lewter (born 2/1909 at Ardmore, TN, married Mabron Lewter, died 2/1998 at Pulaski, TN). The quilt was given to the owner by the maker in 1980.

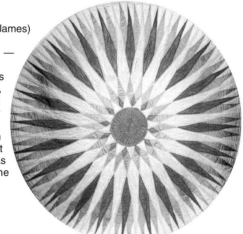

**Stanfill, Barbara Sullivan** (Robert)
Cumberland Chapter
Ancestor: Abel Gower, Jr., NC —#755453
This "Basket" quilt was pieced before 1970 and quilted in 1975. The owner bought the quilt top at a craft fair in Bellevue, TN from a woman who said her mother made it.

**Stanfill, Barbara Sullivan** (Robert)
Cumberland Chapter
Ancestor: Abel Gower, Jr., NC —#755453
This "Basket" quilt was started in 1937 at Nashville, TN by the owner's mother, Bessie Stephens Sullivan (born 8/3/1897 at Nashville, married Everett Vernon Sullivan, died 11/12/1978 at Nashville). The quilt was completed in 1998 by the owner.

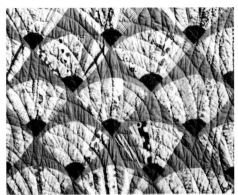

**Stanfill, Barbara Sullivan** (Robert)
Cumberland Chapter
Ancestor: Abel Gower, Jr., NC —#755453
This "Fan" quilt was made circa 1945 at Waverly, TN by the owner's mother-in-law, Hazel Cude Stanfill (born 11/28/1909 at Waverly, TN, married Eldridge Herman Stanfill). The maker gave the quilt to the owner in 1972.

**Stanfill, Barbara Sullivan** (Robert)
Cumberland Chapter
Ancestor: Abel Gower, Jr., NC —#755453
This "Fan" quilt was made circa 1945 at Waverly, TN by the owner's mother-in-law, Hazel Cude Stanfill.

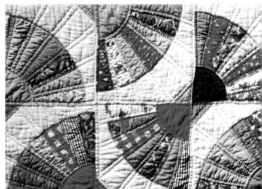

**Stanfill, Barbara Sullivan** (Robert)
Cumberland Chapter
Ancestor: Abel Gower, Jr., NC —#755453
This "Dutch Doll/Sunbonnet Sue" quilt was made circa 1938 at Nashville, TN by the owner's mother, Bessie Stephens Sullivan.

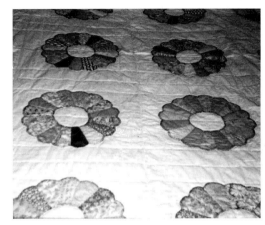

**Stanfill, Barbara Sullivan** (Robert)
Cumberland Chapter
Ancestor: Abel Gower, Jr., NC —#755453
This "Dresden Plate" quilt was made circa 1938 at Nashville, TN by the owner's mother, Bessie Stephens Sullivan.

**Stanfill, Barbara Sullivan** (Robert)
Cumberland Chapter
Ancestor: Abel Gower, Jr., NC —#755453
This "Double Wedding Ring" quilt was made circa 1937 at Nashville, TN by the owner's mother, Bessie Stephens Sullivan.

**Stanfill, Barbara Sullivan** (Robert)
Cumberland Chapter
Ancestor: Abel Gower, Jr., NC —#755453
This embroidered "Butterfly" quilt was made circa 1985 at Waverly, TN by the owner's mother-in-law, Hazel Cude Stanfill.

**Stanfill, Barbara Sullivan** (Robert)
Cumberland Chapter
Ancestor: Abel Gower, Jr., NC —#755453
This "Star" quilt was started before 1950 by the owner's grandmother, Martha Usery Stephens (born 9/16/1867 at Martin, TN, married William Franklin Stephens, died 7/23/1953 at Nashville). The quilt was finished by the owner.

**Stanfill, Barbara Sullivan** (Robert)
Cumberland Chapter
Ancestor: Abel Gower, Jr., NC —#755453
This "Irish Chain" quilt was made before 1950 at Nashville, TN by the owner's grandmother, Martha Usery Stephens (born 9/16/1867 at Martin, TN, married William Frank Stephens, died 7/23/1953 at Nashville, TN).

**Starnes, Rosemary Tarwater** (Billy M.)
Tullahoma Chapter
Ancestor: William Keebler, VA —#481151
This "Sunbonnet Babies" quilt came from the estate of the owner's aunt by marriage, Theo Mashburn Tarwater Hatcher.

**Starnes, Rosemary Tarwater**
(Billy M.)
Tullahoma Chapter
Ancestor: William Keebler, VA —
#481151
This "Grandmother's Flower Garden" quilt was made at Sevierville, TN by the owner's great grandmother, Sally Rule Tarwater (married Matthew Tarwater, died 10/16/1884).

**Steadman, Anna Frank Litz** (Carl)
Samuel Doak Chapter
Ancestor: Edward Smith, VA —#539372
This "Whole Cloth" quilt was made over 50 years ago at Kingsport, TN by the owner's mother-in-law, Myrtle Bariger Steadman (born 11/11/1898 at Sullivan County, TN, married George K. Steadman, Sr., died 5/26/1968 at Hamblen County, TN). This quilt was made from feed sacks.

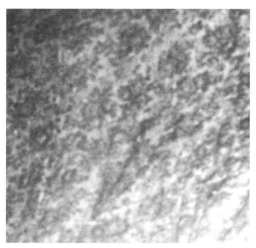

**Steadman, Carla**
Samuel Doak Chapter
Ancestor: Edward Smith, VA —#788377
This "Nine Patch" quilt was made 16 years ago at Hamblen County, TN by the owner's aunt, Elnora Crowder Steadman (born 8/26/1944 at Sullivan County, TN, married Harry Steadman). It was a birthday gift to the owner.

**Steen, Dorothy Lipham** (John W., Jr.)
Robert Cooke Chapter
Ancestor: George Rowe, VA —#724889
This "King's Crown" quilt was made in the 1940's at Heard County, GA by the owner's paternal grandmother, Mary Lucinda (Mollie) Leslie Lipham (born 7/12/1869 at Heard County, GA, married William Watkins Lipham, died 3/15/1947 at Heard County). The maker gave the quilt to Nell R. Lipham, the owner's mother, and she gave the quilt to the owner.

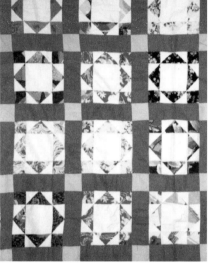

**Steen, Dorothy Lipham**
(John W., Jr.)
Robert Cooke Chapter
Ancestor: George Rowe, VA —#724889
This "Double Wedding Ring" quilt was made during World War II at Ohio County, KY by the owner's maternal grandmother, Minnie Lee Rowe Roeder, and aunt, Anabel Roeder Johnston. Minnie was born 11/9/1873 at Ohio County, KY, married John William Roeder, and died 1/2/1945. Anabel was born 7/13/1912 at Ohio County, KY, married Thomas Henry Johnston, and died 1/14/1997 at Ohio County. The owner has two of these quilts. They were pieced when Aunt Anabel returned to her family while Uncle Tommy was in the South Pacific during WWII. The quilt was given to the owner's mother who gave it to the owner at her marriage 9/2/1952.

**Steen, Dorothy Lipham**
(John W., Jr.)
Robert Cooke Chapter
Ancestor: George Rowe, VA —#724889
This "Strip" quilt was made in the summer and fall of 1995 at Nashville, TN by the owner (born 7/21/1930 at Orlando, FL).

**Steen, Dorothy Lipham**
(John W., Jr.)
Robert Cooke Chapter
Ancestor: George Rowe, VA —#724889
This "Flower In A Star" quilt was made circa 1988 at Ohio, KY by the owner's aunt, Annabel Roeder Johnston.

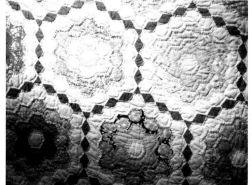

**Steen, Dorothy Lipham**
(John W., Jr.)
Robert Cooke Chapter
Ancestor: George Rowe, VA —#724889
This "Grandmother's Flower Garden" quilt was made circa 1940 at Ohio, KY by the owner's maternal grandmother, Minnie Lee Rowe Roeder.

**Steen, Dorothy Lipham**
(John W., Jr.)
Robert Cooke Chapter
Ancestor: George Rowe,
VA —#724889
This "Sawtooth Star" quilt was made in 1925 at Bloomfield, IN by the owner's great grandmother, Hannah Anne Blancherd Roeder (married John W. Roeder, married 2nd Kramer, died circa 1931). This quilt was made for a wedding present for the owner's mother, Nell Roeder when she married David Lipham 12/25/1925.

**Steen, Dorothy Lipham**
(John W., Jr.)
Robert Cooke Chapter
Ancestor: George Rowe, VA —#724889
This "Young Man's Fancy" quilt was made in 1930 at Ohio County, KY by the owner's maternal grandmother, Minnie Lee Rowe Roeder. The maker came from Kentucky to Florida for the birth of the owner. When she returned home she made this pink and white quilt and gave it to the owner.

**Steen, Dorothy Lipham**
(John W., Jr.)
Robert Cooke Chapter
Ancestor: George Rowe,
VA —#724889
This "Texas Star" quilt was made circa 1938-39 at Ohio County, KY by the owner's maternal grandmother, Minnie Lee Rowe Roeder. It is made from dresses the owner wore in elementary school. The quilt was passed from grandmother, to mother, to owner.

**Stegall, Barbara Greener**
(Risque)
Jackson-Madison Chapter
Ancestor: John Davis, NC
—#729673
This "Cathedral Window" quilt was made in 1988 at Jackson, TN by the owner's mother, Lillie Dodd Greener (born 1895 at Henderson County, TN, married David Greener, died 1992 at Parsons, TN). Lillie made this quilt when she was 93 years old.

**Stegall, Barbara Greener**
(Risque)
Jackson-Madison Chapter
Ancestor: John Davis, NC
—#729673
This "Log Cabin" quilt was made circa 1900 at Henderson County, TN by the owner's grandmother, Betty Eubank Dodd (born 1867 at Henderson County, married Phillip P. Dodd, died 1947 at Henderson County). The lining is dyed brown and the batting is hand-carded cotton grown on the farm.

**Stegall, Barbara Greener**
(Risque)
Jackson-Madison Chapter
Ancestor: John Davis, NC —#729673
This quilt was made in the early 1800's in North Carolina. The owner got this quilt from an elderly lady who was an old family friend. She told the owner that it was made by an ancestor who brought it to Tennessee from North Carolina in a covered wagon.

**Stegall, Barbara Greener** (Risque)
Jackson-Madison Chapter
Ancestor: John Davis, NC —#729673
This "Crazy Patch" quilt was made in the early 1800's at North Carolina. This quilt was also said to have come from North Carolina to Tennessee in a covered wagon.

**Stephens, Helen Nadine Heatherly**
(Arlis Marion)
Clinch Bend Chapter
Ancestor: John Childress, VA —#692385
This "Rainbow Star" quilt was made at Campbell County, TN by the owner's husband's mother, Ethel Lucinda Haggard Stephens (born 4/18/1889 at LaFollette, TN, married the Rev. Arlis McNelson Stephens, died 5/20/1969 at LaFollette). The maker's sister, Martha Ledie Haggard Stephens, helped. The owner's husband remembers his mother and aunt making many quilts. The Stephens and Haggard families are documented in Stephens and Haggard Families, Whitman Hollow On Norris Lake by Nadine H. Stephens.

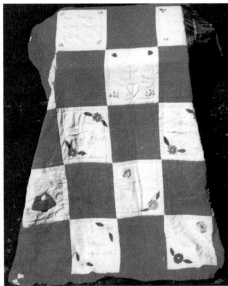

Stephens, Helen Nadine Heatherly (Arlis Marion) Clinch Bend Chapter Ancestor: John Childress, VA —#692385
This "Memory" quilt was made in the summer of 1983 at LaFollette, TN by the owner's niece, Sue Ellen Miller Nidiffer (born 1/23/1950 at LaFollettte, married Larry Nidiffer). She made the quilt for the owner's parents 60th wedding anniversary. The quilt was featured in Heatherlys and Related Families: Our Norris Lake Area Ancestry by Nadine Heatherly Stephens.

Stephens, Helen Nadine Heatherly (Arlis Marion) Clinch Bend Chapter Ancestor: John Childress, VA — #692385
This Christmas "Log Cabin" quilt was made in 1985 at LaFollette, TN by the owner's sister, Dorothy Sue Heatherly Miller (born 10/9/1927 at LaFollette, TN, married William Albert Miller). The maker made the quilt as a Christmas gift for the owner.

Stephens, Helen Nadine Heatherly (Arlis Marion) Clinch Bend Chapter Ancestor: John Childress, VA — #692385
This "Kittens" quilt was made in 1985 at Clinton, TN by the owner. She made this quilt in her first winter after retirement.

Stephens, Helen Nadine Heatherly (Arlis Marion) Clinch Bend Chapter Ancestor: John Childress, VA —#692385
This "Ripe Strawberries" quilt was made at Clinton, TN by the owner (born 7/12/1925 at La Follette). She started the quilt in 1984 after retiring as a school teacher. The pattern was from a childhood friend, Gracie Prater. Lucille Jennings, the mother of a former student, quilted the quilt.

Stephens, Helen Nadine Heatherly (Arlis Marion) Clinch Bend Chapter Ancestor: John Childress, VA —#692385
This "Trip Around the World" quilt was made in the 1930's in West Virginia by the owner's husband's aunt, Atrice Stephens Andrews (born 2/25/1898 at Anderson County, TN, married Joseph Andrews). The maker celebrated her 101 birthday in 1999.

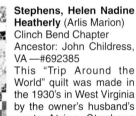

Stephens, Helen Nadine Heatherly (Arlis Marion) Clinch Bend Chapter Ancestor: John Childress, VA —#692385
This "Double Irish Chain" quilt was made in 1880-82 at Campbell, TN by the owner's great aunt and maternal grandmother, Sarah Cannon and Susan Cannon Spangler. Sarah was born in 1848 at Campbell County and died in 1892. Susan was born in 1851 and died in 1942. The sisters made this quilt before Susan's marriage to Ayers Maupin Spangler 8/27/1882. The fabric was purchased from a peddler. The cotton for the batting was grown on the farm. The quilt was featured in Heatherlys and Related Families: Our Norris Lake Area Ancestry by Nadine Heatherly Stephens.

Stephens, Helen Nadine Heatherly (Arlis Marion) Clinch Bend Chapter Ancestor: John Childress, VA —#692385
This "Smoothin' Iron/Sugar Loaf" quilt was made in 1890-1900 at Campbell County, TN by the owner's maternal great aunts, Mary and Lucinda Cannon. Mary was born in 1842 at Campbell County, TN and died in 1930. Lucinda was born in 1852 at Campbell County, married M. George Faust, died in 1925. This quilt was documented in Quilts of Tennessee. It won first place in the Oak Ridge Quilt and Antique Fair 12/7/1986.

Stephens, Helen Nadine Heatherly (Arlis Marion) Clinch Bend Chapter Ancestor: John Childress, VA —#692385
This "Chimney Sweep/Blocks" quilt was made in the early 1920's at Campbell County, TN by the owner's maternal aunts, Mary and Lucinda Cannon. This quilt was documented in Quilts of Tennessee .

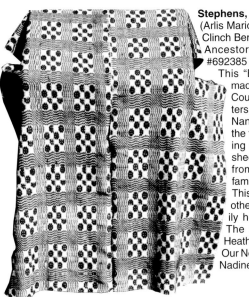

**Stephens, Helen Nadine Heatherly**
(Arlis Marion)
Clinch Bend Chapter
Ancestor: John Childress, VA —
#692385
This "Bear Track" coverlet was made in the 1870's at Campbell County, TN by the Cannon Sisters, Sarah, Mary, Susan and Nancy. The sisters worked in the fields growing flax and taking care of and shearing the sheep. Indigo was purchased from peddlers coming to the family home in a small buggy. This coverlet, along with many others, was woven in the family home in an upstairs room. The coverlet was featured in Heatherlys and Related Families: Our Norris Lake Area Ancestry by Nadine Heatherly Stephens.

**Stephens, Helen Nadine Heatherly** (Arlis Marion)
Clinch Bend Chapter
Ancestor: John Childress, VA —692385
This "Kitten" quilt was made in the late 1940's at Campbell County, TN by the owner's husband's mother, Ethel Haggard Stephens. The makers parents were the Reverend and Mrs. George Marion Haggard (Sarah Jane Sharp).

**Stephens, Helen Nadine Heatherly** (Arlis Marion)
Clinch Bend Chapter
Ancestor: John Childress, VA — #692385
This "Dutch Doll/ Sunbonnet Sue" quilt was made in 1942 at La Follette, TN by the owner. The quilt is made of flour sacks and fabric from the maker's dresses from her childhood.

**Stephens, Helen Nadine Heatherly** (Arlis Marion)
Clinch Bend Chapter
Ancestor: John Childress, VA —#692385
This "Radiant Star" quilt was made in 1898 at Claiborne County, TN by the owner's grandmother, Susan Cannon Spangler and passed from grandmother, to mother, to owner.

**Stephens, Helen Nadine Heatherly** (Arlis Marion)
Clinch Bend Chapter
Ancestor: John Childress, VA —#692385
This "Ocean Wave" quilt was made in 1890-1900 at Powell River, TN by the Cannon Sisters. This quilt was documented in Quilts of Tennessee .

**Stephens, Helen Nadine Heatherly** (Arlis Marion)
Clinch Bend Chapter
Ancestor: John Childress, VA —#692385
This "Prairie Star/Amish Star" quilt was made in 1890-1900 at Campbell County, TN by the Cannon Sisters.

**Stevens, Barbara Brown** (Jim)
Cavett Station Chapter
Ancestor: John Chestnut, VA —#575335
This "Rattle Snake/Rocky Road to Jerico" quilt was made circa 1900 at Somerset, KY by the owner's great grandmother by marriage, Mary Griffin Brown (born 4/1/1860 at Somerset, KY, married John Thomas Brown, died 12/26/1945 at Somerset).

**Stephens, Helen Nadine Heatherly** (Arlis Marion)
Clinch Bend Chapter
Ancestor: John Childress, VA —#692385
This "Broken Star" quilt was pieced in 1956 at La Follette, TN by the owner's friend, Nancy Wilson Rutherford (born 6/1/1884 at Campbell County, TN, married John Rutherford, died 12/9/1970 at La Follette, TN. It was quilted by Thelma Wilson Rutherford at Wartburg, TN.

**Stevens, Barbara Brown** (Jim)
Cavett Station Chapter
Ancestor: John Chestnut, VA —#575335
This "Double Wedding Ring" quilt was made at London, KY by the owner's great aunt, Minnie May Chestnut Estridge (born 9/4/1885 at Laurel, KY, died in 1950 at London, KY). The quilt was given to the owner when she was a baby.

**Stevens, Barbara Brown** (Jim)
Cavett Station Chapter
Ancestor: John Chestnut, VA —#575335
This "Storm At Sea" quilt was made in 1978 at Clinton, TN by the owner's mother, Lillian Irene Brown (born 11/9/1913 at Manchester, KY). The was the maker's first pieced quilt.

**Stevens, Elizabeth Washburn** (James D.)
Sarah Hawkins Chapter
Ancestor: Capt. James Gaines —#488268
This "Crazy" quilt was made circa the 1890's at Afton, TN by the owner's great grandmother, Margaret Marsh Jewell (born 6/7/1840 at Afton, TN, married David Rice Jewell, died 7/25/1911 at Afton).

**Stevens, Elizabeth Washburn** (James D.)
Sarah Hawkins Chapter
Ancestor: Capt. James Gaines —#488268
This "Whole Cloth" tied quilt was made circa the 1950's at Orangeburg, SC by the owner's mother-in-law, Virginia Wohlford Stevens (born 12/6/1909 at Richlands, VA, married Maurice Robert Stevens, died 2/24/1994 at Orangeburg, SC).

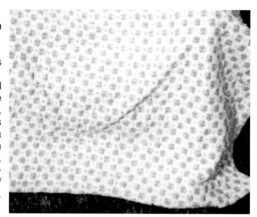

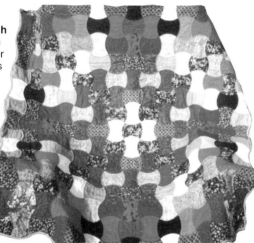

**Stevens, Elizabeth Washburn** (James D.)
Sarah Hawkins Chapter
Ancestor: Capt. James Gaines —#488268
This "Apple Core or Double Ax Handle" quilt was made in 1995 at Tucker, GA by the owner (born 9/18/1940 at Johnson City, TN.

**Stevens, Elizabeth Washburn** (James D.)
Sarah Hawkins Chapter
Ancestor: Capt. James Gaines —#488268
This "Bargello" quilt was made in 1995 at Tucker, GA by the owner.

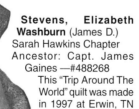

**Stevens, Elizabeth Washburn** (James D.)
Sarah Hawkins Chapter
Ancestor: Capt. James Gaines —#488268
This "Trip Around The World" quilt was made in 1997 at Erwin, TN by the owner.

**Stevens, Elizabeth Washburn** (James D.)
Sarah Hawkins Chapter
Ancestor: Capt. James Gaines —#488268
This "Log Cabin" quilt was made in 1997 at Erwin, TN by the owner.

**Stevens, Elizabeth Washburn** (James D.)
Sarah Hawkins Chapter
Ancestor: Capt. James Gaines —#488268
This "Scrap" quilt was made in the mid 1800's in East Tennessee probably by the owner's great grandmother, Margaret Jewell.

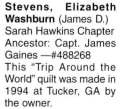

**Stevens, Elizabeth Washburn** (James D.)
Sarah Hawkins Chapter
Ancestor: Capt. James Gaines —#488268
This "Trip Around the World" quilt was made in 1994 at Tucker, GA by the owner.

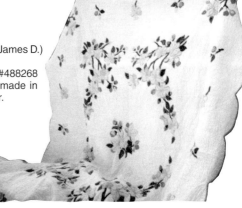

**Stevens, Elizabeth Washburn** (James D.)
Sarah Hawkins Chapter
Ancestor: Capt. James Gaines —#488268
This "Burgoyne Surrounded" quilt was made in 1996 at Tucker, GA by the owner.

**Stevens, Elizabeth Washburn** (James D.)
Sarah Hawkins Chapter
Ancestor: Capt. James Gaines —#488268
This "Apple Blossom" quilt was made in 1963 at Norfolk, VA by the owner.

**Stevens, Elizabeth Washburn** (James D.)
Sarah Hawkins Chapter
Ancestor: Capt. James Gaines —#488268
This "Double Irish Chain" quilt was made in 1994 at Tucker, GA by the owner.

**Stevens, Elizabeth Washburn** (James D.)
Sarah Hawkins Chapter
Ancestor: Capt. James Gaines —#488268
This "Bargello" quilt was made in 1993 at Tucker, GA by the owner.

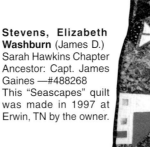

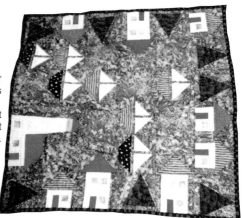

**Stevens, Elizabeth Washburn** (James D.)
Sarah Hawkins Chapter
Ancestor: Capt. James Gaines — #488268
This "Halloween Motif" quilt was made in 1997 at Erwin, TN by the owner.

**Stevens, Elizabeth Washburn** (James D.)
Sarah Hawkins Chapter
Ancestor: Capt. James Gaines —#488268
This "Seascapes" quilt was made in 1997 at Erwin, TN by the owner.

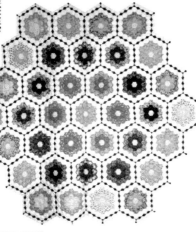

**Stewart, Dorothy England** (James C.)
Chief John Ross Chapter
Ancestor: William Bronough, VA — #526820
This "Grandmother's Flower Garden" quilt was made in 1931 at Caddo, OK by the owner's grandmother, Annie Bronough Pinson (born 2/22/1869 at Honey Grave, TX, married Benjamen Franklin Pinson, died 2/26/1956 at Durant, OK).

**Stover, Paula Swallows** (Donnie)
Roaring River Chapter
Ancestor: John Gore, VA — #774967
This "Eight Pointed Star" quilt was made in the 1870's at Miranda, TN by the owner's paternal great grandmother, Sarah Catherine Hannah Miranda Emeline Dodson (born at Overton County, TN, married in 1878, married 2nd in 1884 William Stanton Swallows, died 9/13/1894 at Overton County, TN). The quiltmaker used left over fabrics from her father's general store located at Miranda, TN. The quilt was passed to the maker's son, Arthur Franklin Swallows. He passed it to Roy E. Swallows who passed it to the current owner.

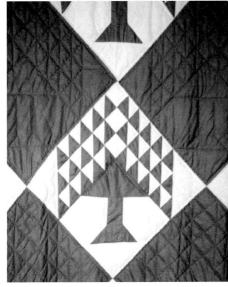

**Stover, Paula Swallows** (Donnie)
Roaring River Chapter
Ancestor: John Gore, VA — #774967
This "Tree of Life" quilt was made in 1960 at Overton County, TN by the owner's mother, Eva Dell Neal Swallows (born 6/28/1923 at Overton County, married Ray Ensor Swallows). She copied the pattern from a quilt made by the owner's great aunt, Polina Elizabeth Gore. This quilt won a blue ribbon at the Overton County Fair and a "Championship A" ribbon for the quilting in 1961.

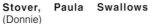

**Stover, Paula Swallows** (Donnie)
Roaring River Chapter
Ancestor: John Gore, VA — #774967
This coverlet was made in the 1870's at Overton County, TN by the owner's maternal great grandmother, Mary Tennessee "Polly" Copeland (born and died in Overton County, TN, married William Thomas Neal). The coverlet was passed to G. Chester

Neal, the maker's son, and then to Eva Dell Neal Swallows, and finally to the current owner. The coverlet won the "Best Antique Coverlet" award in the Overton County Fair in 1959, 1960 and 1961.

**Stover, Paula Swallows**
(Donnie)
Roaring River Chapter
Ancestor: John Gore, VA —
#774967
This "Crazy" quilt was made in the 1830's at Dodson Chapel Community by the owner's paternal grandmother, Mary Ingabird Gibbons Swallows (born 12/10/1890 at Overton County, TN, married Arthur Franklin Swallows, died 2/28/1962 at Overton County).

**Stover, Paula Swallows**
(Donnie)
Roaring River Chapter
Ancestor: John Gore, VA —
#774967
This "Lone Star" quilt was made in 1959 at Overton County, TN by the owner's mother, Eva Dell Neal Swallows .

**Strader, Laura Brawley**
William Cocke Chapter
Ancestor: Capt. Alexander Brevard, NC —#771480
This "Sunshine and Shadows" quilt was made in Cosby, TN at Holloway's Country Home Quilts, a working craft studio located on the Cosby Highway. The owner's twelve year old daughter, Samantha, chose this quilt to finish off her newly decorated room.

**Strader, Laura Brawley**
William Cocke Chapter
Ancestor: Capt. Alexander Brevard, NC —#771480
This "Nautical Star" quilt was also made in Cosby, TN at Holloway's Country Home Quilts.

**Strickland, Hazel Volz**
Clinch Bend Chapter
Ancestor: George Hendricks, VA — #735561
This "Star" quilt was made in 1943 at Cheyenne, WY by the owner's mother, Loyal Volz (born in Iowa, married Earl Volz, died 11/1968 at Cheyenne).

**Strader, Laura Brawley**
William Cocke Chapter
Ancestor: Capt. Alexander Brevard, NC —#771480
This "Variable Star" quilt was made in Cosby, TN at Holloway's Country Home Quilts.

**Sullivan, Carolyn Ramsey** (Nick)
Margaret Gaston Chapter
Ancestor: John Macon, NC —#756739
This " Triple Irish Chain" quilt was made in 1940 at Coffee County, TN. The owner's grandmother had it made for her as a wedding gift.

**Sullivan, Carolyn Ramsey** (Nick)
Margaret Gaston Chapter
Ancestor: John Macon, NC —#756739
This "Tree of Life" quilt was made in 1940 at Coffee County, TN. The owner's grandmother had it made for her as a wedding gift.

**Sullivan, Carolyn Ramsey** (Nick)
Margaret Gaston Chapter
Ancestor: John Macon, NC — #756739
This "Star and Compass" quilt was made in the 1890's at Coffee County, TN by the owner's great great aunt, Kate Cunningham (married Thomas Lenoir Cunningham, died at age 80 circa 1947 at Manchester, TN).

**Sullivan, Carolyn Ramsey** (Nick)
Margaret Gaston Chapter
Ancestor: John Macon, NC — #756739
This "Double Bow Tie" quilt was made before 1920 by the owner's grandmother, Pearl Cunningham Crouch (born 4/30/1882 at Morrison, TN, married Richard Crouch, died 5/1974 at Manchester, TN).

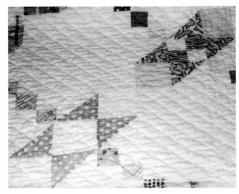

**Stultz, Joan Harris** (Robert)
The Crab Orchard Chapter
Ancestor: Israel Harris —
#352454
This Jacob's Ladder/Stepping Stones" quilt was made in Indiana by the owner's grandmother, Clara Mead (born in the 1870's in Indiana and died in Indiana)

**Summar, Bess Hill** (W.C.)
Jane Knox Chapter
Ancestor:Johnston Easton, VA —#592821
This "Grandmother's Flower Garden" quilt was made in 1940 at Smitheville, TN by the owner's mother-in-law, Mrs. C.A. Summar (born 1881 at Woodbury, TN, died 1963 at McMinnville, TN).

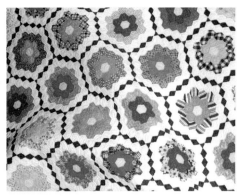

**Summers, Frances Freels** (Joseph)
Chucalissa Chapter
Ancestor: William Tunnell, VA —#636573
This "Bird" quilt was made circa 1979 at Anderson County, TN by the owner's mother, Alma Nichols Freels (born 2/19/1898 at Holden, MO, married Samuel Edgar Freels, died 12/29/1998 at Memphis, TN). The maker bought blocks of fabric with birds printed on them because her son-in-law, Joe Summers, liked birds. She put them together with fabric to match the owner's bedroom.

**Summers, Frances Freels** (Joseph)
Chucalissa Chapter
Ancestor: William Tunnell, VA —#636573
This "Cathedral Window" quilt was made in 1978 in Middle Tennessee by a group of Mennonite ladies.

**Sutton, Donna Susan**
Caney Fork Chapter
Ancestor: William Gregory, NC —#629241
This "Doll" quilt was made in 1981 at Buffalo Creek, TN by Dorothy Foreman. The owner won the quilt at a fundraiser for Defeated Elementary School.

**Sutton, Donna Susan**
Caney Fork Chapter
Ancestor: William Gregory, NC —#629241
This 'Double Wedding Ring" quilt was made in 1937 at Russell Hill, TN by the owner's maternal grandmother, Hallie Russell (born 12/15/1915 at Pleasant Shade, TN, married Robert E. Russell, died 6/20/1995 at Carthage, TN). "The quilt was made for my mother when she was a baby and given to me by my mother."

**Sutton, Nina Russell** (Ernest C).
Caney Fork Chapter
Ancestor: William Gregory, NC —#613946
This "Crazy" quilt was made in the 1880's in Texas by the owner's great aunt, Amanda Cartwright (born 3/29/1847 at Smith County, TN, died 3/1920 at Nashville, TN). At the death of the maker, the quilt was left to the owner's mother, Hallie Russell, who left the quilt to the owner. Amanda was a seamstress who had a dress shop in Texas and on Defeated Creek in the Difficult Community. This quilt is made from scraps of velvet left over from garments made for customers.

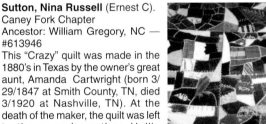

**Sutton, Nina Russell** (Ernest C).
Caney Fork Chapter
Ancestor: William Gregory, NC —#613946
This "Maple Leaf" quilt was made in 1947 in Smith County, TN by the owner's grandmother, Edna McDonald Russell (born 12/12/1881 at Madison County, TN, married Lum Taylor Russell, died 1/19/1963 at Wilson County, TN).

**Swain, Katherine Jane**
Robert Cooke Chapter
Ancestor: Nathaniel Boddie, NC —#476246
This "Jacob's Ladder" quilt was left to the owner by her cousin, Martha Aston Bair (died 2/11/1996). She had purchased the quilt in North Carolina.

**Talley, Mildred Barker** (James Richard)
Judge David Campbell Chapter
Ancestor: John Tipton, VA — #741527
This "White Stuffed" quilt was made in 1862 at Brittsville, TN by the owner's great great grandmother, Elizabeth Wood Wilson (born 4/5/1819, died 3/26/1879). The quilt was made during the War Between the States and is approximately 135 years old. It was in the frame for one year at the home of Elizabeth at Brittsville, TN. Her son, David Wood Wilson, married Emily Ellen Tipton who gave the quilt to their daughter, Icie Wilson Barker, who gave it to her granddaughter, the current owner. Her parents were Alvin and Claytie Barker. The quilt was on display at the Citizen Tri County Bank at Dunlap, TN in 1993. The quilt was given to the owner on her wedding day, July 20, 1952.

**Talley, Mildred Barker** (James Richard)
Judge David Campbell Chapter
Ancestor: John Tipton, VA — #741527
This "Washington's Plume" quilt was made in 1900 at Whiteville, TN by the owner's maternal grandmother, Esther Grayson Hudson (born 11/10/1863 at Whiteville, TN, married Byron Heard Hudson, died 5/25/1939 at Whiteville). The quilt was given to the maker's tenth child, a daughter, Claytie Hudson, who gave the quilt to her only child, the current owner.

**Talley, Mildred Barker** (James Richard)
Judge David Campbell Chapter
Ancestor: John Tipton, VA — #741527
This "Bethlehem Star" quilt was made in 1942 at Dunlap, TN by the owner's mother, Claytie Hudson Barker (born 5/19/1906 at Whiteville, TN, married Alvin Wilson Barker, died 9/2/1974 at Chattanooga, TN). The cotton was grown on the farm. It was picked, seeded and carded to form batts for the quilt.

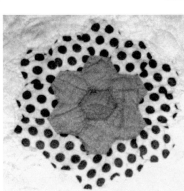

**Talley, Mildred Barker** (James Richard)
Judge David Campbell Chapter
Ancestor: John Tipton, VA — #741527
This "Grandmother's Flower Garden" quilt was made in 1940 at Dunlap, TN by the owner's grandmother, Icie Wilson Barker (born 11/26/1874 at Georgetown, TN, married James Floyd Barker, died 8/24/1968 at Hamilton County, TN). Claytie Hudson Barker helped quilt the quilt. Home grown cotton was used for the quilt. Icie seeded the cotton and Claytie carded the cotton for batts. They used home made quilting frames that were hung so that the quilt could be hoisted to the ceiling at night and when no one was quilting. The maker gave the quilt to the owner's father, Alvin Wilson Barker, who gave it to the owner.

**Talley, Mildred Barker** (James Richard)
Judge David Campbell Chapter
Ancestor: John Tipton, VA — #741527
This "Double Wedding Ring" quilt was pieced in 1948 at Dunlap, TN by the owner's paternal grandmother, Icie Wilson Barker. It was quilted by the maker and Claytie Hudson Barker.

**Talley, Mildred Barker** (James Richard)
Judge David Campbell Chapter
Ancestor: John Tipton, VA — #741527
This "Flower Basket" quilt was made in 1960 at Dunlap, TN by the owner's mother, Claytie Hudson Barker.

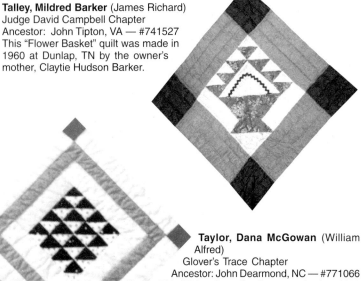

**Talley, Mildred Barker** (James Richard)
Judge David Campbell Chapter
Ancestor: John Tipton, VA — #741527
This "Little Boys' Britches" quilt was made in 1948 at Dunlap, TN by the owner's mother, Claytie Hudson Barker.

**Taylor, Dana McGowan** (William Alfred)
Glover's Trace Chapter
Ancestor: John Dearmond, NC — #771066
This "Flying Geese" quilt was made circa 1918 at Camden, TN by the owner's husband's grandmother, Ella Virginia Weatherly Hudson (born 8/12/1857 at Camden, TN, married Christopher K. Hudson, died 7/18/1921 at Camden). The quilt was passed to the maker's only child, Beulah Hudson Taylor, and then to her son.

**Taylor, Dana McGowan** (William Alfred)
Glover's Trace Chapter
Ancestor: John Dearmond, NC — #771066
This "Tulip" quilt was made in 1918 at Camden, TN by the owner's husband's grandmother, Ella Virginia Weatherly Hudson. The quilt was passed from the owner's husband's mother's estate to the owner.

**Taylor, Dana McGowan** (William Alfred)
Glover's Trace Chapter
Ancestor: John Dearmond, NC — #771066
This "Double Wedding Ring" quilt was made in the 1950's at Camden, TN by the owner's husband's mother, Beulah Hudson Taylor (born 10/24/1884 at Camden, married William Clarence Taylor, died 2/19/1966 at Camden). The quilt was passed from maker to her son's family.

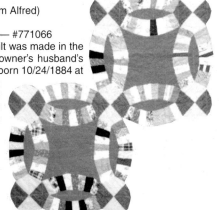

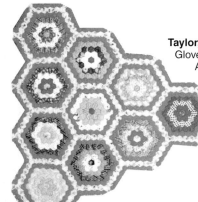

**Taylor, Dana McGowan** (William Alfred)
Glover's Trace Chapter
Ancestor: John Dearmond, NC — #771066
This "Grandmother's Flower Garden" quilt was made in the 1930's at Camden, TN by the owner's husband's mother, Beulah Hudson Taylor.

**Taylor, Dana McGowan**
(William Alfred)
Glover's Trace Chapter
Ancestor: John Dearmond,
NC — #771066
This "Nine Patch" quilt was
made in the 1950's at
Camden, TN by the owner's
husband's mother, Beulah
Hudson Taylor.

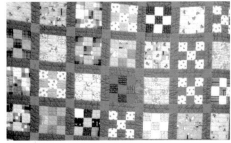

**Teeters, Carol Ruth Reynolds**
(Mitchell)
The Crab Orchard Chapter
Ancestor: Thomas Carleton, NC —
#718209
This "Patch On Patch/Square in a
Square" quilt was made in 1988 at
Parsons, TN by the owner's grand-
mother, Hattie Sue Wheat Reynolds
(born 2/6/1913 at Decatur County,
TN, married William Holland
Reynolds). The quilt was given by the
maker to the owner as a wedding gift.

**Tennessee DAR Centennial
Quilt**
This quilt was made in 1996 by
TSDAR Chapters and Daughters
across the state in celebration of
Tennessee's Centennial.

**Templeton, Annie Glenn
DuBois** (Dick A.)
King's Mountain Messenger
Chapter
Ancestor: Josiah Martin, NC
— #748198
This "Grandmother's Flower
Garden" quilt was made in
the 1930's during the De-
pression by the owner's
mother, Ada B. Reeves
DuBois (born 3/30/1898 at
Brown's Mill, TN, married W.
Hubert DuBois, died 9/4/
1980 at Murfreesboro, TN).

**Templeton, Annie Glenn
DuBois** (Dick A.)
King's Mountain Messenger
Chapter
Ancestor: Josiah Martin, NC —
#748198
This "Whirligig" quilt was made
circa 1890 at Rutherford County,
TN by the owner's grandmother,
Emma Beatrice Fathera Reeves
(born 10/12/1866 at Sharpsville,
TN, married John Chapman
Reeves, died 7/15/1943 at
Murfreesboro, TN). The quilt
was passed from grandmother,
to mother, to current owner.

**Thoma, Margaret Hinkle** (Eldon Bracton)
Tullahoma Chapter
Ancestor: Johann Michael Frey, NC — #768266
This "Grandmother's Flower Garden" quilt
was in the possession of the owner's
mother, Margaret Roundtree Scruggs
Hinkle. It was made by the owner's great
grandmother, Margaretha Kubli (born 10/
22/1839, died in 1919 at Bellbuckle, TN)
or her mother, Maria Magdelina Zweifel
(born 10/12/1806). This family was from
Netstal, Switzerland. They first lived in
Nashville, TN. The owner's maternal great
grandmother was first married to William
Roundtree who died while serving with the Tennessee Calvary. They had two children, the oldest died as
a baby. The quilt is silk and is English stitching.

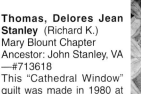

**Thomas, Annice Wear** (Dewell)
Spencer Clack Chapter
Ancestor: Samuel Wear, VA —#
481152
This "Princess Feather" quilt was
made in 1840 at Kodak, TN by the
owner's husband's great grandmother,
Nancy Underwood Smith (born 2/2/
1828 at Kodak, TN, married Pleasent
S. Smith, died 6/8/1898 at Kodak). The
quilt was passed from Nancy, to
Alexander Smith, to Carrie Smith Thomas, to the current owner.

**Thomas, Delores Jean
Stanley** (Richard K.)
Mary Blount Chapter
Ancestor: John Stanley, VA
—#713618
This "Cathedral Window"
quilt was made in 1980 at
New Orleans, LA by the
owner. She was inspired to
make the quilt by a pillow
she saw.

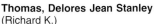

**Thomas, Delores Jean Stanley**
(Richard K.)
Mary Blount Chapter
Ancestor: John Stanley, VA —
#713618
This "Pinwheel/Windmill" quilt was
made in 1930 at Syracuse, NY by
Mrs. Yale. The quilt was pur-
chased by the owner at an estate
sale in Luling, LA.

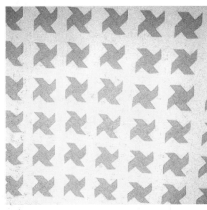

**Thomas, Delores Jean
Stanley** (Richard K.)
Mary Blount Chapter
Ancestor: John Stanley, VA —
#713618
This "Spray of Flowers" quilt was
made in 1954 at Chilliocothe, OH
by a 45 year old woman. The
quilt was a wedding present for
the owner on January 21, 1954.

**Thomas, Delores Jean Stanley**
(Richard K.)
Mary Blount Chapter
Ancestor: John Stanley, VA —
#713618
This "Nine Patch" quilt was made
in 1975 by the owner's aunt, Carrie Billups (born in Hamlin, NY).

**Thomas, Delores Jean Stanley**
(Richard K.)
Mary Blount Chapter
Ancestor: John Stanley, VA —
#713618
This "Butterfly" trapunto quilt was
made in 1975 at Luling, LA by the
owner.

**Thomas, Deona**
Caney Fork Chapter
Ancestor: Powell Hughes, VA —#
718428
This "Crazy" quilt was made in 1878 at
Hickman, TN by the owner's great great
grandmother, Elizabeth Ward Gwaltney
(born 9/1/1831 at Hickman, TN, married
Thomas Gwaltney, died 2/25/1897 at
Hickman). Her daughter, Lucy, helped.
They also weaved the back of the quilt
on a loom with wool. The quilt is signed
"A" for Adelia, the owner's grandmother,
and "Lucy" for the owner's great grandmother. Lucy passed the quilt to her
daughter, Adelia, and on to the owner's
mother, Frances, who passed the quilt
to the owner.

**Thomas, Deona**
Caney Fork Chapter
Ancestor: Powell Hughes, VA —#
718428
This "Square With the World" quilt was
pieced in 1987 at Hickman, TN by the
owner (born 12/15/1955 at Nashville,
TN). When she made this quilt, she was
Womens Missionary Union director of
the New Salem Association for the Centennial Celebration in May, 1988. She
carried the quilt to Richmond, VA in May,
1988 where it won first place (a purple
ribbon) at the Womens Missionary
Union Centennial Celebration. The 24
sections of the world each represent a
part of Women's Missionary Union His-
tory. The quilt was quilted by the owner's aunt, Oleta Gwaltney.

**Thomas, Joyce Carson** (Alfred)
Rhea Craig Chapter
Ancestor: Robert Cooke, VA —
#550833
This "Turkey Track" quilt was
made in 1935 at Madisonville, TN
by the owner's mother, Mrs.
Cooke Carson (born 1897 in Kentucky, married Cooke T. Carson,
died in TN in 1976).

**Thomas, Sarah**
Sarah Hawkins Chapter
Ancestor: Joseph Williams —
#663602
**Thomas, Anna**
Sarah Hawkins Chapter
Ancestor: Joseph Williams —
#663601
This "Bow Tie/Fan Variation" quilt
was purchased by the owners at
an auction in 1975.

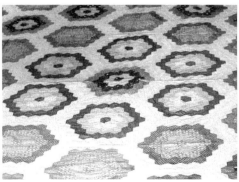

**Thomas, Sarah**
Sarah Hawkins Chapter
Ancestor: Joseph Williams
— #663602
**Thomas, Anna**
Sarah Hawkins Chapter
Ancestor: Joseph Williams
— #663601
This "Grandmother's
Flower Garden" quilt was
pieced in 1860-1900 by the
owners' grandmother.

**Thomas, Sarah**
Sarah Hawkins Chapter
Ancestor: Joseph Williams
— #663602
**Thomas, Anna**
Sarah Hawkins Chapter
Ancestor: Joseph Williams
— #663601
This "Dresden" Plate quilt
was purchased by the own-
ers at an auction in 1975.

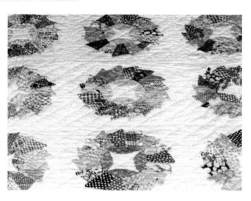

**Thomas, Tedra Hicks** (Thomas)
Andrew Bogle Chapter
Ancestor: Andrew Flesher, VA —
#562600
This crib quilt was made in
1924 at West Frankfort, IL by
the owner's great grand-
mother, Mary McCarnes (born
circa 1852 in Scotland, died circa
1950 in West Frankfort, IL). The
quilt was made for the owner's
mother's birth.

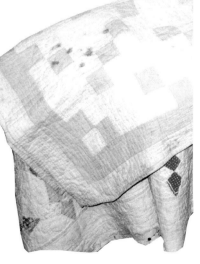

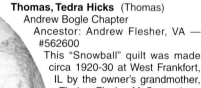

**Thomas, Tedra Hicks** (Thomas)
Andrew Bogle Chapter
Ancestor: Andrew Flesher, VA —
#562600
This "Snowball" quilt was made
circa 1920-30 at West Frankfort,
IL by the owner's grandmother,
Thelma Flesher McCarnes born
2/15/1896 at Taylorsville, IL,
married Joe, died 12/10/1980
at Moumouth, IL). The quilt
was passed from grand-
mother to granddaughter.

**Thomason, Ruth Hopwood**
(Andrew J.)
General William Lenoir Chapter
Ancestor: James Collins, NC —
#761504
This "Dresden Plate" quilt was made in Knoxville, TN around 1965 by the owner (born 7/1/1925 at Florence, AL)

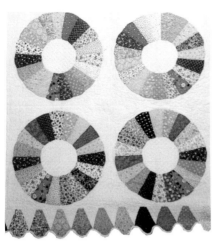

**Thompson, Anna Baker** (Sam W. L.)
Hatchie Chapter
Ancestor: William Hall, NC — #374533
This "Tumbling Blocks" quilt was made circa 1973 at Jackson, TN by the owner's husband's sister, Sarah Elizabeth Thompson Colville (born 9/19/1904 at Chattanooga, TN, married Hugh Winthrope Colville, died 5/9/1996 at Memphis, TN). This small quilt was made of silk scraps and a blue satin backing and border. The maker was very artistic and very generous in sharing her creations with others. The maker gave the owner this quilt as a Christmas present.

**Thompson, Anna Baker**
(Sam W. L.)
Hatchie Chapter
Ancestor: William Hall, NC —#374533
This "Double Wedding Ring" quilt was pieced before 1947 at Union City, TN by the owner's husband's sister, Sarah Elizabeth Thompson Colville. The quilt was quilted by the Circle I Women's Association (formerly known as the Ladies Aide) of the Northside Presbyterian Church in Chattanooga,

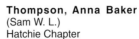

**Thompson, Anna Baker**
(Sam W. L.)
Hatchie Chapter
Ancestor: William Hall, NC — #374533
This "Seth Thomas Rose" quilt was pieced circa 1971 at Jackson, TN by the owner's husband's sister, Sarah Elizabeth Thompson Colville. This quilt was also quilted by the Circle I at the Northside Presbyterian Church in Chattanooga.

TN. This group has been quilting together since the beginning of the church. They contribute their proceeds to the church. This quilt was a wedding gift from the maker to the owner over 50 years ago.

**Thompson, Anna Baker** (Sam W. L.)
Hatchie Chapter
Ancestor: William Hall, NC —#374533
This "Drummer's Samples" quilt was made before 1907 at Hickory Valley, TN by the owner's maternal great grandmother, for whom the owner is named, Ann Eliza Moorman Beck (born 8/1/1845 at Salem, MS, married Col. William Davis Beck, died 5/17/1921 at Bolivar, TN). Col. Beck was the first cousin of Nathan Bedford Forrest. The owner's Grandfather McNaulty's store in Hickory Valley, TN sold general merchandise - even caskets. There were fabric sample books for men's suits. When out of date,

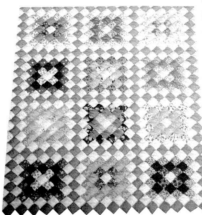

**Thompson, Anna Baker** (Sam W. L.)
Hatchie Chapter
Ancestor: William Hall, NC — #374533
This "Postage Stamp" quilt was pieced circa the 1930's at Chattanooga, TN by the owner's husband's mother, Carrie Elizabeth Lindsay Thompson Post (born 4/23/1878 at Rome, GA, married Fredrick Hampton Thompson, her first husband, died 2/10/1944 at Chattanooga, TN). Many years after the maker died, her sister, Sarah Elizabeth Colville, had the top quilted by the Circle I group at the Northside Presbyterian Church in Chattanooga.

these samples were made into quilts by Grandfather McNaulty's mother-in-law, Mrs. Beck. She pieced these samples into quilts using herring bone stitches.

**Thompson, Anna Baker** (Sam W. L.)
Hatchie Chapter
Ancestor: William Hall, NC —#374533
This coverlet is possibly a variation of the "Dolly Pratt" pattern. It was made circa 1840-50 at Hardeman County, TN by the owner's great great great grandmother's sister, Sarah Robin Legate (born 4/7/1789 at Orange County, NC, married William Legate, died 6/21/1868 at Hardeman County, TN). The coverlet was probably passed from the maker, to the owner's great great great grandmother, Mary Robinson Woods, who passed it to her daughter, Margaret Ann Woods McNaulty, then to her son, David William McNaulty, to his son David Moorman McNaulty, then to his daughter, Annie Lee McNaulty Baker, and then to the current owner. Sarah Robinson Legate was a grandmother of Michael Robinson, Revolutionary War patriot of Orange County, NC, She came with her parents, the James Robinsons, to Hardeman County in the early 1830's. Her husband left her, but she remained in the neighborhood of her sister, Mary Robinson Woods, wife of Squire David Robinson Woods. David was the first chairman of the Hardeman County Court. The Woods had a daughter who married Joseph Spears McNaulty.

**Thomason, Christy Shore** (William M., III)
James Buckley Chapter
Ancestor: John Reden, VA — #742896
This "ABC" nursery quilt was made in 1994 in Obion County, TN by the owner's mother-in-law, Allyson (born at Union City, TN, married William Marvin Thompson, II).

**Thorton, Ann Cox** (W.I.)
Key Corner Chapter
Ancestor: Samuel McClure, VT — # 650051

This "Double Wedding Ring" quilt was pieced in the early 1930's at Dyersburg, TN by the owner's husband's grandmother, Mary Elizabeth Morton Tucker born 10/21/1872 at Double Bridges, TN, married William Henry Tucker, died 1/5/1955 at Dyersburg, TN). It was quilted by someone else. W.I. remembers his grandmother working on the pieces and sewing them together when he was a little boy.

**Thorton, Terry Simmons** (Macon)
Col. Jethro Sumner Chapter
Ancestor: James Curry, Jr., NC —#630399

This "Log Cabin" quilt was pieced circa 1975 at Brownsville, TN by the owner's mother-in-law, Lorraine Regen Thorton (born 10/1/1917 at Nashville, TN, married Dr. John Claiborne Thorton, Jr.). The quilt was quilted by Ruby Timbs. It was given to the owner as a wedding gift in 1975.

**Thorton, Terry Simmons** (Macon)
Col. Jethro Sumner Chapter
Ancestor: James Curry, Jr., NC — #630399

This "Sunbonnet Sue" quilt was pieced in the 1930's and quilted in 1977 at Brownsville, TN. It was pieced by the owner's grandmother, Araminta Ivie Lea Barcroft (born 11/27/1897 at Haywood County, TN, married Robert Jenkins Barcroft, died 9/15/1985 in the same county). It was pieced from scraps of dresses belonging to the maker's daughter, Bobbie Barcroft Simmons. It was presented to the owner's daughter and maker's namesake, Aromonita Lea Thorton, on her first Christmas in 1977. The quilt top was then quilted by a church quilting group.

**Thorton, Terry Simmons** (Macon)
Col. Jethro Sumner Chapter
Ancestor: James Curry, Jr., NC —#630399

This "Trip Around the World" quilt was made in the early 1900's at Brownsville, TN by a long time family friend Sue Nesbitt Forrest (died in the 1940's or 50's at Haywood County, TN). Sue was maker of fine quilts in the Brownsville, TN area and a lifelong family friend of the Thortons. The quilted was passed to her son, Walter, and later to the Thorton Family.

**Thorton, Terry Simmons** (Macon)
Col. Jethro Sumner Chapter
Ancestor: James Curry, Jr., NC — #630399

This "Grandmother's Flower Garden" quilt was made in Brownsville, TN in 1975 by the owner's grandmother, Araminta Ivie Lea Barcroft. The briar stitching is characteristic of the maker's quilts. The maker gave the quilt to the owner as a wedding gift in 1975.

**Thorton, Terry Simmons** (Macon)
Col. Jethro Sumner Chapter
Ancestor: James Curry, Jr., NC — #630399

This "Crazy" quilt was made circa 1940's at Brownsville, TN by the owner's grandmother, Araminta Ivie Lea Barcroft. The quilt was passed from the maker, to her daughter, Bobbie Barcroft Simmons, to her daughter, the current owner.

**Thweatt, Mary Johnson** (John H.)
Captain William Edmiston Chapter
Ancestor: Samuel Abney, Jr., SC — #688085

This "String" quilt was made in the early 1920's at Longview, TX by the owner's great grandmother, Novi Poag Killingsworth (born circa 1860 at Marshall, TX, married A.A. Killingsworth, died 1936 at Longview, TX). The owner inherited the quilt from her mother, Grace Killigsworth Blackwell Johnson. Making quilts was a matter of every day work for women of the owner's family. They made their clothes, kept the scraps, cut the scraps, and gradually combined them into a quilt top. The designs and fabrics were varied and interesting, but also a catalog of the family's clothes over a period of time. The owner often caught her grandmother pointing to some of the pieces, quietly remembering some of the dresses and skirts and the moments when they were worn. They were the last real physical contact she had with the personal items of her mother. The owner says, "you may find two or three quilt tops on a quilt. They were covered regularly and allowed to "wash" in a gentle rain. They smelled wonderful!!"

**Thweatt, Mary Johnson** (John H.)
Captain William Edmiston Chapter
Ancestor: Samuel Abney, Jr., SC — #688085

This "Butterfly" quilt was made in the 1930's Hallsville, TX by the owner's grandmother, Novi Killingsworth Bolding (born 9/24/1882 at Longview, TX, married R.W. Bolding, died 8/25/1968 at Hallsville, TX). The owner believes this is one of the maker's earliest quilts because she is less careful with her designs and color. This reveals more of her personality. "The Butterflies remind me of the fairy moths that flutter around the tall pink and white hollyhocks in my grandmother's garden and along the fence of her chicken yard."

**Thweatt, Mary Johnson** (John H.)
Captain William Edmiston Chapter
Ancestor: Samuel Abney, Jr., SC — #688085

This "Dutch Doll/Sunbonnet Sue" quilt was made in the 1940's at Hallsville, TX by the owner's grandmother, Novi Killingsworth Bolding. Unlike her mother, Novi bought matching fabrics for her "creations." She thought more about her designs and colors. There is still a quality of playfulness. "I get the feeling that nothing ever went wrong in the world this quilt came from."

**Thweatt, Mary Johnson** (John H.)
Captain William Edmiston Chapter
Ancestor: Samuel Abney, Jr., SC — #688085

This "Grandmother's Flower Garden" quilt was pieced in the 1930's at Hallsville, TX by the owner's grandmother, Novi Killingsworth Bolding. This was the maker's last quilt. She had become aware of the close attention to detail and workmanship needed in a more "modern" world. She passed this along only as a quilt top. It was quilted by a lady in Montgomery County in the 1980's. The quilt reflects the "thoughtful and mature" grandmother the owner knew as a "young woman." "But how lucky I was to have known the slightly wild grandmother who thought that making quilts was something fun to do."

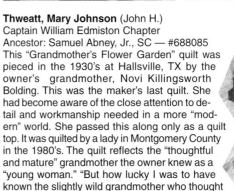

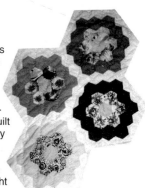

**Tidwell, Janet Malone** (John E.)
French Lick Chapter
Ancestor: Captain David Phillips, PA — #670915
This "Crazy" quilt was made in 1895 at Nashville, TN by the owner's great grandmother, Susannah Pleasants Patterson (born 1853 in England, married the Reverend Alexander

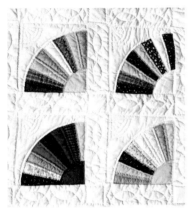

Patterson) died in 1918 at Nashville, TN). Being the wife of an Episcopal minister, the maker incorporated many Christian signs and symbols into the quilt. The quilt was passed from the maker, to her son, Arthur, who gave it to his daughter, who gave it to the owner.

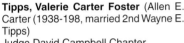

**Tipps, Valerie Carter Foster** (Allen E. Carter (1938-198, married 2nd Wayne E. Tipps)
Judge David Campbell Chapter
Ancestor: William Pinkston, NC — #697875
This "Fan" quilt was made in 1990 at Columbia, TN by the owner's mother, Katie Sue Pinskston Foster (born 7/15/1923 at Columbia, TN, married Robert Allen Foster). The maker learned to piece and quilt from her mother, Argie Grissom Pinkston. Once a top was finished, her friends would gather and help with the quilting. The Pinkstons lived on a farm near Culleoka at Scribners' Mill in Maury County, TN.

**Tipps, Valerie Carter Foster** (Allen E. Carter (1938-198, married 2nd Wayne E. Tipps)
Judge David Campbell Chapter
Ancestor: William Pinkston, NC — #697875
This "Turkey Trot/Goose Tracks" quilt was made between 1900-1912 at Roane County by the owner's first husband's mother, Laura Blair Humphreys, and his aunts, Elizabeth Jane Blair and Susan Caroline Blair. Laura was born 3/25/1866 at Kingston TN, married Abraham Jackson Humphreys and died in 1912 at Kingston. Laura named her daughter, Nancy Susan Carter Sherman after two of her aunts, the Blair sisters. They were commonly referred to as the Blair sisters,

probably because they never married. The Blair sisters are in the Quilts of Tennessee by Ramsey and Waldvogel pp. 81-92. Sue H.C. Sherman was terribly proud of her Blair family heritage. They were prominent citizens of Roane County near Kingston, TN. She valued the quilts and coverlets that came from them. She was equally proud that her father fought in the War Between the States and she had his sword. She said he lied about his age and volunteered as a drummer boy. Both of Sue's parents were dead by the time she was three. She remained in Roane County with relatives until she was ten years old, when she went to live in Athens with her grown half sister, Lucinda Humphreys Riddle.

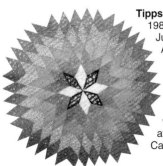

**Tipps, Valerie Carter Foster** (Allen E. Carter (1938-198, married 2nd Wayne E. Tipps)
Judge David Campbell Chapter
Ancestor: William Pinkston, NC — #697875
This "Starburst" quilt was made 1900-1912 at Roane County, TN by the owner's husband's grandmother, Laura Blair Humphreys and Laura's aunts, Elizabeth Jane Blair and Susan Caroline Blair. This quilt was found in the attic of the carriage house after the death of Nancy Susan Humphreys Carter Sherman.

**Tobias, Lois McDaniel** (Harry Dow)
Chickasaw Bluff Chapter
Ancestor: Sgt. James McDaniel, SC —# 781500
This "Hexagon" crib quilt was made in 1894 by the owner's grandmother, Minnie Foote Osborn (born 3/20/1870 at Jefferson, MI, married Elbert Eugene Osborn, died 10/8/1956 at Hillsdale County, MI). In 1894, when Minnie was pregnant with her second child, she made this quilt in the Sewing Circle of Friends who sewed and played cards together for nearly fifteen years. The fabric for quilts was a collection from all the club members and was freely shared. Minnie had also made a quilt for the oldest child, Mable Marie Osborn. That quilt was passed down the other side of the family. This "Hexagon" quilt was made for the owner's mother, Hazel Bernice Osborn McDaniel, who passed it to the current owner.

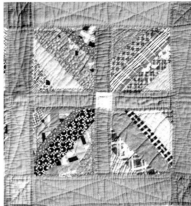

**Tipps, Valerie Carter Foster** (Allen E. Carter (1938-198, married 2nd Wayne E. Tipps)
Judge David Campbell Chapter
Ancestor: William Pinkston, NC — #697875
This "String/Strip" quilt was made circa 1940 at Maury County, TN by the owner's grandmother, Argie Grissom Pinkston (born 11/2/1886 at Columbia, TN, married Merritt Oliver Pinkston, died 4/3/1968 at Columbia). "I remember my grandmother, "Mama Pink," wearing dresses, aprons and smocks made from fabric found in her quilts. Hers are truly memory quilts."

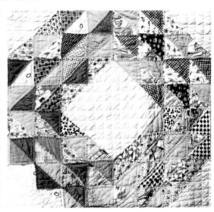

**Tipps, Valerie Carter Foster** (Allen E. Carter (1938-198, married 2nd Wayne E. Tipps)
Judge David Campbell Chapter
Ancestor: William Pinkston, NC — #697875
This "Ocean Waves" quilt was made in Roane County by the owner's first husband's aunt who was more like his "granny." Lucinda Humphreys Riddle was born 12/16/1880 at Roane County, TN, married Miles Riddle, and died at Athens, TN. Miles Riddle founded Riddle's Drug Store in Athens, TN. Their only child, Gussie Rose Riddle, married Harold List and resided in McMinn County. Harold gave the owner two quilts that Lucinda said she helped make when she was a little girl. Lucinda was from Roane County and was among the first set of children born to Abraham Jackson and his first wife, Margaret Lewis. After his wife died, Jack married Laura Blair and they had four children including the quiltmaker's sister, Nancy Susan Humphreys Center Sherman, the mother, of the owner's first husband. She had gone to live in Athens when she was ten years old with her grown half-sister, Lucinda Riddle. Gussie Rose and Pinky never had children.

**Tipps, Valerie Carter Foster** (Allen E. Carter (1938-198, married 2nd Wayne E. Tipps)
Judge David Campbell Chapter
Ancestor: William Pinkston, NC — #697875
This "Connected Flowers" quilt was made 1900-1912 at Kingston, TN by the owner's husband's grandmother, Laura Blair Humphreys and Laura's aunts, Elizabeth Jane Blair (1841-1920) and Susan Caroline Blair (1846-1924).

**Tobias, Lois McDaniel** (Harry Dow)
Chickasaw Bluff Chapter
Ancestor: Sgt. James McDaniel, SC —# 781500
This "Commemorative" original design quilt was made in 1990 at Memphis, TN by the owner's oldest daughter, Lois Janet Tobias (born 5/9/1942 at Memphis, TN). The quilt was made for the owner's 50th wedding anniversary. It was spread on a large table and the guests at the party were asked to sign the squares with a message. The owner says, "this warm and loving gift was used on our bed for nearly eight years, warming a couple and then comforting the one who was left when my husband died."

**Tobias, Virgina Reed** (Joe S.)
James White Chapter
Ancestor: Sgt. James Coffey, PA — #736260
This "Basket of Flowers" quilt was made circa 1930 at Columbia, TN by the owner's paternal grandmother, Ida Virginia Strong Reed (born 5/1/1869 at Pulaski, TN, married James Appleton Reed, died 6/15/1938 at Columbia, TN). This quilt was made as a wedding gift for the owner's mother and father. The owner's mother passed it to her shortly before her death. The quilt was hung in an exhibit of many of the quilts featured in Merikay Waldvogel's book, Soft Covers For Hard Times, at the Knoxville Museum of Art 6/29 - 8/27/1990. It was also featured on the poster advertising the exhibit. Following that exhibit, it was on a tour of six cities in the United States for almost two years. Most recently, the quilt was taken by Waldvogel to the International Quilt Fair in Yokohama, Japan— to hang in an exhibit of antique quilts 10/22-24/1998.

**Toline, Edith McPherson** (Francis)
Old Walton Road Chapter
Ancestor: Maj. John Buchanan, PA — #502561
This "Double Wedding Ring" quilt was made in 1995 at New Johnsonville, TN by the owner's daughter, Gail Toline Miller (born 7/17/1954 at Akron, OH, married Tony Miller). The quilt was a wedding gift for the owner's 50th wedding anniversary and was presented to her 9/3/1995. Names of the owner's five children, thirteen grandchildren and four great grandchildren are embroidered on the quilt.

**Toline, Edith McPherson** (Francis)
Old Walton Road Chapter
Ancestor: Maj. John Buchanan, PA — #502561
This "Eight Pointed Star" quilt was made in 1988 at New Johnsonville, TN by the owner's daughter, Gail Toline Miller.

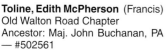

**Toline, Edith McPherson** (Francis)
Old Walton Road Chapter
Ancestor: Maj. John Buchanan, PA — #502561
This "Crazy" quilt was made in the early 1930's at Williamson County, TN by the owner's grandmother, Emma Luretta McPherson (born 4/3/1865 at Humphreys County, TN, married Albert McPherson, Sr., died 1/8/1951 at Nashville, TN). Aunt Lucille Phipps, daughter of the maker, gave the quilt to Eric and Hortense McPherson, the owner's parents, in 1967.

**Toline, Edith McPherson** (Francis)
Old Walton Road Chapter
Ancestor: Maj. John Buchanan, PA — #502561
This "Fan" quilt was pieced in 1940 at Davidson County, TN by the owner's mother, Hortense Sawyer McPherson (born 2/10/1895 at Williamson County, TN, married Eric Coleman McPherson, died 4/23/1989 at Putnam County, TN). The top was quilted by the owner's daughter, Gail Toline Miller in about 1983.

**Toline, Edith McPherson** (Francis)
Old Walton Road Chapter
Ancestor: Maj. John Buchanan, PA — #502561
This "Trip Around the World" quilt was made circa 1948 at Franklin, TN by the owner's mother, Hortense Sawyer McPherson. It was given to the owner by the maker around 1970.

**Toline, Edith McPherson** (Francis)
Old Walton Road Chapter
Ancestor: Maj. John Buchanan, PA — #502561
This "Rose" quilt was made in 1982 at New Johnsonville, TN by the owner's daughter, Gail Toline Miller.

**Toline, Edith McPherson** (Francis)
Old Walton Road Chapter
Ancestor: Maj. John Buchanan, PA — #502561
This "Sunshine and Shade/Log Cabin" quilt was made in 1913 at Franklin, TN by the owner's mother, Hortense Sawyer McPherson. It was given to the owner by the maker around 1970.

**Toline, Edith McPherson** (Francis)
Old Walton Road Chapter
Ancestor: Maj. John Buchanan, PA — #502561
This "Six Pointed Star" quilt was "rescued" by the owner from a yard sale in Lancaster, CA.

**Toline, Edith McPherson** (Francis)
Old Walton Road Chapter
Ancestor: Maj. John Buchanan, PA — #502561
This "Log Cabin Variation/Sunshine and Shade" quilt was made in the early 1930's at Williamson County, TN by Emma Loretta McPherson, the owner's grandmother, and the owner. As a child, the owner made the blocks. Her grandmother offered to finish the quilt. She included all the blocks regardless of how "good" the owner had made them.

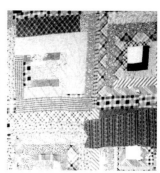

**Toline, Edith McPherson**
(Francis)
Old Walton Road Chapter
Ancestor: Maj. John Buchanan, PA — #502561
This "Star" quilt was "rescued" by the owner from a yard sale in Lancaster, CA.

**Toline, Edith McPherson** (Francis)
Old Walton Road Chapter
Ancestor: Maj. John Buchanan, PA — #502561
This "Dutch Boy/Overall Bill" quilt was made in 1935 at Obion County, TN by the owner's daughter-in-law's aunt, Hazel Nelson (born 1905 at Eldridge, TN, married John Allen Nelson). The owner's daughter-in-law, is Pamela Toline.

**Toline, Edith McPherson** (Francis)
Old Walton Road Chapter
Ancestor: Maj. John Buchanan, PA — #502561
This "Lilies" quilt was made in 1935 at Obion County, TN by the owner's daughter-in-law's aunt, Hazel Nelson.

**Toplovich, Peggie Patton** (J.C.)
Margaret Gaston Chapter
Ancestor Daniel Agee, VA —#702008
This "Turkey Track" quilt was made in the 1860's at Wilson County, TN by the owner's great grandmother, Mary Elizabeth Oakley Patton (born 1845 at Statesville, TN, married Charlie Compton Patton, died 1939 at Watertown, TN). The green, bright yellow, and maroon colors were made from vegetable dyes using, for example, black walnuts. The owner inherited the quilt from her grandfather.

---

The next 25 quilts were made by members of the Young family who have lived at Long Meadow since the 1760's. The following are the quiltmakers of this family: Carolyn Walker Young (born 1743, married William, died 1790), the owner's great great great grandmother, Margaret Galbraith Young (born 1770, married John, died 1853) the owner's great great grandmother, Sarah Miller Young (born 1806, married John, died 1884) the owner's great grandmother, and Ida Whitlock Young (born 1844, married Wylie, died 1924) the owner's grandmother. Longmeadow, the house, farm, and quilts, were left to the owner, her sister, and brother after the deaths of their father, aunt, and uncle. All of the following quilts were made at Long Meadow.

**Torbett, Francis Young** (Vincent)
Cavett Station Chapter
Ancestor: James Fulkerson, VA — #588219
The "Dresden Plate" quilt was made in the 1930's in Knoxville, TN by the owner's maternal aunt, Lula Oldham Fulkerson (born 7/6/1879 at Carter's Valley, TN, died 12/27/1957 at Knoxville, TN). The quilt was made as a special gift for the owner.

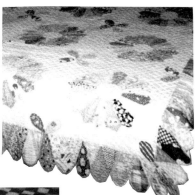

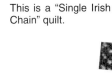

This is a "Sugar Loaf" quilt.

This is a "Triple Irish Chain" quilt.

This is a "Single Irish Chain" quilt.

This is a "Crazy" quilt.

This is a "Nine Patch Checkerboard" quilt.

This is a "Shoo-Fly/Grandmother's Choice" quilt.

This is a "Courthouse Square/ Album Block" quilt.

This is a "Double Irish Chain" quilt.

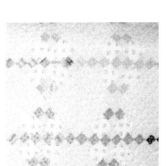

This is a "Nine Patch" quilt.

This is a "Double X" quilt.

This is a "LeMoyne Star" quilt.

This is a "Courthouse Square/ Album Block" quilt.

This is a "Star" quilt.

This is a "Square In A Square" quilt.

This is a "Triangles" tied quilt.

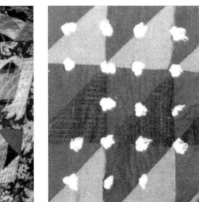

This is a "Patchwork Squares" quilt.

This is a "Nine Patch" quilt.

This is a "Jacob's Ladder" quilt.

This is a "Eight Pointed Star" quilt.

This is a "Double Irish Chain" quilt.

This is a "Nine Patch" quilt.

This is a "Bear's Paw" quilt.

**Travis, Grey Watson** (William C.)
Glover's Trace Chapter
Ancestor: William Robinson, NC — #782571
This "Lover's Trail" quilt was a gift from the owner's son in 1994. He purchased it at a quilt show.

**Treadwell, Alice Murr** (William)
Coytee Chapter
Ancestor: William Robinson, NC
— #782571
This "Trip Around the World" quilt was made in 1960 at Greenback, TN by the owner's great great aunt, Emma Blankenship (born 5/15/1881 at Blount County, TN, married Gilbert James Blankenship, died 4/10/1965 at Loudin County, TN). The quilt was given to the owner's mother who passed it to the owner.

**Trentham, Rachel Watts** (Brent)
Admiral David Farragut Chapter
Ancestor: Nicholas Gibbs, NC — #791915
This "Pineapple" quilt was made in 1930 at Granville, TN by the owner's grandmother, Mary Nell Ferrell Watts (born 9/1897 at Granville, TN, married John Louis Watts, died 8/1997).

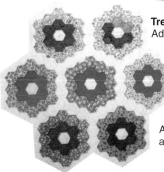

**Trentham, Rachel Watts** (Brent)
Admiral David Farragut Chapter
Ancestor: Nicholas Gibbs, NC —#791915
This "Grandmother's Flower Garden" quilt was made in 1928 at Granville, TN by the owner's great grandmother, Hannah Holleman Hargis (born 11/20/1869 at Granville, TN, married 1st Dr. Albert Ferrell in 1869, married 2nd Abraham B. Hargis in 1907, died 12/17/1961 at Granville).

**Trotter, Mary Alice Stephens** (Rogers E.)
Rhea Craig Chapter
Ancestor: Abraham Glormely, PA — #510381
This "Double T (for Texas and Tennessee)" quilt was made in Monroe County, TN by the owner's great grandmother, Margaret Jane Lee (born 10/14/1839 at Monroe County, TN, married William Edgar Lee, died 11/1/1925 in the same county). William Edgar was a captain in the War Between the States. The maker gave the quilt to the owner.

**Turnage, Janie Mayfield** (Russell)
Old Glory Chapter
Ancestor: James Mayfield, NC — #779154
This "White on White" quilt with a fan quilting pattern was made in 1985 at Williamson County, TN by the owner's niece, Mrs. Paul Tune, Sr. She gave it to the owner as a gift in 1986.

**Turnage, Janie Mayfield** (Russell)
Old Glory Chapter
Ancestor: James Mayfield, NC — #779154
This "Double Wedding Ring" quilt was made in 1978 at Chapel Hill, TN and was purchased as a wedding gift for the owner's daughter, Julie Bryant.

**Turnage, Janie Mayfield** (Russell)
Old Glory Chapter
Ancestor: James Mayfield, NC — #779154
This "Grandmother's Flower Garden" quilt was made in 1956 at Franklin, TN by the owner's sister, Connie Mayfield Talley (born 7/23/1921 at Williamson County, married John Martin Talley, Jr.).

**Turnage, Janie Mayfield** (Russell)
Old Glory Chapter
Ancestor: James Mayfield, NC — #779154
This "Cathedral Window" quilt was made in 1982 at Franklin, TN by the owner (born 8/4/1927 at Williamson County). She made this quilt from materials left over from making her children's clothes. It was made while her mother was living with her.

**Turnage, Janie Mayfield** (Russell)
Old Glory Chapter
Ancestor: James Mayfield, NC — #779154
This "Cathedral Window" quilt was made in 1982 at Franklin, TN by the owner's sister, Connie Mayfield Talley.

**Turnage, Janie Mayfield** (Russell)
Old Glory Chapter
Ancestor: James Mayfield, NC — #779154
This "Inspiration" quilt was made in 1982 at Williamson County, TN by the owner's sister, Connie Mayfield Tallley. It is made with polyester squares crocheted together.

**Turnage, Janie Mayfield** (Russell)
Old Glory Chapter
Ancestor: James Mayfield, NC — #779154
This "Elongated Hexagon Patchwork" quilt was made circa 1959 at Williamson County, TN by the owner's sister, Connie Mayfield Talley. The owner purchased the quilt from the maker.

**Turnage, Janie Mayfield** (Russell)
Old Glory Chapter
Ancestor: James Mayfield, NC — #779154
This "Log Cabin" quilt was made in 1970 at Franklin, TN by the owner. The owner says, "This quilt is special to me because I live in a log cabin 5.2 miles from Franklin, TN."

**Turnage, Janie Mayfield**
(Russell)
Old Glory Chapter
Ancestor: James Mayfield, NC — #779154
This "Blazing Star" quilt was made in 1980 at Centerville, TN by Letha Bryant. She made the quilt for Julie Bryant who gave the quilt to the owner.

**Turner, Eugenia Rodgers** (E. Hamer)
Commodore Perry Chapter
Ancestor: Paul Froman, Sr., VA — #728259
This "Toy Animals" quilt was begun in 1945 and finished in 1965 at Millington, TN by the owner (born 12/13/1926 at Memphis, TN). The top was pieced in 1945 for the birth of Lelia Anne Turner and finished in 1965 for the birth of Elizabeth Louise Turner. These women are daughters of the owner. The batting of the quilt is the owner's baby blanket which is 71 years old.

**Tyner, Janey Cranford**
James Buckley Chapter
Ancestor: Reuben Morgan, VA — #615082
This "Cathedral Window" quilt was made in 1970 at Chester County, TN by the owner's mother, Alice Cranford (born 8/1906 at Chester County).

**Tyner, Janey Cranford**
James Buckley Chapter
Ancestor: Reuben Morgan, VA —#615082
This "State Bird" quilt was made in the 1990's at Martin, TN by the owner's friend, Frances Williams.

**Tyner, Janey Cranford**
James Buckley Chapter
Ancestor: Reuben Morgan, VA — #615082
This "Dutch Sampler" quilt was made in the 1990's at Martin, TN by the owner's friend, Frances Williams (born 3/5/1916 at Martin, TN).

**Vance, Jean Sutherland** (Ray)
King's Mountain Messenger
Ancestor: James Matthews, NC —# 683530
This "Dutchman's Puzzle" quilt was possibly made by the owner's maternal grandmother. It was found in the owner's mother's cedar chest after she died.

**Vance, Jean Sutherland**
(Ray)
King's Mountain Messenger
Ancestor: James Matthews, NC —# 683530
This "Churn Dash/Hole in the Barn Door" quilt was possibly made by the owner's maternal grandmother. It was found in the owner's mother's cedar chest after she died.

**Vance, Jean Sutherland** (Ray)
King's Mountain Messenger
Ancestor: James Matthews, NC —# 683530
This "Jacob's Ladder" quilt was possibly made by the owner's maternal grandmother. It was found in the owner's mother's cedar chest after she died.

**Vance, Jean Sutherland**
(Ray)
King's Mountain Messenger
Ancestor: James Matthews, NC —# 683530
This "Patchwork" tied quilt was made in the 1960's at Bristol, TN by the owner's mother, Betty Jo Liles Sutherland (born 4/24/1922 at Chattanooga, TN, married Parkis Edward Sutherland, died 3/19/1997 at Taft, TN).

**Vandergriff, Sarah Ruth Smithson** (John D.)
Caney Fork Chapter
Ancestor: John Kersey, VA — #780812
This "Double Irish Chain" quilt was made in 1875 at Cannon County, TN by the owner's paternal grandmother, Sarah Octavia Jones Smithson (born 7/25/1855 at Cannon County, TN, married David S. Smithson, died 10/16/1886 in the same county). Sarah married David in 1845. They had four children. The owner's father was their only son. It was decided that he should have this quilt. Since the owner was named in honor of the maker, her father wanted her to have this special quilt. She has had the quilt since her father died in 1974 and cherishes it very much.

**Vandergriff, Sarah Ruth Smithson**
(John D.)
Caney Fork Chapter
Ancestor: John Kersey, VA — #780812
This "Friendship" quilt was made in 1941 at Liberty, TN by the Ladies Aid Society of Liberty Methodist Episcopal Church. Each block has eight names embroidered on it. Each name cost someone ten cents to be put on the block. There are a total of 432 names. The two center blocks are lettered thus, "Ladies Aid Society 1941" and "Pastor John B. Morehead 1941." The owner was a member of that church when the quilt was made. The owner's mother, Nettie Mai Ferrell Smithson, bought the quilt when it was sold at auction. The quilt was passed to the owner in 1975.

**Vandergriff, Sarah Ruth Smithson** (John D.)
Caney Fork Chapter
Ancestor: John Kersey, VA — #780812
This "Rising Sun" quilt was made in 1880 at Cannon County, TN by the owner's maternal great grandmother, Cynthia Ann Melton Campbell (born 5/31/1837 at Cannon County, married Henry Mitchell Campbell, died 8/31/1920 in the same county). The quilt was passed from the maker, to the owner's grandmother, Edna Campbell Ferrell. It was then passed to the owner's mother and finally to the owner.

**Vailes, Jane Phillips** (Andrew)
Stones River Chapter
Ancestor: Joseph Grimsley, VA
—#700536
This "Star of LeMoyne" quilt was made circa 1880 at Putnam County, TN by the owners' great grandmother, Nancy Curtis Matheny (born circa 1830 near Cookeville, TN married Samuel Houston Matheny, died circa 1900 at Cookeville). This quilt was published in The Quilts of Tennessee. This quilt was passed from maker, to her granddaughter, Bertie Bernice Matheny Phillips, (the owner's mother), to the owner.

**Vincent, Patricia L.**
Hatchie Chapter
Ancestor: Fredrick Shearin, NC
— #704049
This "Nine Patch" quilt was made in the 1930's at Hardeman County, TN by the owner's grandmother, Eugenia Whitten Vincent (born 1864, married Joseph Hiran Vincent, died 1944 at Memphis). The quiltmaker had six sons and eight daughters "so a lot of quilting went on, and most of the daughters inherited their mother's needlework ability, but none ever 'bested' her small stitches."

**Vincent, Patricia L.**
Hatchie Chapter
Ancestor: Fredrick Shearin, NC — #704049
This "Star of Bethlehem" quilt was made in Haywood County, TN possibly by Mary Nelle Rice Laney (born 1909 at Haywood County, TN, married J.T. Laney, died 1993 at Memphis, TN). This quilt was being used for padding when the owner found it and asked for it.

**Vincent, Patricia L.**
Hatchie Chapter
Ancestor: Fredrick Shearin, NC — #704049
This "Improved Nine Patch" quilt was made in Haywood County, TN by the owner's brother-in-law's aunt, Lillian Nichols Laney (born circa 1900 at Haywood County, TN, married J. Calvin Laney, died in Texas). "When Aunt Lilly broke up housekeeping, she gave some of her old quilts to different family members. My sister ended up with a few of these keepsakes. I begged her for this quilt until I got it."

**Vincent, Patricia L.**
Hatchie Chapter
Ancestor: Fredrick Shearin, NC — #704049
This "Cathedral Window" quilt was made in 1985 at Bolivar, TN by the owner's mother, Rubye Smalley Vincent. The maker was 75 years old when she made this large quilt. Because her eye sight was not good, she doubled the size of the usual pattern.

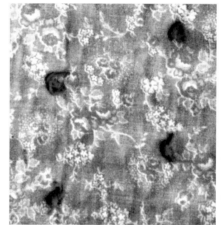

**Vincent, Patricia L.**
Hatchie Chapter
Ancestor: Fredrick Shearin, NC — #704049
This "Whole Cloth" quilt was made in the 1950's at Bolivar, TN by the owner's mother, Rubye Smalley Vincent (born 1910 at Fayette County, TN, married M.O. Vincent). This type of quilt was vogue at the time it was made and may have been the beginning of the modern day comforter.

**Vincent, Sue Emerson** (Marvin)
Hatchie Chapter
Ancestor: Issac Brooks, NC —#771741
This "Tulip" quilt was made in 1948 at Bolivar, TN at the Western State Psychiatric Hospital. The owner's mother-in-law purchased this quilt from the Occupational Therapy shop at the hospital. She gave it to the owner as a wedding gift in 1948.

**Voss, Mayo Holmes** (Edwin)
Campbell Chapter
Ancestor: Ephraim McLean, NC — #735528
This "Ohio Rose" quilt was found in the attic of the owner's husband's uncle, George Hunter Price, after he died.

**Vowell, Mary Pursley Kelly** (Morris A.)
James Buckley Chapter
Ancestor: James Bryan, NC—#556192
This wool coverlet was made circa 1860 at Obion County, TN by the owner's great great grandmother, Elizabeth Martin Murray (born 7/21/1813 at Sumner County, TN, married Daniel Oglesby Pursley, died 11/3/1888 at Union City, TN). The coverlet was passed to the owner's mother, Mary Bird Pursley Kelly, and then to the owner.

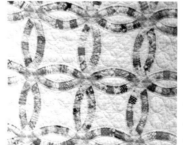
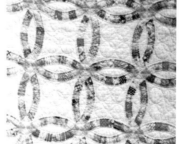

**Vowell, Mary Pursley Kelly** (Morris A.)
James Buckley Chapter
Ancestor: James Bryan, NC —#556192
This "Double Wedding Ring" quilt" was probably made in 1900 at Palestine, TX by the owner's husband's grandmother, Idella Jeannette McDonald (born 2/7/1872 at Anderson, TX, married Oscar Jackson Addington, died 4/4/1951 at Houston, TX). The quilt was passed to the maker's daughter, Mary Sue Addington Vowell, then to the current owner's husband.

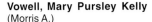

**Vowell, Mary Pursley Kelly**
(Morris A.)
James Buckley Chapter
Ancestor: James Bryan, NC —
#556192
This trapunto "Marseilles" quilt
was made in 1869 at Dyer
County, TN by the owner's great
grandfather's (David Wilson
Pursley) sister-in-law, Blanche
Burton Chitwood (born 1852 at
Dyer County, TN, married Will-
iam Arnette Pursley, died 8/17/
1919 at Obion County, TN).

**Vowell, Mary Pursley Kelly**
(Morris A.)
James Buckley Chapter
Ancestor: James Bryan, NC —
#556192
This "Circular Saw" quilt was
made in the 1930's at Dyer or
Gibson County, TN by the
owner's mother-in-law, Annabel
Phillips Vaughan (born 1893 at
Dyer County, TN, married Frank
Bone Vaughan, died 1958 at
Martin, TN at the home of her
son Wilbur).

**Vowell, Mary Pursley Kelly** (Morris A.)
James Buckley Chapter
Ancestor: James Bryan, NC —
#556192
This "Trip Around the World/Postage
Stamp/Sunshine and Shadow" quilt
was made circa 1900 in Texas by the
owner's husband's grandmother, Idella
Jeannette McDonald. The quilt was
passed to the maker's daughter, Mary
Sue Addington Vowell, then to the cur-
rent owner's husband.

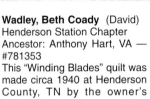

**Wade, Kate Reagan** (Dwight)
Spencer Clack Chapter
Ancestor: Timothy Reagan, MD —
#628645
This "Tree of Life" quilt was made in
the 1960's at Sevierville, TN by the
owner.

**Wadley, Beth Coady** (David)
Henderson Station Chapter
Ancestor: Anthony Hart, VA —
#781353
This "Tree of Life" quilt was
made in 1975 at Chester
County, TN by the owner's
mother, Marie Moore Coady
(born 1939 at Jackson, TN, married Joe Earl Coady). It was
given to the owner as a wedding
gift in 1981.

**Wadley, Beth Coady** (David)
Henderson Station Chapter
Ancestor: Anthony Hart, VA —
#781353
This "Winding Blades" quilt was
made circa 1940 at Henderson
County, TN by the owner's
husband's grandmother, Mary
Bailey Wadley (born 1897 at
Henderson County, TN, married
Frank Wadley, died 1963 in the
same county). The maker
passed the quilt to her daughter-
in-law, Dorothy Wadley, who
passed it to the maker's grandson, David Wadley.

**Wadley, Beth Coady**
(David)
Henderson Station
Chapter
Ancestor: Anthony
Hart, VA —#781353
This "Colonial Girl/
Dresden Doll" quilt
was made in 1975 at
Chester County, TN
by the owner's
mother, Marie Moore
Coady. The quilt is
made from scraps

from the owner's school dresses. The quilt was given to the owner by the maker.

**Wadley, Beth Coady** (David)
Henderson Station Chapter
Ancestor: Anthony Hart, VA —
#781353
This "Jacob's Ladder" quilt was
made circa 1958 at Henderson
County, TN by the owner's
husband's grandmother, Mary
Bailey Wadley. The maker gathered remnants of the flannel from
her five grandson's pajamas and
used these fabrics to piece the
quilt. The quilt was passed from
the maker, to her son Cratus

Wadley, who passed it to her grandson, Robert Wadley.

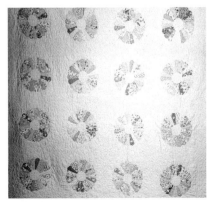

**Wakefield, Marjorie Brown**
(Larimore)
Robert Lewis Chapter
Ancestor: Sgt. William Pickens, SC
—#697394
This "Dresden Plate" quilt was
made circa 1920 at Mooresville,
TN by the owner's great grand-
mother, Sarah Elizabeth Pickens
Orr (born 5/22/1857 at Mooresville,
TN, married henry Warren Orr, died
1/21/1944 in the same town). The
quilt was passed from the owner's
mother to the owner.

**Wakefield, Marjorie Brown**
(Larimore)
Robert Lewis Chapter
Ancestor: Sgt. William Pickens, SC
—#697394
This "Flowers In Baskets" quilt was
made in 1940 at Raymondsville, TX
and given to the owner's grandmother and grandfather as a
Golden Wedding Anniversary
present. It was passed to the owner
in 1973.

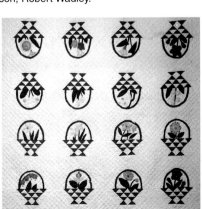

**Walker, Anna Kate Marshall** (Alfred W.)
Spencer Clack Chapter
Ancestor: Spencer Clack, VA —
#762006
This "Nine Patch" quilt was made in 1930 by Mrs. Williams. The quiltmaker was a tenant on the owner's grandfather's (John L. Marshall) farm. It was made for the owner's dolls when her brother, Conley, was born. The quilt is backed with a flour sack.

**Walker, Cynthia Geeslin** (Edward)
William Cocke Chapter
Ancestor: Nicholas Harbuck, GA —
#755782
This "Seven Sisters" quilt was made before 1892 by the aunt of the owner's husband's grandfather's Unity Walker Clifford (born 1/26/1851 at Burkes Garden, VA, married Guilford David Clifford, died 4/28/1922 Eustis, FL). "When my husband's grandmother, Pauline S. Walker, was putting a new back on a quilt made in 1892 by Lottie C. Taylor, she discovered this 'Seven Sisters' quilt had been used as a lining."

**Walker, Cynthia Geeslin** (Edward)
William Cocke Chapter
Ancestor: Nicholas Harbuck, GA —#755782
This "Postage Stamp" quilt was pieced in 1939 at Cocke County, TN by the owner's husband's great grandmother, Josephine McAndrew Shields (born 4/14/1878 at Chestnut Hill, TN, married Dr. J.A.P. Shields, died 11/27/1957 at Tusculum, TN). "The quilt was quilted by a lady on Grassy Fork to satisfy the medical bill she owed Dr. Shields."

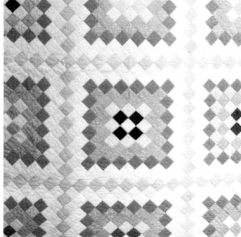

**Walker, Cynthia Geeslin** (Edward)
William Cocke Chapter
Ancestor: Nicholas Harbuck, GA —#755782
This "Nine Patch Variation/Christmas" quilt was made in 1996 at Newport, TN by the owner (born 11/20/1953 at Atlanta, GA). She made the quilt as a Christmas gift for her husband.

**Walker, Katherine Wiseman** (Jack D.)
Tullahoma Chapter
Ancestor: Jacob Leonard, NC —
#581135
This coverlet was made circa 1860 at Lincoln County, TN by the owner's great great grandmother, Mary Waggoner (born 1808 at Lincoln County, TN, married Daniel Waggoner, died circa 1870 at Lincoln County). The quilt was made for the owner's grandmother, Mary Catherine Spencer Wiseman who gave it to the owner.

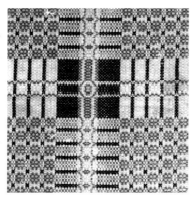

**Walker, Cynthia Geeslin** (Edward)
William Cocke Chapter
Ancestor: Nicholas Harbuck, GA —
#755782
This "Pine Burr/Pineapple" quilt was made at Cocke County, TN by the owner's husband's great uncle's aunt. His great uncle was James A. T. Wood. The quiltmaker is Catherine McNabb Wood (born 10/28/1854 at Cocke County, TN, married William A. Wood, died 1/20/1947 at Knoxville, TN). The quilt was given to Edward Walker by his cousin, Shelia Wood Navarro, in 1997. The quiltmaker grew up in the Wilton Springs community. "She remembered when an Indian looked through the window of their home. She could remember in 1861, her father, Malcolm McNabb, bringing home a new Seth Thomas Clock and placing it on the mantle. As he did so, he remarked that a new president was being inaugurated, Abraham Lincoln."

**Walker, Cynthia Geeslin** (Edward)
William Cocke Chapter
Ancestor: Nicholas Harbuck, GA —#755782
This "Dresden Plate" quilt was made before 1941 at Newport, TN. A cousin of Elna Talley Milne pieced the top. The ladies of the old Methodist Episcopal Church did the quilting.

**Walker, Cynthia Geeslin** (Edward)
William Cocke Chapter
Ancestor: Nicholas Harbuck, GA —#755782
This "Broken Dishes" quilt was made in 1892 in Florida by the owner's husband's father's first cousin, Lottie Clifford Taylor (born 3/5/1873 at Saltville, VA, married Robert Toombs Taylor, died 11/30/1976 at Eustis, FL). The owner's husband received the quilt from Lottie in 1980. This quilt won first prize in the "pre-1900" category at the 1997 Newport-Cocke County Museum Quilt Show.

**Walker, Cynthia Geeslin** (Edward)
William Cocke Chapter
Ancestor: Nicholas Harbuck, GA —
#755782
This "Sunbonnet Sue/Dutch Doll" quilt was made in 1996 at Odessa, FL by the owner's sister, Diane Kummelman (born 6/14/1947 at Atlanta, GA, married Michael Kummelman). Certain pieces in the quilt are labeled as fabrics that came from the owner's mother's (Claranell Bartlett Geeslin) clothes. The maker made the quilt for the owner's daughter, Claire, on the occasion of her first birthday.

**Walker, Katherine Wiseman** (Jack D.)
Tullahoma Chapter
Ancestor: Jacob Leonard, NC —#581135
This coverlet was also made circa 1860 at Lincoln County, TN by the owner's great great grandmother, Mary Waggoner.

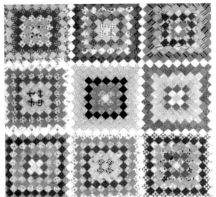

**Walker, Katherine Wiseman** (Jack D.)
Tullahoma Chapter
Ancestor: Jacob Leonard, NC — #581135
This "Postage Stamp" quilt was made in the 1930's at Fayetteville, TN by the owner's husband's grandmother, Harriet Jackson Nichols (born 2/2/1861 at Jefferson County, TN, married John D. Nichols, died 2/1962 at Fayetteville, TN). The quilt was passed from the owner's husband's mother-in-law, to the owner.

**Walker, Mary Helen Hester** (Walter L.)
Chief John Ross Chapter
Ancestor: Andrew Creswell, VA —#701851
This "Old Maid's Ramble" quilt was made before 1929 at Giles County, TN by the owner's paternal grandmother, Lola Elizabeth Crabb Hester (born 4/20/1872 at Giles County, TN, married Joseph Hinton Hester, died 8/15/1934 at Davidson County, TN). When Lillian Geraldine Rawlings married Herbert Hinton Hester 1/27/1929, his mother, the quiltmaker, gave them nine quilts, a feather bed, and two feather pillows for a

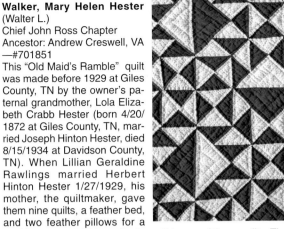

wedding present. This particular quilt is one of those quilts. The owner says, "My grandmother died before I was born. All I know of her is what has been passed down to me in stories, pictures, and the scraps of fabric she lovingly pieced together to make quilts."

**Walker, Patty Kendra S.** (Brian)
Lydia Russell Bean Chapter
Ancestor: Conrad Wilmoit, NC — #760172
This "Trip Around the World" quilt was made in 1998 by the owner's mother-in-law, Charlene Patty (born 4/27/1939 at Maryville, TN, married Dale Patty) and her friends. The quilt is inscribed, "Wedding quilt, Kendra and Brian, 6/6/1998, made with love. Charlene Patty and the Spice Girls." The Spice Girls include Charlene, Aldie King, Margaret Boring, Jerrie Boring and Joy Teffteller. Several years ago they got together and decided to learn to quilt "the old fashioned way."

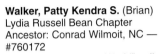

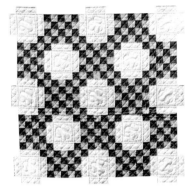

**Walker, Pauline Shields** (Edward)
William Cocke Chapter
Ancestor: Robert Shields, VA —#422329
This "Double Irish Chain" quilt was pieced in 1994 at Newport, TN by the owner (born 9/27/1903 at Chestnut Hill, TN, married Edward R. Walker, Sr.). The quilt was quilted by Estalee B. Wilson.

**Walker, Katie Green** (Ernest L.)
Ann Robertson Chapter
Ancestor John Green, — #753033
This "Kiddie Cover" quilt was made in 1959 at Johnson City, TN by the owner's mother, Alice Young Green (born 8/17/1904 at Bakersville, NC, married James Eugene Green, died 12/18/1991 at Johnson City, TN). The owner says, "My mother ordered this quilt pattern just as soon as she learned I was pregnant. The pattern was ordered from The American Weekly for 25 cents. I still have the picture of the quilt from the magazine. The pattern she ordered was #832 "Kiddie Cover with 9 Faces." The quilt was made for her first grandchild, my first child. When he was born 12/29/1959, the quilt was on the bed. He looked just like the baby on the quilt."

**Walker, Katie Green** (Ernest L.)
Ann Robertson Chapter
Ancestor John Green, — #753033
This "Pyramid" quilt was made by the owner's grandmother, Hettie Blevins Young (born 10/1/1872 at Bakersville, NC, married Zach Henry Young, died 1/5/1953 at Johnson City, TN). The quilt is backed with feed sacks.

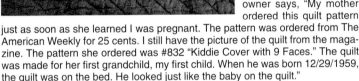

**Walker, Katie Green** (Ernest L.)
Ann Robertson Chapter
Ancestor John Green, —#753033
This "Ohio Star" quilt was made circa 1940 at Johnson City, TN by the owner's mother, Alice Young Green. "It is made from the many pieces of fabric left over from the dresses that mother made for me, especially the seersucker. It is a heavy seersucker that she sewed on my thumb and wrist every night until I no longer sucked my thumb. I still remember how rough and awful it tasted, but it worked."

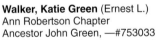

**Walker, Katie Green** (Ernest L.)
Ann Robertson Chapter
Ancestor John Green, — #753033
This "Simplified Basket Block" quilt was made at North Carolina by the owner's mother, Alice Young Green. "This quilt seems to have always been around when I was growing up. I think it is the prettiest of all the quilts my mother had."

**Walker, Katie Green** (Ernest L.)
Ann Robertson Chapter
Ancestor John Green, —#753033
This "Monkey Wrench" quilt was made in 1930 in North Carolina by the owner's mother, Alice Young Green. "This quilt came to me when my mother died. The quilt is backed with a blue print fabric that has the imprint of the rear of a mother pig and her young. Above it is '0 lbs...' This indicates that it must have been the edge of a feed sack."

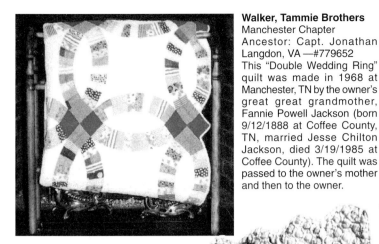

**Walker, Tammie Brothers**
Manchester Chapter
Ancestor: Capt. Jonathan Langdon, VA —#779652
This "Double Wedding Ring" quilt was made in 1968 at Manchester, TN by the owner's great great grandmother, Fannie Powell Jackson (born 9/12/1888 at Coffee County, TN, married Jesse Chilton Jackson, died 3/19/1985 at Coffee County). The quilt was passed to the owner's mother and then to the owner.

**Walton, Jean Fuqua** (James)
Charlotte Reeves Robertson Chapter
Ancestor: Thomas Fuqua, VA —#661572
This "Trip Around the World" doll quilt was made in Portland, TN by the owner's grandmother, Leathia Reid (married Lee Andrews Fuqua, died at Macon County, TN).

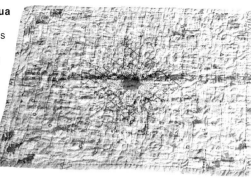

**Walton, Jean Fuqua** (James)
Charlotte Reeves Robertson Chapter
Ancestor: Thomas Fuqua, VA — #661572
This "Grandmother's Flower Garden" doll quilt was made in 1997 at Springfield, TN by Dorothy Fuqua. The owner (born 10/25/1940 at Clarksville, TN) quilted the quilt.

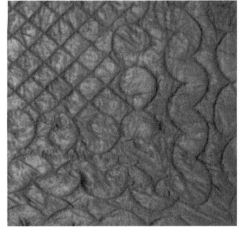

**Ward, Laura Ball** (A. Neal)
General William Lenoir Chapter
Ancestor: Lt. Elisha Reynold, NC —#745032
This "Whole Cloth" quilt was made in 1920 at Carroll County, MS by the owner's cousin, Mrs. James Malcomb Long Sims (died at Carroll County, MS).

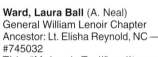

**Ward, Laura Ball** (A. Neal)
General William Lenoir Chapter
Ancestor: Lt. Elisha Reynold, NC — #745032
This "Double Irish Chain" quilt was made at Loudon County, TN by the owner's husband's grandmother, Verna Hair Ward (born 10/24/1871, married Joshua King Ward, died 12/11/1958 at Loudon County).

**Ward, Laura Ball** (A. Neal)
General William Lenoir Chapter
Ancestor: Lt. Elisha Reynold, NC — #745032
This "Snowball" quilt was purchased by the owner in Peoria, IL at an estate sale.

**Ward, Laura Ball** (A. Neal)
General William Lenoir Chapter
Ancestor: Lt. Elisha Reynold, NC — #745032
This "Mohawk Trail" quilt was pieced in the 1930's at Loudon County, TN by the owner's mother-in-law, Irene Ward (born 9/11/1900, married James Clyde Ward, died 3/14/1980).

**Ward, Nelle Kennedy** (A.C.)
Rhea-Craig Chapter
Ancestor: Nimrod Newman, VA —#590650
This "Butterfly" quilt was pieced circa 1939-40 at McMinn County, TN by the owner (born 7/30/1918 at McMinn County, married A.C. Ward). This quilt was made not long after the maker's marriage. It was quilted by her cousin, Mrs. Maggie Simpson Foster.

**Ward, Marilyn**
Rhea-Craig Chapter
Ancestor: Nimrod Newman, Va —#599731
This "They Lived In A Shoe" baby quilt was made circa 1943 at McMinn County, TN by the owner's mother, Nelle Kennedy Ward (born 7/30/1912 at McMinn County, married A. C. Ward). The maker made the quilt for her first child, the owner.

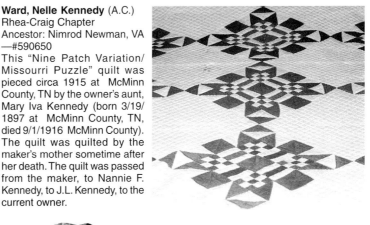

**Ward, Nelle Kennedy** (A.C.)
Rhea-Craig Chapter
Ancestor: Nimrod Newman, VA —#590650
This "Double Irish Chain" quilt was made circa 1936 at McMinn County, TN by the owner's mother, Effie Simpson Kennedy (born 8/20/1890 at McMinn County, TN, married James Lafayette "Fate" Kennedy, died 9/10/1992 at McMinn County). The quilt was given to the owner by the maker. The maker lived to be 102 years old.

**Ward, Nelle Kennedy** (A.C.)
Rhea-Craig Chapter
Ancestor: Nimrod Newman, VA —#590650
This "Nine Patch Variation/ Missourri Puzzle" quilt was pieced circa 1915 at McMinn County, TN by the owner's aunt, Mary Iva Kennedy (born 3/19/1897 at McMinn County, TN, died 9/1/1916 McMinn County). The quilt was quilted by the maker's mother sometime after her death. The quilt was passed from the maker, to Nannie F. Kennedy, to J.L. Kennedy, to the current owner.

**Washburn, Nancy Harton** (Nat I.)
Tullahoma Chapter
Ancestor: Jonathan Foster, MA —#435543
This "Dogwood" quilt was made in 1973 at Tullahoma, TN by the owner's mother, Frances Lewis Harton (born 6/22/1893 at Utica City, NY, married John W. Harton, died 11/27/1989 at Tullahoma).

**Wasson, Mary**
Volunteer Chapter
Ancestor: Godfrey Carriger, NC —#604654
This "Crazy" quilt was made by a maternal ancestor of the owner. Mary inherited the quilt circa 1940. The quilt is pictured in Many Patches Ago by Martha Marshall on page 93.

**Wasson, Mary**
Volunteer Chapter
Ancestor: Godfrey Carriger, NC —#604654
This "Triple Lily" quilt was purchased by the owner at a roadside shop in Tennessee sometime in the 1960's. The quilt is pictured in Many Patches Ago by Martha Marshall on page 34.

**Wasson, Mary**
Volunteer Chapter
Ancestor: Godfrey Carriger, NC —#604654
This original "Amish Mix" quilt was made in 1965 at Bristol, TN by the owner (born 4/26/1911). The quilt is pictured in Many Patches Ago by Martha Marshall on pages 97 and 131.

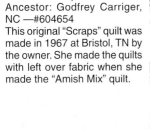

**Wasson, Mary**
Volunteer Chapter
Ancestor: Godfrey Carriger, NC —#604654
This original "Scraps" quilt was made in 1967 at Bristol, TN by the owner. She made the quilts with left over fabric when she made the "Amish Mix" quilt.

**Watson, Velma Sue Black** (J.B.)
Bonnie Kate Chapter
Ancestor: Samuel Sharp, VA —#750401
This "Remella's Butterfly" quilt was pieced in 1941 at McMinn County, TN by the owner's mother-in-law, Remella P. Watson (married Jasper O. Watson) before the birth of her first child. When the owner started learning to quilt, Remella gave her the finished blocks. They are made from sugar and feed sacks. The owner put the blocks together and quilted them in 1988. She named the quilt "Remella's Butterfly".

**Waters, Dixie Dyer** (Donald)
Robert Lewis Chapter
Ancestor: William Abernathy, VA —772704
This "Grandmother's Flower Garden" quilt was made in the early 1900's at Petersburg, TN by the owner's grandmother, Hallie Hobbs Dyer (born 6/7/1872 at Moore County, TN, married William C. Dyer, died 10/31/1943 at Petersburg, TN). The maker gave the quilt to her son who passed it to his daughter, the current owner.

**Watson, Velma Sue Black** (J.B.)
Bonnie Kate Chapter
Ancestor: Samuel Sharp, VA —#750401
This "Dutch Doll" quilt was made in the 1950's at Andersonville, TN by the owner's grandmother, Lizzie Ellen Wilson Longmire (born 3/20/1874 at union County, TN, married Alvis Henderson Longmire, died 4/13/1970 at Andersonville). The owner's aunt had the quilt and when she died, the owner bought it at an estate sale.

**Watson, Velma Sue Black** (J.B.)
Bonnie Kate Chapter
Ancestor: Samuel Sharp, VA —#750401
This quilt was made between 1926 and the early 1930's at Andersonville, TN by the owner's grandmother, Lizzie Ellen Wilson Longmire. The owner's great grandparents, Matilda Heath and James Maston Wilson, left Tennessee in 1920 to go to Oklahoma. They both died by 1926. The owner's grandma Lizzie, got a dress that was her mother's, and made a quilt from the dress. The owner believes this may have been a tradition.

**Watson, Velma Sue Black**(J.B.)
Bonnie Kate Chapter
Ancestor: Samuel Sharp, VA —#750401
This "Grandmother's Flower Garden" quilt was made in the 1950's at Andersonville, TN by the owner's grandmother, Lizzie Ellen Wilson Longmire, and her aunt, Rowena Longmire Lauver. The owner bought the quilt at an estate sale after the death of her aunt.

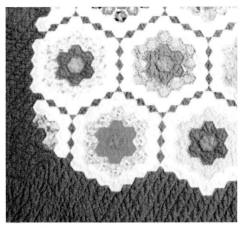

**Watson, Velma Sue Black**(J.B.)
Bonnie Kate Chapter
Ancestor: Samuel Sharp, VA — #750401
This "Bear's Paw" quilt was made in 1992 at Powell, TN by the owner (born 7/1/1945 at Knoxville, TN). This quilt won a blue ribbon at the Tennessee Valley State Fair and honorable mention at the Dogwood Arts Festival. The quilt was made for the owner's young son, Michael.

**Watson, Velma Sue Black**(J.B.)
Bonnie Kate Chapter
Ancestor: Samuel Sharp, VA — #750401
This "Lend and Borrow/Rocky Glen/Indian Meadow" quilt was made sometime in the 1800's by the owner's great great grandmother, Malinda Graves Heath (born 10/18/1815, married Daniel Heath, died 3/2/1888). The quilt was passed from mother, to daughter, to daughter, to daughter.

**Watson, Velma Sue Black**(J.B.)
Bonnie Kate Chapter
Ancestor: Samuel Sharp, VA — #750401
This "Brickwork" quilt was made in the 1920's after 1926 at Andersonville, TN by the owner's grandmother, Lizzie Ellen Wilson Longmire. It was given to the owner by her aunt who was staying with the maker when she died.

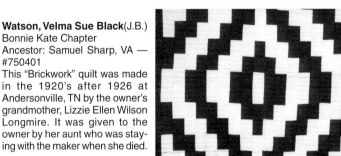

**Watson, Velma Sue Black**(J.B.)
Bonnie Kate Chapter
Ancestor: Samuel Sharp, VA — #750401
This "Colonial Lady" quilt was pieced in the 1950's at Andersonville, TN and quilted in 1999 at Powell, TN. The quilt was pieced by the owner's aunt, Rowena Longmire Lauver (born 7/1920, married George, Whitten Lauver, died 1/4/1998 at Andersonville, TN). The owner bought the quilt top at an estate sale after her aunt died, and in 1999, she quilted the quilt.

**Watson, Velma Sue Black**(J.B.)
Bonnie Kate Chapter
Ancestor: Samuel Sharp, VA — #750401
This "Bow Tie With Cat" quilt was made in 1998 at Powell, TN by the owner. The quilt is made from scraps from the dresses she made for her daughter. She added the cat, wearing a bow tie, because her daughter is "such a cat lover."

**Watson, Velma Sue Black**(J.B.)
Bonnie Kate Chapter
Ancestor: Samuel Sharp, VA — #750401
This "Friendship/Autograph" quilt was made at Powell, TN in 1990 by the owner. She calls the quilt "Hearts and Flowers" because it is quilted in a heart pattern and the print is flowers. The maker made this quilt for her side of the family, the Blacks. It starts with her grandparents -Drury Emory Black (born 2/4/1820's, died 10/26/1906) and Esther Eddington Black (born 6/20/1832, died 11/13/1908), and then she added all descendants to the present generation.

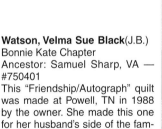

**Watson, Velma Sue Black**(J.B.)
Bonnie Kate Chapter
Ancestor: Samuel Sharp, VA — #750401
This "Friendship/Autograph" quilt was made at Powell, TN in 1988 by the owner. She made this one for her husband's side of the family.

**Watson, Vera Miller** (John)
William Cocke Chapter
Ancestor: Michael Nehs, Jr., VA — #657774
This blue and white geometric coverlet was made in the early 1900's at Cocke County, TN by the owner's great grandmother, Florence Huff Winter (born 12/25/1867 at Greene County, TN, married Issac N, died 7/14/1942 at Cocke County, TN). The coverlet was passed from maker, to her son, to his daughter, to owner.

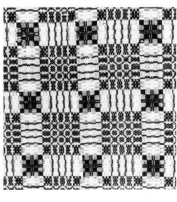

**Watts, Jane Hollingsworth** (Glenn)
Admiral David Farragut Chapter
Ancestor: Nicholas Gibbs, NC — #750496
This "Princess Feather" quilt was made in 1929 at Granville, TN by the owner's husband's maternal grandmother, Hannah Holleman Hargis (born 11/30/1869 at Granville, TN, married Dr. Albert Allison Ferrell, married 2nd Abraham Bohannan Hargis, died 12/17/1961 at Granville). The quilt was made at the birth of the owner's husband.

**Watts, Jane Hollingsworth** (Glenn)
Admiral David Farragut Chapter
Ancestor: Nicholas Gibbs, NC —
#750496
This "Rose Basket" quilt was
pieced in 1925 at Granville,
TN by the owner's
husband's paternal
grandmother, Belle Lee
Hawthorne Watts (born 10/2/
1868 at Granville, TN, married
William Robertson Watts on 4/2/
1889, died 3/19/1947 at Granville).
Both grandmothers quilted the quilt.

**Weakley, Doris Green** (Terry R.)
Jane Knox Chapter
Ancestor: Capt. John Price, VA
—#701963
This "Circle and Squares" quilt
was made in 1938 at Trenton, KY
by the owner's mother for her
"hope chest." The maker, Aileen
Elizabeth Price Green, was born
8/4/1919 at Montgomery County,
TN, married Elzie Martin Green,
and died 1/11/1942 at Montgomery County.

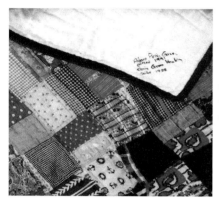

**Weakley, Doris Green** (Terry R.)
Jane Knox Chapter
Ancestor: Capt. John Price, VA —
#701963
This "Crazy Patchwork" quilt was
made in 1940-41 by the owner's
mother, Aileen Elizabeth Price
Green.

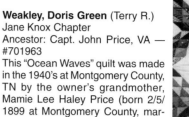

**Weakley, Doris Green** (Terry R.)
Jane Knox Chapter
Ancestor: Capt. John Price, VA —
#701963
This "Ocean Waves" quilt was made
in the 1940's at Montgomery County,
TN by the owner's grandmother,
Mamie Lee Haley Price (born 2/5/
1899 at Montgomery County, mar-
ried Adam Price, died 1979 at Mont-
gomery County).

**Weakley, Doris Green**
(Terry R.)
Jane Knox Chapter
Ancestor: Capt. John
Price, VA —#701963
This "Patchwork String"
quilt was made by the
owner's great grand-
mother, Lucy Elizabeth
Haley (born 1877 at War-
ren County, KY, married
General Marion Haley,
died 1964 at Montgomery
County, TN). Mrs. Genie
Adam Price "Dorothy" got
possession of the quilt in 1964. She passed it to the owner on Mother's Day
1990 in remembrance of the maker. Dorothy said to the current owner, "It will
mean more to you than anyone."

**Wells, Beverly Ann Douglass**
(Louis)
Chief Piomingo Chapter
Ancestor: Hezekiah Kimball,
NJ —#751354
This "Double Wedding Ring"
quilt was made 36 years ago
at Central City, KY by the
owner's husband's grand-
mother, Susie C. Wells. It was
given as a wedding gift to the
owner. The maker lived to be
100 years old.

**Wells, Beverly Ann Douglass**
(Louis)
Chief Piomingo Chapter
Ancestor: Hezekiah Kimball,
NJ —#751354
This "Spirit of 76" quilt was
made in 1976 by the owner
(born 5/4/40 at Calloway
County, KY).

**Wells, Beverly Ann Douglass**
(Louis)
Chief Piomingo Chapter
Ancestor: Hezekiah Kimball, NJ
—#751354
This "Log Cabin" quilt was made
fifteen years ago at Germantown,
TN by the owner.

**Wells, Beverly Ann Douglass**
(Louis)
Chief Piomingo Chapter
Ancestor: Hezekiah Kimball,
NJ —#751354
This cross stitch "Snowball"
quilt was made 40 years ago
at Murray, KY by the owner.
This quilt was made when the
owner was eighteen years old.
It was her first cross stitched
quilt.

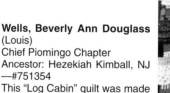

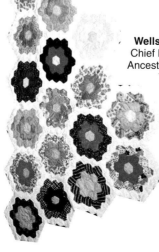

**Wells, Beverly Ann Douglass** (Louis)
Chief Piomingo Chapter
Ancestor: Hezekiah Kimball, NJ —#751354
This "Grandmother's Flower Garden" quilt was
pieced 40-45 years ago at Lynn Grove, KY
by the owner's aunt, Mary Douglass Miller
(born 1097 at Dover, TN, married Kent
Miller, died 1995 at Murray, KY). She was
assisted by her sisters, Emma, Thelma and
Irma. They enjoyed piecing tops together and
"learning all the news." The owner quilted
this quilt when she received the top from
her Aunt Mary.

**Wells, Beverly Ann Douglass** (Louis)
Chief Piomingo Chapter
Ancestor: Hezekiah Kimball, NJ —#751354
This "Flying Bird" quilt was made over 100 years ago at Dover, TN by the owner's grandmother, Mattie Sexton Douglass (born 1870 at Dover, TN, died 1958 at Murray, KY). It has homespun fabric on the back and was given to the owner by "Mother Doug."

**Wells, Beverly Ann Douglass** (Louis)
Chief Piomingo Chapter
Ancestor: Hezekiah Kimball, NJ —#751354
This "Initial H" quilt was made 105 years ago at Calloway County, KY by the owner's grandmother, Mattie Crawford (born 1870, married Lycurus Fields Crawford, died 1958 at Murray, KY). "My grandmother made her sons each a quilt with their initial. Her maiden name was Humphreys and her son was named Humphreys. This was his quilt, which he gave to me to keep in the family since he had no children. My grandmother made her daughters each a quilt with flowers or other patterns."

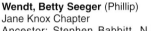

**Wendt, Betty Seeger** (Phillip)
Jane Knox Chapter
Ancestor: Stephen Babbitt, NJ —#753763
This "Maple Leaf" quilt was made at Medford, NJ by the owner (born 11/13/1923 at Greenwood, MN). It has been hung in three quilt shows including the Kirbys Mill Quilt Show in Medford, NJ.

**Wendt, Betty Seeger** (Phillip)
Jane Knox Chapter
Ancestor: Stephen Babbitt, NJ —#753763
This "Butterfly" quilt was made in 1935 in Minnesota by the owner's mother-in-law, Neva K. Wendt (born 12/5/1886 at Pipestone, MN, married August William Wendt, died 10/24/1981 at Cookeville, TN). It has been hung in three quilt shows including the Kirbys Mill Quilt Show in Medford, NJ.

**West, Carlee Dunn** (Earl R.)
Ft. Prudhomme Chapter
Ancestor: Samuel Luck, VA —#783758
This "Friendship/Sunbonnet Sue" quilt was made 1979-80 at Lauderdale County, TN by the owner and members of the Town and Country Homemakers Club of Lauderdale County. "Our club voted to purchase kits or fabrics for quilts and each member would make a block. A lucky member would then receive all blocks made that year for a quilt. Eventually my name was drawn. I had inherited my mother's quilt scraps, so I chose the Sunbonnet Sue pattern and cut them out with matching dresses, bonnets and shoes. I asked the members to decorate them anyway they chose." The owner quilted the quilt.

**West, Carlee Dunn** (Earl R.)
Ft. Prudhomme Chapter
Ancestor: Samuel Luck, VA —#783758
This cross stitch "Rose" quilt was made in 1975 at Ripley, TN by the owner (born 12/4/1925 at Milan, TN). "I cross stitched this quilt over a period of years when I was caring for aged parents in Gibson County, TN. After my mother died in March 1972, I finished it, including the quilting, on 11/18/1975. My name and this date are embroidered in a corner."

**Whitaker, Charlotte Cunningham** (William Mark)
King's Mountain Messenger Chapter
Ancestor: Thomas Boaz, VA —#704935
This "Sampler" quilt was made in 1986 at Fayetteville, TN by the owner. After she retired from teaching, she had the time to pursue a life long interest of quiltmaking.

**Whitaker, Charlotte Cunningham** (William Mark)
King's Mountain Messenger Chapter
Ancestor: Thomas Boaz, VA —#704935
This "Dresden Plate" quilt was pieced in the 1930's by the owner's mother, and completed in 1989 at Lincoln County, TN by the owner (born in 1922 at Lincoln County).

**Whitaker, Charlotte Cunningham** (William Mark)
King's Mountain Messenger Chapter
Ancestor: Thomas Boaz, VA —#704935
This "Boston Commons" quilt was made in 1988 by the owner.

**Whitaker, Linda Hall** (David)
Coyotee Chapter
Ancestor: James Taylor, NC —#627849
This "Butterfly" quilt was made in 1972 at Blount County, TN by the owner's grandmother, Mary Goddard Hall (born 3/12/1902 at Knox County, TN, married Gid Hall, died 1/17/1997 at Blount County). Some of the pieces used are scraps from the owner's dresses when she was a little girl. The quilt was passed from the maker, to the owner's mother, to the owner.

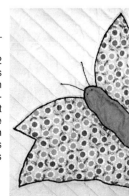

**White, Margaret Starkey**
(Harold Clyde)
Caney Fork Chapter
Ancestor: Enoch Grubbs,
SC —#636357
This "Dogwood" quilt was
made by the owner (born 12/
8/21 at Rockvale, TN).

**White, Margaret Starkey**
(Harold Clyde)
Caney Fork Chapter
Ancestor: Enoch Grubbs,
SC —#636357
This "Cathedral Window"
quilt was made 1980-85 at
Carthage, TN by the owner.

**Whitenton, Margaret Davis**
(Dewey)
Hatchie Chapter
Ancestor: William McLeskey, SC —
#575922
The owner believes that this "Variation of Connecting Stars" quilt was
made during the period of the War
Between the States because of the
colors used. "Shades of brown and
turkey red were prevalent during this
time. This quilt was made by the
owner's great grandmother, Emily
Harriet McCullar Hipps (born 5/9/
1852 at McNairy County, TN, married Thomas A. Hipps, died 3/10/
1918 at McNairy County). At the time
of the quiltmaker's death in 1918, the
quilt was passed on to her daughter,
Minnie Hipps Yarbrough. At Minnie's
death in 1971, the quilt was passed
to her daughter, Nellie Yarbrough
Plunk. At Nellie's death in 1983 the
quilt first went to Nellie's daughter, Marion Plunk Murray, and then to Marion's sister, Imogene Plunk
Johnson. This cousin gave the quilt to the current owner.

**Whitworth, Virginia
Lockhart** (Joe)
Glover's Trace Chapter
Ancestor: Alexander
McCorkle —#527404
This "Sunflower" quilt was
made in 1988 at Camden,
TN by the owner's friend
Floye Markham (born
circa 1910, died circa
1990).

**Whitworth, Virginia
Lockhart** (Joe)
Glover's Trace Chapter
Ancestor: Alexander
McCorkle —#527404
This "Sampler" quilt was
made in 1979 at Camden,
TN by the owner (born in
1932 at Camden). It was the
first quilt she made. It won a
blue ribbon at the Benton
County Fair. The quilt was
made as part of a quilt class
at the Harpeth Quilt and
Clock Shop in Pegram, TN,
Margaret Murray, Instructor.

**Whitworth, Virginia Lockhart**
(Joe)
Glover's Trace Chapter
Ancestor: Alexander McCorkle —
#527404
This "Rocky Mountain Pass" quilt
was pieced in the 1930's or 40's
at Conway, AR by the owner's
aunt and namesake Virginia
Priestly Smith (born 1895 at
Weakley County, TN, died 1986
at Camden, TN). The quilt was
later quilted at the Emory Church
of Christ at Greenfield, TN. It was
a gift to the owner.

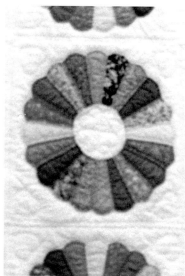

**Whitworth, Virginia Lockhart** (Joe)
Glover's Trace Chapter
Ancestor: Alexander McCorkle —#527404
This "Dresden Plate" quilt was made at Obion, TN by the
quilters of the United Methodist Realfoot Rural Ministry.
It was presented to the owner upon retirement as chair-
man of the Memphis Conference United Methodist
Church Council On Ministries in June, 1988.

**Whitworth, Virginia Lockhart** (Joe)
Glover's Trace Chapter
Ancestor: Alexander McCorkle —#527404
This "Double Irish Chain" quilt was made at Camden,
TN in 1990 by the RSVP Quilters and was purchased by
the owner from them.

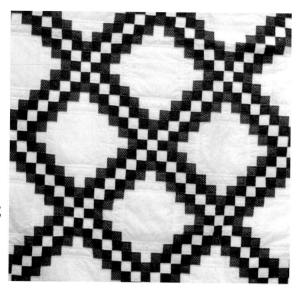

**Whitworth, Virginia Lockhart** (Joe)
Glover's Trace Chapter
Ancestor: Alexander McCorkle —#527404
This "Basket" quilt was made in 1980 at Camden, TN by the owner's friend, Floye Markham.

**Whitworth, Virginia Lockhart** (Joe)
Glover's Trace Chapter
Ancestor: Alexander McCorkle —#527404
This "Swamp Lily" quilt was made before 1865 at Camden, TN by the owner's great grandmother, Sophia Rusing (born 3/22/1828 at Humphreys County, TN, married Willis Crawford Rushing, died 6/23/1913 at Camden, TN). The owner inherited this quilt from her grandmother. The maker was the daughter of Robert and Lively Jane Webb Rushing. They were the parents of thirteen children including Sophia Ann Lockhart (born 2/14/1865). She inherited this quilt from her mother. It lay on the foot of her bed until her death on March 11, 1946.

**Whitworth, Virginia Lockhart** (Joe)
Glover's Trace Chapter
Ancestor: Alexander McCorkle —#527404
This "Hearts and Flowers" quilt was made in 1980 at Obion County, TN at the United Methodist Realfoot Rural Ministry. It was presented to the owner as the outgoing president of the Memphis Conference United Methodist Women.

**Whitworth, Virginia Lockhart** (Joe)
Glover's Trace Chapter
Ancestor: Alexander McCorkle —#527404
This "Double Wedding Ring" quilt was made in 1989 at Camden, TN by the RSVP quilters. It was made for the owner by the volunteers in this program.

**Widger, Lousie Parrott** (John)
Rhea-Craig Chapter
Ancestor: Capt. William Watson, MA —#702040
This "Log Cabin" quilt was made in 1930 at Jackson County, MI by the owner's great grandmother, Ann Marshall Center Jones (born 2/10/1866 at Durham, Lincolnshire, England, married George Center, married 2nd William Jones died 2/25/1952 at Marshall County, MI). Ann Marshall was born in England in 1866 and arrived in America at age six months. She made quilts for her six children and quilt tops for the birth and marriage of her sixteen grandchildren. As one of fifty great grandchildren born before she died, I have two quilt tops, and also have one made for my son. She had started on her great great grandchildren. Many of her first quilts were made from chicken feed sacks.

**Widger, Lousie Parrott** (John)
Rhea-Craig Chapter
Ancestor: Capt. William Watson, MA —#702040
This "States" quilt was made in 1950 at Pontiac, MI by the owner's mother, Aletha Burdette Parrott (born 6/24/1909 at Concord, MI, married Charles E. Parrott, died 1/29/1992 at Pontiac, MI). "After making State birds and State flower quilts for my younger sisters and brothers, I was asked what I would like. I selected the states in order that they were admitted to the union, with the capital named and marked. No such pattern was available then, so my mother took an Atlas and made her own."

**Wilburn, Brenda Green** (John "J.D.")
William Cocke Chapter
Ancestor: Jessee Webb, NC —#771867
This "Nine Patch" scrap quilt was made in 1963-64 at Cocke County, TN by the owner's mother, Doris Sparks Green (born 3/4/1917 at Cocke County, TN, married Horace "Leonard" Green). The maker gave the quilt to the owner. The owner says, "The quilt is made of unusual materials that represent a time period in the history of Cocke County when citizens migrated to other states to obtain employment. Several of my cousins moved to South Carolina to work in the textile mills. Having lived by a code of 'waste not, want not,' these relatives brought mom scraps of fabric from the mills where they worked. They were beautiful upholstery fabrics. Mom used a pattern of squares and rectangles and made a quilt top of corduroy and wool. The lining is from the denim from old jeans we had worn."

**Wilburn, Brenda Green**
(John "J.D.")
William Cocke Chapter
Ancestor: Jessee Webb, NC —#771867
This "Dresden Plate Family Tree" quilt was made in 1991 at Cocke County, TN by the owner's sister-in-law, and mother-in-law, Marie Grigsby (born 1941) and Kate Wilburn (born in 1923 at Cocke County, TN). The quilt was given to the owner as a Christmas present. Each square represents a member of the family. The owner says, "What a wonderful Christmas gift for a family whose hobby is genealogy. "

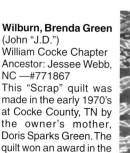

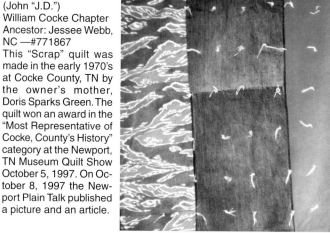

**Wilburn, Brenda Green**
(John "J.D.")
William Cocke Chapter
Ancestor: Jessee Webb,
NC —#771867
This "Tulip" quilt was
bought at a yard sale in
Hartford, TN in 1996.

**Wilburn, Brenda Green**
(John "J.D.")
William Cocke Chapter
Ancestor: Jessee Webb,
NC —#771867
This "Scrap" quilt was
made in the early 1970's
at Cocke County, TN by
the owner's mother,
Doris Sparks Green. The
quilt won an award in the
"Most Representative of
Cocke, County's History"
category at the Newport,
TN Museum Quilt Show
October 5, 1997. On Oc-
tober 8, 1997 the New-
port Plain Talk published
a picture and an article.

**Wilhite, Laura Rogers**
(Melvin B., Sr.)
Cavett Station Chapter
Ancestor: Robert
Cummins, PA —#578390
This "Dresden Plate" quilt
was made by the owner.
She started it in 1939 and
finished it in 1979.

**Wilhite, Laura Rogers**
(Melvin B., Sr.)
Cavett Station Chapter
Ancestor: Robert Cummins,
PA —#578390
This coverlet was made in
the early 1800's in Pennsylvania by the owner's great
great grandmother, Esther
Templeton Brownlee (born
9/17/1792 at PA, married
Joseph Brownlee, died 12/
8/1832). The coverlet is
made of wool from sheep
raised on the farm. The
maker passed the coverlet
to Lucy Jane Mulholland (1837-1920) and James Hamilton Brownlee (1822 -
1894). They passed the coverlet to Laura Jeannette Brownlee (1865-1954 ) and
S.H. Keener (1858-1939). The Keeners passed the coverlet to Lucy Mulholland
Keener 1888-1970) and Bruce T. Rogers (1873-1939). The Rogers passed it to
the owner.

**Wilhite, Laura Rogers**
(Melvin B., Sr.)
Cavett Station Chapter
Ancestor: Robert Cummins,
PA —#578390
This "Wildflowers of the
Smokies" quilt was made in
1984 by twenty five members
of the owner's family.

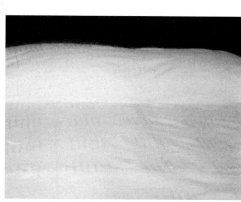

**Wilhite, Laura Rogers**
(Melvin B., Sr.)
Cavett Station Chapter
Ancestor: Robert
Cummins, PA —#578390
This woven coverlet was
made in Knox County, TN
by the owner's great
grandmother, Mary Jane
McCallie Keener, born 9/
8/ 1822 at Knox County,
married LeRoy Scothern
Keener, 2/25/1907 in the
same county). Leona
Watson Rutherford, the
owner's cousin, gave it to
the owner in 1945. The loom on which this coverlet was made, has been given to
"Dollywood" in Sevier County, TN. The loom has a plaque reading "Keener Loom."

**Wilhite, Sarah Vest** (Richard E.)
Hatchie Chapter
Ancestor: Johannes Schaub, NC
—#782339
This "Grandmother's Flower
Garden" quilt was made circa
1930 at Mt. Pleasant, TN by the
owner's mother, Emma Bailey
Vest (born 1/28/1882 at Colum-
bia, KY, married Solomon A.
Vest, died 4/13/1961 at Bolivar,
TN). The maker gave the quilt to
the owner.

**Wilkinson, Marlene Rathbun**
(Capt. Edward L.)
River City Chapter
Ancestor: Jonathan Palmer, CT
—#766672
This "Trip Around the World" quilt
was made circa 1975 at Neosho,
MO by Alice Cain, a friend of the
owner's aunt. Alice was born
circa 1896. Aunt Hazel Giller
gave the quilt to the owner.

**Wilkinson, Marlene Rathbun** (Capt.
Edward L.)
River City Chapter
Ancestor: Jonathan Palmer, CT —
#766672
This "Dresden Plate" quilt was made
in 1982 at Jackson, MS by the
owner's mother-in-law, Lela Mae
Wilkinson (born 7/4/1906 at Pattison,
MS, married Zack Cain Wilkinson).

**Wilkinson, Marlene Rathbun**
(Capt. Edward L.)
River City Chapter
Ancestor: Jonathan Palmer, CT — #766672
This "LeMoyne Star" quilt was made in 1978 at Jackson, MS by the owner's mother-in-law, Lela Mae Wilkinson.

**Willett, Johnnye Shoemaker** (Lee B.)
Alexander Keith Chapter
Ancestor: John Gibbs, NC — #681052
This "Columbia Star" quilt was made in 1900 at McMinn County, TN by the Gentleman of the Jones Chapel Methodist Church. This quilt was presented to the owner's great grandfather, Abraham Crusier Smith, when he was Sunday School Superintendent. The quilt was passed from the first owner to Isabelle Smith Riden to Joe Riden to Bernie Riden to the current owner. The quilt was published in McMinn County Tennessee and Its People: 1819-1997.

**Willhoit, Mary Ruth Smith** (Clyde)
Chief John Ross Chapter
Ancestor: William Calhoun, SC —#571051
This "Flying Geese" quilt was made by the owner's mother-in-law, Ruby Wilhoit (born 4/26/1903 at Bradley County, TN, married Aner P., died 3/3/1991 at Chattanooga, TN). She gave it to the owner.

**Willhoit, Mary Ruth Smith** (Clyde)
Chief John Ross Chapter
Ancestor: William Calhoun, SC — #571051
This "Double Wedding Ring" quilt was made in 1985 at Bradley County, TN by the owner's mother-in-law, Ruby Wilhoit.

**Willhoit, Mary Ruth Smith** (Clyde)
Chief John Ross Chapter
Ancestor: William Calhoun, SC —#571051
This "Grandmother's Flower Garden" quilt was pieced in 1942 at Chattanooga, TN by the owner's aunt, Bernice Varnell (born 10/30/1898 at Chattanooga, married Claude Varnell, died 2/9/1984 at Mettelton, MS). The owner's mother gave the top to Mary Ruth and she quilted it.

**Willhoit, Mary Ruth Smith** (Clyde)
Chief John Ross Chapter
Ancestor: William Calhoun, SC —#571051
This "Iowa Star" quilt was given to the owner by her mother-in-law.

**Williams, Amy**
Spencer Clack Chapter
Ancestor: Benjamin Seaton, PA — #750276
This "Nursery Rhyme" quilt was made in 1973 at Sevier County, TN by the owner's mother, Judy Pat Williams (born 10/15/1951, married Troy Williams). "My mother painted the nursery rhymes and my grandmother, Rowena McFalls, quilted it."

**Williams, Amy**
Spencer Clack Chapter
Ancestor: Benjamin Seaton, PA —#750276
This "Flowers and Birds of the Fifty States" quilt was made by the Smoky Mountains Extension Homemakers Club in Tennessee and Missouri. It was given to the owner by her grandmother who won it in a raffle.

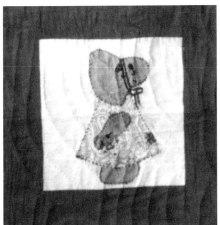

**Williams, Charlotte Raines** (Bruce)
Bonny Kate Chapter
Ancestor: Patrick Ewing, MD —#713426
This "Dutch Girl/Sunbonnet Sue" quilt was made in 1976 at Knoxville, TN by the owner (born 12/25/1921 at Claiborne County, TN). This quilt was made for the 1976 Bicentennial and was displayed at the TVA&I Fair.

**Williams, Diane Moore** (Richard A.)
Charolette Reeves Robertson Chapter
Ancestor: Daniel Duvall, VA —#600207
This "Courthouse Square" quilt was given to the owner by a cousin, Mrs. Jeanette Johns. The owner's uncle Zeb Duvall told her that he wanted this quilt to stay in the Duvall family.

**Williams, Harriet Goodwin**
(John)
General William Lenoir Chapter
Ancestor: Capt. Phillip DeLancey
Maroney, MD —#781736
This "Colonial Lady with Umbrella" made in 1928 at Lenoir City, TN by the owner's great grandmother, Margaret Ellen Maroney Bates (born 3/22/1860 at Knox County, TN, married James Monroe Bates, died 3/8/1962 at St. Petersburg, FL). The quilt was passed from the maker, to the owner's grandmother, Edna Earl Bates Goodwin, to her father Harry Dexter Goodwin, to the owner.

**Williams, Jeannette**
Bonny Kate Chapter
Ancestor: Patrick Ewing, MD —
#713427
This "Sandhills Star" quilt was made in 1978 at Knoxville, TN by the owner's grandmother, Eva Poore Raines (born 7/9/1906 at Claiborne County, TN, married Robert Mack Raines, died 2/28/1979 at Knoxville, TN). The maker gave the quilt to the owner as a Christmas gift.

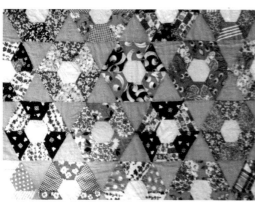

**Williams, Jeannette**
Bonny Kate Chapter
Ancestor: Patrick Ewing, MD — #713427
This "Friendship" quilt was made by the owner's grandmother, Eva Poore Raines, and the owner received the quilt at the death of the maker.

**Williams, Judy McFalls** (Troy)
Spencer Clack Chapter
Ancestor: Benjamin Seaton, PA — #732484
This "State Flowers" quilt was embroidered in 1958 when there were only 48 states. It was quilted in 1963. This quilt was made by the owner's mother, Rowena McFalls (born 4/1929 at Sevierville, TN, married Ben Charles McFalls). She gave the quilt to the owner.

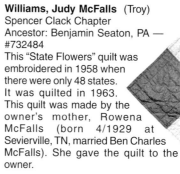

**Williams, Judy McFalls** (Troy)
Spencer Clack Chapter
Ancestor: Benjamin Seaton, PA — #732484
This "Double T" quilt was made in 1936 in Sevier County, TN by the owner's maternal grandmother, Zelma Canupp Henderson (born 5/25/1906 at Sevier County, TN, married Steward Ray Henderson, died 3/6/1937 at Sevier County. The owner passed the quilt to her daughter who passed it to the current owner.

**Williams, Judy McFalls**
(Troy)
Spencer Clack Chapter
Ancestor: Benjamin Seaton, PA —#732484
This "Hexagon" quilt was made in 1975 at Sevier County by the owner's mother, Rowena McFalls.

**Williams, Kristianna Thompson** (Calvin Lee)
Hatchie Chapter
Ancestor: William Austin, VA —#764401
This "Windmill" quilt was made in 1933-35 at Bolivar, TN by the owner's paternal great great grandmother, Willie Moorman Beck McAnulty (born 2/6/1872 at Salem, MS, married David Moorman McAnulty, died 8/3/1940 at Bolivar, TN).

**Williams, Theresa Deanna**
Great Smokies Chapter
Ancestor: Timothy Reagan, MD —#722649
This "Crazy" quilt was bought at a shop on Highway 66 near Sevierville, TN in the late 1970's. The quilt is inscribed as follows: "Twelve Hundredth Performance, London and New York of the Lyequm Theatre success. Sweet Lavendar: under the direction of Mr. Daniel Frohman, matinee, November 27, 1889. Grand Opera House, one year at Lyequm Theatre in New York. Now in the third year at Terr's Theatre, London." The actors are also listed on the quilt.

**Williams, Theresa Deanna**
Great Smokies Chapter
Ancestor: Timothy Reagan, MD —#722649
This "Anniversary Memory" quilt was made in 1998 at Gatlinburg, TN by the owner (born 9/29/1949).

**Williams, Theresa Deanna**
Great Smokies Chapter
Ancestor: Timothy Reagan, MD —#722649
This "Crazy Diamond" quilt was made in 1971 at Gatlinburg, TN by the owner's aunt, Willie Etta Owneby Maples (born 12/8/1928 at Gatlinburg, married Howard C. Maples). The quiltmaker took her mothers dresses and made this memory quilt after her mother's death. The maker gave the quilt to the owner.

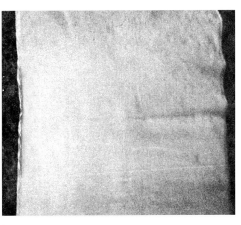

**Williams, Virgina Dare Stallings** (M.V.)
Key Corner Chapter
Ancestor: John Barringer, NC —#731406
This coverlet was made at Friendship, TN by the owner's great grandmother, Mary Hardeman Scales (married William Perkins Scales, died 1893 at Friendship, TN). The coverlet was made from wool from the maker's sheep.

**Williams, Virgina Dare Stallings** (M.V.)
Key Corner Chapter
Ancestor: John Barringer, NC —#731406
This "Butterfly" quilt was made in the 1930's at Friendship, TN by the owner's mother, Lela Scales Stallings (born 3/20/1892 at Friendship, TN, married Dr. W.H. Stallings, died 8/17/1973).

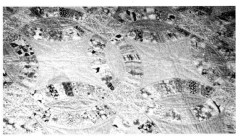

**Williams, Virgina Dare Stallings** (M.V.)
Key Corner Chapter
Ancestor: John Barringer, NC —#731406
This "Double Wedding Ring" quilt was made in the 1930's at Friendship, TN by the owner's mother, Lela Scales Stallings.

**Williams, Virgina Dare Stallings** (M.V.)
Key Corner Chapter
Ancestor: John Barringer, NC —#731406
This "Grandmother's Flower Garden" quilt was made in the 1930's at Friendship, TN by the owner and her mother, Lela Scales Stallings. The owner started this quilt when she was twelve years old and finished piecing about half of it.

**Williams, Virgina Dare Stallings** (M.V.)
Key Corner Chapter
Ancestor: John Barringer, NC —#731406
This "Dutch Doll" quilt was made in the 1930's at Friendship, TN by the owner's mother, Lela Scales Stallings.

**Williams-Hach, Carol Jeanette Killebrew** (Ralph)
Captain William Edmiston Chapter
Ancestor: Robert Killebrew, NC —#748199
This "USA Bicentennial" quilt was made in 1976 at Dover, TN by the owner's mother, Nora Lee Killebrew Strauser (born 1/11/1921 at Trigg County, NY, married Robert K. Strauser).

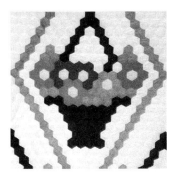

**Williams-Hach, Carol Jeanette Killebrew** (Ralph)
Captain William Edmiston Chapter
Ancestor: Robert Killebrew, NC —#748199
This "Mosaic Flower Basket" quilt was made in 1975 at Dover, TN by the owner's mother, Nora Lee Killebrew Strauser.

**Williamson, Ellen Little** (Fredrick)
Southwest Point Chapter
Ancestor: —#344632
This "Albym Friendship" quilt was made in 1902 by the Women's Guild of the First Baptist Church of Dayton, OH for the wife of the pastor, Henry Frances Colby. Her name was Mary Lizzie Chamberlain Colby. The quilt was inherited by her daughter, Eleanor Thresher Colby, who married Edwin Robert Little of Detroit, MI in 1916. It was inherited in turn by their daughter, Ellen Colby Little, who married Sidney Hall Probert of Detroit in 1947. Sidney died in 1993. After her husband's death, in 1995 Ellen married 2nd Fredrick Royle Williamson of Kingston, TN.

**Willis, Mary Dishongh** (Wylie)
Buffalo River Chapter
Ancestor: Augustine Deshon, NC —#641404
This "LeMoyne Star" quilt was made circa 1880 at Maury County, TN by the owner's grandmother, Mary Catherine Dishongh (born 3/4/1838 at Maury County, married George Butler Dishongh, died 11/27/1884 in the same county).

**Wise, Mary Neil Robinson** (David)
Jane Knox Chapter
Ancestor: John Lindsay, NC —#595101
This coverlet was made in 1860 possibly at Lawrence County, TN by the owner's great uncle's mother, Mrs. Petty.

**Wolfe, Violet Kirkpatrick** (Robert E.)
Coyotee Chapter
Ancestor: Capt. Samuel Ware, VA —#697452
This "Hands of Children" quilt was made in 1995 at Greenback, TN by the owner's friend Nancy Blair (born 1961 at Greenback, married Jerry Blair) and first grader's. " This is my retiring quilt. Logan Blair was in my first grade class. His sister, Kendra Blair, had been in my class in 1992-93. Their mother, Nancy Blair, helped my first graders make this quilt for me and they presented it to me on June 1, 1995, the month I retired."

**Wolfe, Violet Kirkpatrick** (Robert E.)
Coyotee Chapter
Ancestor: Capt. Samuel Ware, VA —#697452
This "Tennessee Homecoming-1986" quilt was made in 1986 at Greenback, TN by the owner's niece Sue Cooper (born 5/7/1943 at Maryville, TN, married Jerry Cooper) and first graders. The maker suggested the owner let her first graders make a quilt to honor the 1986 Tennessee Homecoming. The children drew the pictures on paper, then on the quilt square. The maker applied the fabric paint using the colors directed by the child. A child's mother did the machine quilting. This quilt was hung in the principal's office at Greenback High School Spring 1998 so the seniors could enjoy the quilt they had made as first graders.

**Wolfe, Violet Kirkpatrick** (Robert E.)
Coyotee Chapter
Ancestor: Capt. Samuel Ware, VA —#697452
This "Nine Diamond" quilt was made in 1935 at Madisonville, TN by the owner's mother, Grace Wear Kirkpatrick (born 7/25/1912 at Vonore, TN, married William Elmo Kirkpatrick). This quilt was made during the depression using feed sacks for the lining and backing.

**Wood, Ruby Owens Featherston** (Carl H.)
Travellers Rest Chapter
Ancestor: Capt. John Hardy, GA —#727792
This "Square in a Square" quilt was made in 1969-75 at Jacksonville, FL by the owner's mother, Ruby Owens Featherston (born 10/17/1897 at Evergreen, FL, married John Culp Featherston, died 12/13/1978 at Jacksonville). The maker pieced this quilt traveling, at home, at doctor's offices, to help with arthritic fingers.

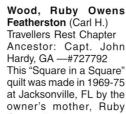

**Wood, Ruby Owens Featherston** (Carl H.)
Travellers Rest Chapter
Ancestor: Capt. John Hardy, GA —#727792
This "Dresden Plate" quilt was made in Evergreen, FL 1900-1915 by the owner's maternal grandmother, Eliza Sophrania H. Owens (born 4/21/1875 at King's Ferry, FL, married Linton L. Owens, died 9/6/1954 at Nassau County, FL). The quilt was passed from grandmother, to mother, to owner.

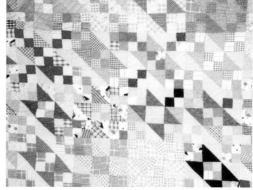

**Wood, Ruby Owens Featherston** (Carl H.)
Travellers Rest Chapter
Ancestor: Capt. John Hardy, GA —#727792
This "Jacob's Ladder" quilt was made in 1900-10 at Nassau County, FL by the owner's maternal grandmother, Eliza Sophrania H. Owens.

**Wood, Ruby Owens Featherston** (Carl H.)
Travellers Rest Chapter
Ancestor: Capt. John Hardy, GA —#727792
This "Tulip" quilt was made in 1925-35 at Nassau County, FL by the owner's maternal grandmother, Eliza Sophrania H. Owens.

**Woods, Rebecca Christopher** (Kenneth E.)
Henderson Station Chapter
Ancestor: Edward Trice, NC —#617127
This "Irish Chain" quilt was made in Henderson County, TN by the owner's great grandmother, Eliza Evaline Boren Trice (born 2/9/1836 at Henderson County, TN, married William Crook Trice, died 9/18/1903 at Chester County, TN). This quilt won first place in the Antique Quilt Show sponsored by Freed-Hardeman College Associates, the women's club of the college. The quiltmaker had five girls and one son. The quilt was passed to one of the girls, the owner's grandmother, Callie Rebecca Trice (married John Enoch Christopher). The quilt was passed to her sister, Martha Evelyn Tomlinson, who never married. She gave the quilt to the owner.

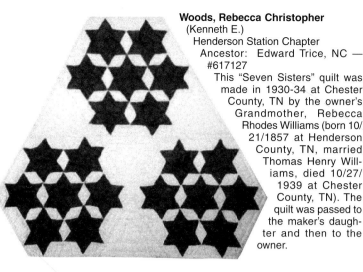

**Woods, Rebecca Christopher**
(Kenneth E.)
Henderson Station Chapter
Ancestor: Edward Trice, NC —
#617127
This "Seven Sisters" quilt was made in 1930-34 at Chester County, TN by the owner's Grandmother, Rebecca Rhodes Williams (born 10/21/1857 at Henderson County, TN, married Thomas Henry Williams, died 10/27/1939 at Chester County, TN). The quilt was passed to the maker's daughter and then to the owner.

**Worrell, Estella Ansley**
(Norman)
Fort Nashborough Chapter
Ancestor: Thomas Ansley, Sr.,
GA —#707065
This "Baby" quilt was made in 1927 at Atchison, KS by the owner's mother-in-law, Charoltte Blomberg Worrell (born 10/11/1889 at Atchinson, married North Chester Earl Worrell, died 8/8/1947 at Nashville, TN). This quilt was made from a kit. The maker's son was born 11/2/1927, but apparently the maker was planning on having a girl because the quilt is made with pinks.

**Wright, Mary Mina Whitener**
(Lucius F.)
Watagua Chapter
Ancestor: Jonathan Knight, NC
—#361423
This "Tulip" quilt was made in 1940 at Spokane, WA by the owner's grandmother, Mary E. Massie Denny (born in Spokane). The maker gave the quilt to the owner.

**Wright, Susan Miller**
Watauga Chapter
Ancestor: Hugh Stephenson, PA —
#765135
This "Double Wedding Ring" quilt was made in 1935 at Haywood County, TN by the owner's great grandmother, Sue Puryear Travis.

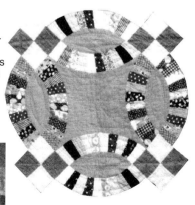

**Wyse, Mary Sue Finley**
(Benjamin DeLaney, Jr.)
Ancestor: Paul Finley, Sr., SC —
#692404
This "Brick" quilt was made in 1925-35 at Saluda, SC by the owner's mother-in-law, Mary Crout Wyse. It is made from large, wool sample swatches used by a traveling salesman.

**Worrell, Estella Ansley**
(Norman)
Fort Nashborough Chapter
Ancestor: Thomas Ansley, Sr.,
GA —#707065
This "Variation of a Mill Wheel" quilt was made in Mt. Pleasant, TN in 1938 by the owner's mother, Viola Henson Ansley (born 5/31/1903 at Mt. Pleasant, TN, married Sterling Price Ansley, died 4/1986 at Winchester, TN). The maker did not originally plan the fabric combinations that ended up in the quilt. She had all of her pieces cut and stacked in her needlework bag. Her cousin was rummaging through the bag and mixed up all the pieces. Rather than spend so much time sorting them again, she just laughed and decided to use them randomly.

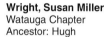

**Worrell, Estella Ansley**
(Norman)
Fort Nashborough Chapter
Ancestor: Thomas Ansley, Sr.,
GA —#707065
This "Pinwheel/Wind Blown Square" quilt was made in 1928-30 at Bessemer, AL by the owner's mother, Viola Henson Ansley, and members of the Four Squares Sewing Club.

**Wright, Susan Miller**
Watauga Chapter
Ancestor: Hugh Stephenson, PA —#765135
This "Grandmother's Flower Garden" quilt was made in the 1920's at Haywood County, TN by the owner's great grandmother, Sue Puryear Travis. She gave the quilt to the owner.

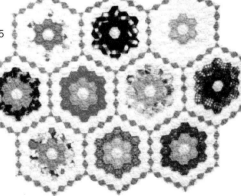

**Wyse, Mary Sue Finley**
(Benjamin DeLaney, Jr.)
Ancestor: Paul Finley, Sr.,
SC —#692404
This "Prairie Star" quilt was made in the 1920's or 30's at Saluda, SC by the owner's mother-in-law, Mary Crout Wyse (born 6/10/1890 at Leesville, SC, married Benjamin DeLaney Wyse, Sr., died 12/1/1982 at Saluda).

**Wyse, Mary Sue Finley** (Benjamin DeLaney, Jr.) Ancestor: Paul Finley, Sr., SC —#692404
This "Brick" quilt was also made in 1925-35 at Saluda, SC by the owner's mother-in-law, Mary Crout Wyse. It is made from large, wool sample swatches used by a traveling salesman.

**Wyse, Mary Sue Finley** (Benjamin DeLaney, Jr.) Ancestor: Paul Finley, Sr., SC —#692404
This "Virginia Star" quilt was made at Saluda, SC by the owner's mother-in-law, Mary Crout Wyse.

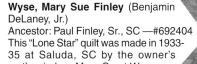

**Wyse, Mary Sue Finley** (Benjamin DeLaney, Jr.) Ancestor: Paul Finley, Sr., SC —#692404
This "Lone Star" quilt was made in 1933-35 at Saluda, SC by the owner's mother-in-law, Mary Crout Wyse.

**Wyse, Mary Sue Finley** (Benjamin DeLaney, Jr.) Ancestor: Paul Finley, Sr., SC —#692404
This "Dresden Plate" quilt was made in 1985-86 at Hartsville, SC by the owner's aunt, Hattie Blackmon Revell (born 8/14/1907 at Wedgefield, SC, married William Rufus Revell). The owner inherited the quilt from her aunt at her death.

**Wyse, Mary Sue Finley** (Benjamin DeLaney, Jr.) Ancestor: Paul Finley, Sr., SC —#692404
This "Crazy" quilt was made circa 1980 at Abbeville County, SC by the owner's aunt, Mary Blackmon Bonner (born 6/23/1904 at Sumter County, SC, married James Neil Bonner, died 4/27/1998 at Greenwood, SC). This quilt was featured at a show at the Fine Arts Center of Erskine College, Due West, SC in the 1980's.

**Wyse, Mary Sue Finley** (Benjamin DeLaney, Jr.) Ancestor: Paul Finley, Sr., SC —#692404
This "Pinwheel" quilt was made in 1986 at Signal Mountain, TN by the Mrs. Leola Vandergriff, the mother of the owner's friend, Elizabeth Haynes.

**Wyse, Mary Sue Finley** (Benjamin DeLaney, Jr.) Ancestor: Paul Finley, Sr., SC —#692404
This "Whole Cloth" quilt was made in 1837 at Newberry District, SC by the owner's husband's great grandmother, Hannah Barrett (born 1/2/1816 at Newberry District, married Dr. DeLaney Lane Wilson, died 6/18/1957 at Aiken, SC). The quilt was passed from maker, to Rebecca Wilson Wyse, to Maude Wyse Bass, to current owner.

**Wyse, Mary Sue Finley** (Benjamin DeLaney, Jr.) Ancestor: Paul Finley, Sr., SC —#692404
This "Grandmother's Flower Garden" quilt was made in the 1930's at Saluda, SC by the owner's mother-in-law, Mary Crout Wyse.

**Wyse, Mary Sue Finley** (Benjamin DeLaney, Jr.) Ancestor: Paul Finley, Sr., SC —#692404
This "Broderie-Perse" quilt was made in 1837 at Newberry District, SC by the owner's husband's great grandmother, Hannah Barrett.

**Wyse, Mary Sue Finley**
(Benjamin DeLaney, Jr.)
Ancestor: Paul Finley, Sr.,
SC —#692404
This "Pine Tree/Tree of
Life" quilt was made in
1950-60 in Tennessee.
The owner's friend, Mrs.
Katherine M. Jones, gave
the quilt to her in 1996.

**Wyse, Mary Sue Finley**
(Benjamin DeLaney, Jr.)
Ancestor: Paul Finley, Sr.,
SC —#692404
This "Flying Geese/Birds
in the Air" quilt was made
in 1925-35 at Saluda, SC
by the owner's mother-in-
law, Mary Crout Wyse.

**Wyse, Mary Sue Finley**
(Benjamin DeLaney, Jr.)
Ancestor: Paul Finley, Sr.,
SC —#692404
This "Grandmother's Fan"
quilt was made in the
1930's at Saluda, SC by
the owner's mother-in-
law, Mary Crout Wyse.

**Wyse, Mary Sue Finley**
(Benjamin DeLaney, Jr.)
Ancestor: Paul Finley, Sr.,
SC —#692404
This "Double Irish Chain"
quilt was made in 1925-35
at Saluda, SC by the
owner's mother, Trannie
Kinard and her mother,
Elizabeth Matthews
Kinard. Trannie was born
1865 at Saluda, married
Jefferson Crout, died 4/
27/1939 at Saluda. Eliza-
beth was born 7/4/1842,
married J. Adam Kinard,
died 1925 at Saluda.

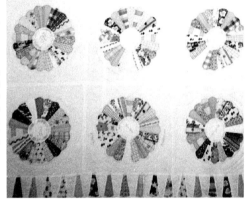

**Wyse, Mary Sue Finley**
(Benjamin DeLaney, Jr.)
Ancestor: Paul Finley, Sr.,
SC —#692404
This "Dresden Plate
Friendship" quilt was
made in 1976 at Due
West, SC by the owner's
aunt, Mary Blackmon
Bonner and the Senior
Citizens of Due West ARP
Church.

**Yearick, Marylee Prince**
(Kenneth)
Robert Cooke Chapter
Ancestor: Maj. John Nelson,
NC —#731940
This "Nine Patch" quilt was
made circa 1940 at Franklin
County, TN by the owner's
great aunt, Lucy Taylor Gre-
gory (born 1883 at Lincoln
County, married Brown Gre-
gory, died 1965 in the same
county).

**Yancey, Maurine Gwaltney**
(James)
Caney Fork Chapter
Ancestor: Powell Hughes, VA
—#720438
This "Lone Star" quilt was
pieced in 1936 at Hickman,
TN by the owner's mother,
Adelia Gwaltney (born 4/15/
1884 at Hickman, married
Finis Edgar Gwaltney, died
4/28/1985 at Hickman). It
was quilted by the owner's
sister, Oleta Gwaltney, in
1973.

**Zimmerman, Carol Ammerson**
(Carl T.)
Cavett Station Chapter
Ancestor: Conrad Harnsberger,
VA —#632066
This "Royal Star" quilt was made
in the 1930's at Mellen, WI by the
owner's husband's grandmother,
Pauline Roeck Zimmerman (born
at Kiel, WS, married Adolf
Fredrick Zimmerman, died at
Mellen, WI).

**Yearick, Marylee Prince** (Kenneth)
Robert Cooke Chapter
Ancestor: Maj. John Nelson, NC
—#731940
This "Grandmother's Flower
Garden" quilt was made in the
1940's at Franklin County, TN
by the owner's great aunt, Lucy
Taylor Gregory.

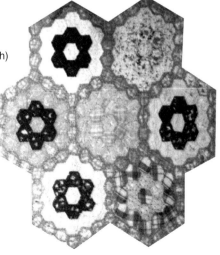

**Zimmerman, Carol Ammerson** (Carl T.)
Cavett Station Chapter
Ancestor: Conrad Harnsberger, VA —#632066
This "Nine Patch Variation" quilt was made in the 1890's at Alabama by the owner's great grand-mother, Hannah E. Hansberger Cooper (born 2/14/1860 at Tallassee, AL, married George Nelson Cooper, died 3/11/1940 at Birmingham, AL). The quiltmaker is remembered as "always having a piece of fabric in her lap and a needle in her hand."

**Zimmerman, Carol Ammerson** (Carl T.)
Cavett Station Chapter
Ancestor: Conrad Harns-berger, VA —#632066
This "Rocky Mountain Road/New York Beauty" quilt was made in 1860 at Alabama by the owner's great great grandmother, Sarah Starr Hansberger (born 12/10/1831 in AL, married Jacob S. Hansberger, died 7/18/1879 in AL).

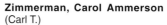

**Zimmerman, Carol Ammerson** (Carl T.)
Cavett Station Chapter
Ancestor: Conrad Harnsberger, VA —#632066
This "Snowball" quilt was made in 1948 by the owner's great aunts, Nannie and Irene Watts. The quilt was given to the owner's mother at a baby shower when she was expecting Carol.

**Zimmerman, Carol Ammerson** (Carl T.)
Cavett Station Chapter
Ancestor: Conrad Harnsberger, VA —#632066
This "Bears and Balloons" quilt was made in 1977 at Birmingham, AL by the owner's mother, Doris McGehee (born 4/16/1928 at Birmingham, married Raymond Lee). It was made for the owner's second son, John Conrad born 12/1977.

**Zimmerman, Carol Ammerson** (Carl T.)
Cavett Station Chapter
Ancestor: Conrad Harnsberger, VA —#632066
This "Clown" quilt was made in 1976 at Birmingham, AL by the owner's mother, Doris McGehee. It was made for the owner's first born son, Carl Jr.

**Zimmerman, Carol Ammerson** (Carl T.)
Cavett Station Chapter
Ancestor: Conrad Harnsberger, VA —#632066
This coverlet was made in Alabama in 1850 by the owner's great great great grandmother, Sarah Starr Hansberger.

**Zimmerman, Carol Ammerson** (Carl T.)
Cavett Station Chapter
Ancestor: Conrad Harnsberger, VA —#632066
This "Checker Board" quilt was made in the late 1800's at Lincoln County, TN by the owner's great great grandmother, Sarah Derina McGehee (born 12/28/1833 at Fayetteville, TN, died 8/30/1922 at Mulberry, TN.

**Zimmerman, Carol Ammerson** (Carl T.)
Cavett Station Chapter
Ancestor: Conrad Harnsberger, VA —#632066
This "String" quilt was made in the 1930's at Birmingham, AL by the owner's grandmother, Addie Lee Amberson (born 2/19/1899 at Argo, AL, married Willie Raymond Amberson, died 4/7/1976 at Birmingham, AL).

**Zimmerman, Carol Ammerson** (Carl T.)
Cavett Station Chapter
Ancestor: Conrad Harnsberger, VA —#632066
This "String" quilt was made in the 1930's at Birmingham, AL by the owner's great grandmother, Hannah Elizabeth Cooper.